OXFORD STUDIES IN ANCIENT PHILOSOPHY

EDITOR: BRAD INWOOD

VOLUME XLVIII

SUMMER 2015

OXFORD
UNIVERSITY PRESS

Great Clarendon Street, Oxford, OX2 6DP,
United Kingdom

Oxford University Press is a department of the University of Oxford.
It furthers the University's objective of excellence in research, scholarship,
and education by publishing worldwide. Oxford is a registered trade mark of
Oxford University Press in the UK and in certain other countries

© Except where otherwise stated, Oxford University Press, 2015

The moral rights of the authors have been asserted

First Edition published in 2015

Impression: 1

All rights reserved. No part of this publication may be reproduced, stored in
a retrieval system, or transmitted, in any form or by any means, without the
prior permission in writing of Oxford University Press, or as expressly permitted
by law, by licence, or under terms agreed with the appropriate reprographics
rights organization. Enquiries concerning reproduction outside the scope of the
above should be sent to the Rights Department, Oxford University Press, at the
address above

You must not circulate this book in any other form
and you must impose this same condition on any acquirer

Published in the United States of America by Oxford University Press
198 Madison Avenue, New York, NY 10016, United States of America

British Library Cataloguing in Publication Data
Data available

Library of Congress Cataloging in Publication Data
Oxford studies in ancient philosophy.—
Vol. xlviii (2015).—Oxford: Clarendon Press;
New York: Oxford University Press, 1983–
v.; 22 cm. Annual.
1. Philosophy, Ancient—Periodicals.
B1.O9   180.'5—dc.19   84–645022
AACR 2   MARC-S

ISBN 978–0–19–873554–0 (hbk.)
ISBN 978–0–19–873555–7 (pbk.)

Printed and bound by
CPI Group (UK) Ltd, Croydon, CR0 4YY

Links to third party websites are provided by Oxford in good faith and
for information only. Oxford disclaims any responsibility for the materials
contained in any third party website referenced in this work

OXFORD STUDIES IN ANCIENT PHILOSOPHY

ADVISORY BOARD

Professor Julia Annas, *University of Arizona*

Professor Susanne Bobzien, *All Souls College, Oxford*

Professor Dorothea Frede, *University of Hamburg*

Professor A. A. Long, *University of California, Berkeley*

Professor Martha Nussbaum, *University of Chicago*

Professor David Sedley, *University of Cambridge*

Professor Richard Sorabji, *King's College, University of London, and Wolfson College, Oxford*

Professor Gisela Striker, *Harvard University*

Professor Christopher Taylor, *Corpus Christi College, Oxford*

Contributions and books for review should be sent to the incoming Editor, Professor Victor Caston, Department of Philosophy, University of Michigan, 435 South State Street, Ann Arbor, MI 48109-1003, USA (e-mail oxfordstudies@umich.edu).

Contributors are asked to observe the 'Notes for Contributors to Oxford Studies in Ancient Philosophy', printed at the end of this volume.

Up-to-date contact details, the latest version of Notes for Contributors, and publication schedules can be checked on the *Oxford Studies in Ancient Philosophy* website:

www.oup.co.uk/philosophy/series/osap

CONTENTS

Explanation in the Epistemology of the *Meno* WHITNEY SCHWAB	1
The Role of Relatives in Plato's Partition Argument, *Republic* 4, 436 B 9–439 C 9 MATTHEW DUNCOMBE	37
Making the Best of Plato's Protagoras MATTHEW EVANS	61
What is a Perfect Syllogism? BENJAMIN MORISON	107
Truth in *Metaphysics E* 4 PAOLO CRIVELLI	167
The Concept of *Ergon*: Towards an Achievement Interpretation of Aristotle's 'Function Argument' SAMUEL H. BAKER	227
Aristotle on Essence and Habitat JESSICA GELBER	267
Index Locorum	295

EXPLANATION IN THE EPISTEMOLOGY OF THE *MENO*

WHITNEY SCHWAB

1. Introduction

AT the end of the *Meno* the character Socrates famously claims that '[true *doxai*] are not worth much until one gets them bound down by a working out of the explanation. . . . When they have been bound down, first they become *epistēmai* and thence permanent' (98 A 3–6).[1] Despite its fame and importance, no consensus exists on what exactly is going on in this passage. Not only do interpreters disagree on the details of Socrates' characterization of *epistēmē*, they disagree on what Socrates takes himself to be characterizing. On one long-standing interpretation, the passage contains the first attempt in Western philosophy to analyse knowledge as justified true belief.[2] Two claims are key to this line of interpretation: first, that *epistēmē* is knowledge; second, that Socrates thinks working out the expla-

© Whitney Schwab 2015

I would like to thank audiences at the 34th Annual Ancient Philosophy Workshop at Washington University in St Louis and the Princeton Workshop in Normative Philosophy for helpful discussion and feedback. For helpful discussion and/or comments on previous drafts I would like to thank Ryan Cook, John Cooper, Adam Crager, Sonny Elizondo, Matthew Evans, Nate Gadd, Sukaina Hirji, Andrew Huddleston, Brad Inwood, David Kaufman, Thomas Kelly, Errol Lord, Brennan McDavid, Barry Maguire, Jimmy Martin, Jessica Moss, Michael Nance, Alexander Nehamas, David Nowakowski, Rachel Parsons, Jessica Pfeifer, Mor Segev, Simon Shogry, Jack Spencer, Jack Woods, and Steve Yalowitz. I would especially like to thank David Bronstein and Scott O'Connor for discussion that led to a major revision of the overall thrust of the paper. Lastly, I would like to thank Hendrik Lorenz and Benjamin Morison, who have discussed this material with me more times, and commented on more drafts, than I can count.

[1] Unless noted, translations are my own (although I have benefited from consulting Grube). Also, unless noted, all further occurrences of 'Socrates' refer to the character Socrates in the *Meno*.

[2] Gail Fine has recently presented the most detailed and rigorous defence of this interpretation (G. Fine, 'Knowledge and True Belief in the *Meno*' ['KTB *Meno*'], *Oxford Studies in Ancient Philosophy*, 27 (2004), 41–81). Dominic Scott has also recently argued for it (D. Scott, *Plato's* Meno (Cambridge, 2006), 184–5), and it is endorsed (if not explicitly argued for) by many others. The interpretation, in fact, enjoys popularity outside of scholarship on ancient philosophy: even E. Gettier suggests it in his famous paper 'Is Justified True Belief Knowledge?', *Analysis*, 23 (1963), 121–3 at 121 n. 1.

nation (*aitias logismos*) upgrades true *doxa* to *epistēmē* by conferring a justification on the *doxa*.³ Opposed to this is an interpretation according to which Socrates is not characterizing knowledge but the distinct, though certainly related, phenomenon of understanding.⁴ Proponents of this interpretation typically insist that working out an explanation is more plausibly taken as a requirement on acquiring understanding than as a requirement on acquiring knowledge.

As interpreters typically cast it, and as I will cast it here, the question of what Socrates takes himself to be characterizing is the question of where his account of *epistēmē* best fits into contemporary epistemological discussion (contemporary to the interpreters, that is).⁵ The question is not, for example, how Socrates' account fares against some allegedly timeless, essentialized conception of knowledge or understanding. Trying to answer this latter question would probably be imprudent, since it would require that one first establish that there is some such conception and then judge Socrates' account against it. Nor is the question, in the first instance, how Socrates' account fares against modern English-language intuitions (I say not 'in the first instance' because presumably there is some connection between what current epistemologists say about knowledge and understanding and the intuitions English-language speakers have). Rather, the question is how Socrates' discussion of *epistēmē* best translates into our contemporary philosophical culture. And, for much of the time that the debate over the status of *epistēmē* in the *Meno* progressed among interpreters of ancient philosophy, contemporary epistemologists focused almost exclusively on knowledge. Thus, it was typically thought that, to the extent that Socrates' account has affinities to current epistemological debates,

---

³ The interpretation also maintains that ἐπιστήμη is a privileged kind of δόξα and that δόξα is belief. More on these claims, and on my use of 'upgrade', in a moment.

⁴ Alexander Nehamas argues for this claim specifically concerning the *Meno* (on which I solely focus) (A. Nehamas, 'Meno's Paradox and Socrates as Teacher' ['Meno's Paradox'], *Oxford Studies in Ancient Philosophy*, 3 (1985), 1–30 at 24–30). Myles Burnyeat alludes to this interpretation of the *Meno* while discussing the jury example in the *Theaetetus* (M. Burnyeat, 'Socrates and the Jury: Paradoxes in Plato's Distinction between Knowledge and True Belief, Part I' ['Jury I'], *Proceedings of the Aristotelian Society*, suppl. 54 (1980), 173–91 at 186–8). Several philosophers have argued that, in Plato generally, ἐπιστήμη more closely approximates understanding than knowledge (see, among others, J. M. E. Moravcsik, 'Understanding and Knowledge in Plato's Philosophy', *Neue Hefte für Philosophie*, 15–16 (1979), 53–69; J. Annas, *An Introduction to Plato's Republic* (Oxford, 1981), chs. 8 and 10; J. Moline, *Plato's Theory of Understanding* (Madison, 1981)).

⁵ Thanks to the editor of this journal for discussion here.

to that extent we should take it to be an account of knowledge. Gail Fine, for example, concludes her argument that Socrates is discussing knowledge and not understanding by saying, '[c]ontemporary epistemology is a large umbrella, and Plato's views fit comfortably under it' ('KTB *Meno*', 71).

The epistemological landscape, however, has changed dramatically, especially in the last ten years. An increasing number of philosophers have turned their attention to discussing the nature and value of understanding as distinct from knowledge.[6] Although accounts of the distinction vary, it is typically held that understanding is a higher cognitive achievement than knowledge: a budding high-school maths student, for example, can know the Pythagorean Theorem in that she can reliably pick it out on lists of mathematical formulae and can apply it to solve certain mathematical problems. But understanding it is a greater achievement, requiring, at the very least, also being able to position the theorem in the broader context of Euclidean geometry. A central worry is that, if we avail ourselves only of the concept of knowledge, we may end up either denying knowledge to people who have it or failing to distinguish adequately between exceptional cognitive achievements and the more humdrum.

Two prominent issues that philosophers are currently exploring in this area warrant special mention: (1) whether scientific enquiry aims at knowledge or some other cognitive achievement, such as understanding, and (2) the difference between moral knowledge and moral understanding.[7] I specifically mention these topics be-

[6] See e.g. L. Zagzebski, 'Recovering Understanding', in M. Steup (ed.), *Knowledge, Truth, and Duty: Essays on Epistemic Justification, Responsibility, and Virtue* (Oxford, 2001), 235–52; J. Kvanvig, *The Value of Knowledge and the Pursuit of Understanding* [*Understanding*] (Cambridge, 2003); W. Riggs, 'Understanding Virtue and the Virtue of Understanding' ['Virtue'], in M. Depaul and L. Zagzebski (eds.), *Intellectual Virtue: Perspectives from Ethics and Epistemology* (Oxford, 2003), 203–26; C. Elgin, 'From Knowledge to Understanding', in S. Hetherington (ed.), *Epistemology Futures* (Oxford, 2006), 199–215; D. Pritchard, 'Knowledge, Understanding, and Epistemic Value', in A. O'Hear (ed.), *Epistemology*, Royal Institute of Philosophy Lectures (Cambridge, 2009), 19–43; S. Grimm, 'Understanding', in D. Pritchard and S. Bernecker (eds.), *The Routledge Companion to Epistemology* (London, 2010), 84–94; M. Strevens, 'No Understanding without Explanation' ['Explanation'], *Studies in History and Philosophy of Science*, 44 (2013), 510–15; J. Greco, 'Episteme: Knowledge and Understanding', in K. Timpe and C. Boyd (eds.), *Virtues and their Vices* (Oxford, 2014), 285–302. Of course, this is not an exhaustive catalogue either of these philosophers' work on understanding or of philosophers currently working on understanding.

[7] For the former see Grimm, 'Understanding', 84, and the references therein. For

cause, as is well known, in the *Meno* Socrates treats *epistēmē* as the aim of rational enquiry and considers the possibility that *epistēmē* (or some kind of *epistēmē*) is virtue. The recent work just cited suggests that these claims could be quite different depending on whether Socrates conceives of *epistēmē* in line with contemporary thinking on knowledge or contemporary thinking on understanding. The time is ripe, then, to reconsider how Socrates' discussion of *epistēmē* maps onto our contemporary epistemological landscape.

In this paper I argue that Socrates' account of *epistēmē* is more charitably taken as an account of understanding than as an account of knowledge. I aim to go beyond the standard defence of this view in two main ways. First, I will provide a substantive reconstruction of Socrates' conception of *epistēmē* by getting clear on what Socrates thinks working out the explanation consists in. According to the interpretation I develop, working out the explanation of some fact is coming to see how it is grounded in facts about the natures of the fundamental entities of the domain to which it belongs. So, for Socrates, to have *epistēmē* of something—for example, a geometrical theorem—is to grasp how the truth of that theorem is grounded in facts about the natures of the fundamental entities of geometry.[8] Second, once my reconstruction is on the table, I appeal to more recent work in epistemology to help identify the cognitive state Socrates takes himself to be discussing and evaluate his account of it. I argue that, while Socrates' account of *epistēmē* fares badly in current discussions of knowledge, it is quite at home in current discussions of understanding. Moreover, I argue that Socrates' account of *epistēmē* provides insights that any philosopher interested in understanding should take seriously. Thus, while I agree with Gail Fine that Socrates' views fit comfortably under the umbrella of contemporary epistemology, I think that this is because contemporary epistemology has recently enlarged its umbrella, rather than because

---

the latter see A. Hills, 'Moral Testimony and Moral Epistemology' ['Testimony'], *Ethics*, 120 (2009), 94–127, esp. 98–106.

[8] The views that come closest to mine in the literature are presented by G. Vlastos, *Socratic Studies* (Cambridge, 1994), esp. 85, and W. Prior, 'Plato and the "Socratic Fallacy"' ['Fallacy'], *Phronesis*, 43 (1998), 97–113, both of whom hold that Socrates takes definitions to be the starting-points of ἐπιστήμη (cf. also S. Menn, 'Plato and the Method of Analysis', *Phronesis*, 47 (2002), 193–223 at 215–23, and Scott, *Plato's Meno*, 183). However, neither of these interpreters develops his view in the way and detail that I do, and so I am unsure how much the overall conception of ἐπιστήμη I develop lines up with theirs.

we can shoehorn Socrates' discussion into current discussions of knowledge. Before I begin I wish to make two terminological and two methodological points. First, in order not to prejudge whether *epistēmē* more closely approximates knowledge or understanding, I leave the Greek word ἐπιστήμη transliterated and use the verb 'to apprehend' in a stipulated sense to denote the cognitive relation that someone with *epistēmē* of some fact bears to that fact. Second, although for the purposes of this paper the reader will not go too far wrong in thinking of *doxa* as belief, I leave the Greek word δόξα transliterated. Third, in this paper I am interested only in the views advanced in the *Meno*. Although I do think that the same or similar views are advanced in other Platonic dialogues, I am not interested, at present, in such connections. Lastly, I wish to emphasize that my argument is one from interpretative charity. I do not attempt to prove conclusively that Socrates' account of *epistēmē* is intended as an account of what current epistemologists are discussing under the heading 'understanding'. Rather, I argue that, since it is both textually legitimate and philosophically fruitful to interpret Socrates in this way, charity should lead us to do so.

2. A preliminary objection

Before discussing the *Meno* directly, I wish to address a serious objection to any attempt to interpret *epistēmē* as something other than knowledge. The objection is levelled by Jonathan Barnes (and cited approvingly by Gail Fine at 'KTB *Meno*', 70 n. 75):

[T]he verb '*epistasthai*', and its cognates '*epistēmē*' and '*epistēmōn*', are not philosophical neologisms; they occur frequently in Greek literature from Homer onwards, and they are there correctly translated by 'know' and its cognates. (At all events, I have found no text which invites the translation 'understand'.) Both Plato and Aristotle talk of *epistēmē* without special qualification or apology; they give no indication that they intend the term in a novel or restricted sense: we are obliged to conclude that they thought they were investigating the ordinary concept of knowledge.[9]

I agree with Barnes's methodological point that we should under-

[9] J. Barnes, 'Socrates and the Jury: Paradoxes in Plato's Distinction between Knowledge and True Belief, Part II' ['Jury II'], *Proceedings of the Aristotelian Society*, suppl. 54 (1980), 193–206 at 204.

stand Plato's characters to be discussing what was denoted by standard uses of '*epistēmē*' in the time surrounding Plato's writing. However, against Barnes, I think that such uses often denote a higher cognitive achievement than what most current epistemologists think would be required for knowledge.[10] The strongest evidence against Barnes comes from passages in which two people or groups are contrasted and the following two conditions are met: (1) only one is said to have *epistēmē*, but (2) both should be taken to have knowledge. Given that those with *epistēmē* are uniformly presented as being cognitively superior to those without it, if conditions (1) and (2) are met, '*epistēmē*' must denote a higher achievement than mere knowledge. Consider the following such passage from Thucydides:[11]

> Hermocrates took the same view, and urged them [sc. the Syracusans] strongly not to be faint-hearted at the prospect of attacking with their ships . . . He was quite sure that if they faced the Athenian navy suddenly and unexpectedly, they would gain more than they would lose; the consternation which they would inspire would more than counterbalance their own inexperience and the *epistēmē* of the Athenians. He told them therefore to try what they could do at sea, and not to be timid. Thus under the influence of Gylippus, Hermocrates, and others, the Syracusans, now eager for the conflict, began to man their ships. (7. 21. 3. 1–22. 1. 1, trans. Jowett)

In this passage Hermocrates implores the Syracusans not to fear the fact that the Athenians have *epistēmē* concerning naval warfare, claiming that a surprise attack will negate any advantage that *epistēmē* might otherwise give the Athenians. We cannot read this, however, as suggesting that only the Athenians, but not the Syracusans, have knowledge concerning naval warfare. If the Syracusans do not know how to sail, how to fight at sea, etc., then their eagerness mentioned at the end would be nothing short of sheer stupidity. Rather, the Syracusans have the relevant knowledge; what they lack, and what the Athenians possess, is some higher achievement. In fact, many translators recognize that Hermocrates must be attributing something more than mere knowledge to the Athenians: Jowett, for example, translates '*epistēmē*' as 'superior skill', where

[10] It is unclear what exactly Barnes means by 'the ordinary concept of knowledge'. Since the question of this paper is how Socrates' discussion of ἐπιστήμη fits into current epistemological debate, Barnes's objection is most pressing in the form in which I have interpreted it.

[11] For similar passages see, among others, Thuc. 1. 142. 6–7 and 2. 87. 4.

The Epistemology of the Meno 7

no separate Greek word corresponds to 'superior'. Jowett is correctly recognizing that the superiority must be built into the meaning of *'epistēmē'* itself.

There are other passages in which it is more natural, if not strictly required, to understand *'epistēmē'* as denoting something superior to knowledge. Isocrates, for example, responds to critics who claim that he does not improve his students because they are not immediately finished orators by insisting that 'on the contrary, *epistēmē* accrues to us scarcely at all' (*Antidosis* 201. 4).[12] While it may be the case that *some* knowledge accrues to us scarcely at all, we can certainly acquire some knowledge quite easily (e.g. by opening our eyes or listening to the experts).[13] It is more plausible, then, to take Isocrates to be claiming that a superior achievement to knowledge is seldom achieved.

I do not wish to labour the point, as Barnes does not support his claim concerning standard uses of *'epistēmē'* by explicitly citing any passages from authors contemporary with or prior to Plato (nor does Fine in citing Barnes). At the very least, I take the above discussion to be sufficient to show that uses of *'epistēmē'* outside of Plato do not force us to understand Socrates as discussing knowledge rather than something superior to knowledge.

3. Working out the explanation

3.1. *The difference between true* doxa *and* epistēmē

At the end of the *Meno* Socrates tries to explain why *epistēmē* is more highly valued than true *doxa* and what the difference between them is:

[ἀληθεῖς δόξαι] οὐ πολλοῦ ἄξιαί εἰσιν, ἕως ἄν τις αὐτὰς δήσῃ αἰτίας λογισμῷ. τοῦτο δ' ἐστίν, ὦ Μένων ἑταῖρε, ἀνάμνησις, ὡς ἐν τοῖς πρόσθεν ἡμῖν ὡμολόγηται. ἐπειδὰν δὲ δεθῶσιν, πρῶτον μὲν ἐπιστῆμαι γίγνονται, ἔπειτα μόνιμοι· καὶ διὰ ταῦτα δὴ τιμιώτερον ἐπιστήμη ὀρθῆς δόξης ἐστίν, καὶ διαφέρει δεσμῷ ἐπιστήμη ὀρθῆς δόξης. (98 A 3–8)

[True *doxai*] are not worth much until one gets them bound down by a working out of the explanation. And this, Meno my friend, is recollection, as we previously agreed. When they have been bound down, first they be-

[12] ἀλλὰ μόλις μὲν ἡμῖν τὰς ἐπιστήμας παραγιγνομένας.
[13] I discuss perception and testimony as sources of knowledge in more detail below (sect. 5.1.3).

come *epistēmai* and thence permanent. It is on account of this that *epistēmē* is more highly valued than correct *doxa*, and *epistēmē* differs from correct *doxa* in virtue of a bond.

This passage shows that Socrates thinks true *doxa* is not sufficient for *epistēmē*. It also shows that Socrates thinks people upgrade from true *doxa* to *epistēmē* by working out an explanation.[14] That is, a person who has *epistēmē* of some fact is distinguished from a person who has a mere true *doxa* concerning it in so far as the former, but not the latter, has worked out the explanation of why that fact obtains.

What, then, does Socrates think is involved in working out an explanation such that it upgrades true *doxa* to *epistēmē*? Unfortunately, this is a difficult question, since the nature of explanation is not an explicit topic of Socrates' and Meno's conversation. From the beginning of the dialogue, however, Socrates emphasizes the epistemic fundamentality of natures or essences.[15] As is well known,

[14] 'Upgrade' is intentionally ambiguous between two options: (1) that true δόξαι remain δόξαι after they have been bound to the soul (just as people can upgrade from a coach plane ticket to a first-class plane ticket); and (2) that true δόξαι lose their status as δόξαι after they have been bound to the soul (just as people can upgrade from a typewriter to a computer). Intense debate surrounds the question whether Socrates takes ἐπιστήμη to be a privileged kind of δόξα. For a sampling see D. Sedley, 'Three Platonist Interpretations of the *Theaetetus*', in C. Gill and M. McCabe (eds.), *Form and Argument in Late Plato* (Oxford, 1996), 79–103 at 93; G. Fine, 'KTB *Meno*', 50–5; C. Perin, 'Knowledge, Stability, and Virtue in the *Meno*', *Ancient Philosophy*, 32 (2012), 15–34 at 16–17; K. Vogt, *Belief and Truth: A Skeptic Reading of Plato* (Oxford, 2012), 13–14. My ultimate position is that Socrates is neutral on this issue and, since my argument here does not depend on it, I ignore it and use the ambiguous 'upgrade'.

[15] According to G. Fine, Socrates claims only that natures or essences are epistemically fundamental to the apprehension of *some* facts ('KTB *Meno*', 56–7; cf. G. Fine, 'Inquiry in the *Meno*', in R. Kraut (ed.), *The Cambridge Companion to Plato* (Cambridge, 1992), 200–26 at 216 n. 6). However, given that Socrates says there is a single process through which explanations are worked out such that ἐπιστήμη comes to be (i.e. recollection), I think that taking natures or essences to be involved in *all* such explanations best maintains the dialogue's unity. Fine, quite naturally, denies that Socrates takes recollection to be the sole process through which explanations are worked out ('KTB *Meno*', 59–60). Her argument rests on the claim that Socrates leaves it open whether disembodied souls do not acquire but, rather, always possess ἐπιστήμη. Thus, she concludes, '[Socrates] presumably would not make it definitionally true that one can know that *p* only if one acquires one's knowledge through recollection' (ibid. 60). Although Fine's argument is important, I only have time to note my main disagreement: although Socrates may leave it open whether discarnate souls acquire ἐπιστήμη, the passage at the end of the *Meno* concerns how ἐπιστήμη comes to be (γίγνεσθαι). I take his discussion, then, to cover only those entities that must acquire (or reacquire) their ἐπιστήμη, and his claim is that such entities do so through recollection.

in the dialogue's opening lines Socrates claims that he cannot answer Meno's question concerning the acquisition of virtue because he does not apprehend what virtue is (70 A 1–71 A 7). According to Socrates, apprehending what something is like—teachable, for example—is epistemically posterior to apprehending what it is (71 B 3–4).[16] In other words, Socrates claims that someone cannot apprehend whether X is F without apprehending what X is. As we learn from Socrates' discussion, apprehending what X is is a matter of apprehending the nature or essence of X. This becomes clear later when he specifies that apprehending what X is requires that one apprehend the definition of X (72 C 6–D 1).[17] Socrates, then, says that he cannot apprehend whether virtue is teachable because he does not apprehend the nature of virtue.

Similarly, in the course of their discussion Socrates implores Meno to specify 'some one same form which they [sc. virtues] all have on account of which [di' ho] they are virtues' (72 C 7–8). The nature of virtue, then, plays a fundamental role in determining (metaphysically) whether a putative virtue is, in fact, a virtue. That is, if justice is a virtue, the fact that justice is a virtue is grounded in facts about the nature of virtue.[18] Thus, apprehending what virtue is will put a person in a position to apprehend whether justice is a virtue.

---

[16] Socrates asks Meno, 'That which I don't know what it is, how could I know what it is like?' (ὃ δὲ μὴ οἶδα τί ἐστιν, πῶς ἂν ὁποῖόν γέ τι εἰδείην;). Although Socrates' question is couched in terms of οἶδα, I take him to be discussing a condition on ἐπιστήμη. One difficulty surrounding the *Meno* is that, while Socrates contrasts true δόξα specifically with ἐπιστήμη in the passage we will focus on, he elsewhere refers to the latter state with a variety of terms (e.g. φρόνησις (cf. 88 B 4 and 88 C 2) and σοφία (cf. 99 B 5, although there he calls the state 'some kind of σοφία')). Thus, like most interpreters, I take the discussion elsewhere in the dialogue to illuminate Socrates' conception of ἐπιστήμη (for further discussion see Prior, 'Fallacy', 101).

[17] The seminal discussion of this notion of definition is in R. Robinson, *Plato's Earlier Dialectic* (Oxford, 1953), 49–60. Kit Fine has recently argued, independently of any concern with interpreting ancient philosophy, that 'the activities of specifying the meaning of a word and of stating what an object is are essentially the same; and hence each of them has an equal right to be regarded as a form of definition' (K. Fine, 'Essence and Modality' ['Essence'], *Philosophical Perspectives*, 14 (1994), 1–16 at 14).

[18] The notion of a fact being grounded in, or holding in virtue of, another fact has received extensive treatment in recent years (although not all philosophers think that grounding is a relation between *facts*). For a 'state-of-the-art' survey of recent literature see M. Clark and D. Liggins, 'Recent Work on Grounding', *Analysis*, 72 (2012), 812–23. Many philosophers who invoke the notion of grounding explicitly present it as an attempt to capture the relation that (they think) ancient philosophers such as Plato and Aristotle were talking about when using 'in virtue of' language.

Generalizing from the last two paragraphs, it seems clear that Socrates takes working out the explanation of some fact to require coming to see how it is grounded in certain other facts, namely facts about the natures of certain things. To develop this idea, I turn to the exchange between Socrates and Meno's slave. This episode is particularly useful as it provides a case in which someone has a true *doxa* yet is said not to have *epistēmē*. Moreover, we are shown exactly how he acquires that true *doxa*. Thus, the exchange provides an opportunity to examine what Socrates thinks a person with mere true *doxa* lacks such that working out an explanation will bring about *epistēmē*.

3.2. The exchange between Socrates and Meno's slave

As part of his effort to quell Meno's famous worry (see 80 D 5–E 5), Socrates engages in a back-and-forth discussion with one of Meno's slaves. After drawing a two-foot by two-foot square, Socrates asks the slave to specify on which line a square with double the area of the drawn square is based (82 D 8–E 2). In the initial stages of the discussion the slave offers two suggestions that are rejected (82 E 2–83 E 10). He then states that he does not apprehend the answer to Socrates' question (84 A 1–2). Socrates then, through additional questioning, gets the slave to evince a further *doxa* on the matter, and this further *doxa* turns out to be true (84 D 3–85 B 7). Although it will be familiar to most readers, we must look at this final stage in some detail since the particular manner in which the slave acquires his true *doxa* is important to evaluating its epistemic status. After Socrates has drawn four adjacent squares of equal size, the discussion proceeds as follows:

SOC. Does not this line from one corner to the other [*pointing to line segment AD*] cut each of these figures in two?
SLAVE. Yes.

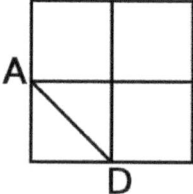

SOC. So these are four equal lines which enclose this figure [*pointing to square* ABCD]?
SLAVE. They are.

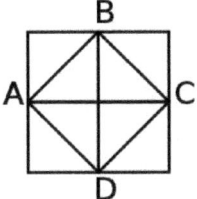

SOC. Consider now: how large is the figure [*pointing again to square* ABCD]?
SLAVE. I do not understand.
SOC. Within these four figures [*pointing to each small square*], each line cuts off half of each, does it not?
SLAVE. Yes.
SOC. How many of this size [*pointing to square* AJDH] are there in this figure [*pointing to square* EFGH]?
SLAVE. Four.

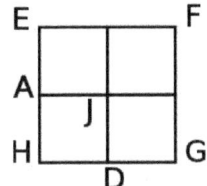

SOC. How many in this [*pointing to square* ABCD]?
SLAVE. Two.

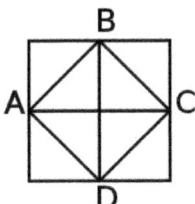

SOC. What is the relation of four to two?
SLAVE. Double.
SOC. How many feet in this [*pointing to square* ABCD]?
SLAVE. Eight.
SOC. Based on what line?
SLAVE. This one [*pointing to line segment* AD].   (84 E 4–85 B 2)

Meno's slave, then, has come to think that (S) is true:

(S) The double-area square is based on the diagonal of the original square.

Despite the slave's coming to think, as a result of this discussion, that (S) is true, Socrates denies that the slave has *epistēmē* of (S):

καὶ νῦν μέν γε αὐτῷ ὥσπερ ὄναρ ἄρτι ἀνακεκίνηνται αἱ δόξαι αὗται· εἰ δὲ αὐτόν τις ἀνερήσεται πολλάκις τὰ αὐτὰ ταῦτα καὶ πολλαχῇ, οἶσθ᾽ ὅτι τελευτῶν οὐδενὸς ἧττον ἀκριβῶς ἐπιστήσεται περὶ τούτων. . . . οὐκοῦν οὐδενὸς διδάξαντος ἀλλ᾽ ἐρωτήσαντος ἐπιστήσεται, ἀναλαβὼν αὐτὸς ἐξ αὑτοῦ τὴν ἐπιστήμην; — ναί. (85 c 9–D 1)

These *doxai* have now just been stirred up in him like a dream, but if he is asked these same questions many times and in various ways, you know that ultimately he will apprehend these things no less precisely than anyone else . . . And will he apprehend without having been taught but only questioned, and take up the *epistēmē* himself from himself? — Yes.

Socrates' claim that the slave does not yet apprehend (S) should give us pause.[19] After all, the slave has acquired his *doxa* in a manner that seems both reliable and illuminating, and it is well justified.[20] Socrates does not say why he thinks that the slave does not yet apprehend (S)—all he says is that, *if* the slave is to apprehend it, he must be asked these questions many times and in various ways.

The passage at the end of the dialogue, quoted above, tells us why Socrates thinks that the slave lacks *epistēmē*: the slave has not worked out the geometrical theorem's explanation. However, this could be taken in two ways. On the one hand, Socrates could think that he has presented the theorem's explanation or, at least, something sufficiently close to it (for example, the discussion might need to be reformulated in a more rigorous form, but the essentials of the explanation are there). The slave's shortcomings, then, would fall entirely on the 'working out' side, in the sense that the slave needs to do more cognitive work in order to grasp that what Socrates presented explains why the theorem is true. On the other hand, Socra-

---

[19] Someone may contend that Socrates commits himself to the claim that ἐπιστήμη comes in degrees of precision (i.e. because he says that the slave will apprehend 'no less precisely'), and this might suggest that the slave does apprehend (S) to some degree. Although such a reading is possible, it is not required. For example, someone who says 'A person who drowns in shallow water drowns no less fatally than a person who drowns in deep water' is not thereby committed to the claim that drowning comes in degrees of fatality. Also note that later in this passage Socrates says simply that the slave, after further questioning, 'will apprehend' (ἐπιστήσεται) the fact in question.   [20] I return to the issue of justification below (sect. 5.1.1).

tes may think that he did not present the slave with the theorem's explanation. On this interpretation, the slave must not only do more cognitive work on the information already presented, he must also acquire substantial additional information.

I think that the overall context of the dialogue makes it clear that the latter represents Socrates' position. First, recall Socrates' commitment to the epistemic priority of apprehending the natures of things. Second, note that in the discussion with the slave Socrates does not appeal to facts about the natures of any entities in such a way that those facts do any explanatory work. Nor does Socrates make it apparent to the slave that natures have any explanatory power at all. Even though Socrates appeals to facts concerning the nature of some entity or that are true of an entity in virtue of its nature, he does not single out a class of facts concerning the natures of squares, triangles, diagonal lines, and so on such that those facts play a basic role in the discussion. For example, Socrates appeals to the fact that a line drawn from one corner of a square to the opposite corner divides the square into two triangles of equal area (84 E 4–85 A 1). This fact does hold in virtue of the nature of squares, the nature of diagonal lines, and the nature of triangles—that is, because a square is what it is, a diagonal line is what it is, and a triangle is what it is, a diagonal line cuts a square into two triangles of equal area. However, Socrates does not make the explanatory role played by the natures of those entities perspicuous in any way. Moreover, he does not indicate that natures play any explanatory role at all. Any explanatory facts that Socrates may deploy, then, are not presented to the slave as having any special status.

If we look at people who were developing geometry in the time surrounding Plato's writing, we can understand better the sense in which natures can be explanatorily basic. Although I will explicitly appeal to Euclid's *Elements*, since it is the fullest extant near-contemporary geometrical treatise we have, scholars agree that this conception of the explanatory role of natures was well established by Plato's time.[21] I should emphasize that I look to Euclid only to

[21] While Ian Mueller, for example, allows that the invocation of Postulates in geometry may post-date Plato (and even Aristotle) and that the invocation of Common Notions may be contemporary with Plato, he maintains that 'it seems to me entirely unlikely that mathematics ever had any kind of articulated deductive structure which did not involve definitions of some kind, some kind of explication of the nature of the things being talked about' (I. Mueller, 'Greek Mathematics (Arithmetic, Geometry, Proportion Theory) to the Time of Euclid', in M. L. Gill and P. Pellegrin (eds.), *A*

illuminate the sense in which natures can be explanatorily fundamental and not to attribute to Socrates the complete conception of geometry that we find in the *Elements*.

At the beginning of book 1, Euclid lays out twenty-three Definitions and then proceeds to prove certain geometrical facts from them, in combination with certain Postulates and Common Notions. An interesting feature of Socrates' discussion with Meno's slave is that one of the facts Socrates appeals to is contained in Proposition 34 of book 1:

> *Proposition* 34: In parallelogrammic figures the opposite sides and angles are equal to one another, and *a diagonal cuts them in half*.[22]

The proof of Proposition 34, however, directly appeals to, and so rests on, Propositions 29, 26, and 4. The proof of Proposition 29, in turn, directly appeals to Propositions 15 and 13. By following this chain of dependences, we see that the proof of Proposition 34 ultimately depends on Propositions 29, 26, 16, 15, 13, 11, 10, 9, 8, 7, 5, 4, 3, 2, and 1. In the proofs of each of these Propositions, however, several of the claims directly depend upon the Definitions stated at the outset of the *Elements*. To take just one such example, consider Proposition 1:

> *Proposition* 1: On a given finite straight line to construct an equilateral triangle.

Contained in the proof of Proposition 1 is the following claim:

> Since [1] point A is the centre of the circle CDB, [2] AC is equal to AB.

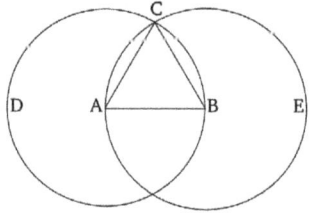

Companion to Ancient Philosophy (Oxford, 2006), 686–718 at 689). It is clear from the discussion of the Divided Line (510 B 9–D 3) that the character Socrates of the *Republic* conceives of natures as explanatorily basic in geometry (cf. M. Burnyeat, 'Plato on Why Mathematics is Good for the Soul', in T. Smiley (ed.), *Mathematics and Necessity: Essays in the History of Philosophy* (Oxford, 2000), 1–81 at 24).

[22] Translations of Euclid's *Elements* are taken, with modifications, from T. Heath, *The Thirteen Books of Euclid's* Elements (1908; repr. New York, 1956).

The Epistemology of the Meno

The move from [1] to [2], in turn, is supported by the Definitions of Circle and Centre:

Definition 15: A Circle is a plane figure contained by one line, such that all of the straight lines falling upon it from one point among those lying within the figure are equal to one another.

Definition 16: And, the point [specified in Definition 15] is called the Centre of the circle.

In other words, it is precisely because a circle is what it is, and the centre is what it is, that the fact that A is the centre of circle CDB makes it the case that AC is equal to AB. In order to see why Proposition 1 is true, then, one must see how its truth depends on the nature of circles and the nature of centre. In an analogous manner, in order to grasp Proposition 34 fully, one must ultimately see how its truth is grounded in the nature of lines, triangles, squares, and so on (which, given the nested nature of geometry, will probably require grasping the natures of additional entities, such as circles).

To return to the discussion between Socrates and Meno's slave, we can now see why Socrates denies that the slave apprehends (S) despite having acquired his *doxa* through the process depicted above. To put the point metaphorically, the slave fails to see a good deal of the 'picture'. To put the point more directly, the slave has accepted many claims without explanation that stand in need of explanation. Specifically, he fails to grasp how the truth of the theorem is grounded in facts about the nature of the entities cited in the theorem (grasping which will probably require him to grasp facts about the natures of additional entities). The slave, through being asked further questions many times and in various ways, must work out why, given what a square is, what a diagonal is, and so on, the double-area square is based on the diagonal of the original square. Presumably this will involve reasoning all the way to facts about the natures of the fundamental entities of geometry. If an appeal is made to facts about the nature of some entity that are grounded in facts about the nature of some more fundamental entity, then facts about the nature of the more fundamental entity would have explanatory power (for example, facts about the nature of squares may be partially grounded in facts about the nature of lines). Such a process would bottom out at the fundamental entities. Thus, the slave must come to grasp what a point is, what a line is, what a figure is, and so on, so that he can see why, given the nature of those entities, the geometrical theorem is true. Only then will he have worked out the geometrical theorem's explanation.[23]

Before we flesh out Socrates' conception of *epistēmē*, I wish to consider an objection to my interpretation thus far. It may seem that I am building too large an edifice on Socrates' claim that the slave will apprehend the theorem after 'he is asked these same questions many times and in various ways' (85 c 10–11). While most interpreters agree that Socrates does not mean that the slave must be asked literally the same questions over and over,[24] my claim that such questioning must take the slave all the way to fundamental entities may seem overblown. Perhaps all Socrates means is that the slave must be questioned a little more to make sure his grasp of the theorem is sufficiently secure.[25]

I agree that if we consider this line in isolation my interpretation is too strong. However, it is precisely because Socrates says only that the slave must be asked further questions, and does not specify the ultimate aim of such questioning, that we must look elsewhere in the dialogue to fill in the details. At the end of the dialogue we learn that acquiring *epistēmē* requires working out an explanation. So, we

---

[23] Similarities exist between Socrates' discussion and current discussions of mathematical explanation. For example, Mark Steiner holds that 'an explanatory [mathematical] proof makes reference to a characterizing property of an entity or structure mentioned in the theorem, such that from the proof it is evident that the result depends on the property' (M. Steiner, 'Mathematical Explanation', *Philosophical Studies*, 34 (1978), 135–51 at 143). Steiner speaks of characterizing properties rather than of natures because he thinks that an entity's or structure's nature consists in its essential properties, and, in turn, he thinks that essential properties just are necessary properties. Given that all the properties of a mathematical entity or structure are necessary, we cannot isolate a proper subset of its properties as constituting its essence. Kit Fine's work on essence and modality (especially his 'Essence'), however, provides a different way of conceiving of the relationship between necessity and essentiality that allows a role for the concept of essence in mathematics.

However, Socrates' discussion differs from these modern discussions in important ways. Foremost, unlike current philosophers of mathematics, Socrates is not attempting to distinguish proofs that merely *prove that* some theorem is true from proofs that also *explain why* some theorem is true (for a general description of issues in 'mathematical explanations within mathematics' see P. Mancosu, 'Explanation in Mathematics', in E. Zalta (ed.), *The Stanford Encyclopedia of Philosophy* (Summer 2011) ⟨http://plato.stanford.edu/archives/sum2011/entries/mathematics-explanation/⟩, § 4). Rather, Socrates is specifying conditions for being in a cognitive state of which he takes himself to have an independent grasp. He is *not* surveying the work of mathematicians and singling out a proper subset of proofs as having some special (i.e. explanatory) status. Thanks to Jimmy Martin for discussion here.

[24] See Scott, *Plato's* Meno, 106–7, for discussion.

[25] Thanks to Rachel Barney and Kirk Ludwig for pressing this objection.

The Epistemology of the Meno 17

can infer that the further questioning must lead the slave to work out the theorem's explanation. The question then becomes: 'What does Socrates think explanation consists in?' By further examining the dialogue and, in particular, by noting the emphasis Socrates places from the beginning on the epistemic priority of facts about what something is (especially at 71 B 3–4), I have argued that he takes explanation to consist in tracing the truth of a fact back to facts about the natures of relevant fundamental entities. Thus, although in isolation the line does not generate my picture, in its broader context it does.

4. Socrates' conception of *epistēmē*

Let us now consider the conception of *epistēmē* that results from Socrates' claim that *epistēmē* of some fact is acquired by working out its explanation. The key characteristic of people with *epistēmē* of some fact is that they have worked out how that fact fits into a broader network of interrelated facts. Such a network crucially includes facts about the nature of the fundamental entities of the domain to which that fact belongs. The person with *epistēmē* of some fact, then, has a synoptic view of the way in which that fact fits into its relevant domain, including, crucially, how the fact is grounded in facts about the natures of certain relevant fundamental entities.

Some interpreters maintain that *epistēmē*, according to Socrates, requires mastery of the entirety of some domain. According to Nehamas, for example, '[w]e have *epistēmē* when we have learned the axiomatic structure of the system in question and can prove any one of its elements' ('Meno's Paradox', 20). Although this claim is consistent with my interpretation, nothing I have said requires it. On the picture thus far, *epistēmē* of some fact *P* requires that one grasps how *P* is grounded in facts about the natures of the fundamental entities of the domain to which *P* belongs. If *P* is wholly grounded in facts about the natures of a proper subset of the fundamental entities of the domain to which *P* belongs, then *epistēmē* of *P* does not require grasping the nature of any irrelevant fundamental entities. On this interpretation, one can have *epistēmē* of a fact *without* having mastery of the entire domain to which it belongs.

However, even if Socrates would accept the further requirement that *epistēmē* of a fact requires mastery of the entirety of its domain, on the picture I have developed *epistēmē* can be had of discrete domains (i.e. domains that do not share fundamental entities) in isolation from one another. For example, if the domain of medicine and the domain of geometry share no fundamental entities, then one can have *epistēmē* of (facts of) medicine without having *epistēmē* of (facts of) geometry. Indeed, Socrates suggests that *epistēmē* is domain-specific in this way when he describes the future course of the slave's education:

οὗτος γὰρ ποιήσει περὶ πάσης γεωμετρίας ταὐτὰ ταῦτα, καὶ τῶν ἄλλων μαθημάτων ἁπάντων. (85 E 1–3)

For he will perform in this same way with all of geometry, and, indeed, all other subjects.

This claim comes *after* Socrates says that further questioning will lead the slave to acquire *epistēmē* of the geometrical theorem, and so it suggests that the slave can first acquire *epistēmē* of geometry and then acquire *epistēmē* of other subjects. However, it may turn out that Socrates thinks reality consists of a single unified domain, such that facts about a single entity or set of entities ground all other facts.[26] What I have provided, then, is Socrates' answer to what I. M. Crombie calls the 'formal' interpretation of the question 'What can be apprehended?' In so far as that question is understood to mean 'What does a fact have to be like for it to be a possible object of *epistēmē*?', the answer is: 'It must belong to a domain structured in terms of fundamental facts concerning natures and derivable facts.' The question whether objects of *epistēmē* belong to discrete domains depends on Socrates' metaphysics.[27]

One last issue I wish to address is how, if at all, someone can have *epistēmē* of facts about the fundamental entities of a given domain. If *epistēmē* of some fact requires grasping its explanation, it seems that facts about fundamental entities cannot be apprehended—since they are fundamental, no further fact explains them. Alternatively, if facts about fundamental entities can be apprehended, the way in

[26] As is well known, *Republic* 6 and 7 suggest that the Form of the Good is *the* fundamental entity of reality.

[27] Crombie helpfully distinguishes between what he calls 'formal' and 'material' interpretations of the question 'What can be apprehended?' as follows (although he couches the questions in terms of 'knowledge'): 'The answer to the formal version of this question will lay down the conditions that anything must satisfy in order to be knowable: the answer to the material version will tell us what things satisfy these conditions' (I. M. Crombie, *An Examination of Plato's Doctrines*, vol. ii (London, 1963), 41).

which they are apprehended must differ from the way in which derivable facts are apprehended.

It is often thought that Plato (or his various characters) maintains that facts about fundamental entities are grasped in the appropriate way by direct intuition. However, my interpretation offers an alternative, and possibly more attractive, view, at least as far as the *Meno* goes. On my reading, apprehending some fact is a matter of grasping how that fact fits into a broader network of interrelated facts that at least partially constitute some domain. For facts that can be derived, *epistēmē* requires grasp of the appropriate derivation. There is, however, no reason why *epistēmē*, on this conception, would be limited only to derivable facts. One can apprehend a fact about the nature of a fundamental entity by grasping how *it* fits into a network of interrelated facts, where this would require grasping the fundamental explanatory role that it plays.[28] Recall the example from Euclid above (sect. 3.2) in which facts about the nature of circles partially grounded a claim made in the course of proving Proposition 1. Socrates could maintain that part of what is required to apprehend facts about the nature of circles is precisely to grasp the role they play in explaining various derivable facts, such as the one cited in the proof of Proposition 1. That claim read as follows:

> Since [1] point A is the centre of the circle CDB, [2] AC is equal to AB.

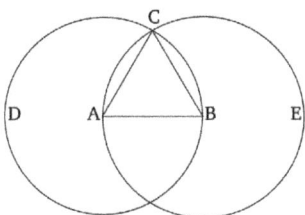

If someone could, for example, recite Definitions 15 and 16, yet did not see that the move from claim [1] to claim [2] is legitimate, this

[28] G. Fine, 'KTB *Meno*', 76–8, presents a somewhat similar view in what she calls Plato's 'interrelation model of knowledge'. However, I disagree strongly with her claim that, for Plato, 'no propositions are known non-inferentially' (ibid. 77). To say that having ἐπιστήμη of facts about natures or essences requires grasping the role they play in explaining subordinate facts is not to say that one infers them from anything. My proposal for distinguishing ἐπιστήμη of provable facts from ἐπιστήμη of fundamental facts is similar to Michael Strevens's distinction between 'understanding why' and 'understanding with' (Strevens, 'Explanation', 513).

would indicate that he or she did not adequately grasp the nature of circles or centres. Accommodating the grasp of first principles in this way would, of course, require broadening Socrates' claim that acquiring *epistēmē* requires working out an explanation, but it is a natural extension of his thinking.[29]

5. What is *epistēmē*?

Now that we have established the details of Socrates' account of *epistēmē*, we can consider where it fits in the current epistemological landscape. In the remainder of this paper I argue that Socrates' account fares badly in current discussions of knowledge but is quite at home in current discussions of understanding. Moreover, I argue that Socrates' account provides possible contributions to the latter that philosophers should take seriously. Thus, I conclude that interpretative charity should lead us to view Socrates' discussion as an attempt to give an account of understanding, rather than an account of knowledge.

5.1. *Is* epistēmē *knowledge?*

I begin by considering what role justification plays in Socrates' account of *epistēmē*. I do so for two reasons. First, as noted in the introduction, on a dominant interpretation of the *Meno*, Socrates characterizes *epistēmē* as *justified* true belief, and I wish to question this long-standing view. Second, and more germane to the specific issue of this section, justification is so centrally tied into the modern conception of knowledge that a characterization of an epistemic state in which justification plays no central role might seem like a change of subject. In fact, Dominic Scott frames the debate over the identity of *epistēmē* in the *Meno* as a debate over the role of justification in Socrates' discussion:

[29] Perhaps Socrates would resist calling such a grasp of facts about fundamental entities ἐπιστήμη strictly speaking. In his discussion of the Divided Line in the *Republic*, for example, the character Socrates claims that we grasp the objects in the highest subsection as a matter of comprehension (νόησιν) (511 D 6–8). However, comprehension seems to be a kind of ἐπιστήμη and, in a related passage in book 7, he explicitly calls this grasp of the highest objects ἐπιστήμη. In connection with this it is worth noting that in *Posterior Analytics* 2. 19 and *Nicomachean Ethics* 6. 6 Aristotle claims that the cognitive grasp we can have of first principles is comprehension (νοῦς) and not ἐπιστήμη strictly speaking.

By giving the notion of explanation centre stage, Socrates in the *Meno*, it has been argued, is not really interested in justification at all. Indeed one might go further and claim that he is not even talking about what we now call knowledge, which is the function of justification, but understanding, the function of explanation. (*Plato's Meno*, 184–5)[30]

According to Scott, in so far as we have reason to doubt whether Socrates thinks that justification plays a role in making it the case that a person counts as having *epistēmē*, we have reason to doubt that Socrates takes himself to be discussing knowledge (I take this to be a consequence of saying that knowledge is the 'function' of justification). Although I will go on to question this claim, it provides a useful place to start, since on many accounts knowledge does share an intimate connection with justification.

5.1.1. *Justification and working out the explanation* Unfortunately, discussion of what role, if any, justification plays in Socrates' account of *epistēmē* has been somewhat vague in the literature. I think that the best way to frame the issue is by asking whether Socrates thinks that working out the explanation of some fact upgrades true *doxa* to *epistēmē* because it confers a justification on the *doxa*.[31] We must distinguish this question from two related questions. First, does Socrates show a general interest in justification? It is entirely possible for Socrates to show a general concern with justification without his thinking that working out the explanation upgrades *doxa* to *epistēmē* because it confers a justification. Second, does working out an explanation confer a justification on a *doxa*? Again, it is entirely possible that working out an explanation would, as a matter of fact, confer a justification on a *doxa* without it being the case that Socrates thinks people count as acquiring *epistēmē* because their *doxa* comes to be justified in that way. Indeed, I think that the prevalence of taking working out the explanation to play a justificatory role in Socrates' epistemology is in part attributable to the fact that working out the explanation would make a *doxa* more justified (on virtually all views of justification). Because most modern discussions of justification focus on its role in upgrading true

---

[30] Scott himself goes on to argue that justification does play a central role in Socrates' account of ἐπιστήμη, and thus that 'there is greater continuity between the concept of knowledge adumbrated in the *Meno* and modern epistemology' (*Plato's Meno*, 185).

[31] As stated above (n. 14), I do not take a stand on whether upgraded δόξαι retain their status as δόξαι.

belief to knowledge, it is tempting to conclude from the fact that working out the explanation would make a *doxa* more justified that *Socrates* thinks it is because the *doxa* acquires that justification that it is upgraded to *epistēmē*. Distinguishing this last question from the question on which I focus, however, shows that such reasoning is invalid.

To begin, note that in reconstructing Socrates' account of *epistēmē* I made no appeal to a notion of justification. This was no mistake. At no point in the discussion does Socrates say that working out an explanation upgrades true *doxa* to *epistēmē* by making that *doxa* justified. Indeed, nowhere in the *Meno* does Socrates, or any character, describe a *doxa* as 'justified'. *A fortiori*, Socrates never explicitly says that *epistēmē* is justified (true) *doxa*. However, concluding from this observation that Socrates does not conceive of working out the explanation as playing a justificatory role would be too quick. Even if Socrates himself does not describe *doxai* as 'justified', it may still be illuminating to understand his position as implicitly employing a notion of justification. That is, given what Socrates says about *doxa*, *epistēmē*, and the role played by working out the explanation in linking the two, it may be best to understand that role as justificatory.[32]

The best way to support appealing to a notion of justification to illuminate Socrates' position is to look at the philosophical concerns that lead epistemologists to invoke it in their discussions. If Socrates is motivated by similar concerns when he claims that *epistēmē* requires working out an explanation, this would provide strong reason for thinking that he conceives of working out the explanation as playing a justificatory role, even if he does not put it that way. In other words, justification serves to scratch a philosophical itch, and we must determine whether Socrates posits working out the explanation to scratch that same itch.

The key feature of justification that interpreters point to is that, roughly speaking, justification is a matter of having good reasons (arguments, evidence, grounds, etc.) for belief (with different conceptions of justification consisting, in large part, in different accounts of what it is for someone to have good reasons to believe).

[32] Thus, I agree with G. Fine that there is little probative force in Burnyeat's observation that 'the *Meno*'s leading condition on knowledge, *aitias logismos* (98 A), is Greek for working out the explanation of something, *not* for assembling a justification for believing it' (G. Fine, 'KTB *Meno*', 61–3, discussing Burnyeat, 'Jury I', 187).

The Epistemology of the Meno 23

Likewise, these interpreters argue, Socrates seems to be concerned with whether people have good reasons for the views they hold. Thus, they conclude, Socrates is interested in justification. Gail Fine offers a representative example of such reasoning:

> Justification (of an internalist sort, at least) is generally thought to require good arguments or good reasons. In so far as Plato is concerned with the latter, it is reasonable to assume that he is concerned with the former, and indeed takes the former to require the latter. ('KTB *Meno*', 66)

Likewise, Dominic Scott maintains that appealing to justification is warranted because '[a] justification consists in a good reason for believing that *p*', and '[h]e [Socrates] wants good reasons for believing that virtue is a form of knowledge, teachable and so on' (*Plato's Meno*, 185).

However, as we saw above, we need to distinguish the question whether Socrates shows any interest in justification from the question whether he thinks that working out the explanation upgrades true *doxa* to *epistēmē because* it plays a justificatory role. The fact that Socrates may be concerned, in general, with whether people have good reasons for their views does *not* show that he intends working out the explanation to rectify a lack of having good reasons. In order to answer our central question, we must determine whether Socrates thinks that mere true *doxa* is debarred from counting as *epistēmē* for the same reasons modern-day epistemologists think true belief is debarred from counting as knowledge such that justification is posited as an additional requirement. If he does think that mere true *doxa* exhibits the same shortcomings as mere true belief, then, since working out the explanation is supposed to rectify those shortcomings, it would be reasonable to understand working out the explanation as playing a justificatory role.

To answer this question, let us return to the episode with Meno's slave. As Burnyeat points out ('Jury I', 187), by most modern accounts of justification, the *doxa* the slave acquires at the end of the discussion is justified (consider, in particular, the portion of the discussion depicted above, sect. 3.2). Even Fine concedes this point. However, she argues that this only shows that:

> Plato rejects a justified-true-belief account of knowledge, if the conditions for justification are construed weakly enough. But we should not infer that he rejects a justified-true-belief account of knowledge as such. Perhaps he favours such an account, but thinks that the sort of justification that is ne-

cessary for knowledge is more demanding than Burnyeat takes it to be. ('KTB *Meno*', 64)

At this point the discussion becomes rather difficult. If someone claims that Socrates, despite never putting it this way, may conceive of working out the explanation as bringing about *epistēmē* by providing a high-powered form of justification, it is difficult to argue against such a position. However, if we were to insist that Socrates thinks working out the explanation plays a justificatory role, this would direct attention away from the most pressing and interesting question. Rather than asking why Socrates offers this conception of *epistēmē*, we must ask why he offers this conception of justification (a conception which even Fine agrees would be highly restrictive). Claiming that Socrates thinks that working out the explanation plays a justificatory role, then, may not help to illuminate his position.

The problem, however, is worse than that. The main reason modern-day epistemologists think true belief is insufficient for knowledge is the problem of epistemic luck.[33] If a person acquires the true belief that *p* merely as a matter of luck, she does not know that *p*. Justification, then, is considered as a further condition to rule out cases of epistemic luck from counting as cases of knowledge.[34] When Socrates denies that the slave has acquired *epistēmē*, however, he gives no indication that this is because the slave may have acquired his true *doxa* by luck. Indeed, we have strong reason to think that luck is not what is at issue: the slave has been led to that *doxa* by a good teacher (i.e. Socrates) who intended him to come to have it, there is nothing deviant in the causal chain leading to the slave's *doxa*, and so on. If Socrates claims that the slave lacks *epistēmē* despite the absence of luck, it cannot be the presence of luck that he is worried about when he posits working out the explanation as a condition on acquiring *epistēmē*. To the

[33] As Mathias Steup puts it: 'Why is [the justification] condition necessary? Why not say that knowledge is true belief? The standard answer is that to identify knowledge with true belief would be implausible because a belief that is true just because of luck does not qualify as knowledge' (M. Steup, 'The Analysis of Knowledge', in E. Zalta (ed.), *The Stanford Encyclopedia of Philosophy* (Fall 2008) ⟨http://plato.stanford.edu/archives/fall2008/entries/knowledge-analysis⟩ § 1).

[34] Of course, one of Gettier's key insights is that even a justified belief can be true because of luck. The issue, however, is not whether philosophers think that justified true belief constitutes knowledge but, rather, what features debar true belief from constituting knowledge such that justification becomes an issue in the first place.

extent that Socrates is not motivated by the problem of epistemic luck, we should hesitate to think that he conceives of working out the explanation as playing a justificatory role. Otherwise we may impute philosophical concerns to Socrates that he does not, in fact, have.[35]

I conclude that appeals to a notion of justification are out of place in reconstructing Socrates' conception of *epistēmē* in the *Meno*. It is best, I think, to understand Socrates as holding that true *doxa* alone is insufficient for *epistēmē*, not because it necessarily lacks a justification, but because its possessor lacks certain relevant information (i.e. the explanation of why it is true). Thus, if the notion of justification is centrally connected to the notion of knowledge (for example, if it plays a role in setting the target for debate), we have strong reason for thinking that Socrates does not intend his account of *epistēmē* to be an account of knowledge.

5.1.2. *Knowledge without justification* Some philosophers, however, afford the notion of justification no central role in discussions that they take to be discussions of knowledge. Indeed, the view of *epistēmē* developed above bears similarities to the account of knowledge recently advanced by Richard Foley. Foley argues that much of recent epistemology has been marred by the mistaken thought that what must be added to true belief to render knowledge must be something different in kind from true belief (such as justification). Foley argues, on the contrary: 'What has to be added to S's true belief P in order to get knowledge? More true beliefs.'[36] Justification, he thinks, need not enter the picture. Moreover, Foley claims that 'whenever an individual S has a true belief P but does not know P, there is important information she lacks', which sounds quite close to my characterization of what Socrates thinks a person with mere true *doxa* lacks.[37] However, it is worth noting two points. First, Foley's account of knowledge is certainly not standard, and our main concern here is the relationship between Socrates' conception of *epistēmē* and current standard views of knowledge. Second, and perhaps more importantly, some philosophers have argued that

---

[35] Moreover, we may be led to assume that when Socrates contrasts true δόξα with ἐπιστήμη, the former only includes cognitive achievements that fall short of what is typically considered knowledge (see n. 44 below).
[36] R. Foley, *When is True Belief Knowledge?* (Princeton, 2012), 8.
[37] Ibid.

Foley's account actually fares better as an account of understanding than as an account of knowledge.[38]

Regardless of the particular details concerning Foley's account, the point stands that showing that justification plays no central role in Socrates' account of *epistēmē* is not sufficient to show that *epistēmē* does not match what current philosophers take themselves to be discussing under the heading 'knowledge'. However, in the next section I argue that Socrates' account of *epistēmē* exhibits such severe extensional differences from most mainstream conceptions of knowledge that, if he had intended his account of *epistēmē* to be an account of what we typically call 'knowledge', it would probably be a very bad one. Now, this does not prove that Socrates did not intend his account in this way, but once we consider how it fares as an account of what is discussed under the heading 'understanding', we will see that the charitable interpretation is to take it in the latter way.

5.1.3. *Extensional differences* A key obstacle to thinking that *epistēmē* approximates knowledge is that *epistēmē*, as Socrates conceives of it, cannot be acquired through many of the mechanisms that are standardly considered paradigm ways of acquiring knowledge. Take two such mechanisms: mere perception and testimony.[39] Consider, first, the case of testimony.[40] Given that Socrates denies that the slave has *epistēmē* at the end of their discussion, he would surely deny that the slave could acquire *epistēmē* merely through the testimony of an authority. Mere testimony is insufficient for acquiring *epistēmē* because Socrates requires that

[38] Cf. Kvanvig, *Understanding*, 199–200.

[39] These two mechanisms are almost unfailingly listed among the 'sources of knowledge' that any adequate account of knowledge must accommodate (cf. R. Audi, *Epistemology: A Contemporary Introduction to the Theory of Knowledge* (London, 2010), and the introduction to J. Adler, 'Epistemological Problems of Testimony', in E. Zalta (ed.), *The Stanford Encyclopedia of Philosophy* (Spring 2014) ⟨http://plato.stanford.edu/archives/spr2014/entries/testimony-episprob/⟩). Although philosophers have long discussed perception as a source of knowledge, they have only recently focused on testimony in its own right, and one of the central epistemological issues concerning it just is the question of 'how we successfully acquire justified belief or knowledge on the basis of what other people tell us' (J. Lackey, 'Introduction', in J. Lackey and E. Sosa (eds.), *The Epistemology of Testimony* (Oxford, 2006), 1–24 at 2). For an in-depth discussion of testimony see C. A. J. Coady, *Testimony: A Philosophical Study* (Oxford, 1992).

[40] Burnyeat, 'Jury I', 186–8, and Nehamas, 'Meno's Paradox', 26–8, also discuss the implications that the fact that ἐπιστήμη cannot be acquired by testimony has for whether it more closely approximates knowledge or understanding.

the slave, by working out the theorem's explanation, come to see for himself why it is true. The slave, that is, must come to have a command of the theorem that cannot be acquired through mere testimony.

Now consider the knowledge that mere perception is supposed to give us of our immediate surroundings. As has been noted by philosophers since Aristotle, perception alone can give us only the *that*, it can never give us the *why* (*Metaph.* 981^{b}10–13). Moreover, not only can mere perception not give us explanations, and certainly not explanations that go back to facts about natures or essences, but requiring a grasp of explanations is an odd requirement to place on most perceptual knowledge. We can certainly grant that there are explanations for facts about our immediate surroundings. The point, however, is that, for many facts about our immediate surroundings, such explanations are bad candidates for that which must be grasped in order to know them. For example, if the chair in my room is black, one explanation of why it is black is that Bob painted it black. It would be odd, however, to think that in order for me to know that *the chair is black* I would have to grasp that *it is black because Bob painted it black*. Or, if the explanation of why the chair is black is a matter of reflectance properties and the structure of our visual system, it is even more implausible to think that one must grasp that kind of explanation in order to know that *the chair is black*.[41]

Two points require comment. First, the claim is not that Socrates thinks it is *harder* to acquire *epistēmē* than philosophers typically think it is to acquire knowledge.[42] Socrates does not, for example, think that we just need to look harder or listen more attentively to acquire *epistēmē*. Rather, he thinks that no matter how hard you try, you cannot acquire *epistēmē* through such means. This strongly suggests that Socrates is discussing something that differs in kind, and not just in degree, from standard philosophical conceptions of knowledge.

Second, the above discussion concerns various modes of acquisition of knowledge and not, in the first instance, possible objects of knowledge. That is, I argued that *epistēmē*, unlike knowledge, cannot be acquired through mere perception, but I did not argue that *epistēmē* of perceptible facts is in principle impossible. On the con-

---
[41] Thanks to Jack Woods for discussion here.
[42] See G. Fine's discussion of such an objection in 'KTB *Meno*', 68–71.

ception of *epistēmē* that I have developed, *epistēmē* of some fact requires tracing the truth of that fact back to facts about fundamental natures or essences. And it is possible that the truth of facts about perceptible objects could be explained in the appropriate way.[43] In other words, if Socrates does rule out *epistēmē* of perceptible objects (as he is often thought to do in the *Republic*, for example), this would not be a consequence solely of the conception of *epistēmē* he presents in the *Meno*. Rather, it would require the further metaphysical claim that facts about perceptible objects are not grounded in the appropriate way in facts about natures or essences.

We have seen, then, that two central ways of acquiring knowledge, namely mere perception and testimony, are not ways in which one can acquire *epistēmē*. However, if *epistēmē* fails to include what are typically taken to be paradigm cases of knowledge, we seem to be faced with two possibilities: either (*a*) Socrates is not discussing knowledge, or (*b*) Socrates is making the grave philosophical error of mistaking a sufficient condition on knowledge for a necessary condition. I say that one option would be to conclude that Socrates is confusing a sufficient condition on knowledge with a necessary condition because someone who has *epistēmē* does seem to have knowledge. On most contemporary accounts of knowledge, once the slave, for example, has come to see why, given the natures of the fundamental entities of geometry, the double-area square is based on the diagonal of the original square, he will count as knowing that fact. Perhaps he even knows it by the end of his discussion with Socrates.[44] Thus, if one can have knowledge without having *epistēmē* but not vice versa, it is more plausible to take *epistēmē* to be a state that overlaps with, but is neither coextensive with nor identical to, knowledge. Charity, then, strongly favours that we accept option

---

[43] Aristotle, for example, also maintains that natures or essences play a fundamental explanatory role but thinks that there can be ἐπιστήμη, at least in some sense, of perceptible objects. In *Posterior Analytics* 1. 8 he claims that, while there is no proof (ἀπόδειξις) *simpliciter* (ἁπλῶς), and so no ἐπιστήμη *simpliciter* of perishable things, there is proof incidentally (κατὰ συμβεβηκός), and so ἐπιστήμη incidentally of them (75^{b}21–6). It is important to note that incidental ἐπιστήμη is still a kind of ἐπιστήμη.

[44] If this is correct, an interesting upshot is that we should include under the heading 'true δόξα' cognitive states that are typically considered knowledge. This, in turn, entails that when Meno asks Socrates how ἐπιστήμη differs from true δόξα, we should understand him to be asking how ἐπιστήμη differs from knowledge. This reconception of Meno's question might lead to a markedly different understanding of Socrates' ensuing answer and the dialogue as a whole.

(a) and say that Socrates is not discussing what contemporary epistemologists are discussing under the heading 'knowledge'.

5.2. Epistēmē *as understanding*

If Socrates is not discussing our current standard view of knowledge, what is he discussing? Let us first consider what the slave will achieve once he has worked out the geometrical theorem's explanation. First, he will have figured out not only *that* the theorem is true but also *why* it is true. Following on from this, he will have come to see how that theorem fits into a broader network of interrelated facts that partially constitute the domain of geometry. Lastly, he will have a command of the theorem that can be gained only by working all of this out *for himself*. This conception of *epistēmē*, as a cognitive state that consists in a synoptic grasp of (at least part of) some domain or phenomenon, fits very well with recent philosophical discussions of understanding. As Jonathan Kvanvig describes understanding:

> Understanding requires the grasping of explanatory and other coherence-making relationships in a large and comprehensive body of information. One may know many unrelated pieces of information, but understanding is achieved only when informational items are pieced together by the subject in question. (*Understanding*, 192)

Wayne Riggs offers a similar description of this type of understanding:

> 'Understanding' has a range of meanings, some of which fall outside the boundaries of what I have in mind. The kind of understanding I have in mind is the appreciation or grasp of order, pattern, and how things 'hang together'. . . . Understanding something like this requires a deep appreciation, grasp, or awareness of how its parts fit together, what role each one plays in the context of the whole, and of the role it plays in the larger scheme of things. ('Virtue', 217)

Indeed, it is worth noting that several philosophers currently working on understanding explicitly present their work as a return to the epistemological concerns of ancient philosophers.[45]

Taking *epistēmē* to be understanding, in the sense in which Kvanvig, Riggs, and others conceive of it, avoids the main objection

[45] Cf. S. Grimm, 'The Value of Understanding', *Philosophy Compass*, 7 (2012), 103–17 at 103, and Greco, 'Episteme'.

I levelled against the claim that *epistēmē* is knowledge. The mechanisms through which knowledge but not *epistēmē* can be acquired are also mechanisms through which understanding cannot be acquired. Mere perception, for example, is not sufficient to generate understanding—merely perceiving that P, even in optimal conditions, will not generate understanding of P. Likewise, mere testimony, even authoritative testimony, will not generate understanding. Simply being told by an expert that P is true will not, on its own, lead a person to acquire understanding of P. Even if an expert tells someone what all the true propositions in a given domain are and lays out the explanatory connections between them, acquiring understanding of that domain will still require the person to do some cognitive work to see for him- or herself how it all 'fits' together.[46] Not only does taking *epistēmē* to approximate understanding avoid these worries, it fits nicely with Socrates' claim that it is through repeated questioning that one upgrades from true *doxa* to *epistēmē*. Asking questions many times and in various ways seems a good procedure for allowing someone to achieve the kind of synoptic grasp that contemporary philosophers think is the hallmark of understanding.[47]

An objection to the claim that understanding cannot be acquired through testimony stems from a comment by Jonathan Barnes. According to Barnes, understanding simply amounts to a special case of knowledge, namely knowledge-*why*, which, in turn, he understands as a special case of knowledge-*that*:

I take the phrase [*x* understands *p*] to mean '*x* knows why *p*'; and I construe that, in the present circumstances, to mean, 'for some *q*, *x* knows that (*p* because *q*)'. ('Jury II', 202)

I disagree with Barnes. Someone can know both that P and that P because Q and yet fail to understand why P obtains. For example, suppose I know, by personal experience, that *the wind speed is accelerating now*. I ask my sister, an expert meteorologist, why this is the case and she tells me that it is because the air pressure is dropping now. On that basis, I come to know that *the wind speed is accelerating now because the air pressure is dropping now*. I can know this last fact without *understanding* why the wind speed is accelerating now because I have no grasp of why the drop in air

---

[46] See Grimm, 'Understanding', 87–8, for a similar claim.
[47] Thanks to the editor of this volume for discussion here.

pressure accounts for the increase in wind speed. Generally speaking, because knowledge-*that* can be acquired by testimony and understanding cannot, understanding cannot be reduced simply to a specific kind of knowledge-*that*. And, if knowledge-*why* is a species of knowledge-*that*, then understanding cannot be reduced to knowledge-*why* either.[48]

One final and important point: thinking of *epistēmē* in terms of what contemporary philosophers discuss under the heading 'understanding' also helps us to understand better why Socrates might be attracted to the idea that virtue is *epistēmē*. If someone has the kind of understanding of moral matters that results from having worked out, for him- or herself, how and why matters stand morally, that person is better equipped than someone who has mere piecemeal knowledge of such matters to act well in *all* facets of human life. For example, in novel circumstances the former person is better positioned than the latter to figure out what action is called for, and so is better positioned to act correctly. Furthermore, it is plausible to think that understanding why the action one is performing is the correct thing to do is a component of being a superlative moral agent.[49] If we think that Socrates' account of *epistēmē* is an account of what is typically called 'knowledge', we may be in danger of missing much of what is interesting and, perhaps, plausible in Socrates' idea that virtue may be *epistēmē*.

5.3. *Merits of Socrates' account*

Now that we have determined that Socrates' account of *epistēmē* is more charitably taken as an account of understanding than as an account of knowledge, it is worth considering how it fares as an account of understanding (of course, the better it fares as such an

[48] On the relationship between understanding and knowledge of causes see Strevens, 'Explanation', 511–12, Hills, 'Testimony', 98–106, and the exchange between S. Grimm, 'Understanding as Knowledge of Causes' ['Knowledge of Causes'], and D. Pritchard, 'Knowledge and Understanding' ['K&U'], in A. Fairweather (ed.), *Virtue Scientia: Essays in Philosophy of Science and Virtue Epistemology* (special issue of *Synthese*), forthcoming.

[49] In connection with these last two points, consider how natural it is for someone to distinguish the value of moral understanding from the value of moral knowledge by claiming that 'one might hold that an agent who possesses moral knowledge in the absence of understanding is not only likely to misapply that knowledge in particular cases (and so do the wrong thing), but also such that his morally right actions are less valuable than they otherwise would be' (S. McGrath, 'Skepticism about Moral Expertise as a Puzzle for Moral Realism', *Journal of Philosophy*, 108 (2011), 111–37 at 132). For extended discussion see Hills, 'Testimony', 106–19.

account, the stronger the argument from charity that it should be taken as such an account). My aim here is not to argue that Socrates' account is the *correct* account of understanding, nor do I wish to analyse all its strengths and weaknesses. Rather, I argue, first, that Socrates' account meets many of the desiderata in an account of understanding and, second, that it provides insights that any philosopher interested in understanding should take seriously.

To begin with, Socrates' account meets many of the desiderata that current philosophers posit for a satisfactory account of understanding.[50] First, it directly ties understanding to explanation, as it should. Intuitively, what distinguishes the person who understands some fact from the person who merely knows it is that the former, but not the latter, can explain why that fact obtains. Secondly, on Socrates' account, understanding is synoptic, again as it should be. Understanding requires being able to place something in a broader context. You cannot understand a single fact in isolation; it necessarily requires seeing how that fact fits into a broader network of facts structured in a certain kind of way. Thirdly, and relatedly, Socrates' account gets the correct entailments between knowledge and understanding. On Socrates' view understanding entails knowledge but not vice versa. Someone can have a good deal of knowledge of some domain without having understanding, but cannot have understanding without having a good deal of knowledge.[51] Fourth, Socrates is right to hold that understanding requires a certain facility with the subject-matter that one understands. Although it is difficult to determine exactly how Socrates conceives of this facility, it certainly involves grasping the relation among facts and being able to 'move around' within the relevant domain (i.e. for explicable facts, to be able to explain them; for fundamental facts, to be able to use them to explain other facts).

Furthermore, I think that the notion of grounding, that is, of one fact holding in virtue of another fact or set of facts, has a central role to play in an account of understanding.[52] When we say that

---

[50] For a list of such desiderata, several of which I restate here, see Greco, 'Episteme', 287–9.

[51] Kvanvig, *Understanding*, ch. 8, has argued that understanding does *not* entail knowledge. For responses to Kvanvig see S. Grimm, 'Is Understanding a Species of Knowledge?', *British Journal for the Philosophy of Science*, 57 (2006), 515–35; Greco, 'Episteme', 298–300; Pritchard, 'K&U'.

[52] See Greco, 'Episteme', who presents what he calls a 'neo-Aristotelian' account of understanding as systematic knowledge of grounding relations.

we understand some fact, what we are claiming is that we grasp why that fact must obtain, given certain other facts. Since we can understand one fact in the light of other facts even when the relation between them is non-causal, we should appeal to the broader notion of grounding rather than to the narrower notion of causation to illuminate the nature of understanding. Mathematics is an obvious case where understanding seems possible but the relationship between facts is non-causal.[53]

If we do think that the notion of grounding can illuminate the nature of understanding, then appealing to the notion of a nature or essence is also attractive. Facts about natures or essences are good candidates for termini of chains of facts connected by the grounding relation. That is, facts about what something is can ground certain other facts without themselves necessarily being grounded in more fundamental facts. For example, the fact that water is H_2O partially grounds the fact that water boils at 100° C (at sea level). But, the fact that water is H_2O is not grounded in some more fundamental fact: that just is what water is.[54] I am not saying that the grounding relation need be well founded in general.[55] But, in so far as the notion of grounding has a role to play in illuminating the nature of understanding, I think that the grounding relation should be well founded. Infinite chains of facts, since they cannot be grasped by finite minds, are ill-suited to be proper objects of understanding. Although much more can, and should, be said about the merits (and shortcomings) of Socrates' account, I think that the above suffices to show that pursuing the idea that his account of *epistēmē* is an account of understanding will be philosophically fruitful.

---

[53] Of course, the weight of these considerations will vary depending on one's conception of causation.
[54] Shamik Dasgupta discusses this issue in his 'Metaphysical Rationalism', forthcoming in *Nous*. According to Dasgupta, it is not that facts about natures or essences could have grounds but, as it happens, lack them (as is the case, he suggests, with facts about the initial conditions). Rather, he contends that facts about natures or essences lack grounds because they are not even *apt* for being grounded in the first place. As an analogy, he considers the way in which definitions can be used to prove things without themselves being apt for being proved.
[55] On this issue see G. Rosen, 'Metaphysical Dependence: Grounding and Reduction', in B. Hale and A. Hoffman (eds.), *Modality: Metaphysics, Logic, and Epistemology* (Oxford, 2010), 109–35 at 116.

6 Conclusion

In this paper I have presented a robust reconstruction of Socrates' account of *epistēmē*. By examining his claim that acquiring *epistēmē* requires working out an explanation, I have argued that *epistēmē*, for Socrates, consists in a synoptic grasp of how some fact fits into a broader network of interrelated facts, including facts about the natures or essences of fundamental entities. I then argued that, whereas this would fare quite poorly in current discussions of knowledge, as an account of understanding it has many attractive features. Thus, in future enquiry, and especially in connecting Socrates' discussion to current discussions in epistemology, I think that it will be more profitable to take *epistēmē* in the *Meno* to be understanding. The consequences that this conclusion has for our understanding of Plato's other dialogues, and the development of ancient epistemology more generally, will have to wait for another time.

University of Maryland, Baltimore County

BIBLIOGRAPHY

Adler, J., 'Epistemological Problems of Testimony', in E. Zalta (ed.), *The Stanford Encyclopedia of Philosophy* (Spring 2014) ⟨http://plato.stanford.edu/archives/spr2014/entries/testimony-episprob/⟩.

Annas, J., *An Introduction to Plato's* Republic (Oxford, 1981).

Audi, R., *Epistemology: A Contemporary Introduction to the Theory of Knowledge* (London, 2010).

Barnes, J., 'Socrates and the Jury: Paradoxes in Plato's Distinction between Knowledge and True Belief, Part II' ['Jury II'], *Proceedings of the Aristotelian Society*, suppl. 54 (1980), 193–206.

Burnyeat, M., 'Plato on Why Mathematics is Good for the Soul', in T. Smiley (ed.), *Mathematics and Necessity: Essays in the History of Philosophy* (Oxford, 2000), 1–81.

Burnyeat, M., 'Socrates and the Jury: Paradoxes in Plato's Distinction between Knowledge and True Belief, Part I' ['Jury I'], *Proceedings of the Aristotelian Society*, suppl. 54 (1980), 173–91.

Clark, M., and Liggins, D., 'Recent Work on Grounding', *Analysis*, 72 (2012), 812–23.

Coady, C. A. J., *Testimony: A Philosophical Study* (Oxford, 1992).

Crombie, I. M., *An Examination of Plato's Doctrines*, vol. ii (London, 1963).
Dasgupta, S., 'Metaphysical Rationalism', forthcoming in *Nous*.
Elgin, C., 'From Knowledge to Understanding', in S. Hetherington (ed.), *Epistemology Futures* (Oxford, 2006), 199–215.
Fairweather, A. (ed.), *Virtue Scientia: Essays in Philosophy of Science and Virtue Epistemology* (special issue of *Synthese*), forthcoming.
Fine, G., 'Inquiry in the *Meno*', in R. Kraut (ed.), *The Cambridge Companion to Plato* (Cambridge, 1992), 200–26.
Fine, G., 'Knowledge and True Belief in the *Meno*' ['KTB *Meno*'], *Oxford Studies in Ancient Philosophy*, 27 (2004), 41–81.
Fine, K., 'Essence and Modality' ['Essence'], *Philosophical Perspectives*, 14 (1994), 1–16.
Foley, R., *When is True Belief Knowledge?* (Princeton, 2012).
Gettier, E., 'Is Justified True Belief Knowledge?', *Analysis*, 23 (1963), 121–3.
Greco, J., 'Episteme: Knowledge and Understanding', in K. Timpe and C. Boyd (eds.), *Virtues and their Vices* (Oxford, 2014), 285–302.
Grimm, S., 'Is Understanding a Species of Knowledge?', *British Journal for the Philosophy of Science*, 57 (2006), 515–35.
Grimm, S., 'The Value of Understanding', *Philosophy Compass*, 7 (2012), 103–17.
Grimm, S., 'Understanding', in D. Pritchard and S. Bernecker (eds.), *The Routledge Companion to Epistemology* (London, 2010), 84–94.
Grimm, S., 'Understanding as Knowledge of Causes' ['Knowledge of Causes'], in Fairweather (ed.), *Virtue Scientia*, forthcoming.
Heath, T., *The Thirteen Books of Euclid's Elements* (1908; repr. New York, 1956).
Hills, A., 'Moral Testimony and Moral Epistemology' ['Testimony'], *Ethics*, 120 (2009), 94–127.
Kvanvig, J., *The Value of Knowledge and the Pursuit of Understanding* [*Understanding*] (Cambridge, 2003).
Lackey, J., and Sosa, E. (eds.), *The Epistemology of Testimony* (Oxford, 2006).
McGrath, S., 'Skepticism about Moral Expertise as a Puzzle for Moral Realism', *Journal of Philosophy*, 108 (2011), 111–37.
Mancosu, P., 'Explanation in Mathematics', in E. Zalta (ed.), *The Stanford Encyclopedia of Philosophy* (Summer 2011) ⟨http://plato.stanford.edu/archives/sum2011/entries/mathematics-explanation/⟩.
Menn, S., 'Plato and the Method of Analysis', *Phronesis*, 47 (2002), 193–223.
Moline, J., *Plato's Theory of Understanding* (Madison, 1981).

Moravcsik, J. M. E., 'Understanding and Knowledge in Plato's Philosophy', *Neue Hefte für Philosophie*, 15–16 (1979), 53–69.
Mueller, I., 'Greek Mathematics (Arithmetic, Geometry, Proportion Theory) to the Time of Euclid', in M. L. Gill and P. Pellegrin (eds.), *A Companion to Ancient Philosophy* (Oxford, 2006), 686–718.
Nehamas, A., 'Meno's Paradox and Socrates as Teacher' ['Meno's Paradox'], *Oxford Studies in Ancient Philosophy*, 3 (1985), 1–30.
Perin, C., 'Knowledge, Stability, and Virtue in the *Meno*', *Ancient Philosophy*, 32 (2012), 15–34.
Prior, W., 'Plato and the "Socratic Fallacy"' ['Fallacy'], *Phronesis*, 43 (1998), 97–113.
Pritchard, D., 'Knowledge and Understanding' ['K&U'], in Fairweather (ed.), *Virtue Scientia*, forthcoming.
Pritchard, D., 'Knowledge, Understanding, and Epistemic Value', in A. O'Hear (ed.), *Epistemology*, Royal Institute of Philosophy Lectures (Cambridge, 2009), 19–43.
Riggs, W., 'Understanding Virtue and the Virtue of Understanding' ['Virtue'], in M. Depaul and L. Zagzebski (eds.), *Intellectual Virtue: Perspectives from Ethics and Epistemology* (Oxford, 2003), 203–26.
Robinson, R., *Plato's Earlier Dialectic* (Oxford, 1953), 49–60.
Rosen, G., 'Metaphysical Dependence: Grounding and Reduction', in B. Hale and A. Hoffman (eds.), *Modality: Metaphysics, Logic, and Epistemology* (Oxford, 2010), 109–35.
Scott, D., *Plato's* Meno (Cambridge, 2006).
Sedley, D., 'Three Platonist Interpretations of the *Theaetetus*', in C. Gill and M. McCabe (eds.), *Form and Argument in Late Plato* (Oxford, 1996), 79–103.
Steiner, M., 'Mathematical Explanation', *Philosophical Studies*, 34 (1978), 135–51.
Steup, M., 'The Analysis of Knowledge', in E. Zalta (ed.), *The Stanford Encyclopedia of Philosophy* (Fall 2008) ⟨http://plato.stanford.edu/archives/fall2008/entries/knowledge-analysis⟩.
Strevens, M., 'No Understanding without Explanation' ['Explanation'], *Studies in History and Philosophy of Science*, 44 (2013), 510–15.
Vlastos, G., *Socratic Studies* (Cambridge, 1994).
Vogt, K., *Belief and Truth: A Skeptic Reading of Plato* (Oxford, 2012).
Zagzebski, L., 'Recovering Understanding', in M. Steup (ed.), *Knowledge, Truth, and Duty: Essays on Epistemic Justification, Responsibility, and Virtue* (Oxford, 2001), 235–52.

THE ROLE OF RELATIVES IN PLATO'S PARTITION ARGUMENT, *REPUBLIC* 4, 436 B 9–439 C 9

MATTHEW DUNCOMBE

ONE of Socrates' central contentions in Plato's *Republic* is that the soul has parts.[1] One argument for this claim runs from 436 B 9 to 439 C 9. Before arguing that the soul has exactly three parts, Socrates argues that it has more than one part. I call this the Partition Argument. Commentators often hold that this argument either under-generates or over-generates parts. On the one hand, if the argument does not involve a genuine conflict, necessary for generating parts, then the argument under-generates. On the other hand, if the key move of the argument can be reiterated indefinitely, the argument over-generates. The Partition Argument contains one of Plato's most important discussions of relatives at 438 A 7–D 9, although scholars rarely consider the significance of this for the argument.[2] In this paper I show that once we see how Plato's

---

© Matthew Duncombe 2015

Nick Denyer and M. M. McCabe commented on this material in its earliest incarnation as the second chapter of my Ph.D. thesis. Audiences in Groningen, Edinburgh, Exeter, and Reading asked helpful questions on the paper in its second life as a talk. David Sedley, Tamer Nawar, and Mabel Wale gave me extensive written feedback when the paper was born again as continuous prose. The editor of this journal kindly suggested some final improvements. Many thanks to you all.

[1] Socrates calls the elements in the soul 'εἴδη' at 435 C 5, 435 E 1, 439 E 1, 'γένη' at 441 C 6, 443 D 3, and 'μέρη' at 442 B 10 and 442 C 4. These are cited by E. Brown, 'The Unity of the Soul in Plato's *Republic*' ['Unity'], in R. Barney, T. Brennan, and C. Brittain (eds.), *Plato and the Divided Self* (Cambridge, 2012), 53–74 at 53. Socrates' usual way of referring to a particular division is with a neuter noun, which could suggest a 'part' in Greek. There is some debate as to whether they are 'parts' in a literal sense or rather 'aspects'. I will not address this question here, since it is not central to the argument of the paper, but on this see R. C. Cross and A. D. Woozley, *Plato's Republic: A Philosophical Commentary* [*Philosophical*] (London, 1966), 116; C. Shields, 'Plato's Divided Soul', in M. McPherran (ed.), *Plato's Republic: A Critical Guide* (Cambridge, 2010), 147–70; and C. Shields, 'Simple Souls', in E. Wagner (ed.), *Essays on Plato's Psychology* (Lanham, Md., 2001), 137–56.

[2] On a terminological point, relatives are items in the world. Relative terms are the linguistic items which express relativity or refer to relatives. Although Aristotle

wider view of relatives is involved in the Partition Argument, the argument avoids the two problems.

I argue for the following three claims. First: both problems arise if desire and rejection can relate to different objects. If desire and rejection each relate exclusively to the same object, then the Partition Argument avoids both problems. Second: Plato thinks that desires, such as thirst, and rejections, such as dipsophobia, both relate to the same object and only that object.[3] He thinks this because desires and rejections are relatives. Each relative relates exclusively to its correlative. In the case of relatives that are intentional mental states, the state correlates with its intentional object.[4] Third: desire and rejection are opposite relatives. In general, opposite relatives need not relate to the same object. However, when Plato discusses how to qualify relatives in *Republic* 4, we discover that in the special case where (*a*) opposite relatives have sorts and (*b*) those sorts arise because the relatives are qualified in the same way, then the opposite relatives relate exclusively to the same object. Thirst and dipsophobia exemplify this special case. So thirst and dipsophobia are opposites that relate to the same object. In this way, Plato can avoid the two problems with the Partition Argument.

Section 1 outlines the Partition Argument and the two problems. Section 2 discusses Plato's wider views of relatives and shows that a relative relates exclusively to its correlative. Section 3 shows why Plato's Partition Argument avoids the problems, as traditionally conceived.

1. The Partition Argument

The Partition Argument has the following structure:

coins the expression '*τὰ πρός τι*' for relatives, we will see that Plato characterizes this class of entities and anticipates many of Aristotle's claims about it.

[3] 'Dipsophobia' names the sort of rejection that corresponds to the sort of desire called 'thirst'. I use 'rejection' to capture the opposite of 'desire'.

[4] I use this expression as a convenient label for whatever an intentional mental state is directed towards, with two caveats. First, in modern discussions of intentionality the intentional object is often discussed as if it were always a single individual, as in 'Caesar loves Cleopatra', where Cleopatra is the intentional object. But in Plato's case, as will become clear, this object can also be general, as in 'Tantalus desires a drink'. Second, to avoid begging any questions, how an object is thought of is not automatically part of the intentional object. 'Tantalus desires a drink' does not in itself imply that Tantalus thinks of the drink in any particular way.

(1) Principle of opposites. If something is a single item, then it cannot act or be acted upon in opposite ways at the same time, in the same respect, and in relation to the same object (436 B 9–C 2) [Premiss].[5]
(2) Desire and rejection are opposite ways of acting or being affected (437 B 1–C 9) [Premiss].
(3) Thirst is the desire for drink (437 E 7–438 A 5; cf. 437 D 1–E 6) [Premiss].
(4) Principle of qualification. (*a*) If a term that is 'of something' is qualified, then it is of a qualified something. (*b*) If a term that is 'of something' is unqualified, then it is of an unqualified something (438 A 7–B 2) [Premiss].[6]
(5) Thirst unqualified is the desire for drink unqualified [Modus Ponens on (4*b*) and (3)].
(6) Someone, *a*, is thirsty and at the same time rejects drink (439 C 3–5) [Premiss].
(7) *a* desires drink unqualified and *a* rejects drink unqualified [Instantiation of (5) with (6)].
(8) *a* acts in opposite ways with respect to drink unqualified [Instantiation of (2) with (7)].
(9) *a* is not a single item (439 B 3–6; cf. 439 C 6–8) [Modus Tollens on (1) and (8)].[7]

Assuming that the soul is the locus of desire and rejection, the argument uses a simple mechanism to show that the soul has parts: the principle of opposites. For any X, the following conditions are individually necessary and jointly sufficient for X to have more than one part. Opposites hold of X: (*a*) at the same time, (*b*) in the same

---

[5] This differs from our principle of non-contradiction: first Plato phrases the principle such that an item cannot have opposite *properties*, while the PNC (roughly) denies that a *proposition* and its negation can be true together. The second difference is that Plato's principle concerns opposites, whereas the PNC concerns negations: if X is opposite to Y, then X and Y are exclusive, but need not be exhaustive. But if X is the negation of Y, then X and Y are exclusive and exhaustive. See Brown, 'Unity'.

[6] H. Lorenz, *The Brute Within: Appetitive Desire in Plato and Aristotle* [*Brute*] (Oxford, 2006), 28–31, discusses this premiss in the most detail of any commentator. In my reconstruction, (4*a*) does not play an explicit role in the statement of the argument. However, in sect. 2, where I give a slightly more rigorous statement of this principle, we will see that (4*a*) is crucial to the validity of the argument.

[7] For other reconstructions see R. F. Stalley, 'Persuasion and the Tripartite Soul in Plato's *Republic*', *Oxford Studies in Ancient Philosophy*, 32 (2007), 63–89 at 69; Lorenz, *Brute*, 25; and T. Irwin, *Plato's Ethics* [*Ethics*] (Oxford, 1995), 204.

respect, and (c) in relation to the same object. The argument under-generates parts if one of the conditions (a)–(c) is not met, while if all conditions (a)–(c) are repeatedly met, the argument over-generates parts. I will examine each possibility in Sections 1.1 and 1.2 respectively.

1.1. Under-generation

Let me stipulate that when an agent desires something, X, as good, (i) the agent desires X; (ii) the agent believes that X is good; and (iii) the agent desires X because she believes X is good. Plato's pre-*Republic* dialogues seem to articulate the 'Socratic' view that whenever an agent desires something, the agent desires it in a qualified way, namely as good.[8] But scholars disagree over Plato's moral psychology in the *Republic*. Traditionalists think the dialogue rejects Socratic psychology, in favour of the view that some desires are good-indifferent. An agent has a 'good-indifferent' desire for X if (i) is satisfied while (ii) and (iii) are not.[9] Such desires may help explain *akrasia*. If an agent desires X irrespective of whether the agent thinks X is good or bad, the agent may act to acquire X, even against what she takes to be her interests. Against this, revisionists

[8] *Prot.* 354 C 4. For the more general claim that what we desire we believe to be good see e.g. *Meno* 77 B 6–78 B 2, *Gorg.* 468 B 1–E 5, and *Prot.* 358 B 6–D 4. The *Protagoras* also gives the famous formulation of the 'Socratic Paradox': 'Now, no one goes towards the bad, or what he believes to be the bad, willingly. Neither is it in human nature to want to go towards what one believes to be bad instead of the good' (358 C 6–E 2). Although finding a satisfying terminology is difficult, I will use 'Socratic' to refer to the moral psychology of the traditionally conceived pre-*Republic* dialogues. This does not imply that the historical Socrates held this view. I use 'Platonic' to refer to the moral psychology of the *Republic*, whatever that may be, even though the character called 'Socrates' evinces it. We cannot be sure that Plato, in the *Republic* or elsewhere, holds the 'Platonic' view *in propria persona*.

[9] R. Parry, *Plato's Craft of Justice* (New York, 1996), 93–4, coins the expression 'good indifferent'. As well as Parry, we might give as 'traditionalists' the following scholars: C. D. C. Reeve, *Philosopher-Kings: The Argument of Plato's Republic* (Indianapolis, 1988), 134–5; Irwin, *Ethics*, 209; N. Smith and T. Brickhouse, *Plato's Socrates* (Oxford, 1994), 90–6; T. Penner, 'Socrates and the Early Dialogues', in R. Kraut (ed.), *The Cambridge Companion to Plato* (Cambridge, 1992), 121–69 at 129; G. Vlastos, 'Socrates', *Proceedings of the British Academy*, 74 (1988), 89–111 at 99 and 105; C. C. W. Taylor, *Protagoras* (Cambridge, 1991), 203. These are cited in G. R. Carone, 'Akrasia in the *Republic*: Does Plato Change his Mind?' ['Akrasia'], *Oxford Studies in Ancient Philosophy*, 20 (2001), 107–48 at 107–8. I would also include T. Penner, 'Thought and Desire in Plato' ['Thought'], in G. Vlastos (ed.), *Plato 2* (Oxford, 1971), 96–118 at 106–7; N. P. White, *A Companion to Plato's Republic* (Indianapolis, 1979), 124–50; P. Hoffman, 'Plato on Appetitive Desires in the *Republic*' ['Appetitive'], *Apeiron*, 36 (2003), 171–4; and Lorenz, *Brute*, 28.

defend the view that Plato still held, in the *Republic*, that there are no good-indifferent desires.[10]

The debate just sketched centres on this passage from *Republic* 4:

[T1] Thus, [Glaucon] said, each desire itself is only of that which it is of by nature, but the things (sc. desires) of a certain sort are due to that which has been added. So don't let someone, I said, disturb us when we are not paying attention, [saying] that no one desires drink, but good drink, and not food, but good food. For, [someone might say], all people desire good things, so, if thirst is a desire, then it would be for good drink, or of good whatever it is, and similarly with the other desires. (437 E 7–438 A 5)[11]

Premisses (3) and (4) summarize the results of this passage. Socrates denies that thirst is a desire for good drink. Rather, thirst, like each desire, is for its natural object. In the case of thirst, drink is the natural object. So thirst, it appears, is good-indifferent.[12] Traditionalists build their case that the *Republic* rejects the Socratic view of desire on this passage. While revisionists have independent evidence for their view (such as *Rep.* 505 D–506 A; cf. 442 C–D; 571 C–572 B; 580 D–581 A), they also try to reclaim [T1].[13]

One revisionist strategy for taming [T1] distinguishes two readings of 'thirst is the desire for drink'. Carone writes: 'It is perfectly consistent to claim that thirst *qua* thirst is for drink while every time we wish to drink we desire drink as good.'[14] That is, divide a conceptual reading from a psychological reading of 'thirst is the desire for drink'. Conceptually, thirst is, by definition, desire for drink,

[10] Revisionists include: G. Lesses, 'Weakness, Reason and the Divided Soul in Plato's *Republic*', *History of Philosophy Quarterly*, 4 (1987), 147–61; G. R. F. Ferrari, 'Akrasia as Neurosis in Plato's *Protagoras*', *Proceedings of the Boston Area Colloquium in Ancient Philosophy*, 6 (1990), 115–40; Carone, 'Akrasia'; R. Weiss, *The Socratic Paradox and its Enemies* (Chicago, 2006), ch. 6; J. Moss, 'Pleasure and Illusion in Plato' ['Pleasure'], *Philosophy and Phenomenological Research*, 72 (2006), 503–35 at 525–7; and J. Moss, 'Appearances and Calculations: Plato's Division of the Soul' ['Calculations'], *Oxford Studies in Ancient Philosophy*, 34 (2008), 35–68 at 60–4; possibly also A. W. Price, *Mental Conflict* [*Conflict*] (London, 1995), 49–52. The 'revisionist' reading actually has some supporters who antedate the 'traditionalist' reading: P. Shorey, *The* Republic [*Republic*] (Cambridge, Mass., 1935), ad loc.; J. Adam, *The* Republic *of Plato* (Cambridge, 1902), ad loc.
[11] My translation, following Shorey, *Republic*, ad loc.
[12] Socrates repeats the same thought, in similar language, at 439 A 4–B 1.
[13] Moss, 'Pleasure', 526, for example, calls the evidence provided by [T1] 'at very best inconclusive'.
[14] Carone, 'Akrasia', 120. Cf. Hoffman, 'Appetitive', 172; Moss, 'Calculations', 62.

so 'thirst is the desire for drink' is true by meaning alone.[15] The psychological reading, on the other hand, could say that whenever some individual thirsts, they desire a drink. As a matter of contingent fact, thirsty individuals always desire a drink as good. But this is an empirical discovery about human psychology. There is no conflict, revisionists say, between the conceptual definition of thirst as the desire for drink and the contingent fact that every time some agent desires a drink, she desires it as a good. The strategy is then to say that (*a*) thirst, as defined above, is for drink and (*b*) in any given case of a thirsty person, Tantalus, say, that person desires drink as a good. But (*a*) is consistent with (*b*), while (*b*) is characteristic of Socratic moral psychology. Thus, [T1] is consistent with Socratic moral psychology.[16]

[T1] is an important step in the Partition Argument. This revisionist reading of [T1] threatens the Partition Argument with under-generation. The principle of opposites asserts that conflict within the agent, under certain conditions, requires a division in the soul. Socrates pinpoints the conflict between being thirsty and rejecting some available drink. But once the revisionist distinguishes definitional and psychological readings of 'thirst is the desire for drink', that situation may not meet the conditions for generating a part. 'Thirst is desire for drink', read as a definition, is consistent with the psychological truth that Tantalus, despite his unfortunate situation, rejects this drink. So there may not be a genuine conflict when Tantalus thirsts but rejects some actual drink: by definition Tantalus' thirst is thirst for drink, but Tantalus may still reject some particular drink in front of him. Such conflict is necessary to posit parts in the soul. So the Partition Argument under-generates.[17]

1.2. *Over-generation*

The under-generation problem parallels an over-generation

[15] Carone, 'Akrasia', 120. This, I take it, is supposed to be a real, rather than nominal, definition.

[16] In fact, Carone herself argues for something stronger: that in the *Republic* Socrates explicitly endorses the earlier Socratic position. See Carone, 'Akrasia', 118–20.

[17] R. W. Jordan, *Plato's Argument for Forms*, Cambridge Philological Society, suppl. 9 (Cambridge, 1983), 36–41, and R. Robinson, 'Plato's Separation of Reason from Desire', *Phronesis*, 16 (1971), 38–48 at 42, raise the under-generation objection independently of revisionist considerations, although the problem is still based on the ambiguity of the claim 'thirst is the desire for drink'.

problem.¹⁸ Suppose that Tantalus' soul does have at least two parts, including an appetitive part. Suppose further that the appetitive part of Tantalus' soul desires to drink. It desires to drink a hot drink because of the presence of coldness.¹⁹ But it also rejects sweetness. So it desires a hot, non-sweet drink. If a hot, sweet drink is available, it seems that the appetitive part both desires and rejects the drink in question. Therefore, according to the principle of opposites, the appetitive part must have two, non-identical parts, one desiring and the other rejecting the drink in question. We could reiterate these moves again and again, to show that, given Plato's principles, the soul has indefinitely many parts.

Some press the over-generation problem independently of wider interpretative concerns.²⁰ But more often commentators use it to motivate the claim that Plato cannot think that just any kind of conflict results in a partition. Some wish to argue that only a specific sort of conflict generates a part in the soul.²¹ For example, some claim that only a conflict between a first-order desire and a second-order aversion to that desire generates a part, e.g. desiring to eat meat, say, but being disgusted by that desire.²² Others argue that the conflict needs to involve a conception of the good in an appropriate way: for example, conflict over what is good or best for the agent.²³ Denying that just any sort of conflict generates a part is the first step towards making the case that the Partition Argument requires a special sort of conflict. Commentators give the over-generation problem as evidence that Plato cannot have inten-

---

¹⁸ See Penner, 'Thought', 108–11; J. Annas, *An Introduction to Plato's Republic* [*Introduction*] (Oxford, 1981), 137; and Reeve, *Philosopher-Kings*, 124–31. Cross and Woozley, *Philosophical*, 116–17, discuss and dismiss a similar objection.
¹⁹ At 437 D–E Socrates evinces his view that the addition of warmth to the desire for drink will produce the desire for cold drink.
²⁰ e.g. Penner, 'Thought', 108–11, and Annas, *Introduction*, 137.
²¹ Irwin, *Ethics*, 205–6; Price, *Conflict*, 45–8. This sort of approach is opposed by C. Bobonich, *Plato's Utopia Recast* [*Utopia*] (Oxford, 2002), 249–54, and Lorenz, *Brute*, 41–52.
²² T. Irwin, *Plato's Moral Theory: The Early and Middle Dialogues* (Oxford, 1977), 327; J. M. Cooper, 'Plato's Theory of Human Motivation' ['Motivation'], *History of Philosophy Quarterly*, 1 (1984), 3–21; Price, *Conflict*, 45–8; Irwin, *Ethics*, 208–12, takes a slightly different line from his earlier self.
²³ Irwin, *Ethics*, 215; cf. Bobonich, *Utopia*, 249. I will not argue against any reading that claims that some specific sort of conflict, e.g. first-order vs. second-order or some conflict involving the good, is needed for a partition. But I take it that the case for such a reading is undermined once we see that there is a satisfactory reading of conflict as between a first-order desire and a first-order aversion.

ded just any conflict between desires to generate a part.[24] If he had intended that any sort of conflict could generate a part, there would be too many parts in the soul.

I have outlined two problems with the Partition Argument.[25] On the one hand, it may under-generate parts; on the other hand, it may over-generate parts. But both problems emanate from the same fact: desires and rejections, e.g. thirst and dipsophobia, need not relate to the same object. We saw that the under-generation problem arises because a necessary condition is not met when applied to the soul. The revisionist reading suggests that thirst may relate to drink, while the corresponding rejection, dipsophobia, may relate, for example, to drink viewed by the agent as a harm. But here a necessary condition on partition is not met, because the opposites thirst and dipsophobia do not relate to the same object, drink: they relate respectively to drink and drink viewed as a harm. If, however, thirst and dipsophobia related exclusively to drink, the under-generation problem would not arise.

Over-generation also arises because thirst and dipsophobia may not relate to one and the same object. In addition to relating to drink, each state may relate to sorts of drink, such as hot drink or sweet drink. If a part of the soul desires and rejects a hot, sweet drink, the sufficient conditions generating a partition within the desiring part are met. If the sufficient conditions on generating a part can be repeatedly met, the Partition Argument over-generates parts. But if drink and dipsophobia related only to drink, rather than also to sorts of drink, reiteration would be impossible. So the Partition Argument would not over-generate parts.

In short, Plato could solve both problems if he had some principled reason to think that thirst and dipsophobia relate exclusively to the same object. I argue that he did have such a reason. For Plato

---

[24] Cooper, 'Motivation', 6.

[25] These are not the only difficulties with the Partition Argument. Some have pointed out that it is hard to see how the partitioned soul is in any sense a unity (e.g. Brown, 'Unity'; Lorenz, *Brute*, 38–40; Bobonich, *Utopia*, 254–7). There are also questions over whether the argument is compatible with the exact parts Socrates wants, i.e. reason, appetite, and spirit (see Cooper, 'Motivation', 4). Note that, even if Whiting is correct that Plato holds in the *Republic* that different individuals can have different numbers of parts in their souls, the over- and under-generation problems still loom (J. Whiting, 'Psychic Contingency in the *Republic*', in Barney et al. (eds.), *Plato and the Divided Self*, 174–208 at 176). The problems with the argument apply as long as this is the argument that at least one soul has at least two parts.

relatives relate only to their objects, a property I call 'exclusivity'. Since thirst and dipsophobia are relatives, each relates exclusively to its object. However, as far as exclusivity shows, opposite relatives could relate to different objects. Mere exclusivity is not sufficient to ensure that thirst and dipsophobia relate to the same object. So I need to attribute a further claim to Plato: in some cases opposite relatives relate exclusively to the same object. Opposites sometimes obey exclusivity. I argue below that Plato's general view of relatives includes a commitment to exclusivity. It turns out that Plato would also accept that opposites sometimes obey exclusivity because of how he thinks relatives are divided into sorts. Given these assumptions by Plato, we can see that for Plato thirst and dipsophobia relate exclusively to the same object and so neither over-generation nor under-generation would trouble him.

2. Relatives in Plato

In this section I argue that Plato endorsed exclusivity and that thirst and dipsophobia must relate to one and the same object. In Section 2.1 I will argue that he held exclusivity. Then, in Section 2.2, I show that desire and rejection are relatives. All relatives exhibit exclusivity; desires and rejections are relatives; so, those mental states exhibit exclusivity. In Section 2.3 I examine Plato's discussion of qualified relatives. This investigation shows that thirst and dipsophobia relate exclusively to one and the same object.

2.1. *Relatives and exclusivity*

Plato discusses relatives in a range of passages.[26] He often returns to the example of larger and smaller: the larger relates to the smaller. This correspondence tells us that relatives, for Plato, are not single. Each relative has a correlative partner. Nothing could be larger if it were the only item that existed. If something is larger, then there is something in relation to which it is larger, i.e. the smaller. Non-relative items, on the other hand, can be single. An item can be a human, for example, even if that item is the only thing there is. Plato's examples reflect the natural thought that relatives come in

[26] e.g. *Charm.* 167 C–168 C; *Parm.* 133 C–134 A; *Rep.* 438 B–E; *Sym.* 199 D–200 A; *Theaet.*152 A–C. Cf. Arist. *Cat.* 6^a36–8^b24.

pairs: the larger is relative to the smaller and the heavier is relative to the lighter. Relatives relate to a correlative.[27]

Since desire relates to the desirable and the desirable relates to desire, the two form a relative–correlative pair. But desire is not just a relative. It is also an intentional mental state. In the special case of relatives that are intentional mental states, the correlative is the intentional object of the state. In the *Charmides* Socrates discusses the claim that 'knowledge is of nothing but itself and other sorts of knowledge' (168 C 1–3). First, in language reminiscent of *Rep.* 438 A 7–B 2, Socrates says that knowledge 'is of something' (τινὸς εἶναι). He asserts that knowledge and its object are like other relative–correlative pairs, giving the examples of larger–smaller, double–half, more–less, heavier–lighter, and older–younger (168 B 5–D 1). Like these relatives, knowledge relates to its correlative (168 D 1–3). But the correlative of knowledge is the intentional object of knowledge, learnings. To confirm this point, Socrates mentions two other intentional mental states, hearing and sight (168 D 6–E 1). Socrates calls the correlative of hearing 'sound' and the correlative of sight 'colour'. Again, each of these is relative, and it relates to its correlative. If the same thought is in the background of *Republic* 4, this suggests that the intentional mental states in the Partition Argument relate to their correlative, which is just the intentional object of that state.

The intentional states mentioned are relatives and relate to their intentional objects. But do such states relate only to their object? They do because all relatives relate only to their correlative. I argue that Plato endorses this principle:

> (Exclusivity) If X and Y are a relative and correlative pair, then X relates only to Y.[28]

Thus stated, the exclusivity principle appears too strong to be plausible. Suppose we replace 'X' and 'Y' in the above schema with 'father' and 'son'. Father and son appear to be a relative–correlative pair, but father does not only relate to son. Fathers can also be fathers of daughters. To rule out such counter-examples, Plato, like Aristotle (*Cat.* 6^b28–7^b14), stipulates that when both relative and

---

[27] There is no evidence that Plato explicitly considered, for example, three-place relations, such as 'x is between y and z'.

[28] This principle cannot be expressed in first-order logic because 'X' and 'Y' range over types, as well as individuals. I use italic capitals to indicate this.

correlative are properly specified, exclusivity holds of each pair. In the above example, father relates exclusively to its correlative if, and only if, that correlative is given as 'offspring' i.e. 'son or daughter'.

The counter-example gets its force because the following statement is ambiguous: (*a*) a father is relative to this-and-such. The subject, 'a father', could be understood to indicate fathers *as such* or some particular father. The former would entail (*a'*) 'For any father, that father is relative to this-and-such'. The latter gives (*a"*) 'For some father, that father is relative to this-and-such'. If we replace 'this-and-such' in (*a'*) with 'son', the result is that (*a'*) is false. Whether (*a"*) is true under the same substitution depends on who that father is. One way to block such counter-examples would be to specify that we are not thinking about any particular father when we make the statement (*a*), but rather fathers as such. That would be to disambiguate in favour of (*a'*). Then it is obvious that the correlative is not son, but offspring, because as fathers, fathers relate to offspring, not just sons or just daughters.[29] In short, when the relative is specified as the relative it is, then it relates only to its correlative, which is also properly specified.

Plato has this sort of move available to ensure exclusivity because he introduces terminology to identify how and when a relative and correlative are specified. In the *Symposium* Socrates mentions the case of brother, another relative, and says: 'Is brother, the very thing that it is [αὐτὸ τοῦθ' ὅπερ ἔστιν], brother of something or not?' (199 E 3–4). From this context it is clear that Socrates intends the expression 'the very thing that it is' at 199 E 3–4 to rule out all improper ways of using 'brother': he means to specify brother as such. Just a few lines above, at 199 D 1–5, Socrates headed off confusion over the proper correlative of love. Socrates is interested in the relative love as such, not in some particular variety of love, such as love of a father or mother. The relative, love as such, always relates exclusively to its correlative.

Socrates clarifies by drawing an analogy with the term 'father' and asks Agathon to imagine he had asked what the correlative of 'father itself' (αὐτὸ τοῦτο πατέρα) is (199 D 4). He receives the answer

---

[29] This way of thinking about relatives is foreign to treatments of relatives descended from Frege and Russell, who give an account in extensional terms. But some modern work on propositional attitudes would find these ideas familiar. See W. V. O. Quine, 'Quantifiers and Propositional Attitudes', *Journal of Philosophy*, 53 (1956), 177–87.

'son or daughter' (ὑέος γε ἢ θυγατρός), which, although a disjunctive expression, picks out an exclusive correlative for father (199 D 7). Father relates to nothing other than a son or a daughter. So the relative, father, under the description 'father', will relate exclusively to its correlative, in this case labelled 'son or daughter'. The 'itself' (αὐτό) and 'the very thing that it is' (αὐτὸ τοῦθ' ὅπερ ἔστιν, transliterated as *auto touth' hoper estin*) vocabulary, applied in the context of relatives, specifies that we should look at the relative under a certain description, that is, as such.[30] In this case we should look at father as a father rather than, say, as a man or a brother or even a father of sons (cf. *Cat.* 7, 7ª31–ᵇ9). When we look at the father in the right way, father relates exclusively to its proper correlative. What that correlative is will be obvious if we read the relative in the general sense.[31]

When properly specified, relative–correlative pairs obey the exclusivity principle. This point can also be seen in our *Republic* 4 passage. The tell-tale use of *hoper estin* crops up at the Partition Argument. At 438 E 5 Socrates uses a different grammatical form of *hoper estin* to refer to the object of knowledge, the knowable, with the periphrasis 'the thing which knowledge is of' (αὐτοῦ οὗπερ ἐπιστήμη ἐστίν). Socrates argues that we could specify knowledge in a certain way. For example, medicine is the specific sort of knowledge that deals with health. However, taken independently of further specification, knowledge is knowledge of the knowable. Moreover, to anticipate my discussion in Section 2.2, Plato confirms that desire, in so far as it is a relative, relates only to its object. Socrates mentions the exclusive object of desire periphrastically at 437 C 1–2, as 'that thing which he desires' (437 C 1–2), then as 'whatever thing he wants' (437 C 3). These expressions designate a correlative to which desire exclusively relates. In the Partition Argument desire relates only to its correlative.

All this suggests that, in general and in the Partition Argument,

[30] Socrates uses this vocabulary of 'itself', 'the very thing that it is', in his crucial moves in the Partition Argument (see sect. 2.3, [T4]).

[31] For further evidence of this use of ὅπερ ἔστιν see my article 'The Greatest Difficulty at *Parmenides* 133 C–134 E and Plato's Relative Terms' ['Greatest'], *Oxford Studies in Ancient Philosophy*, 45 (2013), 43–61 at 55–6, which discusses an occurrence at *Parm.* 133 C 8. Although controversial, I think that the same idea can be found at *Soph.* 255 C–D. I discuss this in detail in 'Plato's Absolute and Relative Categories at *Soph.* 255 C 14' ['Categories'], *Ancient Philosophy*, 32 (2012), 77–86. A more straightforward example of this use of the ὅπερ ἔστιν terminology is found at *Theaet.* 204 E 11.

Plato conceives of each relative as having a correlative, to which it relates exclusively. The technical terminology of *hoper estin* and the concept of exclusivity bound up with it are found across Plato's discussions of relatives and relative terms, including at a crucial point in the Partition Argument. When the relative (and correlative) are properly specified, there will be an exclusive relationship between them.

2.2. Desire and rejection as relatives in Republic 4

The under- and over-generation problems arose because desires and rejections need not relate only to their correlative objects. If desires and rejections were relatives, they would each relate to their proper object because of the exclusivity principle. Then the problems would not arise. I argue below that Plato thinks the mental states in question are relatives, with the attendant formal properties.

The evidence suggests that Plato thinks of desire as a relative in the Partition Argument. There is no doubt that relatives are under discussion in 438 A 7–B 2.[32] Plato's Socrates designates the class as 'a kind such as to be of something' (ὅσα γ' ἐστὶ τοιαῦτα οἷα εἶναί του) in language which adumbrates Aristotle's definition of relatives as 'all the things which are said to be just what they are of other things' (ὅσα αὐτὰ ἅπερ ἐστὶν ἑτέρων εἶναι λέγεται) at *Cat.* 7, 6ᵃ35.[33] Plato tends to identify relatives as a class using similar expressions elsewhere, such as *Sym.* 199 C 4–5. Moreover, the examples of relative–correlative pairs at *Rep.* 4, 438 B 4–D 9, track examples of relatives given elsewhere by Plato and, indeed, Aristotle.[34] Finally, in [T1] Socrates raised the topic of desire and claimed that desire is only for its natural object. In the exchange that follows Socrates wards off Glaucon's worry that desire may only be for the good, rather than the natural object of desire. Socrates does this by appealing to

---

[32] Shorey, *Republic*, ad loc., and Carone, 'Akrasia', 118, make this point.

[33] Although I cannot argue for the point here, I think that there are important conceptual similarities between the way Plato treats relatives and the way Aristotle does in *Cat.* 7, as well as some key differences. Nothing I say will turn on the relationship between Plato's and Aristotle's views. In this paper I do not use Aristotle's explicit statements as evidence for Plato's views, although I do sometimes draw illustrative comparisons with *Cat.* 7.

[34] For larger and smaller see *Charm.* 168 B 5–8 and *Cat.* 7, 6ᵃ36–ᵇ10; for double and half see *Charm.* 168 C 4–5 and *Cat.* 7, 7ᵃ15–17; for heavier and lighter see *Charm.* 168 C 9–10; for desire see *Sym.* 200 A 5 and *Charm.* 167 E 1–2; for knowledge see *Charm.* 168 B 2–3, *Cat.* 7, 6ᵃ36–ᵇ10, 6ᵇ28–35, 7ᵇ15 ff., and *Parm.* 134 A 3–B 1.

the formal properties of relatives at 438 A 8–B 2. Such a move would make sense only if desire were a relative.

As well as this circumstantial evidence, we have direct evidence from the Partition Argument that sorts of desire are relatives. At 439 A 1–2 Socrates says that thirst falls into the class of relatives that he has characterized between 438 A 7 and 438 D 7. Finally, textual parallels tell in favour of my reading, since desire features as a relative in the *Symposium* (200 A 5) and *Charmides* (167 E 1–2). If desire is a relative, then it has the formal, logically relevant, characteristics of that class, in particular, exclusivity.

But is the opposite of desire, rejection, also a relative, with all the relevant characteristics? Plato does not say so in so many words, but the context posits a strict parallelism between opposites such as assent and dissent (437 B 1–4). Desires are in the former class, and rejection is explicitly put in the latter class (437 C 7–9). Since desires are relatives, it is reasonable to hold that their opposites are as well.[35] Moreover, a necessary condition given for partition is that opposites must relate to the same object (436 B 9–C 2); desire and rejection are the pair of opposites in question, so must relate to the same object. But to relate to any object, both desire and rejection must be relatives. As relatives, desires and rejections, in particular, relate exclusively to their correlatives.

2.3. *(Some) opposites relate to the same object*

So far I have argued that relatives for Plato relate exclusively to their correlatives and Plato considers desires and rejections to be relatives. However, nothing I have yet said shows that opposite relatives always relate exclusively to one and the same object. To see that Plato's Partition Argument does not face the over- and undergeneration problems, I must show that he would hold that a particular pair of opposite relatives, in this case thirst and dipsophobia, each relates exclusively to one and the same object, namely, drink.

Opposite relatives sometimes relate to the same object, but sometimes do not. Take knowledge, which is a common example of a relative, for both Plato and Aristotle.[36] Knowledge relates to the knowable (*to epistēton*).[37] The opposite of knowledge is ignorance

---

[35] Aristotle points out that relatives have opposites (*Cat.* 7, 6^{b}15–18).
[36] For Aristotle, see *Cat.* 6^{b}34. For Plato, cf. *Parm.* 134 A 3–B 1; *Theaet.* 201 D 2–3; *Rep.* 438 C 6–9 and 438 E 5.
[37] At least, this is Aristotle's stable terminology. Plato seems to be feeling his way

(*Cat.* 6ᵇ15–18). Ignorance also relates to the knowable: one sense of 'ignorance' is 'not knowing something which one could know'. So in this case both opposite relatives relate to the same object, the knowable. Unfortunately for my argument, not all pairs of opposite relatives are like this. Large and small do not have one and the same correlative. The correlative of large is the small, while the correlative of small is the large, but large and small cannot be the same, since they are opposites. I need to show that Plato thinks that the specific opposite relatives in question, thirst and dipsophobia, relate only to one and the same object. Plato's discussion of qualified relatives helps me to show this.

Plato's Socrates introduces and explains the principle of qualification for relatives at 438 A 7–B 2. Since the Partition Argument deals with sorts of relatives, including the much-larger and the going-to-be-larger, Socrates says something about how such qualified relatives behave. Socrates introduces the principle of qualification thus:

[T2] But surely of all the things which are of such a kind as to be of something [ὅσα γ' ἐστὶ τοιαῦτα οἶα εἶναί του], those that are qualified are of something qualified, so it seems to me, while those that are unqualified are only of things unqualified. (438 A 7–B 2)

In my reconstruction of the Partition Argument in Section 1, I glossed [T2] as two conditionals. I can now formulate the conditionals more precisely, using X' to indicate a sort of X:

(A) If (X and Y are a relative–correlative pair) then (X' is a qualified relative iff Y' is appropriately qualified).[38]

(B) If (X and Y are a relative–correlative pair) then (X is an unqualified relative iff Y is unqualified).

somewhat and avoids coining τὸ ἐπιστητόν as the object of knowledge. The expression Plato uses to refer to the proper correlative of 'knowledge' varies between dialogues. At *Parm.* 134 A 9 the partner is ἀλήθεια; at *Charm.* 168 B–C the partner for knowledge is τὰ μαθήματα, as in *Rep.* 4. In Aristotle the partner is ἐπιστητόν (*Cat.* 6ᵇ34). For further discussion see Duncombe, 'Categories', 84–5.

[38] Although most of his examples concern qualifying the correlative, Socrates does also maintain that when the *relative* is qualified in a certain way, so is the correlative. When discussing thirst as a relative at 437 D 7–E 6, Socrates makes the point that qualifying by addition can also sometimes qualify the correlative. Qualifying thirst with heat leads someone to thirst for cool drink: qualifying thirst with much leads to the desire for much drink. This is why each of (A) and (B) has a biconditional embedded in the consequent.

Socrates illustrates the principle of qualification with the example of knowledge and its sorts:

[T3] But what about knowledges [περὶ τὰς ἐπιστήμας]? Isn't it the same way? Knowledge itself is knowledge of learning itself (or whatever one ought to posit knowledge is of). I mean this sort of thing: did not knowledge of making houses come about when it was divided from other knowledges so as to be called house-building?
Absolutely.
Was this not because it is of a certain kind, which is some different kind from the others?
Yes.
Therefore, when it came to be of a certain sort, it became itself a certain sort [of knowledge]? And the same is true of the other crafts and knowledges.
That's right. (438 C 6–D 8)

For now, I focus on the mechanism for qualifying the relative, in this case knowledge. Knowledge itself is the unqualified relative; learning itself is the corresponding unqualified correlative.[39] Here the expression 'itself' serves to contrast the relative with its sorts, which are qualified somehow or other. The expression could be rendered 'knowledge unqualified'. One sort of knowledge is the (qualified) relative house-building. According to [T3], this 'qualification' came about by a specific mechanism. Knowledge came to relate to a sort of learning, making houses. The sort of knowledge, house-building, resulted from this relationship. This is precisely what (A) leads us to expect. Knowledge and learning constitute a relative and correlative pair: when the latter is qualified, as house-making, so too the former is appropriately qualified, as house-building.[40]

So much for how to identify sorts of relatives. For his argument,

[39] Plato uses two expressions for the object of knowledge in 438 C, which I take to be equivalent: the first is 'learning' at 438 C 7 and the second is 'whatever we ought to say knowledge is of' (ἐπιστήμη μὲν αὐτὴ μαθήματος αὐτοῦ ἐπιστήμη ἐστὶν ἢ ὅτου δὴ δεῖ θεῖναι τὴν ἐπιστήμην) at 438 C 7–8. Plato uses 'knowledge itself' to contrast with some given sort of knowledge. Compare this use with the use we find above where I mentioned that Plato uses the expressions 'itself' (αὐτό) or 'the very thing that it is' (αὐτὸ τοῦθ' ὅπερ ἔστιν) to specify a relative in such a way as to make its correlative exclusive.

[40] The principle of qualification is not true in an unrestricted form. Take master and slave. When we qualify the correlative as a 'good slave', how should we qualify the master? Clearly, not with 'good': a bad or indifferent master might have good slaves. So with what could we qualify the relative? I can think of nothing plausible. So there may be counter-examples to the unrestricted version of the principle,

Relatives in Plato's Partition Argument 53

Socrates also needs to establish that the sorts of relatives relate only to their correlatives. This is straightforward. Take a relative and correlative pair, X and Y. Let X' be a sort of X. By (A), X' is itself relative. X' relates to a sort of the correlative Y, namely, Y'. But by the principle of exclusivity, if X' relates to Y', then X' relates exclusively to Y'. For example, knowledge relates to learning. Knowledge of making houses is itself relative, because it relates to learning about house-building. But, by exclusivity, knowledge of making-houses relates only to house-building. So sorts of relatives relate only to the relevant sorts of correlative.

We can specify a relative as qualified or as unqualified. The same applies to the corresponding correlatives.[41] We have just seen how qualified knowledge, house-making, relates to qualified learning, house-building. In one respect house-making is a sort of knowledge, but in another respect house-making is also a relative in its own right. We could call this unqualified house-making. We can infer by (B) that unqualified house-making is relative to unqualified house-building. Indeed, we may wish to contrast unqualified house-making with some sort of house-making. The sort of house-making that deals with walls is walling and the corresponding sort of house-building is building walls. Walling relates only to building walls; exclusivity applies to relative and correlative pairs whether they are sorts of some other relative–correlative pair or not. Indeed, this point will become crucial below. A key move in diffusing the over- and under-generation problems comes when we see that Socrates takes thirst, which is a sort of desire, as unqualified thirst. When so taken, thirst, now unqualified, will relate only to unqualified drink (439 A 1–7).

So far I have argued that sorts of relatives relate only to sorts of

although I know of no discussion of them in Plato. For an importantly different view of how relatives are qualified, see *Cat.* 11^{a}20–33.

[41] Plato's idea that there are different ways of specifying a relative, as qualified or as unqualifed, is analogous to Aristotle's thought in *Phys.* 2. 3, 195^{a}33–^{b}6, that a cause can be given in different ways. Aristotle invokes the example of the cause of a sculpture. We can specify the cause as 'a sculptor', 'Polyclitus', or indeed 'a man' or 'an animal'. We can pick out the cause in a range of ways. One way of specifying the cause, 'a sculptor', is privileged, because we are trying to explain how a sculpture came about. At *Cat.* 7, 7^{a}31–^{b}9, Aristotle applies this thinking to relatives. A master of a slave can be specified in various ways: ideally as 'a master', but also as 'a man' or as 'a biped'. Plato's idea here is similar. A relative is only relative to its proper correlative. But what counts as a proper correlative depends on how the relative is specified, either as qualified in some way or as unqualifed.

correlatives. But to solve the over- and under-generation problems, I need to show that sorts of *opposite* relatives relate exclusively to one and the same correlative. For example, large and small are a relative–correlative pair. But large and small are also opposites. By (A) both large and small have sorts. Call tallness the sort of largeness related to height and shortness the sort of smallness related to height. Now, in general, sorts of opposites are opposite to each other. Pain opposes pleasure, so physical pain and physical pleasure oppose each other. This is true of opposite relatives: tallness and shortness are opposites, in virtue of being sorts of the opposites large and small. Tallness and shortness are also relatives, in virtue of each having a correlative, namely, height.[42] But, because of the principle of exclusivity, both tallness and shortness relate only to height. So tallness and shortness are opposite relatives, but each is relative to the same thing.

Opposite relatives can have the same correlative object. To put the above argument in its general form, X and its opposite, un-X, are both relatives. According to (A) both can be divided into sorts by specifying a term they relate to, Y. Sorts of opposites are themselves opposites, so X' and un-X' are opposites. The sorts X' and un-X' each have the same correlative, Y. X' and un-X' relate exclusively to Y, but Y can be, and in this case is, one and the same correlative for both X' and un-X'. In this case, X' and un-X' are opposite relatives but relate to the same thing, Y.

The text of the Partition Argument supports this treatment of opposite relatives. At 439 B 3–C 8 Socrates discusses opposing drives relevant to the Partition Argument. At 439 B 8–C 1 he offers an analogy with archery. The archer both pushes and pulls the bow, at the same time. For Socrates' remarks to make sense, both the push and the pull must be relative to the same object, the bow. But this can only be secured with the considerations given above. Pushing is opposite to pulling. I call the sort of pushing relative to a bow 'bow-pushing'.[43] Bow-pushing opposes the sort of pulling that relates to

---

[42] It may seem odd that height, not shortness, is the correlative of tallness. But this is what the principle of qualification dictates: when we identify the sorts of a relative, e.g. large, the sorts are relatives and relate to the sorting concept, in this case height. As I mentioned above, whether we take relatives as qualified or unqualified matters. If we took tall and short as unqualified relatives, rather than as sorts of large and small, presumably tall and short would be a relative–correlative pair.

[43] The action being referred to is obvious to anyone who has seen archery but hard to describe succinctly. When an archer takes aim, she *pushes* the bow towards

Relatives in Plato's Partition Argument 55

the bow, known as 'drawing'. Both bow-pushing and drawing are relatives and so relate only to their object. But in both cases that object is the bow. So there is direct evidence to show that opposite relatives sometimes relate exclusively to the same object in the Partition Argument.[44]

We are now in a position to understand how Socrates applies these general considerations of exclusivity and qualification to desire and thirst and, by extension, rejection and dipsophobia, all of which are key to the Partition Argument. Just after his discussion of the principle of qualification, Socrates continues:

[T4] [i] To return to thirst, then, do you not place it among those things that are such as to be of something and say that it is what it is [τοῦτο ὅπερ ἐστίν] of something? I presume it is thirst . . .?[45]
Yes I do, [it is thirst] for drink.
[ii] Therefore, thirst of a certain sort is for drink of a certain sort.
[iii] But thirst itself is neither of much nor of little nor of good nor

her target with one hand and *pulls* the bowstring towards herself with the other. Both pushing and pulling are done with respect to the bow, not the target. While there is a common term in English for this pulling, namely, 'drawing', there is no common term for the corresponding pushing, so I simply coin 'bow-pushing'.

[44] In discussion, David Sedley pressed the following point about Plato's treatment of qualified opposite relatives. I have defended elsewhere the view that for Plato, like Aristotle, every correlative is also a relative (Duncombe, 'Categories'; Duncombe 'Greatest'; cf. *Cat.* 6^{b}28–35). Just as knowledge relates to the knowable, so the knowable relates to knowledge. I call this reciprocity. Sedley's worry is that exclusivity, reciprocity, and Plato's ideas about opposite relatives are inconsistent. According to Plato, knowledge and ignorance both relate to the knowable. By reciprocity, the knowable relates to knowledge and the knowable relates to ignorance. But, by exclusivity, the knowable can relate to at most one of these. So exclusivity, reciprocity, and Plato's ideas about qualified opposite relatives lead to a contradiction. As far as I can discern, Plato never recognizes this problem. Aristotle, however, rejects Plato's ideas about qualification of relatives (*Cat.* 11^{a}20–33), so may offer a solution. A full discussion of these interesting issues would take us too far from the argument of this paper, but I will briefly note that, in my reconstruction, the Partition Argument does not rely on reciprocity, so, as far as this argument goes, Plato is consistent.

[45] The text here is corrupt. S. R. Slings (ed.), *Platonis Respublica* (Oxford, 2003), prints: Τὸ δὲ δὴ δίψος, ἦν δ' ἐγώ, οὐ τούτων θήσεις τῶν †τινὸς εἶναι τοῦτο ὅπερ ἐστίν†; ἔστι δὲ δήπου δίψος (439 A 1–2). There are two problems with the text as it stands: the first sentence is ungrammatical, and the second sentence is incomplete. My suggestion is that we understand Glaucon's response as having two parts: the ἔγωγε as responding affirmatively to Socrates' first sentence and the πώματος as Glaucon completing the second sentence in the run of the conversation. This seems to reflect a natural enough conversational rhythm, even if not strictly grammatical. That said, the presence of two textual difficulties in as many lines suggests broader difficulties within the text, and so nothing I say hangs on any specific construal of the syntax here.

of bad, nor, in a word, of any particular sort, but [iv] thirst itself by nature is only of drink itself. (439 A 1–7)

In this passage the principles of exclusivity and qualification work in tandem to make Socrates' argument. In [i] Socrates uses the expression *touto hoper estin* to suggest that a relative *as such* relates only to its object. He applies this general thought to the relative thirst. When specified properly, thirst relates only to drink. We might say that thirst as such relates exclusively to drink as such. The principle of exclusivity tells us this about thirst, because thirst is a relative. Next, Socrates invokes the principle of qualification, in [ii] and [iii]. [ii] says that qualified thirst relates to qualified drink, while [iii] says that unqualified thirst relates only to unqualified drink. This rules out that unqualified thirst relates to drink of a certain sort, for example, good drink. Socrates concludes, at [iv], that thirst as such relates only to drink as such, not to thirst qualified somehow. The move to this conclusion relies on both principles. Qualified correlatives are not properly specified correlatives, for the purposes of the principle of exclusivity. So thirst as such relates only to drink as such, not drink qualified in some way.

At first, this may seem a little strange. Is thirst not already a sort of desire? If so, how can thirst, a sort of desire, be thirst as such? But we saw above that sorts of relatives can be viewed simply as relatives *tout court*. Thirst as such is both a sort of desire and relative only to drink. In fact, Socrates applies the *hoper estin* expression to thirst in order to emphasize that, even though it is a sort of desire, we can still view thirst as such. When we do so, we will see that the principle of exclusivity applies to thirst and that thirst is relative only to drink.

I argued in Section 2.1 that relatives have an exclusive correlative, and sorts of relatives relate only to an appropriate sort of their correlative. Section 2.2 showed that desire and rejection are relatives. Finally, we saw in Section 2.3 that opposite relatives can relate to the same object, and indeed must when they are divided into sorts by relating to the same object. We saw that this applies also in the case of thirst. With these resources, we can now see that the Partition Argument, as Plato understood it, neither over-generates nor under-generates parts.

3. Solving the problems

I will first outline my construal of the argument, then show how the argument faces neither problem. I pointed out in Section 1 that the principle of opposites specifies three individually necessary and jointly sufficient conditions on anything, X, having parts: X bears opposite relations (*a*) to the same thing, (*b*) at the same time, and (*c*) in the same respect. The Partition Argument assumes that the locus of drives is the soul, and applies these conditions to the soul of an individual, Tantalus, in my example. We make the plausible assumption that Tantalus sometimes thirsts for drink and is dipsophobic for drink, at the same time.

When construed my way, Tantalus' soul meets condition (*a*) since, when specified as thirst, Tantalus' thirst relates to drink. Drink is the object of thirst because thirst is a sort of desire, identified as desire for drink. We saw in Sections 2.2 and 2.3 that sorts of relatives, including desires, are identified by the correlative to which they exclusively relate. In the case of mental states such as desires, those correlatives are the intentional object. For similar reasons, Tantalus' dipsophobia relates to drink. So Tantalus' soul has opposite relations to the same object. Condition (*b*) is met by stipulation: we assumed that Tantalus thirsts and is dipsophobic at the same time. Since the soul is the locus of thirst and dipsophobia, Tantalus' soul does both. It is also easy to see how condition (*c*) is met on my reading. For (*c*) to hold of Tantalus' soul, it must thirst for and reject drink in the same respect. Section 2.3 showed that sorts of relatives, such as thirst and dipsophobia, when specified as such, relate to their object specified as such. Tantalus' thirst is for drink as such and Tantalus' dipsophobia is for drink as such. In both cases Tantalus' attitude is towards drink as such. Hence, there is no room for Tantalus, or his soul, to thirst for drink in one respect and reject it in another. All the individually necessary and jointly sufficient conditions on there being more than one part in Tantalus' soul are met.

Construed this way, the argument does not face the over- and under-generation problems. To save the Partition Argument from under-generation, Socrates would have to ensure that the same object, under the same aspect, is both desired and rejected, at the same time. Desire and rejection are opposite relatives. We saw in

Section 2.3 that opposite relatives are divided into sorts according to their object. Desire for drink is thirst; rejection of drink is dipsophobia. In virtue of being sorts of opposites, thirst and dipsophobia are opposites. But the principle of exclusivity ensures that thirst and dipsophobia each relate only to drink. The fact that the object of thirst as such and dipsophobia as such is drink as such rules out the possibility that it is desired and rejected under different aspects or at different times. But thirst and dipsophobia are opposite attitudes towards the same object. So there is guaranteed to be a genuine violation of the principle of opposites, which is sufficient to generate a part in the soul.

My reading also avoids over-generation. If all conflict in the soul generated a part, then conflict within a part may be sufficient for a partition within that part. Specifically, many readers hold that a thirst for drink and the rejection of some particular drink on offer—say, a hot, sweet drink—would suffice to generate a part within the appetitive part. But now it is easy to see that Plato's Socrates is not committed to anything that would lead to unrestrained over-generation of parts. Thirst as such relates to drink as such. Dipsophobia as such relates to drink as such. An agent cannot have thirst and dipsophobia without psychic conflict. But an agent can thirst and reject a warm drink without conflict. Thirst is relative to drink as such, while the rejection is for warm drink. But drink as such and warm drink are not the same object, so there is not a conflict sufficient to generate a part.

4. Conclusion

The aim of this paper was to show that two principal problems raised against the Partition Argument can be solved, once we understand the notion of relatives at play in the argument. The over- and under-generation problems threaten because thirst and dipsophobia may relate to different objects. Plato's conception of relatives blocks this possibility. For Plato, a relative relates to, and only to, its proper correlative. I showed that Plato considers the mental states at stake in the Partition Argument—desire, rejection, thirst, and dipsophobia—to be relatives. In virtue of the way that the principle of qualification divides relatives into sorts, opposite relatives, including thirst and dipsophobia, exclusively relate to the same object. So the argument, as Plato would have understood it, does not face the over- and under-generation problems.

Durham University

BIBLIOGRAPHY

Adam, J., *The Republic of Plato* (Cambridge, 1902).
Annas, J., *An Introduction to Plato's Republic* [*Introduction*] (Oxford, 1981).
Barney, R., Brennan, T., and Brittain, C. (eds.), *Plato and the Divided Self* (Cambridge, 2012).
Bobonich, C., *Plato's Utopia Recast* [*Utopia*] (Oxford, 2002).
Brown, E., 'The Unity of the Soul in Plato's *Republic*' ['Unity'], in Barney et al. (eds.), *Plato and the Divided Self*, 53–74.
Carone, G. R., 'Akrasia in the *Republic*: Does Plato Change his Mind?' ['Akrasia'], *Oxford Studies in Ancient Philosophy*, 20 (2001), 107–48.
Cooper, J. M., 'Plato's Theory of Human Motivation' ['Motivation'], *History of Philosophy Quarterly*, 1 (1984), 3–21.
Cross, R. C., and Woozley, A. D., *Plato's Republic: A Philosophical Commentary* [*Philosophical*] (London, 1966).
Duncombe, M., 'Plato's Absolute and Relative Categories at *Soph*. 255 C 14' ['Categories'], *Ancient Philosophy*, 32 (2012), 77–86.
Duncombe, M., 'The Greatest Difficulty at *Parmenides* 133 C–134 E and Plato's Relative Terms' ['Greatest'], *Oxford Studies in Ancient Philosophy*, 45 (2013), 43–61.
Ferrari, G. R. F., 'Akrasia as Neurosis in Plato's *Protagoras*', *Proceedings of the Boston Area Colloquium in Ancient Philosophy*, 6 (1990), 115–40.
Hoffman, P., 'Plato on Appetitive Desires in the *Republic*' ['Appetitive'], *Apeiron*, 36 (2003), 171–4.
Irwin, T., *Plato's Ethics* [*Ethics*] (Oxford, 1995).
Irwin, T., *Plato's Moral Theory: The Early and Middle Dialogues* (Oxford, 1977).
Jordan, R. W., *Plato's Argument for Forms*, Cambridge Philological Society, suppl. 9 (Cambridge, 1983).
Lesses, G., 'Weakness, Reason and the Divided Soul in Plato's *Republic*', *History of Philosophy Quarterly*, 4 (1987), 147–61.
Lorenz, H., *The Brute Within: Appetitive Desire in Plato and Aristotle* [*Brute*] (Oxford, 2006).
Moss, J., 'Appearances and Calculations: Plato's Division of the Soul' ['Calculations'], *Oxford Studies in Ancient Philosophy*, 34 (2008), 35–68.

Moss, J., 'Pleasure and Illusion in Plato' ['Pleasure'], *Philosophy and Phenomenological Research*, 72 (2006), 503–35.
Parry, R., *Plato's Craft of Justice* (New York, 1996).
Penner, T., 'Socrates and the Early Dialogues', in R. Kraut (ed.), *The Cambridge Companion to Plato* (Cambridge, 1992), 121–69.
Penner, T., 'Thought and Desire in Plato' ['Thought'], in G. Vlastos (ed.), *Plato 2* (Oxford, 1971), 96–118.
Price, A.W., *Mental Conflict [Conflict]* (London, 1995).
Quine, W. V. O., 'Quantifiers and Propositional Attitudes', *Journal of Philosophy*, 53 (1956), 177–87.
Reeve, C. D. C., *Philosopher-Kings: The Argument of Plato's Republic* (Indianapolis, 1988).
Robinson, R., 'Plato's Separation of Reason from Desire', *Phronesis*, 16 (1971), 38–48.
Shields, C., 'Plato's Divided Soul', in M. McPherran (ed.), *Plato's Republic: A Critical Guide* (Cambridge, 2010), 147–70.
Shields, C., 'Simple Souls', in E. Wagner (ed.), *Essays on Plato's Psychology* (Lanham, Md., 2001), 137–56.
Shorey, P., *The* Republic *[Republic]* (Cambridge, Mass., 1935).
Slings, S. R. (ed.), *Platonis Respublica* (Oxford, 2003).
Smith, N., and Brickhouse, T., *Plato's Socrates* (Oxford, 1994).
Stalley, R. F., 'Persuasion and the Tripartite Soul in Plato's *Republic*', *Oxford Studies in Ancient Philosophy*, 32 (2007), 63–89.
Taylor, C. C. W., *Protagoras* (Cambridge, 1991).
Vlastos, G., 'Socrates', *Proceedings of the British Academy*, 74 (1988), 89–111.
Weiss, R., *The Socratic Paradox and its Enemies* (Chicago, 2006).
White, N. P., *A Companion to Plato's* Republic (Indianapolis, 1979).
Whiting, J., 'Psychic Contingency in the *Republic*', in Barney *et al.* (eds.), *Plato and the Divided Self*, 174–208.

MAKING THE BEST OF PLATO'S PROTAGORAS

MATTHEW EVANS

WHAT if some highly regarded public intellectual pulled you aside at a party and told you, in all seriousness, that any belief anyone has ever had—or ever will have—is, without exception, correct? How would you respond? If you are anything like me, you would probably take a moment to express some heartfelt shock and contempt before stopping to ask yourself, in a more sustained way, how anyone could possibly believe such a thing. After all, if *this* belief is correct, then so is *every* belief; and if *every* belief is correct, then so is the belief that *not* every belief is correct! How then could anyone— even a highly regarded public intellectual—expect to defend this belief against those, like you, who believe the opposite? Would it even be possible to engage such a person in a meaningful and worthwhile debate?

Your predicament here would be similar, I think, to the one that Plato's Socrates takes himself to be in when he realizes (or pretends to realize) that his fellow enquirer Theaetetus has, in proposing to define knowledge as perception, inherited from the sophist Protagoras a deeply puzzling view about the epistemic authority of all human beings:[1]

© Matthew Evans 2015
Many thanks to Emily Austin, Paul DiRado, Mehmet Erginel, Verity Harte, Sean Kelsey, Whitney Schwab, David Sosa, Iakovos Vasiliou, Paul Woodruff, an anonymous referee, and Brad Inwood for their detailed comments on earlier versions of this paper. Thanks also to audiences at the New York Colloquium in Ancient Philosophy, the University of Toronto, the State University of New York at Albany, UMass Amherst, Harvard, Oxford, Yale, the University of Texas at Austin, and Notre Dame, and to the students in my seminars at Yale, New York University, and Michigan in 2010, 2011, and 2012.

[1] My translations of *Theaetetus* passages will modify those of J. McDowell (trans. and comm.), *Plato: Theaetetus* [*Plato*] (Oxford, 1973), and M. J. Levett (trans.), *Theaetetus*, in *The Theaetetus of Plato*, ed. M. Burnyeat (Indianapolis, 1990), and will follow the text of W. F. Hicken in *Platonis opera*, i, ed. E. A. Duke *et al.* (Oxford, 1995), 277–382.

TEXT ONE

SOC. This is no meagre account of knowledge you're proposing to give: it's what Protagoras used to say. He said the same thing, but in a different way. [T1] For he claims somewhere that human beings are the measure of all things, of things that are, that they are, and of things that are not, that they are not. You've read this somewhere, right?

THEAET. Yes, I've read it many times.

SOC. [T2] And doesn't he say something like this, that each thing is to me as it appears to me, and is to you as it appears to you [ὡς οἷα μὲν ἕκαστα ἐμοὶ φαίνεται τοιαῦτα μὲν ἔστιν ἐμοί, οἷα δὲ σοί, τοιαῦτα δὲ αὖ σοί]—since you and I are human beings?

THEAET. He does say that.

SOC. Well, it's not likely that a wise man would speak foolishly. So let's give him our full attention. [T3] Now isn't it the case that sometimes [ἐνίοτε], when the same wind is blowing [πνέοντος ἀνέμου τοῦ αὐτοῦ], one of us shivers and the other does not? Or one shivers slightly and the other shivers intensely?

THEAET. That certainly does happen.

SOC. [T4] Then will we say that at that time [τότε] the wind itself, by itself [αὐτὸ ἐφ' ἑαυτοῦ τὸ πνεῦμα], is either cold or not cold? Or will we be persuaded by Protagoras that it is cold to the one who shivers, and not [cold] to the one who doesn't?

THEAET. That seems plausible.

SOC. [T5] And [the wind] appears [φαίνεται] this way to each [of them]?

THEAET. Yes.

SOC. [T6] And this appearing is a kind of perceiving?

THEAET. Yes.

SOC. [T7] So appearance [φαντασία] and perception are the same in cases of heat and all such [qualities]. For things turn out to be, to each [person], as each [person] perceives them [to be].

THEAET. That seems plausible.

SOC. [T8] Perception, then, is always of what is, and is falsehood-free [αἴσθησις ἄρα τοῦ ὄντος ἀεί ἐστιν καὶ ἀψευδές], as befits knowledge.

(*Theaet.* 151 E 8–152 C 6)

In this passage Socrates seems to cast the Protagorean view as a thoughtful way of analysing what I will call a **contrast case**—a case in which the same thing, at the same time, appears one way to one person, and another way to another person. The wind case, as Socrates unpacks it in [T3], [T4], and [T5], looks like a straightforward contrast case: the same wind, at the same time, blows on two different people (I will call them Mark and Janet), but while it appears cold to one (Mark), it appears not cold to the other (Janet).[2] To analyse a case like this properly, Socrates seems to think, we need to make a couple of important decisions. First we need to decide how things stand with respect to the two people, the appearances they undergo, and the object that each of these appearances is *of* or *about*. Then we need to decide how to assess the *epistemic status* of each of these appearances—is it correct, incorrect, or neither? To assess it as *correct* would be to hold that it constitutes (or is poised to constitute) knowledge, and to assess it as *incorrect* or *neither* would be to hold that it does not (or is not). Very loosely speaking, the first is a decision in metaphysics and the second is a decision in epistemology.

In [T2], [T4], and [T5] Socrates claims that, according to Protagoras, the thing that each of these appearances is of or about—the wind—is to each person as it appears to that person: it is cold to Mark, since it appears cold to Mark; and it is not cold to Janet, since it appears not cold to Janet. This seems to be the *metaphysical* component of his analysis.

Then in [T6], [T7], and [T8] Socrates implies that, according to Protagoras, if a thing is to a person as it appears to that person, then this appearance is *correct*: it constitutes (or is poised to constitute) knowledge. Thus the fact that the wind *is* cold to Mark and not cold to Janet, together with the fact that the wind *appears* cold to Mark and not cold to Janet, guarantees—according to Protagoras—that *both* of their appearances are correct. This seems to be the *epistemological* component of his analysis.

Though there is some suggestion in [T7] that Protagoras might want to restrict his analysis to contrast cases involving perceptual qualities such as *small, heavy, white*, and the like (152 D 2–6), it becomes clear in the ensuing discussion that, as Socrates understands

---

[2] Burnyeat claims that in this passage 'it was not said that the second person feels warm in the wind, or even that he feels the wind is not cold . . . [it was said] simply that he does not feel cold'. See M. Burnyeat, 'Protagoras and Self-Refutation in Plato's *Theaetetus*' ['Protagoras'], *Philosophical Review*, 85 (1976), 172–95 at 178. But this is a mistake. As Ketchum and Fine have emphasized, Socrates says in [T5] (152 B 10) that the wind 'appears this way to each' of them, thereby implying that it appears *not cold* to the one who does not shiver. See R. Ketchum, 'Plato's "Refutation" of Protagorean Relativism' ['Relativism'], *Oxford Studies in Ancient Philosophy*, 10 (1992), 73–105 at 77, and G. Fine, 'Relativism and Self-Refutation: Plato, Protagoras, and Burnyeat' ['Relativism'], in J. Gentzler (ed.), *Method in Ancient Philosophy* (Oxford, 2001), 137–63 at 140–1 n. 11.

him anyway, Protagoras wants to extend his analysis to *all* contrast cases—even those involving *non*-perceptual qualities such as *just*, *shameful*, and *pious* (167 C 4–7; 172 A 1–C 1). It also becomes clear that he is not interested in exploiting any sort of conceptual distinction between something's *appearing* a certain way to someone, perceptually or otherwise, and someone's *believing* it to be that way (166 E 2–167 A 8; 171 A 6–9).[3]

Now what troubles Socrates about the view that emerges from all this, and what should probably trouble us as well, is that it seems to rule out the possibility of contrast cases in which one of the two appearances is *epistemically inferior* to the other. For if there could be no cases of this sort, then presumably it would be pointless for anyone to try to resolve a given contrast case by submitting the two contrasting appearances to critical scrutiny—no matter how striking or momentous the contrast between them might be. Here is how Socrates puts the worry:

TEXT TWO

if what each person believes . . . will in fact be true for that person, and no one will assess anyone else's experience better, and no one will have greater authority to examine whether anyone else's belief is correct or false [μήτε τὴν δόξαν κυριώτερος ἔσται ἐπισκέψασθαι ἕτερος τὴν ἑτέρου ὀρθὴ ἢ ψευδής], but . . . each person himself alone has his own beliefs, and all of them are correct and true, then how could it be, my friend, that Protagoras is wise, so that he rightly thinks himself worthy to be a teacher of others and to receive enormous fees, while we are more ignorant and ought to follow him around—if each himself is the measure of his own wisdom? How can we not claim that Protagoras is pandering to the crowd when he says these things? I keep silent about myself and my own skill of midwifery, and the ridicule we deserve, but I think the entire practice of dialectic [σύμπασα ἡ τοῦ διαλέγεσθαι πραγματεία] deserves it too. For examining and attempting to refute one another's appearances and beliefs, given that each person's [appearances and beliefs] are correct [τὸ γὰρ ἐπισκοπεῖν καὶ ἐπιχειρεῖν ἐλέγχειν τὰς ἀλλήλων φαντασίας τε καὶ δόξας, ὀρθὰς ἑκάστου οὔσας]—is that not an immensely tedious bit of nonsense [φλυαρία] if [what he says] is true . . . ? (*Theaet.* 161 D 2–162 A 3)

---

[3] For this reason I will assume in what follows that there is no fundamental difference in meaning between claims about what appears to a person and claims about what that person believes. This assumption would be contentious in other interpretative contexts, but nothing substantive rides on it (or should ride on it) in this one. For an example of the sort of interpretative context in which it clearly would be contentious see G. Fine, *Plato on Knowledge and Forms: Selected Essays* [*Plato*] (Oxford, 2003), 132–41.

In this passage Socrates seems to be arguing that Protagoras, by denying the possibility of incorrect belief, commits himself to denying something that he *elsewhere* commits himself to *accepting*, namely, the possibility of superior wisdom. The argument, as I understand it, goes more or less as follows:

(W1) If the Protagorean analysis of contrast cases is right, then incorrect belief is impossible.
(W2) If incorrect belief is impossible, then the practice of dialectic—assertion and counter-assertion, argument and counter-argument—is pointless.
(W3) If some people are wiser than others, then the practice of dialectic is *not* pointless.
(W4) Some people are wiser than others. Therefore:
(W5) The Protagorean analysis of contrast cases is wrong.

This line of reasoning—which I will call the **wisdom argument**—strikes me as extremely powerful, and I see no obviously plausible way for Plato's Protagoras to resist it.[4] He cannot deny (W1), since the impossibility of incorrect belief is an acknowledged implication of his proposed analysis of contrast cases. Nor can he deny (W4), the claim that some people are wiser than others, since this is something he explicitly accepts a few pages later (166 D 1–7). Nor, I think, can he deny (W3)—and just allow that the practice of dialectic is pointless—since he plainly takes himself to be justified in defending his analysis of contrast cases against those (such as Socrates) who would attempt to undermine it (166 A 7–B 2; 166 C 2–9; 167 D 5–168 C 2).[5] In the end, then, it would seem that Protagoras' only remotely viable option here is to deny (W2), the claim that the practice of dialectic is pointless if incorrect belief is impossible.

Of course we might wonder how viable this option really is, since (W2)—at least on the face of it—is very hard to deny. After all, if incorrect belief is impossible, then what reason could there be for us to probe and test our beliefs in the context of a dialectical exchange? Why should we bother to submit our beliefs to critical scrutiny, as

[4] In this paper I will be limiting my attention to the views of *Plato's* Protagoras—the possibly imaginary figure who actually does hold the views that Socrates attributes to him in this dialogue—and I will not consider the views of *the historical* Protagoras. For ease of exposition I will often use the name 'Protagoras' to refer to the former figure; I will never use it to refer to the latter.

[5] For a useful discussion of these passages see Alex Long, 'Refutation and Relativism in *Theaetetus* 161–171', *Phronesis*, 49 (2004), 24–40 at 29–33.

Protagoras thinks we (sometimes) should, if it is not so much as *possible* for *any* of them to be wrong? This, I take it, is the intuitive crux of the challenge that Socrates poses to Protagoras in the form of the wisdom argument.

But could it be that Protagoras actually has what he needs to *meet* this challenge? Can he tell a clear and coherent story about why it is (sometimes) worthwhile for people to argue with each other, even if no one's epistemic authority is ever any greater than anyone else's?[6] As far as I know, none of the major commentators on the *Theaetetus* has ever dared to suggest that he can.[7] Yet that is exactly what I will try to do in this paper. My specific argument will be that Socrates himself—in a passage commonly known as 'The Defence of Protagoras' (166 C–167 D)—provides his opponent with just enough resources to explain how it could be reasonable for people to participate in a dialectical exchange with each other, even if it is already clear to both of them that neither of their beliefs falls anywhere short of perfect knowledge.

Before I begin, however, let me emphasize that I do not expect to demonstrate, nor do I intend to suggest, that the Protagorean analysis is the right one, or a good one, or even an especially plausible one. Nor do I wish to defend any particular view about whether and to what extent Plato himself would endorse the argument he has Socrates press against it.[8] All I want to establish here is that Plato's own clarification and development of this analysis shows *how it can*

---

[6] The question here is inspired by one of Burnyeat's: 'Can a thorough-going relativist tell a *consistent* story about expertise, about teaching and learning, about discussion and debate, without conceding a role to objective truth?' See M. Burnyeat, 'Introduction', in M. Burnyeat (ed.), *The* Theaetetus *of Plato* (Indianapolis, 1990), 1–255 at 27.

[7] Many have held that the so-called περιτροπή argument at 170 A 6–171 D 7 is unsuccessful in one way or another. See G. Vlastos, 'Introduction', in G. Vlastos (ed.), *Plato's* Protagoras (New York, 1956), vii–lviii at xiv n. 27; K. Sayre, *Plato's Analytic Method* [*Method*] (Chicago, 1969), 87–90; McDowell, *Plato*, 169–71; D. Bostock, *Plato's* Theaetetus [*Theaetetus*] (Oxford, 1988), 89–92; Ketchum, 'Relativism'; and T. Chappell, 'Does Protagoras Refute Himself?' ['Protagoras'], *Classical Quarterly*, NS 45 (1995), 333–8. But none of these commentators has gone so far as to claim that Protagoras' view is consistent with all of the basic presuppositions of the practice of dialectic.

[8] My instinct is to suppose that he would endorse it wholeheartedly, but at the moment I have trouble convincing myself of this. After all, it is Theodorus (not Theaetetus) who is responsible for defending Protagoras against the wisdom argument, and Plato repeatedly depicts Theodorus as a reticent and unreliable advocate (162 A 4–C 2; 168 C 2–169 A 1). Is Plato actually provoking us to take up the task that Theodorus has proved unwilling or unable to perform?

survive that argument. If I am right about even this much, then—as I hope will become clear shortly—Plato's Protagoras is a far more resilient and intriguing philosopher than he is standardly thought to be.

I

Up to this point I have claimed that Protagoras can successfully defend himself against the wisdom argument just in case he can coherently maintain that people sometimes have a reason to engage in the practice of dialectic with each other. Also I have claimed, or at least have promised to claim, that he *can* coherently maintain this.

But my promise might seem empty, right from the start, since most of the leading commentators on the *Theaetetus* have held that, according to Protagoras, it is not even possible for people to *disagree* with each other.[9] If these commentators are right, then it is not easy to see how Protagoras could manage to establish that people sometimes have a reason to argue with each other, since it is no longer clear what there could be for them to argue *about*. They believe *different* things, to be sure; but if the things they believe are in no way *opposed*, then they seem not to be under any rational pressure to participate in a dialectical exchange with each other. Or so, at any rate, we might think.[10]

[9] This view is held by so many different commentators, on so many different grounds, that it would be tedious to cite them all here. But a few especially clear formulations can be found in E. N. Lee, '"Hoist with his Own Petard": Ironic and Comic Elements in Plato's Critique of Protagoras (*Tht.* 161–171)' ['Hoist'], in E. N. Lee, A. P. D. Mourelatos, and R. M. Rorty (eds.), *Exegesis and Argument: Studies in Greek Philosophy Presented to Gregory Vlastos* (New York, 1973), 225–61 at 237 n. 24: 'on [Protagoras'] own principles, the entire notion of real disagreement—the sheer logical *collision* of one man's assertion and another man's denial *of the same thing*—is in fact ruled out'; M. M. McCabe, *Plato and his Predecessors: The Dramatisation of Reason* [*Plato*] (Cambridge, 2000), 34–5: 'In the relativist world of Protagoras . . . [n]o proposition can stand in any relation to another proposition which might allow one to contradict another'; and K. Vogt, *Belief and Truth: A Skeptic Reading of Plato* (Oxford, 2012), 110: '[Protagoras] does not envisage [Mark] and [Janet] as genuinely disagreeing: there is no conflict between what they say.'

[10] See McDowell, *Plato*, 171; Lee, 'Hoist', 248; S. Waterlow, 'Protagoras and Inconsistency: *Theaetetus* 171 A 6–C 7' ['Protagoras'], *Archiv für Geschichte der Philosophie*, 59 (1977), 19–36 at 35–6; Bostock, *Theaetetus*, 94–5; Chappell, 'Protagoras', 337; McCabe, *Plato*, 45–6; M. Erginel, 'Relativism and Self-Refutation in the *Theaetetus*' ['Relativism'], *Oxford Studies in Ancient Philosophy*, 37 (2009), 1–45 at 42; and Z. Giannopoulou, 'Objectivizing Protagorean Relativism: The Socratic Underpinnings of Protagoras' Apology in Plato's *Theaetetus*' ['Objectivizing'], *Ancient Philosophy*, 29 (2009), 67–88 at 71.

Actually I suspect that we need not think this,[11] but for the purposes of this paper I will assume that we should. I will assume, in other words, that Protagoras can adequately defend himself against the wisdom argument only if he can accept something that most commentators think he *cannot* accept—namely, that it is possible for one person to believe the opposite of what another person believes. Part of my aim in what follows will be to establish that he *can* accept this, regardless of whether he *must*.

One reason why so many commentators have arrived at a different conclusion, I take it, is that Protagoras clearly thinks of each of the two beliefs in a given contrast case as being accurately responsive to a reality that is somehow *private* to each of the two believers;[12] and it is tempting to infer from this that he thinks of *the things these believers believe* as being private to them as well.[13] For example, if Protagoras holds that the wind Mark feels, or *the coldness of* the wind Mark feels, is private to Mark, then—we might suppose—he must also hold that what Mark believes, strictly speaking, is not that the wind is cold, but that *his* wind is cold or that the wind is cold *to him*.[14] On this interpretation, then, Protagoras holds something like the following view:

Content Relativism: In all contrast cases, the content of each person's belief—that is, *what each person believes*—is relative to that person.

As I have just suggested, this view will need to be filled out in one

[11] Suppose it turned out that, for obscure psychological reasons, one of the foreseeable effects of every dialectical discussion is an improvement in the emotional well-being of both of its participants. Then people would seem to be under some sort of rational pressure to engage in the practice of dialectic with each other, even if the things they believed were in no way opposed.

[12] See 152 D 2–E 1; 153 E 4–154 A 4; 156 D 2–157 C 1; 160 B 5–D 3; and 166 C 2–7.

[13] More or less explicit versions of this interpretation can be found in F. Cornford, *Plato's Theory of Knowledge: The* Theaetetus *and the* Sophist *of Plato* [*Theory*] (London, 1935), 73; Lee, 'Hoist', 246–7; D. K. Glidden, 'Protagorean Relativism and Physis' ['Physis'], *Phronesis*, 20 (1975), 209–27 at 217; R. M. Dancy, 'Theaetetus' First Baby: *Theaetetus* 151 E–160 E', *Philosophical Topics*, 15 (1987), 61–108 at 71; B. Williams, 'Introduction', in B. Williams (ed.), *Plato:* Theaetetus (Indianapolis, 1992), vii–xx at x; McCabe, *Plato*, 32; and Giannopoulou, 'Objectivizing', 71.

[14] As I understand it, this interpretation does not require Protagoras to hold that Mark would *express* his belief by *saying* 'my wind is cold' or 'the wind is cold to me'. All it requires him to hold is that the belief Mark would express by saying 'the wind is cold' is different from the belief that *anyone else* would express by saying *the very same thing*—since each of these beliefs would really be about a different private world.

of two different ways, each of which relativizes (to the believer) a different component of what the believer believes. **Predicate Relativism** relativizes the predicate; on this view, what Mark believes is not that *his* wind is cold, but that the wind is cold *to him*. **Subject Relativism**, on the other hand, relativizes the subject;[15] on this view, what Mark believes is not that the wind is cold *to him*, but that *his* wind is cold.[16]

Now it is quite clear that Protagoras, if he is a content relativist of either sort, cannot accept that it is possible for anyone to believe the opposite of what anyone else believes. For if what Mark believes is that the wind is cold *to him* or that *his* wind is cold, then the *opposite* of what Mark believes is that the wind is *not* cold to him or that his wind is *not* cold; and that is certainly not what Janet believes. What Janet believes, according to the content relativist, is that the wind is not cold *to her* or that *her* wind is not cold. So if Protagoras is a content relativist, then (we are assuming) he has no chance of defeating the wisdom argument, since he cannot accept that—let alone explain how—it is possible for one person to believe the opposite of what another person believes.

But is Protagoras a content relativist? He does often say things that suggest such a view, but—as many commentators have emphasized—he also often says things that suggest an importantly different view:[17]

Truth Relativism: In all contrast cases, *the truth or false-*

---

[15] Note that my use of the term 'subject' here is meant to pick out the syntactic subject of the content of a belief, not the phenomenological subject of a perceptual encounter.

[16] The distinction between predicate relativism and subject relativism is clearly marked, in different terms, by Bostock, *Theaetetus*, 47–8 and Ketchum, 'Relativism', 89–90. But are these the only two views available to the content relativist here? What if we propose, for example, that the content of Mark's belief is neither that *his* wind is cold, nor that the wind is cold *to him*, but simply that *to him* or *at his world* the wind is cold? The problem with this proposal, I think, is that it fails to specify the content of the definite description 'the wind' as it occurs in Mark's belief. Is this content supposed to be the same as, or different from, the content of the definite description 'the wind' as it occurs in *Janet's* belief—the belief that *to her* or *at her world* the wind is *not* cold? If it is different, then we seem to get the equivalent of subject relativism; and if it is the same, then we seem to get the equivalent of predicate relativism. So this third view appears not to be a stable alternative to the first two. Maybe there are other, more stable alternatives in the vicinity here, but if so they have escaped my notice.

[17] See 158 E 6; 160 C 7; 161 D 2; 170 D 5–6; 170 E 4–5; 170 E 9; and 171 C 5–7.

hood of the content of each person's belief is relative to each person.[18]

While these two views—content relativism and truth relativism—might at first appear similar (or even equivalent) to each other, it is important to realize that in fact they are profoundly at odds with each other.[19]

To see why, suppose Protagoras is a content relativist who thinks that what Mark believes is that the wind is cold to him. (Suppose, in other words, that Protagoras is a predicate relativist.) In that case nothing prevents him from claiming that the content of Mark's belief is *absolutely true* if the wind is cold to Mark, and *absolutely false* if the wind is *not* cold to Mark. So the semantic apparatus of relative truth and falsehood is of no use to him here. Because he has built all of the necessary relativity into *what each person believes*, he has

[18] Commentators who emphasize these passages in their interpretation include Vlastos, 'Introduction', xiii–xiv; Burnyeat, 'Protagoras'; M. Matthen, 'Perception, Relativism, and Truth: Reflections on Plato's *Theaetetus* 152–160' ['Perception'], *Dialogue*, 24 (1985), 33–58; N. Denyer, *Language, Truth, and Falsehood in Ancient Greek Philosophy* [*Truth*] (London, 1991), 83–94; Chappell, 'Protagoras'; and L. Castagnoli, 'Protagoras Refuted: How Clever is Socrates' "Most Clever" Argument at *Theaetetus* 171 A–C?' ['Refuted'], *Topoi*, 23 (2004), 3–32. Among these commentators, and between these commentators and others, there is a long-standing debate about what Protagoras means when he says that such-and-such is 'true for' so-and-so, and about whether the various things he says in this vein add up to a 'theory of truth'. We may be in a position to contribute something to this debate, but not for a while yet. See below, n. 31.

[19] It is also worth noting that I am not using the labels 'content relativism' and 'truth relativism' in the way they are typically used by philosophers today. Thanks in large part to the work of John MacFarlane, it is now widely accepted that the content or the truth of a sentence or a belief can be relativized, in a semantic framework, not only to the context of the *speaker* (or the *believer*) of that sentence or that belief but also to the context of the *assessor* of that sentence or that belief. The views currently known as 'content relativism' and 'truth relativism' hold that, in certain domains of talk and thought, the content or the truth of each sentence or belief in that domain is relative to the context of the assessor. But the views I have baptized with those names do not hold this. According to the view I am calling 'content relativism', for example, *what Mark believes* is not relative to the person who *decides* or *determines* what Mark believes; it is simply relative to Mark. Likewise, on the view I am calling 'truth relativism', *the truth or falsehood of* what Mark believes—in so far as this is relevant to fixing the epistemic status of his belief—is not relative to the person who *decides* or *determines* the truth or falsehood of that belief; it is simply relative to Mark. These latter two views, as I understand them, are very crude versions of the ones that tend to circulate now under the somewhat cumbersome headings of 'contextualism' and 'nonindexical contextualism' respectively. For a useful map of this complex and difficult territory see J. MacFarlane, 'Relativism', in G. Russell and D. Graff Fara (eds.), *The Routledge Companion to Philosophy of Language* (New York, 2012), 132–42.

no reason to build any of it into *the truth or falsehood of* what each person believes.²⁰

Suppose next that he is a truth relativist, so that in his view what Mark believes is neither absolutely true nor absolutely false, but true relative to Mark and false relative to Janet. Here the situation is reversed: because Protagoras has built all of the necessary relativity into *the truth or falsehood of* what each person believes, he has no reason to build any of it into *what each person believes*. What Mark believes, on this view, is simply *that the wind is cold*; and it is this—the non-relativized content of Mark's belief—that is true for Mark if the wind is cold to Mark, and false for Janet if the wind is not cold to Janet.

That is why I think it would be unreasonable for anyone, including Protagoras, to be *both* a content relativist *and* a truth relativist. But which is he, then, assuming he is one or the other?²¹

II

If Protagoras is a content relativist, then (as we have seen) he must be either a subject relativist or a predicate relativist. Yet TEXT ONE makes it quite clear, in my view, that he is not a subject relativist. For in [T3] and [T4] he explicitly grants that it is *the same wind* that blows on, and appears to, both Mark and Janet together.²² But if he wants to deny that there are really *two* winds blowing here— one that appears to Mark and another that appears to Janet—then presumably he *also* wants to deny that what Mark believes is that *his* wind is cold, and that what Janet believes is that *her* wind is *not*

---

²⁰ A parallel argument will establish the same conclusion if we suppose instead that he is a subject relativist.
²¹ Of course it is not logically necessary that he be one or the other, but as far as I can see there is no plausible interpretation of the relevant texts that yields a comparably clear third alternative.
²² This point is emphasized also by G. B. Kerferd, 'Plato's Account of the Relativism of Protagoras' ['Relativism'], *Durham University Journal*, 42 (1949), 20–6 at 20–1, and Matthen, 'Perception', 35–6. For some recent attempts to undermine the authority of TEXT ONE on this issue, however, see R. Waterfield, *Plato:* Theaetetus [*Theaetetus*] (London, 1987), 152–3; Fine, *Plato*, 144 n. 28; D. Sedley, *The Midwife of Platonism: Text and Subtext in Plato's* Theaetetus [*Midwife*] (Oxford, 2004), 38 n. 1; and Erginel, 'Relativism', 9–10 n. 29. Each of these attempts is motivated by subtle and important exegetical considerations that, for reasons of length, I cannot expect to address adequately in this paper. My hope is to do them greater justice in future work.

cold. For how could the contents of their beliefs be relativized in this way, let alone be true, if there is only one wind for their beliefs to be about in the first place?[23]

Instead Protagoras seems to want to insist that this same wind *is the way it is*—cold or not cold—*only relative to* Mark and Janet. So a suitably generalized version of this part of his view would have to look something like the following:

> **Property Relativism**: In all contrast cases, the thing each person's belief is about has whatever (relevant) properties it has only relative to each person.

On a view of this sort, the things our beliefs are about in a given contrast case do not have whatever properties they have *in their own right* or *in themselves*; whatever properties they have, they have *only relative to us*. In the wind case, for example, the wind is in itself neither cold nor not cold; it is cold relative to Mark, and not cold relative to Janet.[24] Similarly, in the wine case (159 B 2–E 5), the wine is in itself neither sweet nor bitter; it is sweet relative to healthy Socrates and bitter relative to sick Socrates.

Once we accept that Protagoras is a property relativist, however, we might be tempted to infer from this that he is also a *predicate* relativist. For the way the predicate relativist thinks *we believe things to be*—cold to us, sweet to us, and the like—is exactly the way the property relativist thinks *things are*. So property relativism and pre-

[23] Moreover, it would make no sense for Protagoras to suggest (as he does in [T4]) that the wind is cold and not cold only relative to Mark and Janet if he thought that in fact there are two winds here, one private to Mark and the other private to Janet. On this point see especially Matthen, 'Perception', 49–50.

[24] Though this strikes me as the plain upshot of [T4], Sayre disagrees. For in his view Protagoras cannot intelligibly claim that the wind is in itself neither cold nor not cold, since that would be to claim, in effect, that the wind is in itself *both* not cold *and not* not cold! See Sayre, *Method*, 65–6. This concern would be warranted, perhaps, if it were clear that in TEXT ONE 'cold' and 'not cold' are to be understood as contradictories rather than contraries. But that is not so clear. In fact I would suggest that, when Protagoras says that the wind is cold to Mark and not cold to Janet, he means that the wind is to Mark *somewhere cold* on the hot/cold scale, and is to Janet *somewhere not cold* on the hot/cold scale—since this is how he thinks the wind perceptually appears to each of them. So when he claims that the wind is in itself neither cold nor not cold, I take it he means that the wind is in itself *nowhere at all* on the hot/cold scale. But if that is what he means, then Sayre's concern is unwarranted: Protagoras can intelligibly claim that the wind is in itself *both* not somewhere cold on the hot/cold scale *and not* somewhere not cold on the hot/cold scale. For some useful further discussion of this issue see T. Chappell, *Reading Plato's* Theaetetus [*Theaetetus*] (Indianapolis, 2005), 59–61, and T. Chappell, 'Reading the περιτροπή' ['Reading'], *Phronesis*, 51 (2006), 109–39 at 123–4.

dicate relativism, taken together, support the epistemological component of the Protagorean analysis perfectly: if the things we form our beliefs about are exactly the way we believe them to be when we form our beliefs about them, then of course all of our beliefs will end up being correct.

But at the same time it is difficult to see how Protagoras *could* be a predicate relativist. For predicate relativism turns out to be straightforwardly inconsistent with the canonical formulation of his own view. Recall [T2] in TEXT ONE: 'each thing is to me as it appears to me, and is to you as it appears to you'.[25] Here Socrates tells us that, according to Protagoras, there is some sort of equivalence relation between the way things *appear* to the believer, or the way the believer *believes* things *to be*, and the way things *are* to the believer. So if we want to know how Mark believes the wind to be—that is, what the content of Mark's belief is—all Protagoras thinks we have to do is find out how the wind is to Mark. How, then, is the wind to Mark? According to Protagoras, it is *cold* to Mark; it is not *cold to Mark* to Mark. But then, according to Protagoras, the way Mark believes the wind to be is *cold*, not *cold to Mark*. Therefore Protagoras is not a predicate relativist.

Though this strikes me as the simplest and most decisive reason to deny that Protagoras is a predicate relativist, two other reasons are worth mentioning here as well. First, there is an important passage later in the discussion where Socrates supposes that, according to Protagoras, the content of one person's belief might be true for that person and false for another person (170 D 4–E 6). If we assume that according to Protagoras something's being false for a person entails that this person believes the opposite of it—a reasonable assumption, I think—then we can infer that according to him it is possible for one person to believe the opposite of what another person believes. Yet he cannot consistently accept this possibility if he is a predicate relativist.

Second, when Socrates discusses the wine case (159 B 2–E 5), he suggests that according to Protagoras the healthy man and the sick man believe opposite things about the wine they both drink. He then seems to confirm this interpretation a bit later, at 166 D 7–E 4, where he says (in the voice of Protagoras): 'Don't go after my ac-

---

[25] This formulation reappears in various structurally isomorphic guises throughout the rest of the dialogue. See 162 C 8–D 1; 166 E 2–4; 167 C 4–5; 171 E 1–3; and 177 C 7–8.

count by its letter, but instead learn with even greater clarity what I mean as follows. Remember, for example, what was said earlier: that to the sick man the things he eats appear and are bitter, whereas to the healthy man they appear and are the opposite [τἀvαvτία].'[26] But if Protagoras is a predicate relativist, then he cannot consistently accept that it is possible for one thing to appear one way to one person, and *another* thing to appear *the opposite* way to *another* person. Since this remark is supposed to be an especially clear expression of his view, it suggests even more strongly that he is not a predicate relativist.

To my mind these three considerations make a very powerful case against interpreting Protagoras as a predicate relativist. Yet at the same time I admit I am surprised by this result. For, as we have just seen, property relativism and predicate relativism, taken together, provide the perfect support structure for Protagoras' epistemology. So if we are going to deny that he is a predicate relativist, as it currently seems we should, then we need to make sure that our preferred alternative interpretation will allow us to explain how his account of what we believe, combined with his account of the way things are, will yield—in a similarly satisfying way—his account of what we know.

III

Is there some such alternative interpretation available? I believe there is. But to get an adequate sense of it, we need to remind ourselves of what we have in place so far: two lines of argument, one with the conclusion that Protagoras is not a subject relativist, and the other with the conclusion that he is a not a predicate relativist. If these two lines of argument are sound, then Protagoras is not a content relativist; and if he is not a content relativist, then (we are assuming) he is a *truth* relativist.[27] So what we have now, in effect, is an extended argument for the conclusion that Protagoras is a truth relativist—someone who holds that, in all contrast cases, the truth or falsehood of what each person believes is relative to each person. We also have an additional, partly independent, line of argument

[26] Here Protagoras seems to have forgotten that it was drink, not food, that was under discussion at 159 B 2–E 5. But I take it that this does not seriously compromise the doctrinal continuity between the two passages.

[27] Recall my assumption, at the end of sect. 1, that he is one or the other.

for the conclusion that Protagoras is a *property* relativist—someone who holds that, in all contrast cases, the thing each person's belief is about has whatever (relevant) properties it has only relative to each person.[28]

What would this combination of views look like, more concretely, if Protagoras were to apply them to the wind case in TEXT ONE? As a property relativist, he would presumably start by claiming that at a certain moment there comes to be between Mark and the wind a particular coldness that is unique to the triple of Mark, the wind, and the moment, such that at that moment the wind is cold to him; and, at that same moment, there comes to be between Janet and the wind a particular not-coldness that is unique to the triple of Janet, the wind, and the moment, such that at that moment the wind is not cold to her.[29] Now if Protagoras were a predicate relativist, he would go on to claim that, since what Mark believes is *that the wind is cold to him* and what Janet believes is *that the wind is not cold to her*, each of their beliefs is absolutely true. But we are supposing instead that Protagoras is a truth relativist, and as a truth relativist he would claim that, since what Mark believes is *that the wind is cold* and what Janet believes is *that the wind is not cold*, neither of their beliefs is absolutely true; Mark's is true for Mark because the wind is cold to him, and Janet's is true for Janet because the wind is not cold to her.[30]

It seems to me that this combination of property relativism and truth relativism will support Protagoras' epistemology just as effectively as the combination of property relativism and predicate relativism does, but in a slightly less straightforward way. According to the latter combination, remember, Mark's belief is correct because the content of his belief is absolutely true; and the content of his belief is absolutely true because the way he believes the wind to be corresponds perfectly to the way the wind is—namely, cold *to him*.

---

[28] If we assume that truth is a property of (some of) the things people believe, and that part of what it is to believe something is to believe that it is true, then we can—in accordance with Ketchum, 'Relativism', 76—*derive* truth relativism *from* property relativism. But it is not clear to me that Protagoras would accept either of these two assumptions. In fact I strongly suspect, for reasons I discuss briefly in n. 56 below, that he would reject the second. So for the moment I am inclined to think that we should see his commitment to truth relativism as something over and above his commitment to property relativism.

[29] This is the model that seems to emerge most naturally from passages such as 153 D 8–154 A 4; 156 C 7–E 7; and 159 B 2–E 5.

[30] For a broadly similar reconstruction see Castagnoli, 'Refuted', 7–9.

According to the former combination, by contrast, Mark's belief is correct because the content of his belief is true *for him*; and the content of his belief is true *for him* because the way he believes the wind to be corresponds perfectly to the way the wind is *to him*—namely, cold.³¹ Since either of these combinations will yield the result that all beliefs are equally correct, neither of them strikes me as significantly less able than the other to support Protagoras' epistemology. So we now seem to have lost our last salient reason to interpret him as a predicate relativist.

³¹ As I mentioned earlier, in n. 18, there is a great deal of disagreement about what Protagoras means when he says that such-and-such is 'true for' so-and-so, and about whether the various things he says in this vein add up to a 'theory of truth'. Most of the commentators agree that, according to Protagoras, *it is true for Mark that the wind is cold* if and only if *Mark believes that the wind is cold*. But they disagree about why Protagoras thinks this. As Burnyeat, 'Protagoras', 180–1, points out, it need not be because he holds that 'it is true for Mark that the wind is cold' *just means* 'Mark believes that the wind is cold'. In fact Protagoras *does not* hold this—or so Burnyeat argues, followed by Denyer, *Truth*, 85–7; Ketchum, 'Relativism', 81–2; E. K. Emilsson, 'Plato's Self-Refutation Argument in *Theaetetus* 171 A–C Revisited', *Phronesis*, 39 (1994), 136–49 at 147–8; Castagnoli, 'Refuted', 27 n. 73; and many others. For if he did, they argue, this seemingly central component of his view would turn out to be nothing but a boring tautology. Fine disagrees, arguing—with Bostock, *Theaetetus*, 91 n. 6—that even if this component of his view is in some sense a tautology, it is a deliberately informative, potentially deep, and (to that extent) philosophically interesting one. See Fine, 'Relativism', 142–3, and Fine, *Plato*, 139–40 and 187–8. Fine's argument has not been widely accepted, however, and as a result her interpretation remains unpopular. But if Burnyeat and the others are right, and Protagoras *does not* think that 'it is true for Mark that the wind is cold' means 'Mark believes that the wind is cold', then what *does* he think it means? Recent proposals abound. See especially M. Lee, *Epistemology after Protagoras: Responses to Relativism in Plato, Aristotle, and Democritus* (Oxford, 2005), 41–5; Chappell, 'Reading', 129; and Erginel, 'Relativism', 14–15 n. 42. My own recommendation is that we focus our attention on the distinctively *epistemic* significance this sort of talk seems to have in passages such as TEXT TWO and 160 C 7–D 3, where Protagoras implies that what makes Mark's belief *correct*—what makes it meet the relevant standard for knowledge—is that its content is true *for him*. If we take this approach, then we will be inclined to suppose that the relativized (dyadic) truth predicate in Protagoras' lexicon has very roughly the same epistemically validating force, as applied to beliefs, that the non-relativized (monadic) truth predicate has in ours. This by itself might not amount to a 'theory of truth', since it says nothing about *what makes* something *true for* someone. But I agree with Burnyeat, 'Protagoras', 180–2, and Denyer, *Truth*, 85–7, that Protagoras has a view about this as well. For he pretty clearly wants to say that what makes the content of a particular person's belief true for that person is that things are, to that person, the way that person believes them to be. If we were then to ask him what he means when he says that something is some way 'to' someone, he would presumably appeal to the familiar formulation of property relativism on offer in passages such as 156 C 7–157 A 4 and 159 C 4–D 6. As I see it, then, his overall position exhibits a fairly transparent explanatory structure: his hyper-permissive epistemology is supported by his truth relativism, and his truth relativism is supported by his property relativism.

IV

Suppose we decide, on the basis of all this, that Protagoras is a truth relativist rather than a content relativist. Would that make an important difference for our overall assessment of his view? Earlier we assumed that he can successfully defend himself against the wisdom argument only if he can accept that it is possible for one person to believe the opposite of what another person believes. Now we discover that, if he is a truth relativist, he *can* accept this. For the semantic apparatus of relative truth allows him to say that the content of Mark's belief is *that the wind is cold* and the content of Janet's belief is *that the wind is not cold*; since these two contents are plainly opposed to each other, he now seems free to claim that one person can believe the opposite of what another person believes. Yet at the same time he *also* seems free to claim that the content of each person's belief, no matter how opposed it might be to the content of anyone else's, is true *for that person*. So apparently he has all he needs in order to maintain that, although what Mark believes is the opposite of what Janet believes, both of their beliefs are correct!

Of course we might start to worry at this point that we have lost our grip on what it would be for one person to believe the opposite of what another person believes. Is it not some sort of conceptual necessity that, if the content of your belief is opposed to the content of mine, then at least one of our beliefs is *not* correct?

To my mind, at any rate, the answer to this question is not obvious.[32] Certainly we could insist that there is a particular *kind* of opposition between contents that would ensure the incorrectness of at least one of the beliefs whose contents they are. Call this kind of opposition **controversion**. But is there any *other* kind of opposition that Protagoras would be entitled to recognize here? It seems to me that there is. For I take it he is free to deny that at one and the same moment the wind could be *both* cold to Mark *and not*

---

[32] Max Kölbel, a contemporary philosopher with relativist sympathies, proposes that this very possibility—the possibility of error-free opposition in belief—is a kind of 'criterion' for non-objectivity in any given domain of thought. Here is the crux of his formulation: 'For any p: it is an objective matter whether p, just if: For all thinkers A and B: . . . if A believes that p and B believes that not-p then either A has made a mistake or B has made a mistake.' By this criterion, then, Protagoras would want to insist that, for any p, it is *not* an objective matter whether p. See M. Kölbel, *Truth without Objectivity* [*Truth*] (London, 2002), 28–31.

cold to Mark;[33] and if he is free to deny this, then he is also free to deny that at one and the same moment Mark could believe *both* that the wind is cold *and* that the wind is *not* cold.[34] So it would appear that Protagoras can claim, along with most of the rest of us, that these two contents—*that the wind is cold* and *that the wind is not cold*—stand in a certain relation to each other that would make it impossible for anyone to believe both of them at the same time. But what relation is this exactly? Here I think Protagoras would be entitled to hold that, whatever it is, it is a *kind* of opposition. Call it **exclusion**.[35]

The question now is whether Protagoras can coherently maintain *both* that it is possible for contents to exclude each other *and* that it is *not* possible for contents to controvert each other. We might be tempted to suppose that he cannot coherently maintain this, since we tend to assume that if any two contents exclude each other, then *that is because* they controvert each other. But I think we need to acknowledge that this assumption is not mandatory. For there does seem to be room in logical space for a view according to which (i) each thing always is to each person as that person believes it to be, (ii) nothing ever both is and is not any way to any person, and (iii) if a thing is to a person as that person believes it to be, then that person's belief is correct. If these three claims are so much as *consistent* with each other—and I see no reason to doubt that they are—then we have yet to discover any conceptual incoherence at the heart of the Protagorean view. For while (ii) and truth relativism together make it possible for contents to exclude each other, (i) and (iii) together make it impossible for contents to controvert each other. So this view really does seem to deliver for Protagoras the remarkable result that, at one and the same time, one person could be correct in believing the *opposite* of what *another* person is correct in believing.

---

[33] On this issue I stand with Glidden, 'Physis', 215 n. 28, Fine, *Plato*, 189, Chappell, 'Reading', 123–4, and Erginel, 'Relativism', 9 n. 28, against Kerferd, 'Relativism', 21, and Waterlow, 'Protagoras', 25–6.

[34] Recall that according to Protagoras the way the wind is to Mark is the way Mark believes it to be. So if the wind cannot at any moment be both cold to Mark and not cold to Mark, then—as Protagoras sees it—Mark cannot at any moment believe both that the wind is cold and that the wind is not cold.

[35] The kinds of opposition in content I am calling 'controversion' and 'exclusion' correspond loosely to the kinds of disagreement in attitude MacFarlane calls 'preclusion of joint accuracy' and 'doxastic noncotenability'. See J. MacFarlane, *Assessment Sensitivity: Relative Truth and its Applications* [*Assessment*] (Oxford, 2014), 121–8.

V

But even if Protagoras can get away with claiming that the content of one person's correct belief could be opposed to the content of another's, we might still wonder whether he can get away with claiming that it sometimes makes sense for such people to participate in a dialectical exchange with each other. After all, if both of their beliefs are guaranteed in advance to be correct, then why should they bother to discuss the matter with each other in the first place? What would be the point of airing their opposition if it is not so much as *possible* for *either* of them to be wrong?

Here we might try to respond, on Protagoras' behalf, that it is somehow exciting or enjoyable or ennobling to challenge someone else's beliefs—or to have one's own beliefs challenged—in the context of a dialectical discussion. If that were the case, then maybe people like Mark and Janet could expect a significant payoff from arguing with each other, even if it is already clear to them that both of their beliefs are correct.

Regardless of the merits of this line of response, however, it is not the one that Protagoras himself decides to pursue. Instead he explores the possibility of a *non-epistemic standard of assessment* for beliefs—one that would allow us to distinguish between beliefs worth having and beliefs worth avoiding, but would not thereby require us to concede that the former are correct and the latter are not. He explores this possibility in greatest detail during his attempt to give an account of wisdom that would escape the trap Socrates has set for him with the wisdom argument. The relevant passage is long, but illuminating:

TEXT THREE

[E]ach of us is the measure of things that are and are not, yet we differ from each other in myriad ways for this very reason, that some things are and appear to one, while other things are and appear to another. [G1] And far be it from me to deny the existence of wisdom and a wise man, but I say that this wise man himself is the one who, by working a change, makes good things be and appear to anyone of us to whom bad things are and appear [or: makes things be and appear good to anyone of us to whom things are and appear bad] [ὃς ἄν τινι ἡμῶν, ᾧ φαίνεται καὶ ἔστι κακά, μεταβάλλων ποιήσῃ ἀγαθὰ φαίνεσθαί τε καὶ εἶναι]. [G2] So don't go after my account by its letter, but instead learn with even greater clarity what I mean as follows. Remember, for example, what was said earlier: that to the sick man the things he eats appear and are bitter, whereas to the healthy man they appear and are the opposite. Now it's not that one should make either of them wiser—for that is not possible—nor should one make the accusation that the ill man is ignorant because he believes *these* things, and the healthy man is wise because he believes *those* things, but one should work a change [from *these*] to *those*. For that other condition is better. [G3] In this way too, in education, one should work a change from this [worse] condition to that better one. But while the doctor works the change with drugs, the sophist does it with arguments. Now one doesn't ever make someone who believes false things later believe true things—for it is neither possible to believe things that are not, nor [possible to believe] things other than those one experiences, and these are always true. But I think that someone whose soul is in a harmful condition believes things that are akin to it, while a beneficial condition makes him believe things of the other kind, which are the very appearances [φαντάσματα] that some people—out of inexperience—call true. But I call these things *better* than those, not *truer*. [G4] And I say that those who are wise . . . concerning bodies are doctors, and those who are wise concerning plants are gardeners—for I claim that gardeners produce in plants beneficial and healthy perceptions and truths in place of harmful perceptions, whenever any of them is sick. [G5] Likewise [I say that] wise and good orators make beneficial things, instead of harmful things, seem just to cities [ταῖς πόλεσι τὰ χρηστὰ ἀντὶ τῶν πονηρῶν δίκαια δοκεῖν εἶναι ποιεῖν]. Whichever things *seem* just and fine to each city also *are* just and fine to it, for however long it recognizes them as such; but the wise man makes *beneficial* things be and seem [just and fine] to them in place of each of the *harmful* things that are [just and fine] to them. And, according to the same account, the sophist who is able to teach his students in this way is wise and worth a lot of money to those he teaches. (*Theaet.* 166 D 1–167 D 2)

Many of the claims Protagoras makes in this passage are problematic in various ways, and it is unclear whether we can interpret all of them together so as to provide him with a fully consistent view. But the question I want to ask here is a relatively narrow one: has he given himself the resources he needs in order to explain, in a coherent way, how it might make sense for people with opposed beliefs to engage in the practice of dialectic with each other? My contention will be that he has.[36]

The crucial part of TEXT THREE is [G1], where Protagoras provides his first general formulation of the account of wisdom he

[36] As far as I know, the only other commentator who would agree with me about this is Michel Narcy, and his reasons are significantly different from mine. See below, n. 40.

favours. As McDowell and Burnyeat have emphasized, however, this formulation can be interpreted in two very different ways:

The Committed Reading: The wise person makes good things instead of bad things be and appear a certain way to the patient.

The Uncommitted Reading: The wise person makes certain things be and appear good to the patient instead of bad to the patient.[37]

Nearly all of the commentators who have attended closely to this passage—I will call them **the critics**—hold that the committed reading saddles Protagoras with an incoherent view.[38] For on this reading he is not claiming that it is a relative matter whether the things the patient believes (or could be brought to believe) are beneficial or harmful for the patient to believe; he is implying, without any qualification whatsoever, that some things are beneficial for the patient to believe and other things are harmful for the patient to believe. But in that case, the critics suggest, he must be presupposing that someone could have an *incorrect belief* about whether a particular thing is beneficial or harmful for the patient to believe. If the critics are right about this, then the committed reading does indeed spell doom for Protagoras. For, as we have seen, he cannot accept the possibility that *anyone* has an incorrect belief about *anything*.[39]

We might then conclude, as some commentators seem to, that the

[37] See McDowell, *Plato*, 165–6, and Burnyeat, 'Introduction', 24–5. Burnyeat calls these readings 'the compromising interpretation' and 'the uncompromising interpretation' respectively. But I find these labels somewhat misleading, for reasons that should become clear shortly.

[38] See Vlastos, 'Introduction', xxi–xxii n. 47; A. T. Cole, 'The Apology of Protagoras' ['Apology'], *Yale Classical Studies*, 19 (1966), 103–18 at 111; W. K. C. Guthrie, *The Sophists* (Cambridge, 1971), 187; McDowell, *Plato*, 167; Glidden, 'Physis', 218–19; Waterfield, *Theaetetus*, 169–70; Burnyeat, 'Introduction', 24–5; R. Polansky, *Philosophy and Knowledge: A Commentary on Plato's* Theaetetus (Lewisburg, 1992), 122–5; Sedley, *Midwife*, 56; Chappell, *Theaetetus*, 105–7; and Giannopoulou, 'Objectivizing', 74–83.

[39] Although this strikes me as a straightforward implication of his view, some commentators—such as Kerferd, 'Relativism', 25—disagree. They think that Protagoras wants to leave room for the possibility of incorrect belief about certain things, such as whether a particular belief is beneficial, or whether a particular person is wise, or whether things are for each person as that person believes them to be. On interpretations of this sort, Protagoras is a *local* relativist rather than a *global* one. But for the sake of simplicity I am going to set these interpretations aside and just assume that he is a global relativist. Needless to say, this will not make the *philosophical* task of defending him any less difficult than it already is.

uncommitted reading leaves Protagoras in a better position.[40] But in fact it does no such thing. For if the committed reading forces him to accept the possibility of incorrect belief, in just the way the critics think it does, then the uncommitted reading *also* forces him to accept that possibility. After all, on this reading he is not claiming that it is a relative matter whether the patient believes (or will believe) that such-and-such is bad (or good); he is implying, without any qualification whatsoever, that the patient believes (or will believe) this.[41] But then, according to the same line of argument as before, he must be presupposing that someone could have an incorrect belief about whether the patient believes (or will believe) this.[42] So if the committed reading saddles him with an incoherent view, then evidently the *uncommitted* reading saddles him with an *equally* incoherent view.

[40] See Vlastos, 'Introduction', xxi–xxii; Glidden, 'Physis', 218–19; M. Narcy, *Platon: Théétète* (Paris, 1995), 114–21; Burnyeat, 'Introduction', 25–6; and Sedley, *Midwife*, 56. Of these commentators, Narcy seems to be alone in thinking that the uncommitted reading not only makes good sense of what Protagoras says in TEXT THREE, but also leaves Protagoras in a *fully satisfactory* position. As I will argue in a moment, however, the uncommitted reading *does not* make good sense of what Protagoras says in TEXT THREE, *whether or not* it leaves him in a fully satisfactory position.

[41] It is worth considering in this connection the so-called 'future argument' at 178 A 5–179 B 5.

[42] The difficulty here is anticipated in various ways by J. Jordan, 'Protagoras and Relativism: Criticisms Bad and Good' ['Protagoras'], *Southwestern Journal of Philosophy*, 2 (1971), 7–29 at 24–5; McDowell, *Plato*, 171; Chappell, 'Protagoras', 336–7; and Fine, *Plato*, 193–4. A possible escape route is at least suggested by Sedley, *Midwife*, 58–9, who holds that according to Protagoras 'there are no truths of the form "For X, such and such is the case for Y"'. Sedley calls this the 'single-relativization assumption' (SRA). If Sedley is right, and Protagoras accepts the SRA, then something extraordinary seems to follow. For Protagoras is committed to the view that, if Z believes that such-and-such, then such-and-such is the case for Z. So suppose Protagoras believes that W believes that such-and-such. Then his view will have the consequence that, for Protagoras, such-and-such is the case for W. But this consequence is inconsistent with the SRA! Therefore, if Protagoras accepts the SRA, he must deny that he believes *anything* about what *anyone* believes. Obviously this would allow him to avoid having to say that someone has, or could have, an incorrect belief about whether so-and-so believes such-and-such. (That is the possible escape route I had in mind.) But surely this goes too far. Socrates consistently and unreservedly attributes to Protagoras all sorts of beliefs about what other people believe, especially—but not exclusively—in TEXT THREE. This is why I find it implausible that Protagoras would accept the SRA in the first place. For a broadly similar argument against Sedley on this issue see Chappell, 'Reading', 118–20, and for a counter-argument against Chappell see Z. Giannopoulou, 'In and out of Worlds: Socrates' Refutation of Protagorean Relativism in *Theaetetus* 170 A–171 C', *Ancient Philosophy*, 31 (2011), 275–94 at 279–80.

Regardless of whether the uncommitted reading leaves Protagoras in a better position, however, it plainly fails to fit the case of the orator in [G5].[43] For Protagoras does not say here that the orator's healing power consists in making certain things seem beneficial to the city instead of harmful to the city; rather he says that it consists in making things that *are* beneficial to the city *seem just* to the city. His view, apparently, is that there are some things such that, if and when they seem just to the city, the city does *well*, and other things such that, if and when they seem just to the city, the city does *badly*; the orator makes the former, instead of the latter, seem just to the city.[44] What the orator is supposed to discover, then, is not how to make the city believe *that it is better off believing something*, but how to make the city believe *something it is better off believing*.

The other three cases—the doctor in [G2], the sophist in [G3], and the gardener in [G4]—are not quite as transparent as that of the orator in [G5]. But all of them can be interpreted along the same lines: the patient starts off believing something she is worse off believing (for example, that the wine is bitter), so the wise person makes her believe something she is *better* off believing—namely, the *opposite* thing (for example, that the wine is sweet). Since all four cases *can* be interpreted in this way, and since at least one of them (the orator) *must* be, the committed reading strikes me as manifestly superior to the uncommitted reading, simply as an interpretation of what Protagoras says in TEXT THREE.

This is an important result for our purposes, I think, because the committed reading gives us a very clear indication of how Protagoras might at least *hope* to resist the wisdom argument. For if he can maintain that there are certain venerable figures among us who have the power to make people believe things they are better off believing, then he can also explain why having these figures around would make it reasonable for people with opposed beliefs to engage in the practice of dialectic with each other. He need only be able to claim something that is implicit in much of what he says in TEXT THREE anyway—namely, that there are some contrast cases in which one person would be better off believing what the other person believes. If he can make this claim, then presumably he can also insist that it

---

[43] Many of the critics explicitly acknowledge this. See especially Cole, 'Apology', 109–11; McDowell, *Plato*, 166; and Burnyeat, 'Introduction', 26.

[44] This interpretation of [G5] seems to be telegraphed by the last two sentences of [G2], and then seems to be confirmed by 172 A 1–B 6 and 177 C 6–D 7.

sometimes makes sense for people to argue with each other. For by doing so, especially in the company of the wise, they stand a decent chance of having their minds changed for the better.[45]

VI

Can Protagoras make this claim, however? Can he coherently maintain that, in at least some contrast cases, one person would be better off believing what the other person believes? According to the critics, of course, the answer is no.[46] For if Protagoras sincerely claims that so-and-so would be better off believing such-and-such, then—the critics seem to assume—he must hold that *the belief that* so-and-so would *not* be better off believing such-and-such *is incorrect*. Obviously Protagoras is in serious trouble if this is a fair assumption for the critics to make. But is it?

One way to try to answer this question would be to consider what I will call a **second-order contrast case**—a case in which what one person believes about a certain contrast case is different from what *someone else* believes about *that same* contrast case. Suppose, for instance, that Protagoras believes that Mark would be better off agreeing with Janet, and Diotima believes the opposite. Then suppose Diotima confronts Protagoras on this very question, and attempts to engage him in a dialectical discussion. Could Protagoras coherently permit himself to claim, against Diotima, that Mark would be better off agreeing with Janet? Or would he, by making this very claim, be presupposing that Diotima's belief is incorrect?

Since this second-order contrast case is itself just another contrast case, the question whether Protagoras could coherently per-

[45] Like me, the great humanist Ferdinand Schiller thinks there is something worth exploring in this broadly pragmatic account of wisdom. See F. C. S. Schiller, *Plato or Protagoras? Being a Critical Examination of the Protagoras Speech in the* Theaetetus *with Some Remarks upon Error* (Oxford, 1908). But unlike me, Schiller wants to argue that—according to *the historical* Protagoras—what makes a proposition true (or false) is nothing other than its being beneficial (or harmful) to believe. Whether or not Schiller's argument on this point is convincing, the view he attributes to the historical Protagoras is certainly not held by *Plato's* Protagoras, since this latter character goes well out of his way to deny that the things we are better off believing are any more true than the things we are worse off believing. Here I concur with Cornford, *Theory*, 73 n. 1; Burnyeat, 'Introduction', 23–4; and Chappell, *Theaetetus*, 106.

[46] According to Protagoras, on the other hand, the answer is clearly yes. See 167 D 2–3.

mit himself to claim that Mark would be better off agreeing with Janet is equivalent, I take it, to the question whether Protagoras could coherently permit *Mark* to claim *that the wind is cold*. For the first-order contrast case between Mark and Janet has the same fundamental structure as the second-order contrast case between himself and Diotima.[47] So if Protagoras can coherently permit Mark to make his claim about the wind, then he can also coherently permit *himself* to make *his own* claim about *Mark*.

But can Protagoras coherently permit Mark to make his claim about the wind? At a quick first glance, anyway, I think it should seem fairly obvious that he can. He certainly thinks that Mark is entitled to *believe* that the wind is cold, since he thinks that this belief is guaranteed in advance to be correct. And it would be odd for anyone to insist that we are not permitted to assert what we correctly believe (let alone what we know). So we might well conclude, on the basis of this very simple line of argument, that Protagoras can *easily* permit himself to claim, against Diotima, that Mark would be better off agreeing with Janet.

On reflection, however, we might come to suspect that this simple line of argument is a bit too simple. For if Protagoras thinks that Diotima's claim is no less true for her than his own claim is for him, then he must also think that these two claims are on a par with respect to truth. But if that is what he thinks, then we might well suppose that he is confused about *what it is to make a claim* in the first place. We might be convinced, for example, that in order to make a claim—especially in the context of a dialectical discussion—one must commit oneself to the *absolute truth* of that claim, and (thus also) to the *absolute falsehood* of the *opposite* claim.

Many of the critics seem to be convinced of this at any rate. Here is Burnyeat:

to assert anything is to assert it as a truth, as something which is the case. . . . The relativist may reply that 'All truth is relative' is not asserted as an absolute truth, . . . but only as a relative one: *it is true for me that all truth is relative*. This is no help. The second proposition is . . . still an assertion. 'It is true for me that all truth is relative' is put forward as itself true without qualification. A commitment to truth absolute is bound up with the very act of assertion.[48]

---

[47] Here I am taking it for granted that Protagoras, as a global relativist, will want to handle all contrast cases in roughly the same way. See above, n. 39.

[48] Burnyeat, 'Introduction', 30. This is a compressed version of the same line of

It would seem, then, that Burnyeat wishes to endorse something like the following general claim about assertion:

The Absolute Truth Rule: In asserting something, one commits oneself to the absolute truth of what one asserts.

As Burnyeat rightly suggests, it is a consequence of this claim that the truth relativist cannot coherently assert anything at all. For if part of what it is to assert something is to commit oneself to the absolute truth of what one asserts, then by asserting anything at all the truth relativist commits herself to there being some absolute truths. But as a truth relativist she *also* commits herself to there being *no* absolute truths. So, according to the absolute truth rule, the truth relativist cannot coherently assert her own view—or any other view for that matter. This is why we would need to accuse Protagoras of a certain sort of incoherence if we, like Burnyeat and the others, were to endorse the absolute truth rule.

But it is far from clear that we, Protagoras, or anyone else *should* endorse the absolute truth rule. Many leading philosophers of language now recommend a relativistic account of truth in certain narrowly defined domains of discourse, such as epistemic modals, future contingents, knowledge attributions, vague terms, and predicates of personal taste.[49] Though none of these philosophers

reasoning developed more carefully in Burnyeat, 'Protagoras', 190–5. In both places Burnyeat cites John Passmore, who writes: 'The fundamental criticism of Protagoras can now be put thus: to engage in discourse at all he has to assert that something is the case. . . . it is presupposed in all discourse that some propositions are true, that there is a difference between being the case and not being the case, and to deny this in discourse is already to presume the existence of the difference. . . . To assert that, for example, 'there are no truths' is to assert both that there are and that there are not truths because, precisely, to assert is to *assert to be true*.' See J. Passmore, *Philosophical Reasoning* (New York, 1961), 67–8. Similar views, as applied to the case of Protagoras, can also be found in J. L. Mackie, 'Self-Refutation: A Formal Analysis', *Philosophical Quarterly*, 14 (1964), 193–203 at 200; Lee, 'Hoist', 248–9; Bostock, *Theaetetus*, 91; R. Wardy, *Doing Greek Philosophy* (London, 2006), 99; and L. Castagnoli, *Ancient Self-Refutation: The Logic and History of the Self-Refutation Argument from Democritus to Augustine* (Cambridge, 2010), 39.

[49] On epistemic modals see A. Egan, J. Hawthorne, and B. Weatherson, 'Epistemic Modals in Context', in G. Preyer and G. Peter (eds.), *Contextualism in Philosophy: Knowledge, Meaning, and Truth* (Oxford, 2005), 131–68; on future contingents see J. MacFarlane, 'Future Contingents and Relative Truth', *Philosophical Quarterly*, 53 (2003), 321–36; on knowledge attributions see M. Richard, 'Contextualism and Relativism', *Philosophical Studies*, 119 (2004), 215–42; on vague terms see M. Richard, *When Truth Gives Out* (Oxford, 2008), ch. 4; on predicates of personal taste see P. Lasersohn, 'Context Dependence, Disagreement, and Predicates

would follow Protagoras in recommending a relativistic account of truth in *all* domains of discourse, every single one of them (as far as I can tell) would recommend a *unified account of assertion across* all domains of discourse.[50] So even the less radical relativists among us would want to deny that a commitment to absolute truth is bound up with *any* act of assertion—no matter what domain of discourse that act of assertion might belong to.[51] In other words, the absolute truth rule is no longer uncontroversial, if it ever was, and we would be in good company today if we opted to reject it.

Even if we opted to accept it, however, I think the damage to Burnyeat's argument would already be done. For the aim of that argument is to show that as a truth relativist Protagoras is required, by conceptual necessity alone, not to assert anything. Yet now we discover that the putative conceptual necessity on which this argument depends is in fact denied by a wide swath of leading experts in the field today. So if this argument is going to succeed on its own terms, it will have to be powerful enough to show not only that *Protagoras* is confused, but also—and on the basis of the same line of reasoning—that *these experts* are confused. Since I think we can agree that it fails to show the latter,[52] I think we should also agree that it fails to show the former.

---

of Personal Taste', *Linguistics and Philosophy*, 28 (2005), 643–86; and in general see Kölbel, *Truth*; F. Recanati, *Perspectival Truth: A Plea for (Moderate) Relativism* (Oxford, 2007); and MacFarlane, *Assessment*.

[50] On this point see especially Kölbel, *Truth*, ch. 6; A. Egan, 'Epistemic Modals, Relativism, and Assertion', *Philosophical Studies*, 133 (2007), 1–22; J. MacFarlane, 'What is Assertion?' ['Assertion'], in J. Brown and H. Cappelen (eds.), *Assertion: New Philosophical Essays* (Oxford, 2011), 79–96; and MacFarlane, *Assessment*, 34–5 and 97–117. By an 'account of assertion' here I just mean an attempt to specify what makes a given speech act an assertion rather than (say) a promise, a request, a command, or a question.

[51] It is also worth noting that there are several other leading contemporary philosophers of language who are not relativists of any kind, but who nonetheless favour broadly *expressivist* accounts of assertion—accounts that make no appeal to truth at the fundamental level of analysis. These philosophers, if I understand them correctly, would also want to deny the absolute truth rule. See e.g. S. Yalcin, 'Epistemic Modals', *Mind*, 116 (2007), 983–1026; and E. Swanson, 'How Not to Theorize about the Language of Subjective Uncertainty', in A. Egan and B. Weatherson (eds.), *Epistemic Modality* (Oxford, 2011), 249–69.

[52] It fails to show the latter simply because it presupposes what needs to be shown—namely, the absolute truth rule itself.

VII

Of course this does not mean that we should just let Protagoras off the hook. He may have some powerful companions in guilt when it comes to rejecting the absolute truth rule, but—unlike these companions of his—he has not yet told us anything about what sort of account he would put in its place. And he needs to tell us *something* about this, I take it, if he expects to defend himself successfully against the wisdom argument. For only then will he be able to explain how it could make sense for people to continue to argue with each other even when it is clear to both of them that neither of their assertions is in any way deficient with respect to truth.[53] This is why I think he needs to replace the absolute truth rule with some alternative account—one that tells us what the asserter *could be* committing herself to *if not* the absolute truth of what she asserts.[54]

Does Protagoras have the resources to develop such an account? Some commentators seem to think that he does, and that the account in question is precisely the one that Burnyeat (in the passage quoted above) rejects as hopeless:

The Relative Truth Rule: In asserting something, one commits oneself to the truth *for oneself* of what one asserts.[55]

---

[53] Note that Protagoras, as I interpret him, is not telling us what people *already are* doing when they argue with each other; he is telling us what they *should be* doing when they argue with each other. The openly prescriptive tone of passages such as 166 E 4–167 A 6 ([G2] and [G3] in TEXT THREE above) and 160 B 8–C 2 (TEXT FIVE below) makes it plain, in my view, that he sees himself as advancing a *revolutionary* view rather than a *hermeneutic* one. So we would be treating his view unfairly if we were to judge it by its power to justify the currently dominant way of engaging in the practice of dialectic. His whole point is that there is a better way.

[54] Here I am assuming, along with Burnyeat and most of the other critics, that any adequate account of assertion will specify some distinctive commitment that is undertaken by the asserter in relation to what she asserts. But I should emphasize that I am interpreting the term 'commitment' very broadly here, so that it will apply across the board to any act that is governed by a norm. So what I am assuming, in effect, is that any adequate account of assertion will specify some distinctive norm that governs every act of assertion as such. This is the approach favoured by such figures as J. Searle, *Speech Acts: An Essay in the Philosophy of Language* (Cambridge, 1969), ch. 2; R. Brandom, 'Asserting', *Noûs*, 17 (1983), 637–50; and T. Williamson, 'Knowing and Asserting', *Philosophical Review*, 105 (1996), 489–523. But it is not the only one. See MacFarlane, 'Assertion', for a useful comparative analysis of the options.

[55] See especially Jordan, 'Protagoras', 19–21; Ketchum, 'Relativism', 91–4; and Chappell, *Theaetetus*, 116–17.

Making the Best of Plato's Protagoras 89

But other commentators have argued, following in the footsteps of Burnyeat, that this account will generate a vicious regress of some kind, and so is not a coherent alternative after all. Here again is Burnyeat:

> [Protagoras'] position is supposed to be that x is F or p is true for a just in case a judges that x is F or p is true;[56] and this is not an arbitrary connection or one that can be abandoned without our losing grip on the notion of relative truth. Protagoras, as Socrates keeps saying, is a clever fellow, but he is not so clever that there is no limit to the complexity of the propositions he can understand . . . Therefore, the relativistic prefix 'It is true for Protagoras that . . .' . . . admits of only limited reiteration. At some point, though we may not be able to say just where, Protagoras must stop and take a stand. And once committed, if only in principle, to an absolute truth, he can no longer maintain that all truth is relative and any judgment whatsoever true only for the person(s) whose judgment it is.[57]

According to Burnyeat, then, the relative truth rule somehow requires that it be possible for people to believe things of unlimited complexity. Since this is not possible, he thinks, the relative truth rule cannot be coherently sustained.

But why exactly does he think that the relative truth rule requires that this be possible? His argument seems to run along the following lines. If Protagoras is a truth relativist who accepts the relative truth rule, then as soon as he asserts something—*that the wind is cold*, say—we can ask him whether *it is absolutely true* that the wind is cold. Because he is a truth relativist, he will have to say no, it is only true *for him* that the wind is cold. As soon as he says this, however, we can ask him whether *it is absolutely true* that it is true for him that the wind is cold. Again he will have to say no, it is only true *for him* that it is true for him that the wind is cold. Since this procedure can be repeated indefinitely, it would appear that—as soon as Protagoras asserts that the wind is cold—he commits himself to its being true for him that it is true for him that it is true for him

---

[56] This formulation contains what I take to be a small but important mistake. Contrary to what Burnyeat says here, Protagoras' position—as I understand it—is supposed to be (i) that p is true for a just in case a judges that p, *not* (ii) that p is true for a just in case a judges that p is (absolutely) *true*. For if Protagoras holds (ii), then he will quickly be forced to accept that, if a judges that p, then a judges that p is (absolutely) true. But he cannot coherently accept this, as I interpret him, because as a truth relativist he must judge that *nothing* is (absolutely) true. This may not matter much for our purposes here, however, since as far as I can tell it has no direct relevance to the argument Burnyeat proceeds to give against the relative truth rule.   [57] Burnyeat, 'Protagoras', 194–5.

(and so on indefinitely) that the wind is cold. So, as soon as he asserts anything at all, he commits himself to the truth *for himself* of something of unlimited complexity.⁵⁸

One concern we might have about this argument right away is that Protagoras seems free to turn it back against those who accept the *absolute* truth rule.⁵⁹ For suppose Aspasia is a truth absolutist who accepts the absolute truth rule. Then as soon as she asserts that the wind is cold, we can ask her whether *it is only true for her* that the wind is cold. Because she accepts the absolute truth rule, she will have to say no, it is *absolutely* true that the wind is cold. But then we can ask her whether it is only true for her that it is absolutely true that the wind is cold. Again she will have to say no, it is absolutely true that it is absolutely true that the wind is cold. Since this procedure can be repeated indefinitely, it would appear that—as soon as Aspasia asserts that the wind is cold—she commits herself to its being absolutely true that it is absolutely true that it is absolutely true (and so on indefinitely) that the wind is cold. So she likewise commits herself to the *absolute* truth of something of unlimited complexity.

⁵⁸ Contrast this with the deceptively similar line of argument canvased by H. Putnam, *Reason, Truth and History* (Cambridge, 1981), 120: 'Protagoras . . . claimed that . . . when I say "Snow is white", I am using this utterance to claim that *snow is white* is true-for-me, whereas when Robert Nozick says the same words he would . . . be claiming that *snow is white* is true-for-*him*. . . . It follows (on Protagoras' view) that no utterance has the same meaning for me and for anyone else . . . Plato's counter-argument was that, if every statement X means "I think that X", then . . . the ultimate meaning of "Snow is white" is . . . "I think that I think that I think that I [think] (with infinitely many 'I thinks') that snow is white." This Plato took to be a *reductio ad absurdum*.' Leaving aside the merits of Putnam's interpretation of Plato here, I think we can see that his interpretation of Protagoras—unlike Burnyeat's—is dubious at best. He seems to assume, for example, that committing oneself to its being true for oneself that the wind is cold is equivalent to *asserting* (or 'claiming') *that it is* true for oneself that the wind is cold. But this assumption is highly questionable in its own right, and it certainly does not fit the view we have been developing on Protagoras' behalf up to this point. According to that view, remember, what is true for Mark is the same as what he believes, namely, *that the wind is cold*. So if Mark is sincere, then what he asserts—when he commits himself to its being true for him that the wind is cold—is simply *that the wind is cold*, not *that it is true for him* that the wind is cold. In effect, Putnam's interpretation holds that Protagoras is a sort of *content* relativist about *assertion*; and this clashes rather badly with our current interpretation, which holds that he is a *truth* relativist about *belief*. Other variants of this dubious, Putnam-style interpretation of Protagoras as a sort of content relativist about assertion can be found in Lee, 'Hoist', 246–7; Glidden, 'Physis', 216–17; Williams, 'Introduction', x; and Chappell, *Theaetetus*, 116.

⁵⁹ This is the concern that preoccupies J. W. Meiland, 'Is Protagorean Relativism Self-Refuting?', *Grazer philosophische Studien*, 9 (1979), 51–68 at 59–63.

Making the Best of Plato's Protagoras 91

As Burnyeat suggests, however, there does seem to be an important difference between the two situations here.⁶⁰ For while Protagoras' view entails that people believe everything that is true for them, Aspasia's view *does not* entail that people believe everything that is *absolutely* true.⁶¹

But I suspect that this difference will not be enough, by itself, to vindicate the argument. It *would* be enough, I think, if we could legitimately rely on the assumption that, according to Protagoras, people believe not only everything that is true for them, but also everything that *they commit themselves to being* true for them. Then we would be able to infer, on the basis of the reasoning sketched out above, that according to Protagoras it is possible for people to believe things of unlimited complexity.

The problem is that we cannot legitimately rely on this assumption. To see why, consider the *parallel* assumption that, according to Aspasia, people believe everything that they commit themselves to being *absolutely* true. Should Aspasia accept this parallel assumption or not? Certainly she will want to accept that people commit themselves, not only to the absolute truth of what they believe, but also to the absolute truth of *the logical consequences of* what they believe. After all, it is obvious that people are under some sort of obligation to revise their beliefs if they detect an inconsistency somewhere in the logical consequences of those beliefs. Would her acceptance of this rather obvious fact then force her to conclude that people *believe* the logical consequences of what they believe? If she accepts the parallel assumption—that people believe everything that they commit themselves to being absolutely true—then yes, it would. But in that case she too will have to conclude that it is possible for people to believe things of unlimited complexity; for, as we have just seen, every believed thing can be nested recursively in an infinite sequence of 'it is absolutely true that' operators, each of which will yield a fresh logical consequence of the initially believed thing.⁶² Of course she may be entitled to deny the parallel assump-

---

⁶⁰ See Burnyeat, 'Protagoras', 194.

⁶¹ Here I am accepting for the sake of argument Burnyeat's claim that, according to Protagoras, people believe everything that is true for them. For an important recent attack on this claim see M. V. Wedin, 'Animadversions on Burnyeat's *Theaetetus*: On the Logic of the Exquisite Argument' ['Animadversions'], *Oxford Studies in Ancient Philosophy*, 29 (2005), 171–91 at 181–4.

⁶² Moreover, it is reasonable to assume that one of the logical consequences of every believed thing is an infinite disjunction containing that thing as one of its

tion instead. But if she is, then I take it *Protagoras* is entitled to deny the *original* assumption—that people believe everything that they commit themselves to being true *for them*. So I think Burnyeat is mistaken in concluding that Protagoras is at a significant dialectical disadvantage here.[63]

In the end, then, the relative truth rule does not seem to saddle Protagoras with the sort of vicious regress that Burnyeat and others have suggested it does. So we should not accept, on the basis of their arguments alone, that this account of assertion cannot be coherently sustained. As far as we know at this point, it remains a live option—not only for Protagoras, but also for us.

VIII

Earlier we asked ourselves whether a truth relativist like Protagoras can coherently permit Mark to claim that the wind is cold. We then determined that, if he *can* coherently permit this, then he can *also* coherently permit *himself* to claim *that Mark would be better off agreeing with Janet*. Though some commentators have joined Burnyeat in arguing, on purely philosophical grounds, that Protagoras cannot coherently permit anyone to claim anything, we have not found their arguments compelling so far.

Nevertheless, we might imagine that we could reach a similar conclusion on purely *exegetical* grounds. For Protagoras often seems to admonish us *not* to speak in the way that Mark *would have* to speak if he were going to claim that the wind is cold. Consider, for example, the following passage, which appears near the beginning of the entire discussion, almost directly after TEXT ONE:

TEXT FOUR

[according to Protagoras,] nothing is one thing itself, by itself, nor is there anything that you could correctly speak of either as some [one] thing or as some [one] sort of thing [ἓν μὲν αὐτὸ καθ' αὑτὸ οὐδέν ἐστιν, οὐδ' ἄν τι

disjuncts. This assumption—sometimes called 'the disjunction introduction rule'—is not completely uncontroversial, since the defenders of some paraconsistent systems will want to deny it. But it too would be sufficient to establish that, if we believe all the logical consequences of what we believe, then we believe things of unlimited complexity.

[63] For some other recent critical responses to Burnyeat on this issue see T. Bennigson, 'Is Relativism Really Self-Refuting?', *Philosophical Studies*, 94 (1999), 211–36 at 224–6; Wedin, 'Animadversions', 184–7; and MacFarlane, *Assessment*, 32.

προσείποις ὀρθῶς οὐδ' ὁποιονοῦν τι], but if you address it as big [ὡς μέγα προσαγορεύῃς], it will also appear small, and if [you address it as] heavy, [it will also appear] light, and likewise with everything, since nothing is one thing, neither some [one] thing nor some [one] sort of thing. But in fact it is from movement, change, and mixture in relation to each other that all things *come to be*—those very things which we say *are*, [thereby] addressing them incorrectly [οὐκ ὀρθῶς προσαγορεύοντες]. For nothing ever *is*, but [everything] always *comes to be*.[64] (*Theaet.* 152 D 2–E 1)

Now compare this passage with the next one, which seems to function as a brief synopsis of the view Socrates has been developing on Protagoras' behalf from 152 D 2—the beginning of the just-quoted TEXT FOUR—all the way to 160 B 3:

TEXT FIVE

The result, then, I think, is that we [i.e. the perceiving thing and the perceived thing]—whether we *are* or *come to be*—are or come to be *to each other*, since necessity binds together our being, but does not bind it together with anything else, not even with ourselves. . . . So whether one applies the term [ὀνομάζει] 'being' or 'becoming' to something, one must say [ῥητέον] '*to* someone' or '*of* something' or '*relative to* something'. One must not speak [οὔτε . . . λεκτέον] of anything itself, by itself, as being or becoming; and one must not allow anyone else to speak in this manner either. That is the meaning of the account we have just worked through. (*Theaet.* 160 B 5–C 2)

These two passages, taken together, make it very difficult to see how Protagoras could coherently permit Mark to claim that the wind is cold. For in making this claim Mark would seem to be violating both of the constraints Protagoras imposes on us in these passages: he would be using 'is' rather than 'becomes', and—more importantly—he would be using 'is' rather than 'is to [me]'.[65] So it seems hard to escape the conclusion that, according to Protagoras, Mark would be making some sort of *mistake* in claiming that the wind is cold.[66] Moreover, I think we can safely assume that this alleged mistake would not be merely *linguistic* in nature; it would be, at bottom, *doxastic*—it would consist in a certain *belief* on Mark's

---

[64] See also 157 A 7–C 1.
[65] In TEXT FIVE Socrates makes it quite clear that according to Protagoras the second violation is somehow more basic or more significant than the first.
[66] Compare M. Lee, 'The Secret Doctrine: Plato's Defence of Protagoras in the *Theaetetus*', *Oxford Studies in Ancient Philosophy*, 19 (2000), 47–86 at 85.

part, whether expressed in speech or not, to the effect that the wind is cold.

But now we should find this result extremely puzzling. For we saw earlier that Protagoras is explicitly and profoundly wedded to the view that Mark is *correct* in believing that the wind is cold. How then could he *also* think that Mark is *incorrect* in believing that the wind is cold? One possibility is that Protagoras is simply confused, and that his confusion comes into full view at precisely this point.[67] Another possibility—and I suspect the *only* other possibility—is that Protagoras, despite appearances, *does not* think that Mark is incorrect in believing that the wind is cold.

This second possibility, if it can be fleshed out in a satisfactory way, strikes me as significantly more appealing—because significantly more charitable—than the first. But we cannot be expected to take it seriously until we see how it could be consistent with the constraints Protagoras imposes on us (and Mark) in TEXT FOUR and TEXT FIVE.

To see how it *might* be consistent with those constraints, consider the short but consequential exchange that occurs directly after TEXT ONE and directly before TEXT FOUR—an exchange in which Socrates announces a transition of sorts in his ongoing discussion of Protagoras:

> SOC. But . . . was Protagoras really then some sort of all-wise person? Did he make [his analysis of contrast cases in TEXT ONE] a riddle for us, the vulgar crowd, and then tell the truth to his disciples in secret?
> THEAET. What sort of [truth] do you mean, Socrates?
> SOC. I will tell you. It's certainly no worthless account . . . (152 C 8–D 2)

Everything Socrates attributes to Protagoras in the wake of this passage, from the beginning of TEXT FOUR to the end of TEXT FIVE, is part of what commentators have come to call 'the secret doctrine'— a comprehensive account of reality that Protagoras allegedly reveals only to his inner circle. Why he wishes to keep this account secret is never made entirely plain, and for our purposes here I doubt it matters. All I want to point out is that when Socrates introduces this account he signals an important shift, in the context of discussion, from something like an assembly hall to something like a seminar room. He also implies that the view he will attribute to Protagoras

---

[67] This is the verdict ultimately reached by Denyer, *Truth*, 87–100.

after this shift will somehow explain or support the view he attributed to Protagoras before it.

What motivates this shift in the first place, I take it, is the *sheer strangeness* of the view Protagoras endorses at the end of TEXT ONE. According to that view, remember, Mark knows at a certain moment that the wind is cold, even though *Janet* knows at *the same* moment that *the same* wind is *not* cold! Socrates finds this perplexing, and rightly so: it is a bizarre view, and in order to make sense of it we need Protagoras to explain how Mark's belief and Janet's belief could be so starkly opposed to each other and yet still be, both of them, perfectly correct. This is the explanatory enterprise that Socrates seems to take up, on Protagoras' behalf, at the beginning of TEXT FOUR.

But now notice that it is only in the context of this explanatory enterprise that Socrates has Protagoras impose the constraints we noted earlier. So Protagoras' aim in imposing these constraints cannot be to prohibit Mark from believing that the wind is cold, or to prohibit Janet from believing that the wind is not cold. After all, what he is trying to explain here is how they could both be *correct* in believing what they believe, not how they could both be *incorrect* in believing what they believe. His aim must rather be to prohibit *his fellow theorists*—the ones in the seminar room—from believing that the wind is *in itself* (independently of Mark and Janet) *either* cold *or* not cold. For if they were to believe this, he must think, they would be unable to explain how Mark's belief and Janet's belief could both be correct: Mark's could be correct only if the wind were not in itself the way Janet believes it to be, and Janet's could be correct only if the wind were not in itself the way Mark believes it to be. That, more than anything else, seems to be the primary message of TEXT FOUR and TEXT FIVE.

On this interpretation, then, Protagoras implicitly observes a distinction between those beliefs that carry a commitment to the incorrectness of their opposites, and those beliefs that do not.[68] The ones he aims to prohibit wholesale in TEXT FOUR and TEXT FIVE are the former, not the latter. So he need not forbid Mark from believing that the wind is cold; he need only forbid Mark from believing

---

[68] Here I am assuming that what troubles Protagoras about the belief *that the wind is in itself cold* is that this belief carries a commitment to the *incorrectness* of the belief *that the wind is not cold*. So if nothing troubles him about the belief *that the wind is cold*—as his discussion in TEXT ONE makes fairly clear—then he must think that this belief does not carry the same commitment.

that the wind is *in itself* cold—something that Mark presumably does not (yet) believe anyway.[69]

IX

But even if Protagoras need not forbid Mark from believing that the wind is cold, it is unclear whether he can coherently forbid *anyone* from believing *anything*. For suppose Janet spends a couple of hours in the seminar room with Protagoras, becomes belligerent, and sincerely asserts—to Protagoras' face—that the wind is *in itself not* cold. Certainly Protagoras would want to prohibit her from asserting this, but how could he? Since this new dispute between him and Janet is yet another contrast case, he will be forced to accept that she is correct in believing—and so is permitted to assert—that the wind is in itself not cold. After all, if she believes it, then according to Protagoras it is true for her; and if it is true for her, then (by the relative truth rule) she is permitted to assert it.[70]

This is why I suspect that the relative truth rule, by itself, will not be enough to save Protagoras from his critics. For when this rule is conjoined with the other components of his view, it yields the unfortunate result that *all sincere assertions are fully permitted*. But what Protagoras eventually needs, I think, is an account of assertion that will allow him to explain how *some* sincere assertions *could fail to be* fully permitted. Otherwise he will not be able to accept that in the disputes he himself is a party to—such as his dispute with Diotima over what Mark is better off believing, or his dispute with Janet over whether the wind is in itself not cold—his assertions are somehow superior to his opponent's.

Could he simply refuse to accept this, and just allow that in these

---

[69] Is it fair for Protagoras to assume that Mark does not (yet) believe this? My sense is that it is. For he could simply stipulate that Mark has not yet entered the seminar room, and so has not yet been given an opportunity to consider how the wind is in itself.

[70] Suppose Janet becomes docile instead, and sincerely asserts that the wind is not cold *to her*. Would Protagoras then have to admit that this new belief of hers is *absolutely* true? No. For although he *agrees* with her that the wind is not cold to her, someone else in the seminar room—call him Dan—might *disagree* with her (and him). In that case Protagoras would want to say that it is neither absolutely true that the wind is *not* cold to Janet nor absolutely true that the wind *is* cold to Janet; it is true for Janet (and for him) that the wind is *not* cold to Janet, and it is true for Dan that the wind *is* cold to Janet.

cases his own assertions are *in no way* superior to his opponent's? I have trouble seeing how. Maybe he could get away with claiming, as he must, that his own assertions and his opponent's are on a par with respect to truth. But if he tries to insist that they are on a par with respect to *everything*, then he seems to strip himself of any reason he might otherwise have had to engage his opponent in a dialectical discussion. He would be under no rational pressure to defend his own assertions against his opponent's if he were convinced, right from the start, that all assertions are on a par in every way.[71] Moreover, and perhaps more importantly, we know that he is *not* convinced of this; for, as we have seen, he thinks it would be a serious mistake for Janet to assert that the wind is in itself not cold.

What Protagoras needs, then, is an account of assertion that will allow him to assess his own assertions as superior to those of his opponents *with respect to something other than truth*.[72] But does he have the resources to develop such an account, even if only in outline? I believe he does. In fact I suspect that Socrates leaves him with *at least two* potentially promising lines of thought here, one in the Digression (172 C–177 C), and the other in the Defence of Protagoras (166 A–168 C).

Consider first the Digression. In this part of the dialogue Socrates seeks to establish, among other things, that the linguistic practice of orators is fundamentally distinct from the linguistic practice of philosophers. Orators, he says,

> can't make their speeches [τοὺς λόγους ποιεῖσθαι] about whatever they want... their speeches are always ... addressed to a seated master, who sits there holding some lawsuit or other in his hand. And the contests are never a matter of indifference [to the speaker], but are always a matter of concern to him, and often the race is for [the speaker's] life [περὶ ψυχῆς ὁ δρόμος]. As a result of all this they become keen and shrewd, knowing how to flatter the master in speech and beguile him in deed... and in the end they grow up from adolescents into men with nothing healthy in their minds, having become clever and wise—or so they think. (172 E 2–173 B 2)

Throughout the Digression, and in this passage especially, Socrates suggests that people like Protagoras are trained—and train others— to think of the very act of speaking as a manipulative exercise in

---

[71] On this narrow point I concur with many of the critics, especially Waterlow, 'Protagoras', 35–6; Castagnoli, 'Refuted', 23–4; Chappell, 'Reading', 136–7; and Erginel, 'Relativism', 41–3.
[72] Compare Ketchum, 'Relativism', 104–5.

self-protection. So if we were to take this suggestion as the basis of an account of what one commits oneself to in so far as one asserts something, we would end up with a view according to which success in assertion is partly a matter of convincing others, and partly a matter of benefiting oneself.[73] Here is a very rough formulation of the sort of view I have in mind:

> **The Self-Benefit Rule**: In asserting something, one commits oneself to one's being better off as a result of one's listener's believing what one asserts.

Although this is an intriguing and in some ways attractive interpretation of Protagoras' view, I think it falls short of what he needs in at least one crucial respect. For it seems incapable of explaining why either participant in a dialectical discussion would be justified in listening with an open mind to whatever the other has to say. Once each of them realizes that the other is engaged in a practice of narrowly self-interested manipulation, it is hard to see why either of them would be receptive enough to participate in the sort of conversation that the other had anything to gain from.[74] So I doubt that the self-benefit rule is enough, by itself, to get Protagoras completely out of trouble here.

But Socrates seems to have given him another, more promising route of escape as well. For recall that in TEXT THREE he implicitly attributes to Protagoras the view that, in at least some contrast cases, one person would be better off believing what the other person believes. From this it is safe to assume, I think, that Protagoras is sensitive to the benefit that one might at least hope to *receive from* someone else (by coming to believe what that person asserts) or to *confer upon* someone else (by getting that person to believe what one asserts) in the context of a dialectical discussion. So if we were to take *this very hope* as the basis of an account of what one commits oneself to in so far as one asserts something, we would end up with a view that is subtly but importantly different from the self-benefit rule:

[73] As far as I know, this approach to Protagoras' view of assertion has never been discussed in print. A more refined version of it was originally suggested to me in person by Sean Kelsey.
[74] There might be some cases in which the interests of both parties are aligned for some reason. But these cases would have to be highly unusual, maybe even as a matter of necessity, given the overtly polemical model of discourse we find in the Digression.

The Other-Benefit Rule: In asserting something, one commits oneself to one's listener's being better off believing what one asserts.

Now the first thing to notice about this new account is that it, unlike the previous one, seems fully capable of explaining how each participant in a given dialectical exchange could be justified in listening receptively to what the other has to say. For if both of them realize at the outset that their common aim is to help *each other*, rather than *themselves alone*, it is easy to see why each of them would be willing to keep an open mind. So the other-benefit rule seems to leave Protagoras in a much better position.[75]

But does it leave him in a *good enough* position to rank his own assertions as superior to those of his opponents with respect to something other than truth? Perhaps it does. For he now seems free to claim, based on his remarks in TEXT THREE, that there are some dialectical disputes in which *both* participants would be better off believing what *one* of them asserts. Then he can insist that all of the disputes he himself is involved in—such as his dispute with Diotima about Mark, or his dispute with Janet about the wind—are disputes *of just this kind*. So in the end it would appear that the other-benefit rule will allow him to maintain that, although *no* sincere assertions are less *true* than others, *some* sincere assertions are less *permitted* than others.

X

Once Protagoras endorses the other-benefit rule, however, many of the critics will (reasonably) demand to be told what he thinks it is to commit oneself to someone's being better off believing something. Is it not, even in part, to commit oneself to the *absolute truth* of the claim that this person *would* be better off believing it? Clearly Protagoras must deny this, but what else can he say?

Though there is not much textual evidence to support a detailed answer to this question, I think we could make a good start by looking with some care at his famously deferential *fee structure*. As Soc-

---

[75] Note, however, that the two accounts are not mutually exclusive. They could be refined, adjusted, and combined in a number of different ways. But for the sake of simplicity I will limit my attention to what I take to be the more promising of the two accounts, namely, the other-benefit rule.

rates reminds us, both in the *Theaetetus* and elsewhere, Protagoras routinely asks his students to pay him in proportion to the benefit they think they have received from his teachings.[76] Here is how Protagoras describes this policy in the dialogue named after him:

> if there is someone among us who is the least bit distinguished in excellence, that person is to be cherished. And I consider myself to be such a person, distinguished from everyone else in my ability to help people become noble and good, and worth the fee that I charge, and even more—or so it seems to my students themselves. That is why I charge according to the following system: if he wishes to, my student gives me the money I ask for; if not, he goes to the temple, states under oath how much he thinks my teachings are worth, and pays that much. (*Prot.* 328 A 7–C 2)

It seems to me that this distinctive compensation scheme suggests an equally distinctive view about what it is to commit oneself to someone's being better off believing something. For in these remarks we find a clear willingness on Protagoras' part to absorb the consequences *for another person* of that person's believing what he says—a willingness to take on a certain burden with respect to the *well-being* of that other person—without any insistence on his own way of assessing either those consequences or that burden. What we find here, in other words, are the rudiments of something like the following view:

> **The Pragmatic Account of Benefit Commitment**: To commit oneself to someone's being better off believing what one asserts is to take responsibility for the consequences of bringing that person to believe it, as those consequences are assessed by that person.

Once Protagoras arms himself with a view of this sort, he has a straightforward reply he can give to his critics. He can insist that we need not commit ourselves to the absolute truth of *anything* when we commit ourselves to someone's being better off believing what we say; we need only take responsibility for the consequences of bringing that person to believe it, as those consequences are assessed by that person.

Of course the critics might object at this point that Protagoras cannot hope to explain how we might take responsibility for the consequences of what we say unless he presupposes the absolute

---

[76] See especially 165 E 1–4 and the last sentence of TEXT THREE.

truth of various assertions about what those consequences are. But this objection strikes me as weak. Assertions about consequences are not fundamentally different in kind from assertions about winds, wines, therapies, beliefs, and even assertions themselves. So if he can give us a fully general account of assertion that makes no appeal to absolute truth, then he can use that account to explain what he is doing when he makes *any assertion at all*—about what people are better off believing, about the consequences of someone's believing what he says, about how others assess those consequences, and even about *what it is to make an assertion in the first place.*

Consider, for example, the familiar second-order contrast case between Protagoras and Diotima over whether Mark would be better off agreeing with Janet. As we have seen, Protagoras needs to be able to say that Mark *would* be better off, without thereby challenging the correctness of Diotima's belief that he would not. But now it looks as though the other-benefit rule, taken in conjunction with the pragmatic account of benefit commitment, allows Protagoras to do just that. For this combination of views does not require him, in his dispute with Diotima, to commit himself to the incorrectness of Diotima's belief about Mark. It requires him only to commit himself to Diotima's being better off believing what *he* believes about Mark. Of course this means that he must take responsibility for the consequences of bringing her to believe this, as those consequences are assessed by her. But he need not, for this reason alone, hold that her belief about Mark is any less correct than his own.

Suppose, however, that Protagoras succeeds in bringing Diotima to believe what he believes, so that by his own lights he must now take responsibility for the consequences of bringing her to believe this, as those consequences are assessed by her. What would this demand of him, more concretely? According to the pragmatic account of benefit commitment, it would have to depend on what Diotima goes on to tell him about how she thinks her change of mind has worked out for her. She might claim that it has made her better off, or she might claim that it has not. If she claims that it has, then at that point Protagoras would have to believe that he is entitled to some benefit from her; if she claims that it has not, then he would have to believe the opposite. But as far as I can tell he would *never* have to believe that any of his or her past or present beliefs is *incorrect*. If some further dispute were to arise between them about what the relevant consequences have been, or about what he or she has said, or about some further feature of their dispute, he could simply analyse it in the same way he analysed their *original* dispute. So there seems not to be any difficulty here that he cannot handle with the resources he already has.

Moreover, it would appear that this general approach can be applied to any contrast case that Protagoras might ever be involved in. Recall, for instance, the dispute between Protagoras and Janet about whether the wind is in itself not cold. As we have seen, Protagoras must—in asserting that the wind is *not* in itself not cold—accept that his assertion is superior to Janet's *somehow*. But he will not be compelled, for this reason alone, to accept that it is superior *with respect to truth*. He need only accept that it is superior with respect to *goodness*—in so far as both he and Janet would be better off believing it. If she disputes this point as well, and asserts that she would *not* be better off believing it, then Protagoras will in turn be able to reply that no, she *would* be better off believing it; he need only *also* accept that she would be better off believing *that she would be better off believing it*. Because this procedure can be reiterated indefinitely for each additional dispute that Protagoras might be involved in, there seems not to be any point at which he will be forced by his own commitments to concede that any of his opponent's claims is any less correct than his own. So it looks as though he has got clean away!

XI

At the beginning of this paper we asked ourselves whether Protagoras can, by using only the resources Socrates gives him, defend his overall view against the argument Socrates advances against it in TEXT TWO (161 D 2–162 A 3). Early on I maintained that he can do this if, but only if, he can coherently explain how people might be justified in making and heeding various claims in the context of a dialectical discussion. My claim then was that he *can* explain this, and I now take myself to have made good on that claim. As far as I know, every major commentator before me who has considered this issue in any detail has defended the opposite claim. What I hope I have managed to do here, if nothing else, is to have shaken up this consensus a bit.

Before I conclude, however, let me reiterate that I do not expect to have shown that the Protagorean analysis of contrast cases is accurate, appealing, or even especially plausible. My assumption all along has been that nobody (sane) would think that. All I expect to have shown is that one of the main reasons we have been given by the scholarly authorities to reject this analysis simply does not hold up. As I see it, the interesting question here is not whether we should *agree* with Protagoras—because obviously we should not— but whether we should *disagree* with him *because he cannot make coherent sense of the practice of dialectic*. If the answer to this second question is *no*, as I have been arguing it is, then our next task is to figure out, in a more satisfying way, exactly why we *should* disagree with him.

University of Texas at Austin

BIBLIOGRAPHY

Bennigson, T., 'Is Relativism Really Self-Refuting?', *Philosophical Studies*, 94 (1999), 211–36.

Bostock, D., *Plato's* Theaetetus [*Theaetetus*] (Oxford, 1988).

Brandom, R., 'Asserting', *Noûs*, 17 (1983), 637–50.

Burnyeat, M., 'Introduction', in M. Burnyeat (ed.), *The* Theaetetus *of Plato* (Indianapolis, 1990), 1–255.

Burnyeat, M., 'Protagoras and Self-Refutation in Plato's *Theaetetus*' ['Protagoras'], *Philosophical Review*, 85 (1976), 172–95.

Castagnoli, L., *Ancient Self-Refutation: The Logic and History of the Self-Refutation Argument from Democritus to Augustine* (Cambridge, 2010).

Castagnoli, L., 'Protagoras Refuted: How Clever is Socrates' "Most Clever" Argument at *Theaetetus* 171 A–C?' ['Refuted'], *Topoi*, 23 (2004), 3–32.

Chappell, T., 'Does Protagoras Refute Himself?' ['Protagoras'], *Classical Quarterly*, NS 45 (1995), 333–8.

Chappell, T., *Reading Plato's* Theaetetus [*Theaetetus*] (Indianapolis, 2005).

Chappell, T., 'Reading the περιτροπή' ['Reading'], *Phronesis*, 51 (2006), 109–39.

Cole, A. T., 'The Apology of Protagoras' ['Apology'], *Yale Classical Studies*, 19 (1966), 103–18.

Cornford, F., *Plato's Theory of Knowledge: The* Theaetetus *and the* Sophist *of Plato* [*Theory*] (London, 1935).

Dancy, R. M., 'Theaetetus' First Baby: Theaetetus 151 E–160 E', *Philosophical Topics*, 15 (1987), 61–108.

Denyer, N., *Language, Truth, and Falsehood in Ancient Greek Philosophy* [*Truth*] (London, 1991).

Egan, A., 'Epistemic Modals, Relativism, and Assertion', *Philosophical Studies*, 133 (2007), 1–22.

Egan, A., Hawthorne, J., and Weatherson, B., 'Epistemic Modals in Context', in G. Preyer and G. Peter (eds.), *Contextualism in Philosophy: Knowledge, Meaning, and Truth* (Oxford, 2005), 131–68.

Emilsson, E. K., 'Plato's Self-Refutation Argument in Theaetetus 171 A–C Revisited', *Phronesis*, 39 (1994), 136–49.

Erginel, M., 'Relativism and Self-Refutation in the *Theaetetus*' ['Relativism'], *Oxford Studies in Ancient Philosophy*, 37 (2009), 1–45.

Fine, G., *Plato on Knowledge and Forms: Selected Essays* [*Plato*] (Oxford, 2003).

Fine, G., 'Relativism and Self-Refutation: Plato, Protagoras, and Burnyeat' ['Relativism'], in J. Gentzler (ed.), *Method in Ancient Philosophy* (Oxford, 2001), 137–63.

Giannopoulou, Z., 'In and out of Worlds: Socrates' Refutation of Protagorean Relativism in Theaetetus 170 A–171 C', *Ancient Philosophy*, 31 (2011), 275–94.

Giannopoulou, Z., 'Objectivizing Protagorean Relativism: The Socratic Underpinnings of Protagoras' Apology in Plato's *Theaetetus*' ['Objectivizing'], *Ancient Philosophy*, 29 (2009), 67–88.

Glidden, D. K., 'Protagorean Relativism and Physis' ['Physis'], *Phronesis*, 20 (1975), 209–27.

Guthrie, W. K. C., *The Sophists* (Cambridge, 1971).

Hicken, W. F. (ed.), *Theaetetus*, in *Platonis opera*, i, ed. E. A. Duke *et al.* (Oxford, 1995), 277–382.

Jordan, J., 'Protagoras and Relativism: Criticisms Bad and Good' ['Protagoras'], *Southwestern Journal of Philosophy*, 2 (1971), 7–29.

Kerferd, G. B., 'Plato's Account of the Relativism of Protagoras' ['Relativism'], *Durham University Journal*, 42 (1949), 20–6.

Ketchum, R., 'Plato's "Refutation" of Protagorean Relativism' ['Relativism'], *Oxford Studies in Ancient Philosophy*, 10 (1992), 73–105.

Kölbel, M., *Truth without Objectivity* [*Truth*] (London, 2002).

Lasersohn, P., 'Context Dependence, Disagreement, and Predicates of Personal Taste', *Linguistics and Philosophy*, 28 (2005), 643–86.

Lee, E. N., '"Hoist with his Own Petard": Ironic and Comic Elements in Plato's Critique of Protagoras (*Tht.* 161–171)' ['Hoist'], in E. N. Lee, A. P. D. Mourelatos, and R. M. Rorty (eds.), *Exegesis and Argument: Studies in Greek Philosophy Presented to Gregory Vlastos* (New York, 1973), 225–61.

Lee, M., *Epistemology after Protagoras: Responses to Relativism in Plato, Aristotle, and Democritus* (Oxford, 2005).
Lee, M., 'The Secret Doctrine: Plato's Defence of Protagoras in the *Theaetetus*', *Oxford Studies in Ancient Philosophy*, 19 (2000), 47–86.
Levett, M. J. (trans.), *Theaetetus*, in *The Theaetetus of Plato*, ed. M. Burnyeat (Indianapolis, 1990).
Long, Alex, 'Refutation and Relativism in *Theaetetus* 161–171', *Phronesis*, 49 (2004), 24–40.
McCabe, M. M., *Plato and his Predecessors: The Dramatisation of Reason* [*Plato*] (Cambridge, 2000).
McDowell, J. (trans. and comm.), *Plato: Theaetetus* [*Plato*] (Oxford, 1973).
MacFarlane, J., *Assessment Sensitivity: Relative Truth and its Applications* [*Assessment*] (Oxford, 2014).
MacFarlane, J., 'Future Contingents and Relative Truth', *Philosophical Quarterly*, 53 (2003), 321–36.
MacFarlane, J., 'Relativism', in G. Russell and D. Graff Fara (eds.), *The Routledge Companion to Philosophy of Language* (New York, 2012), 132–42.
MacFarlane, J., 'What is Assertion?' ['Assertion'], in J. Brown and H. Cappelen (eds.), *Assertion: New Philosophical Essays* (Oxford, 2011), 79–96.
Mackie, J. L., 'Self-Refutation: A Formal Analysis', *Philosophical Quarterly*, 14 (1964), 193–203.
Matthen, M., 'Perception, Relativism, and Truth: Reflections on Plato's *Theaetetus* 152–160' ['Perception'], *Dialogue*, 24 (1985), 33–58.
Meiland, J. W., 'Is Protagorean Relativism Self-Refuting?', *Grazer philosophische Studien*, 9 (1979), 51–68.
Narcy, M., *Platon: Théétète* [*Platon*] (Paris, 1995).
Passmore, J., *Philosophical Reasoning* (New York, 1961).
Polansky, R., *Philosophy and Knowledge: A Commentary on Plato's Theaetetus* (Lewisburg, 1992).
Putnam, H., *Reason, Truth and History* (Cambridge, 1981).
Recanati, F., *Perspectival Truth: A Plea for (Moderate) Relativism* (Oxford, 2007).
Richard, M., 'Contextualism and Relativism', *Philosophical Studies*, 119 (2004), 215–42.
Richard, M., *When Truth Gives Out* (Oxford, 2008).
Sayre, K., *Plato's Analytic Method* [*Method*] (Chicago, 1969).
Schiller, F. C. S., *Plato or Protagoras? Being a Critical Examination of the Protagoras Speech in the Theaetetus with Some Remarks upon Error* (Oxford, 1908).

Searle, J., *Speech Acts: An Essay in the Philosophy of Language* (Cambridge, 1969).
Sedley, D., *The Midwife of Platonism: Text and Subtext in Plato's Theaetetus* [*Midwife*] (Oxford, 2004).
Swanson, E., 'How Not to Theorize about the Language of Subjective Uncertainty', in A. Egan and B. Weatherson (eds.), *Epistemic Modality* (Oxford, 2011), 249–69.
Vlastos, G., 'Introduction', in G. Vlastos (ed.), *Plato's Protagoras* (New York, 1956), vii–lviii.
Vogt, K., *Belief and Truth: A Skeptic Reading of Plato* (Oxford, 2012).
Wardy, R., *Doing Greek Philosophy* (London, 2006).
Waterfield, R., *Plato:* Theaetetus [*Theaetetus*] (London, 1987).
Waterlow, S., 'Protagoras and Inconsistency: Theaetetus 171 A 6–C 7' ['Protagoras'], *Archiv für Geschichte der Philosophie*, 59 (1977), 19–36.
Wedin, M. V., 'Animadversions on Burnyeat's *Theaetetus*: On the Logic of the Exquisite Argument' ['Animadversions'], *Oxford Studies in Ancient Philosophy*, 29 (2005), 171–91.
Williams, B., 'Introduction', in B. Williams (ed.), *Plato:* Theaetetus (Indianapolis, 1992), vii–xx.
Williamson, T., 'Knowing and Asserting', *Philosophical Review*, 105 (1996), 489–523.
Yalcin, S., 'Epistemic Modals', *Mind*, 116 (2007), 983–1026.

WHAT IS A PERFECT SYLLOGISM?

BENJAMIN MORISON

THE answer to the question forming the title of this paper might seem rather easy. Recent commentators are in universal agreement. In 1951, in his pioneering work on Aristotle's syllogistic, Łukasiewicz wrote: 'Perfect syllogisms are self-evident statements which do not possess and do not need a demonstration.'[1] In the 1960s Patzig did not find much to disagree with (not here, at least): 'a perfect argument is an argument in which the defined necessity not only occurs but "*appears*" or is transparent . . . In a word, perfect syllogisms are *self-evident* syllogisms [evidente Schlüsse]'.[2] A decade or so after that, in 1980, Lear refers to the perfect syllogisms as 'obviously valid inferences',[3] adding that 'to establish that the conclusion of a perfect syllogism follows from the premisses, one should need to do no more than state the syllogism itself' (ibid.); 'No argument is given for their [sc. the first-figure syllogisms'] validity. For if the syllogisms are perfect, no argument need be given' (3). On one more decade, and in 1995 Ebert agrees with Patzig that what differentiates perfect from imperfect syllogisms is that the one kind is evident and the other not: 'Patzig hat insbesondere gezeigt, daß die Differenz zwischen

© Benjamin Morison 2015

Particular thanks go to Marko Malink and Jacob Rosen for several long discussions, as well as to Jonathan Barnes, Alexander Bown, Laura Castelli, Alan Code, John Cooper, Adam Crager, Paolo Crivelli, Gabriel Richardson Lear, Jonathan Lear, Hendrik Lorenz, Stephen Menn, Calvin Normore, Emily Perry, Christian Pfeiffer, Oliver Primavesi, Christof Rapp, Gideon Rosen, Christopher Roser, Carrie Swanson, and audiences at Princeton, Indiana, Chicago, Geneva, Munich, and Berlin. I got thinking about perfect syllogisms as a result of seeing my former teachers Jonathan Barnes and Michael Frede argue over the *dictum de omni et nullo* at Barnes's 2004 Locke Lectures in Oxford. My 2008 book notes on Barnes's resulting book, *Truth etc.*, contained germs of the idea worked out in detail here.

[1] J. Łukasiewicz, *Aristotle's Syllogistic from the Standpoint of Modern Formal Logic* [*Syllogistic*] (Oxford, 1951), 43.

[2] G. Patzig, *Die Aristotelische Syllogistik: Logisch-philologische Untersuchungen über das Buch A der 'Ersten Analytiken'*, 2nd edn. (Göttingen, 1963), trans. J. Barnes as *Aristotle's Theory of the Syllogism: A Logico-Philological Study of Book A of the Prior Analytics* [*Theory*] (Dordrecht, 1968), 45.

[3] J. Lear, *Aristotle and Logical Theory* [*Logical*] (Cambridge, 1980), 2.

vollkommenen und unvollkommenen Syllogismen nicht mit dem Unterschied zwischen gültigen und ungültigen, sondern mit dem zwischen evidenten und nicht evidenten (gültigen) Syllogismen zu tun hat',[4] although Ebert has a different explanation of why the assertoric perfect syllogisms are evident. And into the twenty-first century, Ebert and Nortmann's massive commentary by and large endorses Patzig's interpretation: 'Für den Begriff des vollkommenen Syllogismus, der hier eingeführt wird, ist der Begriff der *Evidenz* ausschlaggebend: Vollkommen ist ein Syllogismus, bei dem das notwendige Folgen (der Konklusion aus den Prämissen) ohne weiteres *einleuchtet*.'[5] Barnes, in his seminal *Truth etc.* (2007), says: 'A syllogism is perfect if and only if its validity can be grasped without being proved. That is to say, if and only if its validity is evident.'[6] And finally, Striker, in her 2009 commentary for the Clarendon Aristotle Series, writes: 'Syllogisms are called perfect if the necessity of the inference is evident once the premisses are given.'[7]

Commentators mostly agree, then, a perfect syllogism is an evident one. (Conversely, an imperfect syllogism is non-evident.) For a syllogism to be evident is for the necessity of the conclusion's following from the premisses to be evident (it is not that the premisses or the conclusion have themselves to be evidently true), or as we might put it, the *validity* of the argument must be evident for the argument to count as perfect.

In this paper, I am going to argue against this consensus. I claim that Aristotle never defines perfect syllogisms as the evident ones or ones whose validity is evident or self-evident, but rather defines them as ones which meet a rather precise logical condition, namely, that the proof or explanation that its conclusion follows necessarily from its premisses is conducted without making any detours through any propositions other than its premisses. I shall argue that commentators have misunderstood Aristotle's use of the verb

---

[4] T. Ebert, 'Was ist ein vollkommener Syllogismus des Aristoteles?', *Archiv für Geschichte der Philosophie*, 77 (1995), 221–47 at 222.

[5] T. Ebert and U. Nortmann, *Aristoteles: Analytica Priora Buch I*, übersetzt und erläutert [*Buch I*] (Aristoteles: Werke in deutscher Übersetzung, 3.I/1; Berlin, 2007), 228. Elsewhere in their commentary they propose a slightly different interpretation, which I discuss below, n. 50.

[6] J. Barnes, *Truth etc.* [*Truth*] (Oxford, 2007), 417.

[7] G. Striker, *Aristotle:* Prior Analytics Book I [*Book I*], translated with an introduction and commentary (Clarendon Aristotle Series; Oxford, 2009), 82.

What is a Perfect Syllogism? 109

phanēnai in his definition of perfection and have erroneously concluded that perfect syllogisms must be evident. Rather, what makes a syllogism perfect is that the explanation or proof of its validity— what it takes for the necessity of its conclusion given its premisses to *become* apparent—takes a certain form.

The desire on the part of the above-mentioned commentators to identify perfect syllogisms with those whose validity is evident is encouraged by a natural philosophical thought. If perfect syllogisms are evident, then it would be an attractive proof strategy to state the perfect syllogisms (arguments which are *evidently* or *obviously* syllogisms), and then use them as the basis for the subsequent proofs that other arguments (which are not evidently syllogisms) are syllogisms. This is more or less what Aristotle does: he does indeed prove the validity of imperfect syllogisms using the perfect syllogisms as his base arguments and then employing conversion and reductio to relate the imperfect syllogisms to the perfect ones. The perfect syllogisms would then seem to function rather like axioms (they could not actually *be* axioms, since, *pace* Łukasiewicz and Patzig, syllogisms are not statements).[8] In fact, Łukasiewicz states outright that '[t]he perfect syllogisms . . . are the axioms of the syllogistic' (*Syllogistic*, 43). But even if it were true that Aristotle uses the perfect syllogisms similarly to axioms or principles or whatever, why should that mean he took them to be *evident*? Did Aristotle think axioms, or first principles, must be obvious or evident? The answer is no. Axioms must be 'true and primitive and immediate and more familiar than and prior to and explanatory of the conclusions' (*Post. An.* 1. 2, 71^{b}21–2), but, as Barnes points out, 'the later notion that the axioms of a science must be in some way evidently and patently true is not at all Aristotelian'.[9] Aristotle is surely right about this. *Obviousness* is neither a sufficient condition for being an axiom (plenty of theorems are obvious, e.g. $1+1=2$), nor a necessary condition (plenty of first principles are not obvious, e.g. the parallels postulate, or, in some logical systems, formulae of the form '$a \rightarrow \forall x\, a$, where x does not occur free in a'[10]). Thus acknowledging

---

[8] For an extended reflection on whether syllogistic is like a science, with axioms and theorems, see Barnes, *Truth*, chapter 5: 'The Science of Logic'.

[9] *Aristotle:* Posterior Analytics, translated with an introduction and commentary, 2nd edn. (Clarendon Aristotle Series; Oxford, 1994), 97.

[10] H. B. Enderton, *A Mathematical Introduction to Logic* (San Diego, 1972), 112. Such formulae are liable to strike one as ill-formed, rather than true, let alone *obviously* true. Adam Crager also suggests to me the common axiom for propositional

that perfect syllogisms play a role similar to that of axioms in no way puts pressure on us to interpret Aristotle as saying that perfect syllogisms are the evident or obvious ones. (In fact, I shall be arguing that perfect syllogisms are not principles in Aristotle's system; to be sure, they are the basic *syllogisms* of his system, but they are arguments which are *shown* or *proven* by Aristotle to be valid using genuine principles of his system, the *dictum de omni et nullo*.)

If this is the *philosophical* reason commentators have been keen to saddle Aristotle with the idea that perfect syllogisms are the obvious ones, the *textual* motivation is the explanation that Aristotle gives at *Pr. An.* 1. 1, 24^{b}22–6, of what perfection is (in Striker's translation, which I shall be modifying later):

Now I call a syllogism perfect if it requires nothing beyond the things posited for the necessity to be evident [*phanēnai*]; I call a syllogism imperfect if it requires one or more things that are indeed necessary because of the terms laid down, but that have not been taken among the premisses.

It is the word *phanēnai* that has led commentators to suppose that what is at issue is obviousness or something like it. The sentence is understood as claiming that nothing is needed for the necessity of the conclusion's following from the premisses to be *obvious* apart from the premisses themselves. This in turn is understood as meaning that the validity of perfect syllogisms (the fact that the conclusion follows from the premisses) is obvious when you just look at the conclusion in the light of the premisses. Look at Lear again: 'to establish that the conclusion of a perfect syllogism follows from the premisses, one should need to do no more than state the syllogism itself' (*Logical*, 2), or Striker: 'the necessity of the inference is evident once the premisses are given' (*Book I*, 82).

Philosophically speaking, this proposal is rather problematic. First, commentators have searched for ways in which Barbara and Celarent might be *obviously* valid, in a way in which Cesare (for instance) is not. This is a tough ask. Consider what happens if you try to dramatize the obviousness of Celarent (AeB, BaC; AeC), say by appealing to Euler or Venn diagrams. Then try arguing that Cesare (BeA, BaC; AeC) is not just as obvious, or Camestres (BaA, BeC; AeC) for that matter—the Euler diagrams for these

logic '$p \to (q \to p)$', which has struck some as having outright *false* instances ('If it is raining, then if it is not raining, it is raining') and, *a fortiori*, as not being obviously true.

syllogisms are structurally identical! (I have been caught out too many times in lectures trying just such a tactic.) Or conversely, try constructing the Euler or Venn diagram for Darii, a perfect syllogism; it is not at all straightforward, because it is indeterminate how big you should draw the circle for C.

One might attempt a different route, and try to get oneself to find the conclusions of perfect syllogisms evident 'by reminding oneself of the truth conditions of their premises' (Striker, *Book I*, 83). This seems unpromising for a similar reason, as Striker herself acknowledges: 'it is doubtful whether one could still find a difference in degree of obviousness between, say, Celarent (first figure) and Cesare or Camestres (second figure) in this way' (ibid.).

Patzig goes down a slightly different route. As we saw, he thinks that a 'perfect argument is an argument in which the defined necessity not only occurs but "*appears*" or is transparent' (*Theory*, 45). This raises the natural question: 'What justification did Aristotle have for asserting some syllogisms to be evident and others not?' (46). Patzig's answer is that 'a normally endowed man[11] would be convinced of the truth of the first class of syllogisms substantially more easily than he would be of the truth of the second class' (48). He then offers an explanation for why the 'normally endowed man' finds the syllogisms of the first class so compelling: in the case of Barbara, its obviousness is due to the transitivity of the 'is predicated of all' relation. But there are severe difficulties with this. For a start, this explanation will not work for the other three perfect assertoric syllogisms. But even in the case of Barbara, Patzig is led to assert that one must get the order of the premises right, otherwise this obviousness will be lost.[12] But that Aristotle did not think the order of premises was important jumps out at any reader when working through the proofs of *Prior Analytics* I. 1–22 (cf. e.g. I. 6, 28^{a}26–8, Felapton), so if Patzig were right, we would be faced with the awkward fact that Barbara would be *valid* whether you expressed its premises as 'AaB, BaC' or 'BaC, AaB', but would only be *perfect* if you expressed its premises in the first way. However, Aristotle never says that Barbara *when expressed a certain way* is perfect. He holds that Barbara is perfect, *tout court*.

[11] Barnes's naughty translation of 'ein normalbegabter Mensch'. The well-endowed man finds even *Baroco* easy. (That's a joke.)
[12] '[T]he order of the premises chosen by Aristotle, supposing the formula "A belongs to B", leads in the first figure to evident syllogisms; this evidence disappears if the order of the premises is altered' (*Theory*, 60).

In a nutshell, then, the orthodox view of what the perfection of a perfect syllogism consists in is this: a syllogism 'P, Q; therefore, R' is perfect iff it is clear that R follows from P and Q, or alternatively, iff the conditional 'If P, Q, then clearly it must be the case that Q' is true. We have seen that there are philosophical difficulties with the account, but it does not follow that it is not a correct interpretation of Aristotle. And as we shall see, there are indeed one or two texts, cited by Patzig and those who share this view, which push in that direction. But the alternative I argue for is that what makes a perfect syllogism perfect is the nature of the *explanation* of why it counts as a syllogism. That fact is straightforward: it is that the explanation makes no reference to any proposition involving the terms of the syllogism other than its premises. Put it another way: in a perfect syllogism, the explanation of *why* the conclusion follows of necessity from the premises as a result of them being the premises they are (that is my rendering of the definition of a syllogism) will make reference only to the propositions featuring as the premises and the relation they stand in to each other and to the conclusion. That relation will turn out to be the relation described in the *dictum de omni et nullo*; thus, an argument counts as a perfect syllogism iff the explanation of why it is a syllogism consists in adverting to its premises and conclusion being related in the way described in the *dictum de omni et nullo*. This makes the *dictum de omni et nullo* a governing principle in Aristotle's logic.

Other commentators have seen the importance of the *dictum de omni et nullo* in the account of why the four perfect syllogisms are perfect.[13] Barnes attributes one such view to Alexander of Aphrodisias: a perfect syllogism is one whose 'validity is evident inasmuch as it is underwritten by the *dictum de omni et nullo*. That was Alexander's view of the matter' (*Truth*, 393). Whether or not Barnes is right to trace this view back to Alexander,[14] it differs from Patzig's only in its proposed explanation for *why* the perfect syllogisms are evident. However, as we shall see in the course of looking in detail at the evidence, it is misleading to say that Aristotle thinks the *dictum de omni et nullo* explains the *perfection* of perfect syllogisms.

---

[13] The recent German commentators are a case in point. I discuss their interpretation in more detail in n. 50.

[14] Ian Mueller, in his introduction to I. Mueller and J. Gould (trans.), *Alexander of Aphrodisias: On Aristotle,* Prior Analytics *1. 8–13* (Ancient Commentators on Aristotle; London, 1999), 6, *contrasts* Alexander's view with the view that the perfect syllogisms are self-evident.

What is a Perfect Syllogism? 113

Rather, it explains the *validity* of perfect syllogisms. But it is time to look at that evidence.

1. Aristotle on perfect syllogisms

The definition itself runs as follows (*Pr. An.* 1. 1, 24^{b}22–6):

τέλειον μὲν οὖν
καλῶ συλλογισμὸν τὸν μηδενὸς ἄλλου προσδεόμενον παρὰ τὰ
εἰλημμένα πρὸς τὸ φανῆναι τὸ ἀναγκαῖον, ἀτελῆ δὲ τὸν προσδεόμενον ἢ ἑνὸς ἢ πλειόνων, ἃ ἔστι μὲν ἀναγκαῖα διὰ τῶν   24^{b}25
ὑποκειμένων ὅρων, οὐ μὴν εἴληπται διὰ προτάσεων.

Here is my rather literal translation:

So then I call 'perfect' a syllogism which needs nothing else in addition to the things supposed for its necessity to be made apparent, whereas [I call] 'imperfect' that which is in need of one or more things [for its necessity to be made apparent], things which are necessary through the underlying terms but which have not been taken through propositions.

This definition of perfection comes immediately after Aristotle's celebrated definition of what a syllogism (*sullogismos*) is.[15] Given the importance of perfect syllogisms in Aristotle's deductive system— they are the syllogisms on the basis of which all other syllogisms are proven to be valid—it is not surprising that he should define what a perfect syllogism is immediately after defining what a syllogism is. Aristotle defines a syllogism as an argument where the conclusion necessarily follows from the premises because the premises are those ones (τῷ ταῦτα εἶναι, 24^{b}20).[16] In the course of elaborating what he means by that qualifier, Aristotle glosses it as meaning that no terms other than the ones featuring in the premises of the argument are needed for the necessity[17] (of the conclusion's following

---

[15] I stick with the transliteration 'syllogism' out of habit and conformity; a better translation might be 'valid deductive argument' (Striker, *Book I*, 79) or 'deduction' (R. Smith, *Aristotle: Prior Analytics* [*Prior*] (Indianapolis, 1989), *passim*).

[16] I am being rather dogmatic in my interpretation here; for more details on the difficult phrase τῷ ταῦτα εἶναι see J. Barnes, 'Proof Destroyed', in M. Schofield, M. Burnyeat, and J. Barnes (eds.), *Doubt and Dogmatism: Studies in Hellenistic Epistemology* (Oxford, 1980), 168–9, with M. Mignucci, 'Syllogism and Deduction in Aristotle's Logic', in M. Canto-Sperber and P. Pellegrin (eds.), *Le Style de la pensée: recueil de textes en hommage à J. Brunschwig* (Paris, 2002), 244–66. What I say about perfect syllogisms is independent of this or that construal of τῷ ταῦτα εἶναι.

[17] Jacob Rosen points out that τὸ ἀναγκαῖον could mean 'the necessary [item]', i.e.

from the premisses) *to come about* (πρὸς τὸ γενέσθαι τὸ ἀναγκαῖον, 24^{b}22). The definitions of perfection and imperfection which immediately follow concern not what it takes for the necessity of the conclusion's following from the premisses *to come about* (γενέσθαι) but rather what it takes for the necessity of the conclusion's following from the premisses *to become apparent* (πρὸς τὸ φανῆναι τὸ ἀναγκαῖον, 24^{b}24). This is as it should be. *All* syllogisms meet the conditions for being a syllogism—in other words, all syllogisms require no more terms than those in the premisses for the necessity *to come about*. What differs between perfect and imperfect syllogisms is what it takes for that necessity *to become apparent*.

What we learn in the definitions of perfect and imperfect syllogisms is that in the case of perfect syllogisms, by definition, the premisses ('the things supposed') are just what we need for that necessity to become apparent, whereas in the case of imperfect syllogisms, by definition, other things need to be supplied in addition to the premisses in order for that necessity to become apparent or be made apparent. Notice that the phrase πρὸς τὸ φανῆναι τὸ ἀναγκαῖον has to be supplied in the definition of imperfect syllogisms: the imperfect ones need one or more things *for their necessity to become apparent*. Both sets of syllogisms will have their necessity made apparent; what it takes to make that necessity apparent is what will distinguish the two classes of syllogism.

The phrase describing those extra things you need to supply to make the necessity of imperfect syllogisms apparent is rather obscure: 'things which are necessary through the underlying terms but which have not been taken through propositions'. The word I have translated 'propositions' here is normally translated 'premisses'; I do not like that as a *translation*,[18] but Aristotle is undoubtedly here making the point that the extra things you need to supply for the necessity of imperfect syllogisms to become apparent are propositions which were not taken as premisses of the imperfect syllogism but which are other, different, propositions. (The meaning of the phrase οὐ μὴν εἴληπται διὰ προτάσεων, containing as it does one of Aristotle's favourite verbs for what one does when putting forward a

---

the necessary proposition, i.e. the conclusion. This is still consonant with the proposal I put forward for how to understand γενέσθαι and φανῆναι.

[18] For more on why 'premiss' is not the right *translation* of the word πρότασις see P. Crivelli and D. Charles, '"Πρότασις" in Aristotle's *Prior Analytics*', *Phronesis*, 56 (2011), 193–203.

What is a Perfect Syllogism? 115

proposition as a premiss, λαμβάνειν, is not controversial.) The point about these extra propositions being 'necessary through the underlying terms' is that the propositions to be supplied in the course of making clear the validity of the syllogism are not just any old propositions, but ones which must be made out of the terms which feature in the syllogism. So Aristotle is saying that when you show the validity of an imperfect syllogism, you will have to adduce propositions in addition to the premisses of the syllogism, albeit propositions that must be composed of terms in the syllogism. There is no mystery about what these propositions are: we shall see later that Aristotle is referring to the propositions that will be deployed in the course of conversion and reductio proofs of the imperfect syllogisms.

I take it, therefore, that Aristotle is *not* saying in his definition of perfection that the validity (or better: the necessity of the conclusion's following from the premisses—but in general I just say 'validity') of a perfect syllogism is evident, in the sense that a perfect syllogism is *obviously* or *self-evidently* valid. (This was the position that seemed philosophically so hard to defend.) Instead, in the definitions of perfection and imperfection Aristotle is talking about what it takes for *the validity of the syllogism to become apparent*. The validity of perfect syllogisms is made clear one way (through reference to its premisses alone) whereas the validity of imperfect syllogisms has to be made clear another way (through reference to one or more propositions in addition). Note, then, that the difference between perfect and imperfect syllogisms will reside not in whether the validity of the two kinds of syllogism will successfully be made apparent, but rather in the explanatory resources that one deploys in the course of making their validity apparent. It is not that perfect syllogisms can have their validity made clear, but the validity of imperfect syllogisms cannot become or be made clear; rather, there is a difference in what it takes to make their respective validity apparent.

There are several things we need to check to see whether this interpretation is possible. First, we need to satisfy ourselves that the verb *phanēnai* can refer to *something's becoming clear*, or *being made clear*, rather than to something's *being* clear all on its own. Second, we need to look at Aristotle's actual practice in the *Prior Analytics*. Does he offer explanations of the validity of the perfect syllogisms? That is, does he attempt to make apparent their validity, rather than just letting their validity shine forth, so to speak? Third, we need to see whether Aristotle, when giving his explanations of the validity of imperfect syllogisms, sees himself as making clear or apparent *their* validity.

(*a*) *The meaning of* phanēnai

No doubt, aorist passive forms of that verb can be used to express that something is clear in itself, or evident all on its own. For instance, at *Meteorologica* 1.6, when Aristotle is explaining the nature of comets, he refers to a great comet which came to be 'at the time of the earthquake in Achaea and the tidal wave' (343^b1) and says that it 'appeared to the west in winter in frosty weather when the sky was clear' (ἐφάνη μὲν χειμῶνος ἐν πάγοις καὶ αἰθρίαις ἀφ' ἑσπέρας, 343^b18–19). The comet was, simply, apparent in the sky.

But there is another, very familiar, use of the verb, to mean that something has been *made clear* or has *become* clear, by being *explained* or *shown*. Some particularly good examples are to be found in the *Parmenides* of Plato. At 139 E 7, for instance, Plato is setting up a complex argument to the effect that the one is neither similar to something nor dissimilar to something, either to itself or to something else. Plato signals the introduction of a new premiss in the argument with the word που ('presumably' or 'I suppose'; in the translation below, 'surely'), and the introduction of a proposition already established with the word *ephanē* (139 E 7–140 A 6):

οὐδὲ μὴν ὅμοιόν τινι ἔσται οὐδ' ἀνόμοιον οὔτε αὐτῷ οὔτε ἑτέρῳ. — τί δή; — ὅτι τὸ ταὐτόν που πεπονθὸς ὅμοιον. — ναί. — τοῦ δέ γε ἑνὸς χωρὶς ἐφάνη τὴν φύσιν τὸ ταὐτόν. — ἐφάνη γάρ. — ἀλλὰ μὴν εἴ τι πέπονθε χωρὶς τοῦ ἓν εἶναι τὸ ἕν, πλείω ἂν εἴη πεπόνθοι ἢ ἕν, τοῦτο δὲ ἀδύνατον. — ναί. — οὐδαμῶς ἔστιν ἄρα ταὐτὸν πεπονθὸς εἶναι τὸ ἓν οὔτε ἄλλῳ οὔτε ἑαυτῷ. — οὐ φαίνεται. — οὐδὲ ὅμοιον ἄρα δυνατὸν αὐτὸ εἶναι οὔτε ἄλλῳ οὔτε ἑαυτῷ. — οὐκ ἔοικεν. 140 A 1

'Furthermore, it will be neither like nor unlike anything, either itself or another.' — 'Why?' — 'Because whatever has a property the same is surely like.' — 'Yes.' — 'But it was shown that the same is separate in its nature from the one.' — 'Yes, it was.' — 'But if the one has any property apart from being one, it would be more than one; and that is impossible.' — 'Yes.' — 'Therefore, the one can in no way have a property the same as another or itself.' — 'Apparently not.' — 'So it cannot be like another or itself either.' — 'It seems not.' (trans. Gill and Ryan, in *Plato: Complete Works*, ed. J. M. Cooper with D. H. Hutchinson (Indianapolis and Cambridge, 1997))

The key phrase for our purposes is τοῦ δέ γε ἑνὸς χωρὶς ἐφάνη τὴν φύσιν τὸ ταὐτόν ('But it was shown that the same is separate in its nature from the one', 139 E 9–140 A 1). *Ephanē* here refers back to the conclusion of the argument spanning 139 D 1–E 3. The same use occurs at 138 D 5 (with reference to the proposition 'it is impossible for the one to be somewhere in something', proven earlier in an argument whose conclusion is at 138 B 5–6), 140 D 3 (referring to the proposition 'it is impossible for the one to be equal to something', proven earlier at 140 C 6–7), and several other places. Now, no one is tempted to infer from this kind of use of the verb that a proposition such as 'the same is separate in its nature from the one' or 'it is impossible for the one to be somewhere in something' is clear in the sense of self-evident! In saying that a proposition *ephanē*, Plato has in mind that this proposition has been *shown to be the case*, or that it has *become clear in the light of other considerations* (the premises used to show it).

Lest one thinks this is a use restricted to Plato, here is an Aristotelian example, at *GC* 2. 11, 338[a]18:

ταῦτα μὲν δὴ εὐλόγως,   338[a]17
ἐπεὶ ἀΐδιος καὶ ἄλλως ἐφάνη ἡ κύκλῳ κίνησις καὶ ἡ τοῦ
οὐρανοῦ, ὅτι ταῦτα ἐξ ἀνάγκης γίνεται καὶ ἔσται, ὅσαι
ταύτης κινήσεις καὶ ὅσαι διὰ ταύτην.   338[b]1

And this is reasonable; for circular motion, i.e. the revolution of the heavens, was seen on other grounds to be eternal, since precisely those movements which belong to and depend upon this eternal revolution come-to-be of necessity, and of necessity will be.

As Joachim notes, 'The conclusion just established is logically concordant with the eternity of the revolution of the οὐρανός which Aristotle had proved on other grounds in *Phys.* Θ 7–9.'[19] Joachim rightly points out that when Aristotle says here that the eternity of the heavenly motion *ephanē*, he means that he has shown or proven it.

So the natural interpretation of these uses of the word *ephanē* in Plato and Aristotle is that they are being used to track the making clear of something by the giving of proofs or explanations; our

[19] H. H. Joachim, *Aristotle: On Coming-to-Be and Passing-Away (De generatione et corruptione)*, a revised text with introduction and commentary (Oxford, 1922), 275.

translators even went so far as to translate the word as 'was shown' or 'was seen'.

This use of the verb *ephanē* is a matter of indicating that something has become clear *after an argument has been offered for it*.[20] For something to become clear in this way is not the same as its being self-evident, or not needing explanation. In fact, it is very common for Aristotle to finish a complex explanation by saying that it is *therefore* clear that such-and-such, using the adjective *phaneros*, etymologically linked to the verb *phainesthai*, and an inferential connective such as *oun*. In these contexts the locution 'therefore it is clear that . . .' indicates that the issue has become clear *in the light of* the explanation given. The chapters of the *Prior Analytics* presenting the assertoric and modal syllogistic, stuffed as they are with proofs of validity and non-concludence, are replete with this locution. In 1. 4–6 alone we have the following: 1. 4, 26^b18, $^b26$; 1. 5, 27^a16 (an especially important example, to which I shall return), $^a23$, 28^a1; 1. 6, 28^a36, $^b30$, 29^a11.[21] This kind of clarity is a sort of 'conditional' clarity; the idea is not that the claim in question was all along clear or self-evident, but rather that light has been shed on it by the considerations offered.[22]

On the view I am offering, then, *phanēnai* in the definition of perfection means 'to *become* clear'. Aristotle means to indicate in his definition of perfect syllogisms that nothing more is required for the validity of those syllogisms to become clear than what is provided in the premisses. Alternatively: the *explanation* for their validity makes reference to the premisses alone. After the explanation of the validity of the syllogism—one which makes reference only to the premisses—it will be clear that the syllogism is valid.[23]

[20] In this paragraph I am grateful to Laura Castelli for discussion.
[21] Examples of δῆλον with an inferential connective from the same chapters: 1. 4, 26^a13 (assuming that the οὖν in the same line is a genuine οὖν and not part of μὲν οὖν); 26^b29 (δῆλον followed by γάρ); 1. 5, 28^a4 (δῆλον followed by γάρ again).
[22] For a very nice Aristotelian example of the difference between the two types of clarity see *Phys.* 1. 7, 190^a31–$^b3$: it *is* clear (φανερὸν ὅτι, $^a33$) in the case of non-substances that there must be something underlying, but it should *become* clear to someone who looks at things in Aristotle's way (ἐπισκοποῦντι γένοιτο ἂν φανερόν, $^b3$)— i.e. someone who follows the argument through—that the same holds for substances.
[23] The distinction between things which *are* clear and things which will *become* clear—or clearer—in the light of an argument surely underlies the Stoic theory of demonstration, according to which a proof is revelatory of its unclear conclusion: 'This being so, a proof must first of all be an *argument*, secondly *concludent*, thirdly *true*, fourthly *having a non-evident conclusion*, fifthly *revealing this by the force of the premisses*' (S.E. *M.* 8. 310; translation from Brunschwig, 'Proof Defined', in

What is a Perfect Syllogism?

(*b*) *Does Aristotle offer explanations for the validity of the perfect syllogisms?*

We have just seen that *phanēnai can* be used to indicate that something has become clear through having an explanation offered for it. The question now is: does Aristotle offer explanations for the validity of the perfect syllogisms, or does he think their validity shines forth like the comet? To this question, the simple answer is: yes, he does offer explanations for their validity. Here is the evidence.

(i) *Assertoric syllogistic.* In *Prior Analytics* 1. 4 Aristotle discusses the first figure of assertoric syllogisms (those whose premisses are of the form AxB, BxC), and presents Barbara, Celarent, Darii, and Ferio as perfect syllogisms. In every one of those cases Aristotle explains why it is that their premisses entail the conclusion. Now admittedly, these explanations tend to be rather short and mysterious. For Barbara, he says: 'if A is predicated of all B and B of all C, it is necessary for A to be predicated of all C. *For it was said previously what we mean by '[predicated] of all*' (1. 4, 25ᵇ37–40). For Celarent, he simply continues: '*Similarly* also if A is predicated of no B, and B is predicated of no C, A will belong to no C' (25ᵇ40–26ᵃ2). The whole explanation of why this is the case is contained in the innocent word 'similarly' (ὁμοίως). For Darii: 'Let A belong to all B and B to some C. Then *if being predicated of all is what it was said to be in the beginning*, it is necessary that A belong to some C' (26ᵃ23–5). Finally, Ferio: 'And if A belongs to no B and B to some C, it is necessary that A does not belong to some C: *for it was determined also what we mean by [being predicated] of none*' (26ᵃ25–7). In each case—albeit implicitly in the case of Celarent—Aristotle explains why the conclusion follows from the relevant premisses, with an explanation introduced by 'for' or 'if'. Moreover, in each case—albeit implicitly in the case of Celarent—he refers us back to what he had previously said about the nature of a- and e-predication, i.e. the famous *dictum de omni et nullo*.

How exactly the *dictum de omni et nullo* can explain why these syllogisms are valid is a question to which I shall return at length. But for the moment, I want to observe that Aristotle does indeed explain

---

Schofield, Burnyeat, and Barnes (eds.), *Doubt and Dogmatism*, 125–60 at 144). The conclusion, which is unclear in the sense of not being self-evident, has light shone on it by the premisses which entail it. See the discussions in Brunschwig, op. cit., and Barnes, 'Proof Destroyed', in the same volume.

or justify why it is that the conclusion follows from the premisses, *even in the case of the four perfect syllogisms of the first figure*.

In *Prior Analytics* 1. 5 and 6 he discusses the second (MxN, MxX) and third (PxS, RxS) figures, all of whose syllogisms are imperfect, and all of which receive explanations, as you would expect. The very first syllogism of the second figure that he discusses (Cesare) sets the scene for us (1. 5, 27ᵃ5–9): 'For let M be predicated of no N and all X. Now since the negative premiss converts, N will belong to no M; but it was assumed that M belongs to all X, so that N will belong to no X—for this was shown before [τοῦτο γὰρ δέδεικται πρότερον].' Here, Aristotle states the premisses of the syllogism whose validity will be proven, and then gives his explanation of why the conclusion follows from them (the explanation starts at 'since'). The explanation turns on converting the first proposition, MeN, into NeM, which then, taken together with the other proposition, MaX, gives us the premisses of Celarent, and so together they entail NeX. The point for our purposes is that Aristotle states that he takes himself to have *shown* (δέδεικται) that Celarent's conclusion (NeX) follows from its premisses. This is a somewhat bold claim, since, as we just saw, his explanation in 1. 4 for the validity of Celarent consisted in the single, cryptic word 'similarly' (ὁμοίως, 26ᵃ2) but it is relatively straightforward to provide the fully worked-out proof to which he is alluding (and I do so in what follows; see below, Section 2: 'How does the *dictum de omni et nullo* explain the validity of Barbara and Celarent?').[24] Thus, Aristotle thinks of himself as having *shown* the validity of Celarent.

Now, it is true that Aristotle does not refer again in 1. 5–6 to having *shown* any of the perfect syllogisms which serve as the probative base for syllogisms in the second and third figures, and which are pressed into that duty at every turn. Instead, in the remainder of 1. 5–6 he contents himself in his explanations with saying things like 'for the first figure has come about again' (1. 5, 27ᵃ12–13), or 'then we get a syllogism in the first figure' (1. 5, 27ᵃ36; 1. 6, 28ᵃ22), etc. But it is no accident that it is in the very *first* proof of an imperfect syllogism (Cesare in chapter 5) that he reminds the reader that the validity of the relevant first-figure syllogism (Celarent) has been *shown*, for we can then see what his whole strategy for the second

---

[24] It hardly needs saying that if Aristotle's cryptic one-word explanation of the validity of Celarent counts as showing its validity, then his fuller explanations in the case of Barbara, Darii, and Ferio count as showing their validity too.

What is a Perfect Syllogism? 121

and third figures is going to be: he is going to prove the validity of the syllogisms in those figures by relating them back to the first-figure syllogisms from 1. 4, whose validity has already been shown. The evidence is, then, that Aristotle not only gave *explanations* of the validity of the assertoric perfect syllogisms (in 1. 4), but also thought of these explanations as *showing* their validity (as is clear from his back reference in 1. 5). (I shall be arguing that these explanations all take the same form, a reference back to the *dictum de omni et nullo* stated in 1. 1, but that is for later.)

(ii) *Modal syllogistic.* The modal syllogistic is brutally difficult to comprehend in its entirety, despite the heroic efforts of commentators over the centuries, most recently Marko Malink,[25] on whose account I largely rely. But about the identity of the perfect syllogisms there is no doubt. They are:

1. 8: Barbara NNN, Celarent NNN, Darii NNN, Ferio NNN ($29^{b}36$–7);[26]
1. 9: Barbara NXN, Celarent NXN ($30^{a}17$–23); Darii NXN ($30^{a}37$–$^{b}1$); Ferio NXN ($30^{b}1$–2);[27]
1. 14: Barbara QQQ ($32^{b}38$–$33^{a}1$); Celarent QQQ ($33^{a}1$–5); Darii QQQ ($33^{a}23$–5); Ferio QQQ ($33^{a}25$–7);
1. 15: Barbara QXQ ($33^{b}33$–6); Celarent QXQ ($33^{b}36$–40); Darii QXQ, Ferio QXQ ($35^{a}30$–5);
1. 16: Barbara QNQ ($36^{a}2$–7); Celarent QNQ ($36^{a}17$–25); Darii QNQ (described only abstractly at $35^{b}23$–6); Ferio QNQ ($36^{a}39$–$^{b}2$).

Question: in how many of these cases does Aristotle offer an explanation for why the conclusion follows necessarily from the premisses?

NNN. Aristotle offers precious little in the way of explanation for any of the NNN syllogisms, perfect or otherwise. But the little he

[25] *Aristotle's Modal Syllogistic* [*Modal*] (Cambridge, Mass., 2013).
[26] These four syllogisms are never described by Aristotle as perfect, but commentators agree they must be: 'Barbara, Celarent, Darii, and Ferio NNN are valid and perfect moods' (Malink, *Modal*, 103); cf. Patzig, *Theory*, 61–7.
[27] Again, Aristotle never calls these four syllogisms perfect, but commentators agree they must be: 'Barbara, Celarent, Darii, and Ferio are valid and perfect as NXN-moods' (Malink, *Modal*, 104); 'The syllogisms in the four valid moods (Barbara NXN, Celarent NXN, Darii NXN, Ferio NXN) are perfect' (Striker, *Book I*, 114).

does say is highly suggestive of what we have seen so far. His tactic is simple. He opens up his description of NNN syllogisms, the first modal cases he considers, by saying:

The case of necessary terms is much the same as that of terms that belong. For the same order of terms will or will not produce a syllogism in the case of belonging as in the case of belonging or not belonging of necessity, the only difference being that 'belonging (or not belonging) of necessity' is added to the terms. For the privative proposition converts in the same way, and 'being in something as in a whole' and 'predicated of all' will be explained in a similar fashion. (1. 8, 29^{b}36–30^{a}3)

It is that final sentence which is telling. Aristotle remarks that the conversion of e-propositions still holds when e-propositions have 'necessarily' added to them, and that 'predicated of all' will be understood 'in a similar fashion'. The best explanation for why he draws attention to those two logical features in particular is that e-conversion forms the basis of all the other conversions, and the *dictum de omni et nullo* serves as a basis for the perfect syllogisms. In this way, Aristotle can immediately continue to say that 'in the other cases the conclusion will be shown to be necessary by conversion, in the same way as in the case of belonging' (30^{a}3–5), to cover those NNN syllogisms which are proved by conversion from perfect syllogisms. That leaves only those syllogisms which cannot be proven in this way, of which there are just two, namely Baroco NNN and Bocardo NNN, which he immediately goes on to discuss in 30^{a}6–14. So—albeit rather abstractly—Aristotle does still offer an explanation for the validity of the perfect syllogisms, by referring them to the *dictum de omni et nullo* (or some suitably modalized version of it).

NXN. Both Barbara and Celarent NXN are asserted to be syllogisms at 1. 9, 30^{a}17–20, with the following explanation: 'for since A belongs (or does not belong) to every B of necessity, and C is one of the Bs, it is evident that one or the other will hold of C also of necessity' (30^{a}21–3). This is an explanation of validity: it justifies the previous assertion of the validity of Barbara NXN and Celarent NXN. Now, there are two schools of thought about this explanation. One is that it is an explanation of the validity of Barbara NXN and Celarent NXN calling upon the *dictum de omni et nullo* via the telling locution 'C is one of the Bs'.[28] This is the view I shall be ar-

[28] For the link between this locution and the *dictum de omni et nullo*, see also M.

guing for. The other school of thought is that it is a justification of the perfection of Barbara NXN and Celarent NXN, since it asserts that if their premisses are true then it is *evident* that their conclusions must be true. This is exactly the interpretation of perfection I am arguing against: namely, that it is a necessary and sufficient condition for a syllogism PQR to be perfect that the conditional 'If P and Q, then clearly R' is true. So I shall have to return to this example to make my case (see below, Section 6: 'Objection: texts which suggest the prevailing interpretation of what a perfect syllogism is'). Darii NXN receives its own little explanation at 30^a40–$^b1$: after laying out the syllogism (Aa_NB, Bi_XC, therefore Aa_NC), Aristotle justifies it by saying 'for C is under B, and A belonged to every B of necessity'. I shall also be arguing that the locution 'C is under B' (τὸ γὰρ Γ ὑπὸ τὸ Β ἐστί) is a locution deployed by Aristotle to signal that the *dictum de omni et nullo* is being called upon. But the more important point for now is that an explanation is given of Darii NXN's validity. What Aristotle immediately goes on to say about Ferio NXN confirms this: 'Similarly if the syllogism were privative, for the demonstration [ἀπόδειξις] is the same [as the one for Darii NXN]' (30^b1–2). Thus, Aristotle signals that Ferio NXN is also valid, and that one can construct an explanation for why that is the case along similar lines to the one constructed for Darii NXN. For the perfect NXN syllogisms, then, Aristotle not only gives explanations for their validity, but also is prepared to call those explanations *demonstrations*. Moreover, although this is something that will take some more argument, the explanations seem to call upon the *dictum de omni et nullo* (presumably a suitably modalized one), just as in the case of the NNN syllogisms, and analogously to the assertoric perfect syllogisms.

QQQ. Barbara QQQ is explicitly called perfect at i. 14, 32^b39, and its validity is 'evident from the definition [ὁρισμοῦ], for we have explained [ἐλέγομεν] "possibly belonging to all" in this way' (32^b40–33^a1). So Barbara's validity is explained or made clear by reference to a modalized version of the *dictum de omni*. Aristotle introduces Celarent QQQ by saying 'similarly' (33^a1), and offers an explanation of its validity in lines 33^a3–5: 'for A's possibly not belonging to what B may be said of was just the same as nothing that could

Malink, 'Τῷ vs. τῶν in *Prior Analytics* i. 1–22' ['Text'], *Classical Quarterly*, NS 58 (2008), 519–36 at 530–1.

possibly be under B being left out'. Whatever one makes of that explanation (which is not easy to translate), it is clearly an explanation that calls upon a modalized *dictum de nullo*. Darii QQQ is called perfect at 33ᵃ23 (if one goes with the received text), and its validity is said to be 'evident from the definition of "possibly belonging"' (33ᵃ24–5), just as in the case of Barbara QQQ. For Ferio QQQ, 'the demonstration [ἀπόδειξις] is the same' (33ᵃ27). So once again, the perfect syllogisms get explanations, and once again, these explanations are also described as *demonstrations*. Furthermore, we have seen that Aristotle justifies the perfect QQQ syllogisms by reference to a modalized *dictum de omni et nullo*.

QXQ. Barbara, Celarent, Darii, and Ferio QXQ are called perfect at 1. 15, 33ᵇ25–8. Barbara QXQ is explained at 33ᵇ33–6: 'let A possibly belong to every B and let B be posited to belong to every C. Now since C is under B [ὑπὸ τὸ B ἐστί τὸ Γ] and A possibly belongs to every B, it is evident that it also possibly belongs to every C; so a perfect syllogism comes about.' This explanation is minimal, and interesting in two ways. First, it offers some solace to those who hold that it is necessary and sufficient for a syllogism to be perfect that it is evident that its conclusion follows from its premises, since Aristotle says here that *because* the conclusion evidently follows from its premises, the syllogism is perfect. (Thus, it is an important text for the view that I am arguing against, and I will be tackling it below.) But the explanation also employs the mysterious locution 'C is under B' which we saw above for Darii NXN (and implicitly for Ferio NXN). If I am right—and this remains to be seen—that this locution betrays a usage of the *dictum de omni et nullo*, then here again we have a perfect syllogism being explained by the *dictum*. Celarent QXQ is said to be 'similarly' (33ᵇ36) valid and perfect. Darii and Ferio QXQ are said to be valid and perfect at 35ᵃ30–5; 'the demonstration [ἀπόδειξις] is the same as before' (35ᵃ35–6), i.e. the same as the ones given at 33ᵇ33–40 for Barbara and Celarent.[29]

QNQ. The QNQ syllogisms are called perfect at 1. 16, 35ᵇ25. Barbara QNQ is described at 36ᵃ2–7; its status as perfect is justified by the fact that 'it is perfected straightaway through the initial premisses' (36ᵃ6–7), but there is no attempt to explain or justify its validity. The situation with Celarent QNQ is even stranger.

[29] Cf. Striker, *Book I*, 150.

What is a Perfect Syllogism? 125

It is asserted to be a syllogism, and called perfect, at 36ª17–21, but there is no explanation of why the conclusion follows from the premises or why the syllogism is perfect; instead there is an explanation of why the plain assertoric conclusion *does not* follow. Darii QNQ is not mentioned explicitly at all,[30] although a remark at the beginning of the chapter commits Aristotle to thinking that it is valid and perfect: 'When one of the premises signifies belonging of necessity, the other possibly belonging, there will be a syllogism when the terms are related in the same way, and the syllogisms will be perfect when the necessity is posited with the minor extreme' (when Aristotle says 'in the same way', he means 'as in the previous chapter' (Striker, *Book I*, 151), which is how we know that these lines in 1. 16 are describing Barbara, Celarent, Darii, and Ferio QNQ). As for Ferio QNQ, Aristotle has a few lines in 36ª39–^{b}2 where he asserts that the premises of Ferio QNQ do not entail an assertoric conclusion, and he says 'the demonstration is the same' (presumably the same as with Celarent QNQ), but, as with Celarent, there is no explicit explanation of why the Q-conclusion *does* follow.

What is the take-home message of this brief tour of the perfect modal syllogisms? Answer: perfect modal syllogisms have explanations too! Only very few perfect modal syllogisms are described without any explanation whatsoever. In the vast majority of cases, Aristotle gives explanations, sometimes quite elaborate. And at several turns he calls those explanations 'demonstrations', most notably at 1. 9, 30^{b}1–2, 1. 14, 33ª27, and 1. 15, 35ª35–6. Thus, it is simply not true that for Aristotle, perfect modal syllogisms are stated as self-evident. They demand—and in the vast majority of cases are given—explanation. As for the nature of those explanations, we saw that the *dictum de omni et nullo*, or some suitable modalized version of it, was called upon, although exactly how remains to be seen.

So putting together what we have found out about perfect assertoric syllogisms and perfect modal syllogisms, we can say the following:

- They receive in the vast majority of cases explicit explanations, and Aristotle is prepared to use words such as *dedeiktai* (1. 5,

[30] 'Aristotle forgets to mention Darii QNQ, which should also be perfect' (Striker, *Book I*, 153–4).

27^{a}8–9) or *apodeixis* (see the references in the previous paragraph) of these explanations.
- In those cases where an explanation is offered, their validity is explained by reference to the *dictum de omni et nullo*, or some suitable modalized version of it.
- In some cases (Barbara QQQ and Darii QQQ), their validity is said to be *clear* from, or in the light of, the *dictum*. Since quite generally the explanations of the validity of perfect syllogisms appeal to the *dictum*, it is safe to conclude that Aristotle conceived of the explanations he gives of the validity of perfect syllogisms as *making their validity clear*.

So, the evidence is that Aristotle did not think perfect syllogisms were self-evident. He did not think that they did not stand in need of explanation, or that their validity can be seen just by stating them. Rather—as the definition of perfect syllogisms suggested all along—he thought of them as ones for which the explanations of their validity, the making clear of their validity, look a certain way.

(c) What about imperfect syllogisms?

An imperfect syllogism, you will recall, is one 'which is in need of one or more things [for its necessity to become apparent], things which are necessary through the underlying terms but which have not been taken through propositions' (24^{b}24–6). I claimed above that Aristotle thinks imperfect syllogisms have their validity made clear through a different type of explanation from the explanation of the validity of perfect syllogisms. So we need to see whether Aristotle ever describes the validity of an imperfect syllogism as clear in the light of the explanation he gives for it. And he does, at 1. 5, 27^{a}9–18:

Again, if M belongs to all N and to no X, X will belong to no N. For if M belongs to no X, neither does X belong to any M; but it was assumed that M belongs to all X; therefore X will belong to no N—for the first figure has come about again. And since the privative one converts, neither will N belong to any X, so that there will be the same *sullogismos*. (These things can also be proved by reduction to the impossible.) It is evident [φανερόν], then [οὖν], that a syllogism comes about when the terms are so related, but not a perfect syllogism, for the necessity is brought to perfection [ἐπιτελεῖται] not only from the initial assumptions, but from others as well. (trans. Striker, adapted)

What is a Perfect Syllogism? 127

This is the second proof of chapter 5, the proof of Camestres in the second figure (MaN, MeX, therefore NeX). Aristotle proceeds by first taking the two premisses, MaN and MeX, and pointing out that they produce the conclusion XeN, because you can convert MeX to XeM, which, taken together with MaN, yields XeN by Celarent ('the first figure has come about again'). So we have shown that MaN and MeX yield XeN, and now one converts the conclusion XeN into NeX to yield us Camestres: MaN, MeX, therefore NeX. (Aristotle then points out that the same *sullogismos* has come about: he means either that Camestres has reduced to the same first-figure syllogism as Cesare, namely Celarent (Ross's interpretation[31]), or that Camestres has the same conclusion as Cesare, namely NeX (Striker's interpretation[32]).)

The important part is what comes next: Aristotle says that it is therefore clear that a syllogism comes about when the terms are so related (i.e. when the premisses are MaN, MeX), *but that this does not make the syllogism perfect*. This shows us immediately that the fact that it has become *clear* that a syllogism is valid is not *sufficient* for it to be perfect. We can see that Aristotle thinks of himself as having made Camestres clear with the explanation he gives, but that this explanation does not qualify the syllogism to be perfect. Instead, he says, the syllogism is imperfect, because the explanation of the validity of Camestres (here referred to as the process of being brought to perfection) did not proceed *only* ($\mu \acute{o} \nu o \nu$, 27^{a}17) from the premisses ($\dot{\epsilon} \kappa$ $\tau \hat{\omega} \nu$ $\dot{\epsilon} \xi$ $\dot{\alpha} \rho \chi \hat{\eta} s$, ibid.) but from other things too. So we needed to draw on propositions other than the premisses in order to explain the validity of Camestres, in this case the propositions XeM (obtained by converting the minor premiss) and XeN (the interim conclusion obtained from MaN and XeM).

This text therefore confirms the following about perfect and imperfect syllogisms. (*a*) Aristotle does sometimes acknowledge in the course of his proofs of imperfect syllogisms what his definition of imperfect syllogisms implied: that these proofs *make clear* that the conclusions of the syllogisms follow necessarily from their premisses.[33] This is no surprise, given the language of proof (*deixis*)

---

[31] W. D. Ross, *Aristotle's* Prior *and* Posterior Analytics: *A Revised Text with Introduction and Commentary* (Oxford, 1949), ad loc.

[32] Striker: 'Here as in many other places Aristotle uses the word "syllogism" both for an entire argument and its conclusion' (*Book I*, 101).

[33] There is another, albeit less compelling, text where Aristotle discusses an imperfect syllogism and offers an explanation for why its conclusion follows, stating

and demonstration (*apodeixis*) which is systematically employed to characterize the explanations of the imperfect syllogisms, as well as explanations of the perfect syllogisms; LSJ gives as the first meaning of *both deiknumi* and *phainō* 'to bring to light'. (*b*) The explanations of the validity of imperfect syllogisms have to proceed through propositions in addition to the premisses, whereas the explanations of the validity of perfect syllogisms just call on the premisses themselves (cf. 1. 4, 26^{b}30, where Aristotle tells us that Barbara, Celarent, Darii, and Ferio are all perfect because they were all 'brought to perfection through their premisses': πάντες γὰρ ἐπιτελοῦνται διὰ τῶν ἐξ ἀρχῆς ληφθέντων).

In further support of (*b*), there is evidence elsewhere that imperfection is a feature of a syllogism which is revealed by examining the nature of the explanation given for its validity. At 1. 15, 34^{a}1–5, Aristotle discusses the validity of syllogisms whose premisses are of the form Ax_XB, Bx_QC (i.e. first-figure syllogisms whose major premiss is assertoric and whose minor premiss is problematic). He says:

> It is evident, then, that when belonging is used in the proposition with the minor extreme, perfect syllogisms come about. But that there will be syllogisms when it is the opposite way has to be shown through the impossible. It will also be clear at the same time [ἅμα] that these syllogisms are imperfect, for the proof [δεῖξις] is not from the premisses as taken.

at the end of that explanation that it is clear that it does. It is when he is discussing the particularly difficult syllogism Celarent XQM (Ae$_X$B, Ba$_Q$C, therefore Ae$_M$C), at 1. 15, 34^{b}19–35^{a}2. You might have thought from its name that this is a perfect syllogism, but at 1. 15, 33^{b}25–9, Aristotle denies that any syllogism coming from XQ premisses is perfect: 'If one of the premisses asserts belonging, the other possibly belonging, then when the premiss with the major extreme signifies the possible, all the syllogisms will be perfect and conclude to the possible in the sense of the definition stated. But when the premiss with the minor extreme does so [i.e. signifies the possible], the syllogisms will all be imperfect.' The proof of Celarent XQM is horribly difficult (see M. Malink and J. Rosen, 'Proof by Assumption of the Possible in *Prior Analytics* I. 15', *Mind* (forthcoming)) but the paragraph in which it is contained finishes as follows: 'It is clear, then [δῆλον οὖν], that the conclusion is for belonging to none of necessity' (35^{a}1–2). This looks like another example of the conclusion of an imperfect syllogism being said to be clear, after a suitable explanation. However, the conclusion of the syllogism had already been offered (complete with proof) earlier in the paragraph, at 34^{b}25–6, and the intervening text has explained why *other* putative conclusions *do not* follow (Ae$_Q$C, Ae$_N$C). So when Aristotle states at the end of the paragraph that it is clear that the conclusion is Ae$_M$C, this strictly speaking does not refer to the clarity we have obtained from the initial proof of the conclusion's following from the premisses, but to the clarity we have obtained from the whole paragraph. For this reason, I do not want to rest my case on this text.

What is a Perfect Syllogism?

In other words: prove the validity of these latter syllogisms (the ones with mere belonging in their major premiss) and *at the same time* you can read off from the nature of the proof—viz. the fact that it refers to propositions other than the premisses alone—that the syllogisms are imperfect. To see that a syllogism is imperfect you need do nothing more than inspect the proof given for its validity. The same thought surfaces in 1. 16, 36^{a}1, when Aristotle is talking about the syllogism with premisses Aa$_N$B, Ba$_Q$C: 'that the syllogism is imperfect is clear from the demonstration [$ἀποδείξεως$]'.

Scrutiny of what Aristotle says about imperfect syllogisms yields one further piece of evidence about the nature of imperfection. We have already seen that a syllogism is revealed to be imperfect when the proof of its validity has to proceed through propositions in addition to its premisses, e.g. as a result of conversion. Aristotle also points out that a syllogism is imperfect if you have to use *reductio ad impossibile* to prove it: 'It is also clear that all the syllogisms in this figure are imperfect, for all of them are brought to perfection by adding some things that are either necessarily inherent in the terms or assumed as hypotheses, as when we give a proof through the impossible' (1. 5, 28^{a}4). Since Aristotle thought that all imperfect syllogisms could be proven either through conversion (resulting in the addition to the proof of propositions 'necessarily inherent in the terms') or through the impossible (resulting in the addition to the proof of propositions 'assumed as hypotheses'), we now have a good grip on what it takes for a syllogism to be imperfect, and how this is manifested through the proof of its validity.

2. How does the *dictum de omni et nullo* explain the validity of Barbara and Celarent?

Grant for the moment that I am right that according to Aristotle, perfect syllogisms are the ones which become clear through an explanation of a certain sort, and imperfect syllogisms become clear through an explanation of another sort. (I shall later consider the few textual objections to this view that remain.) I argued that the *definition* of perfect syllogisms emphasizes that the explanation of their validity will make reference to the premisses alone and not other propositions. Yet, the *explanations* that Aristotle actually gives for perfect syllogisms all refer to the *dictum de omni et nullo*. This is most obvious in the case of the assertoric perfect syllogisms:[34]

Barbara: 'If A is predicated of all B and B of all C, it is necessary for A to be predicated of all C. *For it was said previously what we mean by "[predicated] of all"*' (1. 4, 25^{b}37–40).

Celarent: '*Similarly* also if A is predicated of no B, and B is predicated of no C, A will belong to no C' (25^{b}40–26^{a}2).

Darii: 'Let A belong to all B and B to some C. Then *if being predicated of all is what it was said to be in the beginning*, it is necessary that A belong to some C' (26^{a}23–5).

Ferio: 'And if A belongs to no B and B to some C, it is necessary that A does not belong to some C: *for it was determined also what we mean by [being predicated] of none*' (26^{a}25–7).

Thus, it looks as though Aristotle goes flatly against his own definition of perfect syllogisms: according to the definition of perfection, their validity was supposed to become clear through an explanation referring only to their *premisses*, and yet here we see the explanations of their validity making reference not to the premisses of the syllogisms at all, but to a claim about *the nature of a- and e-predications*![35] What I need to do, then, on Aristotle's behalf, is show how these two explanations come to the same thing. In a nutshell, my view is this: the *dictum de omni et nullo* is an abstract rule of inference which licenses a certain conclusion to be drawn from premisses that are related in a certain way, so to explain the validity of a syllogism by a simple reference to the *dictum* is *shorthand* for observing that the premisses of the syllogism you are dealing with are related in just the way demanded by the *dictum*. No conversion or reductio is needed to explain why the conclusion follows, unlike the case of imperfect syllogisms, where conversion or reductio is needed, thus bringing in propositions other than the premisses in the course of the explanation. *Thus, to attribute the validity of a syllogism to the*

---

[34] Noted by Barnes, *Truth*, 392.

[35] In fact, Aristotle does more than refer to the nature of a- and e-predications; he also refers to the fact that *he has already characterized* a- or e-predication: πρότερον γὰρ εἴρηται πῶς τὸ κατὰ παντὸς λέγομεν (26^{a}39–40); εἰ ἔστι παντὸς κατηγορεῖσθαι τὸ ἐν ἀρχῇ λεχθέν (26^{b}24); ὥρισται γὰρ καὶ τὸ κατὰ μηδενὸς πῶς λέγομεν (26^{b}27). Presumably Aristotle imagines someone challenging him on his assertion that a given conclusion follows from the premisses: 'What right do you have to assert *that*?' To this, the answer is: 'I have the right because I've already said what a- and e-predications are in a way that will explain how the conclusion follows from the premisses!' Thanks to Stephen Menn for discussion here.

What is a Perfect Syllogism? 131

dictum de omni et nullo alone just is to explain its validity on the basis of the relation the two premisses bear to each other without bringing in other propositions.

Obviously, we now have to look at the *dictum* to see what it says, and whether we can extract this interpretation out of it (1. 1, 24^{b}28–30):

λέγομεν δὲ τὸ κατὰ παντὸς
κατηγορεῖσθαι ὅταν μηδὲν ᾖ λαβεῖν τοῦ ὑποκειμένου[36]
καθ' οὗ θάτερον οὐ λεχθήσεται· καὶ τὸ κατὰ μηδενὸς ὡσαύτως.   24^{b}30

We say that something is predicated of every whenever it is possible to take nothing of the subject of which the other will not be said; and similarly for predicated of none.

Aristotle states a principle concerning universal affirmative predication, and then (in the last five words) states that what he has just says goes for universal negative predication too, *mutatis mutandis* (ὡσαύτως). The conjunction of the two principles is known as the *dictum de omni et nullo*, but it can be separated into a *dictum de omni* and a *dictum de nullo*. The *dictum de omni* states that we say X is predicated of all Y whenever one can take nothing of Y of which X will not hold (and presumably the *dictum de nullo* then states that we say X is predicated of no Y whenever one can take nothing of Y of which X *does* hold). There has been a lot of scholarly literature on the *dictum*, especially recently, and, roughly speaking, two strands of thought have emerged. What is known in the literature as the 'orthodox' reading[37] of the *dictum* is that it states the following:

AaB ↔ For any x, if B holds of x then A holds of x.
AeB ↔ For any x, if B holds of x then A does not hold of x.[38]

The orthodox reading assumes that the expression 'nothing of Y' means 'no individual member of Y' (hence the individual variable

---

[36] There is a debate about what text to print here. I have printed a conservative text, following the majority of manuscripts. (This is not my preferred text. See below, n. 52)

[37] The terminology was introduced by Barnes (*Truth*, 406–12).

[38] This is Malink's formulation of the orthodox *dictum de omni et nullo* (*Modal*, 46). Barnes endorses the orthodox reading of the *dictum* in *Truth*, but does not offer a formal rendering. The closest he gets is this (for the *dictum de omni*): 'A is predicated of every B if and only if there isn't any B of which A is not predicated' (389), which would more naturally be represented by this: 'There is no x such that B is predicated of x and A is not predicated of x.' In standard first-order predicate logic, this formulation is equivalent to the one in my main text.

'x' on the RHS of the biconditional above). 'Heterodox' readings of the *dictum* argue that the phrase 'nothing of Y' could just as well mean 'no plurality contained in Y'.[39] Marko Malink has adopted a heterodox reading of the *dictum* in his pioneering work on Aristotle's modal syllogistic;[40] his parallel principles to the two principles above are these:

$AaB \leftrightarrow$ For any Z, if BaZ then AaZ.
$AeB \leftrightarrow$ For any Z, if BaZ then $\sim$AaZ.[41]

The important thing to note here is that the quantifier 'For any Z' ranges over whatever it is that the letters A and B stand for in Aristotelian logic—universals, or classes, or whatever.[42]

Despite the important differences between Malink's heterodox version of the *dictum* and Barnes's orthodox one in the semantics they offer for a- and e-predication, they share three features as interpretations of what Aristotle wrote:

(1) Both present their interpretations of the *dictum* as biconditionals. They take Aristotle to be offering something like a *paraphrase* or *elucidation* of the meaning of 'AaB'. Barnes goes so far as to call the alleged paraphrase a *definition* of 'AaB' (412), whereas Malink thinks that it is merely a characterization of some key logical features of 'AaB' (66, endorsing Morison, 'Notes', 214). (Malink cannot think that the *dictum* offers a definition of a-predication since a-predication also appears on the right-hand side of his biconditional.) There is one feature, then, of the *dictum de omni* that they both gloss over, namely the modality in the phrase 'it is possible to take nothing of the subject' ($\mu\eta\delta\grave{\epsilon}\nu\ \mathring{\eta}\ \lambda\alpha\beta\epsilon\hat{\iota}\nu\ \tau o\hat{v}\ \dot{v}\pi o\kappa\epsilon\iota\mu\acute{\epsilon}\nu o\nu$; note the 'potential' meaning of the verb 'to be'). Or rather, they do not gloss over it, but merely push it to the side: 'I think that the modal element, which is very lightly indicated in the Greek, is not to be taken seriously' (Barnes, *Truth*, 389); 'The phrase "none . . . can be taken" may be understood to mean "there is none . . ."' (Malink,

---

[39] Barnes, *Truth*, 412, argues that the Greek of the *dictum* could not mean this; for dissent see B. Morison, 'Aristotle etc.' ['Notes'], *Phronesis*, 53 (2008), 209–22 at 214.
[40] He lists other scholars who have gone with a 'heterodox' view at *Modal*, 47 n. 2.
[41] *Modal*, 63. Malink's renderings derive from Barnes, *Truth*, 409.
[42] There is an inexplicable error in Morison, 'Notes', 214, where it is said that the quantifiers in Barnes's heterodox version of the *dictum de omni* range over individuals.

Modal, 35).⁴³ However, there is also modality in the second half of the *dictum*, namely in the expression 'of which the other will not be said' (καθ' οὗ θάτερον οὐ λεχθήσεται). 'Will not be said' (λεχθήσεται) is a 'future of implication', very common in Aristotle.⁴⁴ Hence, it would be nice to have an interpretation which accounts for this double modality, and I shall be offering one shortly.⁴⁵

(2) Both Barnes⁴⁶ and Malink agree that the way to employ the *dictum* in the justification of the perfect syllogisms is by replacing the occurrences of the statements of a- and e- predication in their premisses by the paraphrases offered by the *dictum*. Let us see how this is supposed to work with Barbara. You start with the premisses:

A is predicated of all B;
B is predicated of all C.

Then you replace each occurrence of '. . . is predicated of all . . .' with the paraphrase that the *dictum* licenses. For Barnes, this yields:

For any x, if B holds of x then A holds of x;
For any x, if C holds of x then B holds of x.

What then? We are supposed to see that they entail 'For any x, if C holds of x then A holds of x',⁴⁷ or perhaps we employ the machinery of first-order predicate logic to generate that conclusion.⁴⁸ For Malink, the story is similar: Barbara is validated because 'given that the . . . *dictum de omni et nullo* holds for any A and B, it follows logically that for any A, B, and C: if Aa$_X$B and Ba$_X$C, then Aa$_X$C'

---

⁴³ Note how Malink takes μηδέν as subject of the phrase: 'nothing (or "none") can be taken', which is also a possible translation (thanks to Stephen Menn for pointing this out to me).
⁴⁴ Start with *Pr. An.* 1. 2, 25ᵃ7, 11, 15, 16, 18, 19, all in the very first examples given by Aristotle of one thing necessarily following from another (the conversion rules). For the appearance of the future in the descriptions of the syllogisms themselves see e.g. 1. 4, 26ᵃ2 (Celarent).
⁴⁵ It was Scott O'Connor who first drew my attention to the importance of accounting for that modality.
⁴⁶ It is worth stressing that Barnes's discussion of perfect syllogisms is sceptical in intent; he does not think there is a way of making good on the idea that the *dictum de omni et nullo* underwrites the validity of the perfect syllogisms, and so many of the positions I attribute to him are not positions that he endorses, but positions he adopts in the course of the dialectic.
⁴⁷ Barnes, *Truth*, 416: 'How do I know that Barbara is valid? "You know it immediately, if you know it at all".'
⁴⁸ Barnes, *Truth*, 417: 'in the context of modern logic . . . it is something [tiro logicians] will be invited to prove'.

(*Modal*, 38). What does 'logically' mean here? Answer: according to the rules of 'classical propositional and quantifier logic' (ibid. 38 n. 9).[49]

For both Malink and Barnes, then, the idea behind the *dictum* is that it licenses paraphrases of a- and e-predications in such a way that either one can then just see the validity of the perfect syllogisms or one can use the logical machinery of our best post-Fregean logic to infer that they are valid.[50] Both their accounts of how the *dictum* serves to validate Barbara seem rather unsatisfactory. Quite apart from the troubling anachronistic deployment of post-Fregean logical machinery, there is the obvious problem that if we are allowed to deploy all that machinery in the proving of Barbara (and Celarent),

[49] Strictly speaking, Malink is talking about his 'abstract' *dictum de omni et nullo*, which uses the relation '... is a member of the plurality associated with ...' ('*mpaw*') rather than the relation '... is predicated of all ...', but the point stands: Malink calls upon a background logic in addition to the *dictum* in order to validate Barbara. The premises of Barbara are Aa_XB and Ba_XC, i.e., in the language of Malink's abstract *dictum* (*Modal*, 37), $\forall X$ (B *mpaw* $X \to A$ *mpaw* X) and $\forall X$ (C *mpaw* $X \to B$ *mpaw* X). 'X' is here a second-order variable (for classes, sets, or pluralities, or whatever). So in order to validate the conclusion of Barbara, $\forall X$ (C *mpaw* $X \to A$ *mpaw* X), we will need to instantiate the second-order variable, use the 'transitivity' of '$\to$', and then universally generalize on whatever second-order entity we took for 'X'. Thus, we need some tools of second-order logic too and not just standard first-order quantifier logic; when Malink speaks of 'quantifier logic' he means a general logic of quantifiers ranging over all types. (Thanks to Marko Malink for discussion of this point.)

[50] Ebert and Nortmann offer a similar strategy to that adopted by Barnes and Malink, but in more informal terms. They think that Aristotle's lead idea in treating Barbara as perfect is 'daß sich die Gültigkeit der logischen Folgerung bei diesem Modus durch folgende Überlegung unmittelbar und unwiderleglich plausibel machen läßt: Man wähle ein beliebiges Individuum aus dem Umfang des Subjektterminus der unteren Prämisse; diesem muß der Prädikatterminus dieser Prämisse ebenfalls zukommen, wegen der Explikation des Von-jedem-Ausgesagtwerdens. Da der Prädikatterminus der unteren Prämisse zugleich der Subjektterminus der oberen *a*-Prämisse ist, muß diesem Individuum aus demselben Grunde der Prädikatterminus der oberen Prämisse ebenfalls zukommen' (*Buch I*, 293). Note that this explanation is resolutely orthodox with its reference to taking an *individual* (as with Barnes), and that the major and minor premisses are both translated or explicated in the same way ('aus demselben Grunde') and then fitted together, as with both Barnes and Malink. Notice also, however, that they are clear that this is an attempt on Aristotle's part to make plausible the fact that the conclusion of Barbara follows from its premisses: this much is in the spirit of the thesis of the first part of this paper, that Aristotle feels the need to explain why the conclusions even of perfect syllogisms follow from their premisses. (This part of their commentary sits rather uneasily with what they say elsewhere (228): 'Für den Begriff des vollkommenen Syllogismus, der hier eingeführt wird, ist der Begriff der *Evidenz* ausschlaggebend: Vollkommen ist ein Syllogismus, bei dem das notwendige Folgen (der Konklusion aus den Prämissen) ohne weiteres *einleuchtet*.' Their explanation at 293 appears to contradict 'ohne weiteres'.) I am grateful to Oliver Primavesi for bringing this to my attention.

What is a Perfect Syllogism? 135

then we should be allowed to continue to use that machinery for proving all the other syllogisms, in which case we no longer have an account of the syllogistic which respects the way *Aristotle* sets up his logic, with Barbara, Celarent, Darii, and Ferio as the 'base' syllogisms, and the conversion rules and reductio as the logical tools from which to derive the others.[51]

(3) Since Barnes and Malink take the *dictum de omni et nullo* to be licences to paraphrase a- and e-predications, they both run into a difficulty when it comes to accounting for the validity of Darii and Ferio. For the minor premiss of Darii and Ferio is an i-predication, and the *dictum de omni et nullo* says nothing (on their interpretation) about the semantics of i-predications. Moreover, the conclusion of Ferio is an o-predication, about which they think the *dictum* is also silent. They both offer solutions to this 'desperate' (Barnes, *Truth*, 403) conundrum. Barnes suggests that 'we might reinforce the *dictum* by the addition of a couple of extra clauses—a *de aliquo* dealing with "of some" and a *de aliquo non* with "not some"' (*Truth*, 403–4). Malink suggests a similar supplementation: 'Aristotle does not mention a *dictum de aliquo* characterizing the semantics of i_x-propositions, or a *dictum de aliquo non* characterizing the semantics of o_x-propositions. However, these two *dicta* can easily be supplied with the help of Aristotle's claims concerning the contradictoriness of assertoric propositions' (*Modal*, 36). No doubt one *can* supply such extra *dicta*, but Barnes and Malink would be the first to admit that Aristotle never mentions them, never suggests that they are involved in accounting for the validity of the perfect syllogisms, and is therefore highly misleading when he intimates that the *dictum de omni et nullo* alone is responsible for the validity of the perfect syllogisms.

Putting these three worries together, we get three desiderata for how we should interpret the *dictum de omni et nullo* (if possible):

- to take account of the modality in it;
- to make the *dictum* validate the perfect syllogisms without bringing in extra logical machinery, anachronistic or otherwise;

[51] This is part of what Malink had in mind when he concedes that his interpretation 'does not explain why Aristotle took the four first-figure moods to be perfect (as opposed to merely valid), but it is not my intention here to enter into a discussion of this question' (*Modal*, 39).

- in particular, to make the *dictum* validate the perfect syllogisms without bringing in a *dictum de aliquo* or *de aliquo non*.

The third constraint is especially suggestive of a way forward. If the explanation of all four perfect assertoric syllogisms must use the *dictum de omni et nullo* and no other *dictum*, then let us look at which parts of the *dictum de omni et nullo* Aristotle actually appeals to for those syllogisms. In the case of Barbara, it is the *dictum de omni* ('For it was said previously what we mean by "[predicated] of all"', $25^b 39$–40); in the case of Darii also ('if being predicated of all is what it was said to be in the beginning', $26^a 24$). For Ferio, it is the *dictum de nullo* ('for it was determined also what we mean by [being predicated] of none', $26^a 27$). For Celarent, we are not told explicitly which *dictum* to employ (remember that cryptic 'similarly' at $25^b 40$), although pretty clearly it is the *dictum de nullo*. Thus, it seems as though Aristotle refers us to the relevant part of the *dictum de omni et nullo* according to what the *major premiss* of the syllogism is. The suggestion is, then, that we find an interpretation of the *dictum* which does not involve using it to paraphrase *both* premisses of a syllogism, but which instead involves applying it to the major premiss *alone*, thus respecting the third desideratum.

But how could this possibly work? The key text that will guide my interpretation is the one from *Prior Analytics* 1. 9 where Aristotle is laying out Barbara and Celarent NXN ($30^a 15$–23):

συμβαίνει δέ ποτε καὶ τῆς ἑτέρας προτάσεως ἀναγ- $30^a 15$
καίας οὔσης ἀναγκαῖον γίνεσθαι τὸν συλλογισμόν, πλὴν οὐχ
ὁποτέρας ἔτυχεν, ἀλλὰ τῆς πρὸς τὸ μεῖζον ἄκρον, οἷον εἰ τὸ
μὲν Α τῷ Β ἐξ ἀνάγκης εἴληπται ὑπάρχον ἢ μὴ ὑπάρχον,
τὸ δὲ Β τῷ Γ ὑπάρχον μόνον· οὕτως γὰρ εἰλημμένων τῶν
προτάσεων ἐξ ἀνάγκης τὸ Α τῷ Γ ὑπάρξει ἢ οὐχ ὑπάρξει. $30^a 20$
ἐπεὶ γὰρ παντὶ τῷ Β ἐξ ἀνάγκης ὑπάρχει ἢ οὐχ ὑπάρχει
τὸ Α, τὸ δὲ Γ τι τῶν Β ἐστί, φανερὸν ὅτι καὶ τῷ Γ ἐξ ἀνάγκης ἔσται θάτερον τούτων.

It sometimes results that the syllogism becomes necessary when only one of the propositions is necessary (not whatever proposition it might be, however, but only the proposition in relation to the major extreme). For instance, if A has been taken to belong or not to belong of necessity in this way, then A will belong or not belong to C of necessity. For since A belongs or does not belong to all of B of necessity, but C is something of the Bs, it is clear that one or the other of these will also apply to C of necessity. (trans. Striker, lightly adapted)

What is a Perfect Syllogism? 137

Abstracting for the moment from the difficulties associated with the modal syllogistic, it is clear that in his explanation (γάρ, 30ᵃ21) in 30ᵃ21–3 of *why* Barbara NXN and Celarent NXN are valid, Aristotle reformulates the shared minor premiss of Barbara NXN and Celarent NXN, viz. BaC, as 'C is something of the Bs' (τὸ δὲ Γ τι τῶν Β ἐστί, 30ᵃ22). This is crucial because the *dictum de omni* tells us this: we say AaB when it is possible to take nothing of B (μηδὲν ᾗ λαβεῖν τοῦ ὑποκειμένου) of which A will not be said. So if our major premiss is AaB, and our minor premiss tells us that 'C is something of the Bs'—that C is a subclass of the Bs—then the *dictum* tells us that A *must* be 'said of' C. For the minor premiss precisely tells us that there is *something* (τι) of the Bs (namely the Cs), and the *dictum* tells us that when A holds of all B (as the major premiss states), it is possible to take *nothing* (μηδέν) of B of which A will not be said. The way in which Aristotle expresses the minor premiss of Barbara NXN and Celarent NXN using the locution 'something'+ genitive (τὸ δὲ Γ τι τῶν Β ἐστί) is a nod to the language of the *dictum*, which uses the locution 'nothing'+genitive.⁵² Moreover, we should note that Aristotle does *not* similarly reformulate the major premiss. Whatever Aristotle's strategy is here, it is clear that it involves reformulating the minor premiss with the locution 'something'+genitive, but not the major one.

Let us see how this works with assertoric Barbara. The premisses of Barbara are AaB and BaC. The *dictum de omni* tells us that we say

⁵² The *dictum* as I printed it above, following the vast majority of manuscripts, uses the locution μηδέν+genitive, and this is the text followed by e.g. Striker and Smith, to take two recent authoritative commentators. The reference to the *dictum* in the phrase τὸ δὲ Γ τι τῶν Β ἐστί at 1. 9, 30ᵃ22, is even clearer if you accept the text that Malink and I prefer for the *dictum*: λέγομεν δὲ τὸ κατὰ παντὸς κατηγορεῖσθαι ὅταν μηδὲν ᾗ λαβεῖν τῶν τοῦ ὑποκειμένου καθ' οὗ θάτερον οὐ λεχθήσεται (this text follows the only manuscript which does not have the text as I printed it, namely MS A; see Malink, 'Text', for details). τι τῶν Β at 30ᵃ22 would correspond word for word to μηδέν . . . τῶν τοῦ ὑποκειμένου at 24ᵇ29.

The OCT text of the *dictum* excises τοῦ ὑποκειμένου, following Alexander (but no manuscript of the *Prior Analytics*): λέγομεν δὲ τὸ κατὰ παντὸς κατηγορεῖσθαι ὅταν μηδὲν ᾗ λαβεῖν καθ' οὗ θάτερον οὐ λεχθήσεται. With this text, my point about the language of 30ᵃ22 recalling the language of the *dictum* might appear to be somewhat diminished (since the reference in the *dictum* to the subject term drops out). Nonetheless, the word μηδέν in this version of the *dictum* still means 'nothing *of the subject*', otherwise the *dictum* makes no sense, and indeed those who follow Ross in going along with Alexander's text and excising τοῦ ὑποκειμένου do so because they think 'nothing' *already means* 'nothing of the subject': Barnes, for instance, excises τοῦ ὑποκειμένου on the grounds that it is 'an obvious gloss' (*Truth*, 387 n. 34) which adds nothing to the sense of the *dictum*. So even with the OCT's minimal text, we would have good reason to construe the phrase at 1. 9, 30ᵃ22, as referring back to the *dictum*.

AaB when 'it is impossible to take something of B of which A will not be said'. But if BaC, then 'C is something of the Bs' (following the lead of 30ª22). Now, if it is impossible to take something of B of which A will not be said, and C is something of the Bs, then, putting these two together, we get that it is impossible for A not to be said of C: in other words, A must be said of C, i.e. AaC. (This last move from 'A must be said of C' to 'AaC' needs explanation; see below.) What role, on this account, does the *dictum de omni* actually play? I want to suggest that it is a rule of inference, which one could express as follows:

> Given as a premiss AaB, whenever you have another premiss which postulates[53] a subclass of B, it necessarily follows that A is said of that subclass.

The *dictum de omni* as expressed by Aristotle is 'We say that something is predicated of every whenever it is possible to take nothing of the subject of which the other will not be said'. The modality in the *dictum* implicit in 'it is possible' and 'will not be said' is cashed out as 'it necessarily follows' in my version; it expresses *necessitas consequentiae*. Far from being a trivial or eliminable feature of the *dictum*, it gets to the heart of what it is: it is not a paraphrase of a-predications, but a characterization of a key *logical* or *inferential* property of those predications.[54] (In my version, I have also rephrased, for clarity, the locution '[some]thing of' as 'a subclass of'.) So let us apply the *dictum* to the case of Barbara. The major premiss is AaB. But the *dictum de omni* tells us something about a-predications: if an argument has a predication of the form AaB as a premiss and another premiss postulating the existence of a subclass of the Bs, then A must hold of that subclass. But the second premiss of Barbara, BaC, precisely postulates there being a subclass of the Bs, namely C ('C is something of the Bs')! Hence, given our major premiss AaB, we can infer using the *dictum* that A is said of the subclass the minor premiss postulated of B, namely C, thus AaC.

[53] This verb is a nod to the verb λαβεῖν as it appears in the *dictum*. It is Aristotle's standard verb for what one does with a premiss of an argument (see e.g. the reference to τὰ εἰλημμένα in the definition of a perfect syllogism, 1. 1, 24ᵇ23–4). So on my interpretation, when Aristotle says 'it is impossible to take something of B of which A is not said' he means something like this: 'it is impossible to *assume* or *postulate* a subclass of B of which A is not said'.

[54] Morison, 'Notes', 214: the *dictum* 'is a *characterisation* of the relations of "being predicated of every" and "being predicated of no" in which we are told precisely those facts about the relations which are needed to explain the perfect syllogisms'.

What is a Perfect Syllogism? 139

This interpretation of the *dictum* is 'heterodox', in Barnes's sense, since in its reference to a *subclass*, it generalizes over classes or pluralities, and not over individuals. However, it is different from Malink's 'heterodox' interpretation because it takes the modality seriously, it validates Barbara *on its own* without recourse to other logical apparatus, and it does not interpret the *dictum* as offering a paraphrase of a-predications.

Next, let us take Celarent. We will need to do two things: extract the *dictum de nullo* from Aristotle's hand-waving gesture at it (καὶ τὸ κατὰ μηδενὸς ὡσαύτως, 24^{b}30), and extract Aristotle's proof of Celarent from his similarly vague reference (ὁμοίως δὲ καὶ εἰ τὸ μὲν Α κατὰ μηδενὸς τοῦ Β, τὸ δὲ Β κατὰ παντὸς τοῦ Γ, ὅτι τὸ Α οὐδενὶ τῷ Γ ὑπάρξει, 25^{b}40–26^{a}2). The *dictum de omni* was this:

> Given as a premiss AaB, whenever you have another premiss which postulates a subclass of B, it necessarily follows that A is said of that subclass.

This suggests that the *dictum de nullo* is this:

> Given as a premiss AeB, whenever you have another premiss which postulates a subclass of B, it necessarily follows that A is *not* said of that subclass.

Since the minor premiss of Celarent is BaC, the same as with Barbara, we know that Aristotle will allow us to rewrite it as 'C is something of the Bs', following the example of 30^{a}22. Then we can link this up with the *dictum de nullo* to infer that A is not said of C, thus AeC.

This interpretation of what is going on with Barbara and Celarent is not without difficulties. In the case of Barbara, application of the *dictum de omni* gave us 'A is said of C' as the conclusion, and in the case of Celarent, application of the *dictum de nullo* gaves us 'A is not said of C'. How do we get from those descriptions to 'AaC' and 'AeC'? There are two problems. First, Aristotle does not explain anywhere what the locution 'said of' means. Second, my paraphrases (AaC and AeC) are not contradictories, which you might have expected given that the *dictum de omni* and the *dictum de nullo* are supposed to differ from one another in the presence or absence of the word 'not'.[55] My solution is that, encouraged by the

---

[55] I am grateful to Marko Malink for pressing me on the second of these problems.

lack of an explanation for the locution 'X is said of Y', I am assuming that 'X is said of Y' is another way of saying 'Y is X', and hence that 'A is said of C' means 'C is A', and 'A is not said of C' means 'C is not A'. These two phrases differ from one another in the presence or absence of a negation, just as you would expect, and yet their meaning seems to be precisely 'AaC' and 'AeC' respectively.[56] (I am helped in this by the absence of explicit quantifiers in the description of the conclusion in the *dictum*.[57])

Now we have seen how the *dictum* is supposed to underwrite or generate Barbara and Celarent, it is worth taking a step back and thinking about what sort of thing the *dictum* is. On the picture I have been presenting, the *dictum* tells you what follows from what. It is, in that respect, like a rule of inference. For like a rule of inference, it instructs us in the inferential power of a proposition. The *dictum de omni* tells us about the inferential power of a-propositions, and the *dictum de nullo* tells us about the inferential power of e-propositions. The *dictum de omni* tells us this about the inferential power of a-propositions: in the presence of the a-proposition AaB, and another proposition which postulates the existence of a subclass of B, it cannot fail to be the case that a further proposition is true, namely the proposition stating that A holds of that subclass. The *dictum de nullo* tells us this about the inferential power of e-propositions: in the presence of the e-proposition AeB, and another proposition which postulates the existence of a subclass of B, it cannot fail to be the case that a further proposition is true, namely the proposition stating that A fails to hold of that subclass. As a comparison, think of how the inference rule *modus ponens* tells you about the inferential power of the conditional: in the presence of a conditional, and another proposition which is the antecedent of that conditional, it cannot fail to be the case that a further proposition is true, namely the proposition which is the consequent of the conditional. The *dictum* tells you about the inferential power of a-

[56] For other examples in Aristotle of where the presence or absence of a negation does not lead to two *contradictory* propositions, see *De int.* 7.

[57] Notice that although the description of the conclusion contains no quantifiers, the way I have phrased the two rules for a- and e-predication precludes that they validate the subaltern modes Barbari and Celaront. Barbari is 'AaB; BaC; therefore AiC'. When applying the *dictum* to the premisses of this argument, we get that the conclusion will predicate A of *that subclass of B which the minor premiss postulated to exist*. But this subclass is C—all of it—not some part of C. So Barbari is not validated by the *dictum*. Similarly for Celaront. (I am grateful to Adam Crager for pressing this point.)

and e-predications, just as *modus ponens* tells you about the inferential power of the conditional. So in this sense, the *dictum* is like a rule of inference.

Notice that I have been formulating rules of inference not as imperatives ('from X infer Y') or permissions ('from X you can infer Y'), but rather as truth-evaluable *factual* claims about what cannot fail to be the case given what: 'given as a premiss AaB, whenever you have another premiss which postulates a subclass of B, it necessarily follows that A is said of that subclass' and 'given as a premiss AeB, whenever you have another premiss which postulates a subclass of B, it necessarily follows that A is not said of that subclass'. I have done this in order to remain faithful to the fact that the *dictum* is a factual statement about a- and e-predications and yet contains modalities: 'We say that something is predicated of every whenever it is possible to take nothing of the subject of which the other will not be said: and similarly for predicated of none' (λέγομεν δὲ τὸ κατὰ παντὸς κατηγορεῖσθαι ὅταν μηδὲν ᾖ λαβεῖν τοῦ ὑποκειμένου καθ' οὗ θάτερον οὐ λεχθήσεται· καὶ τὸ κατὰ μηδενὸς ὡσαύτως, 24^{b}28–30). But although the *dictum* is formulated as a factual claim, it is not, on my interpretation, an unpacking of the *truth-conditions* of a- and e-predications. This puts me at odds with Barnes and Malink, who see the *dictum* as precisely that—an unpacking of the truth conditions of a- and e-predications—and who therefore adopt the strategy of using the *dictum* to *paraphrase* a- and e-predications.[58] In contrast, on my view, the *dictum* is a statement of what you can use a- and e-predications to do, inferentially speaking, and not an elucidation of the truth-conditions of a- and e-predications. But even though it is not an unpacking of the *truth-conditions* of a- and e-predications, it still does tell us something important about *what* a- and e-predication are, or what we *mean* when we make an a- or e-predication. It tells us that a-predication is a predication such that when two terms A and B are related in that way, it will follow, if there is a subclass of B, that A holds of that subclass. (*Mutatis mutandis*, as Aristotle might put it, for e-predication.) And just as one can view inference rules in modern logic as telling us something about the meaning of the connectives whose behaviour they regulate,[59] so we should view Aristotle's inference rules for a-

---

[58] It also puts me at odds with Ebert and Nortmann; see n. 50 above.

[59] What I say in the text is neutral on the question of whether the meaning of the connectives is *exhausted* by giving such inference rules.

and e-predications as telling us something about the meaning of a- and e- predications (or, if you prefer, about the quantifiers 'all' and 'none'). This is as it should be. For at the start of *Prior Analytics* 1.1 Aristotle announced his intention to define or delimit (διορί-σαι, 24ᵃ11) what we mean by 'predicated of all' or 'predicated of none' (τί λέγομεν τὸ κατὰ παντὸς ἢ μηδενὸς κατηγορεῖσθαι, 24ᵃ14–15). There is no need to assume that this means that Aristotle intends to give a full-blooded definition of a- and e-predication (I am not sure whether he even thinks they are the sort of thing which *have* full-blooded definitions), but it certainly means that we expect a characterization of them. I have been arguing that he does exactly that: he gives a characterization of a key logical property of both predications.[60] So, the *dictum* is a factual statement about the inferential properties of a- and e-predications, and thereby tells us something about the meaning of those kinds of predication—just not by giving truth-conditions for those predications.[61]

Lastly, it is worth stressing that the *dictum* has explanatory value. It is not, for instance, merely an abstract description of Barbara or Celarent. The *dictum tells* or *informs* you what follows from what; it asserts that something follows from something else. (No argument schema does that.) This is why an appeal to it will serve to explain why a given argument form (Barbara, say, or Celarent) is a form whose instances are syllogisms. It is not just an abstract description of Barbara or Celarent, but rather an isolation of the inferential property of a- and e-predications which serves to explain why Barbara and Celarent are syllogisms. This is why I think Aristotle is happy to describe himself as proving or showing the validity of perfect syllogisms (see above, Section 1(*b*): '*Does Aristotle offer explanations for the validity of the perfect syllogisms?*'); he is thinking of the fact that he is deriving the conclusions of the perfect syllogisms using a

[60] Cf. again Morison, 'Notes', 214, quoted above, n. 54. I am particularly grateful to Alexander Bown and Christian Pfeiffer for help with the issues discussed in this paragraph.

[61] In fact, Aristotle does *elsewhere* give something resembling an unpacking of the truth-conditions of a-predication: 'I say that something holds of every case if it does not hold of some cases and not of others, nor at some times and not at others' (κατὰ παντὸς μὲν οὖν τοῦτο λέγω ὃ ἂν ᾖ μὴ ἐπὶ τινὸς μὲν τινὸς δὲ μή, μηδὲ ποτὲ μὲν ποτὲ δὲ μή, *Post. An.* 1. 4, 73ᵃ28–9). I submit that this unpacking of the truth-conditions of a-predication is couched in rather different terms from the *dictum de omni* in the *Prior Analytics*: 'We say that something is predicated of every whenever it is possible to take nothing of the subject of which the other will not be said' (24ᵇ28–30). In the *Posterior Analytics* there is no modality and in particular no 'implicative future'. (I am grateful to Adam Crager for urging me to consider the *Posterior Analytics* text.)

rule of inference. So Striker is right when she writes: 'it is clear that Aristotle does not think of the perfect moods as being in any sense deduced' from the *dictum* (*Book I*, 84). You do not deduce things *from* rules of inference; you deduce things *from* propositions, *using* a rule of inference. And Aristotle does deduce the conclusions of perfect syllogisms from their premisses, using the *dictum* as a rule of inference.

3. How does the *dictum de omni et nullo* explain the validity of Darii and Ferio?

Darii and Ferio present problems for any interpretation of Aristotle's syllogistic. As we saw before, it was a major stumbling-block for prior interpretations of the *dictum de omni et nullo* that it could not be used to validate Darii and Ferio, despite Aristotle's appeals to that very *dictum* (and nothing else) when he explains the validity of those two perfect syllogisms. Barnes and Malink resorted to importing new *dicta* to cover i- and o-predications. It is not clear to me that my interpretation is entirely successful here either, but let us see what happens. Since the major premiss of Darii is AaB, it is the *dictum de omni* which is at issue. The *dictum*, you will recall, states this:

> Given as a premiss AaB, whenever you have another premiss which postulates a subclass of B, it necessarily follows that A is said of that subclass.

The second premiss of Darii is BiC, i.e. that B belongs to some of the Cs. Does this premiss postulate there to be a subclass of B? Well, it does, in this sense: it postulates that there is a subclass of B which consists of part of C (those among the Cs which are B). So we can infer using the *dictum* that A is said of part of C (those Cs which are B), i.e. that A is said of *some* of the Cs (namely, those which are B), i.e. AiC.

A similar story will be told for Ferio. We take the *dictum de nullo*, since the major premiss is a universal negative:

> Given as a premiss AaB, whenever you have another premiss which postulates a subclass of B, it necessarily follows that A is not said of that subclass.

The second premiss of Ferio is BiC. Once again, we take this premiss to postulate there to be a subclass of B, namely the subclass of B which consists of *the part of C which is B* (those among the Cs which are B). So we can infer using the *dictum de nullo* that A is not said of that part of C (those Cs which are B), i.e. that A is not said of *some* of the Cs (namely, those which are B), i.e. AoC.

For both Darii and Ferio, the difficulty is in coming up with the description of the minor premiss in terms of subclasses (respecting the locution '[some]thing of the subject' in the *dictum*), and in recovering the description of the relevant conclusion. In the case of the minor premiss of Barbara, we do at least get some help from Aristotle when he paraphrases 'BaC' into 'C is one of the Bs' (τὸ δὲ Γ τι τῶν B ἐστί) at 1. 9, 30ᵃ22, but we are on our own when it comes to paraphrasing the minor premiss of Darii, 'BiC', into something like 'part of C is a subclass of B'. The same is true of the conclusions of Darii and Ferio, as licensed by the *dictum*: nothing prepares us for paraphrasing 'A is said of part of C' into 'A holds of some C' (AiC), or 'A does not hold of part of C' into 'A does not hold of some C' (AoC). The 'translation schema' that I have been urging goes like this:

A is said of C → AaC;
A is not said of C → AeC;
A is said of part of C → AiC;
A is not said of part of C → AoC.

But of course, I accept that Aristotle does not help us with these translations. Indeed, any commentator who puts forward a theory about the meaning or use of the *dictum* has to take a stance on what 'said of' means in the *dictum*, and has to do so without any help from Aristotle, who is silent on the matter.

Aristotle's silence on this matter is rather revealing of his own logical habits. In contemporary logical systems, a rule of inference such as *modus ponens* might be expressed as follows: 'From ϕ and "If ϕ then ψ", infer ψ.' With this rule, there is some work to be done to see that two propositions in front of us (as it might be, 'If it is day it is not night' and 'If if it is day it is not night, then it is not the case that it is both day and night') meet the description of the first two propositions described in the rule, and to see what the conclusion we are invited to draw is (in this case, 'it is not the case that it is both day and night'). The work that needs to be done is,

What is a Perfect Syllogism? 145

roughly speaking, the work of *syntactic substitution*. Now, the *dictum de omni et nullo* is a rule of inference which is formulated in semantic terms, in contrast to the way I just specified *modus ponens*, which was in syntactic terms.[62] Suppose one attempted to express *modus ponens* in semantic terms: 'When a proposition expresses that one proposition follows a second proposition, and the first proposition is assumed, then the second proposition necessarily follows.' The challenge in applying the rule so formulated would be to assess whether the propositions that lie in front of you meet the description of the premisses in the rule of inference, and to extract the relevant conclusion. I want to claim that Aristotle's *dictum de omni et nullo* functions similarly to a rule formulated in this way. It says that when AaB, then if you postulate the existence of a subclass of B, A cannot fail to hold of that subclass. We have to do the work of assessing whether the proposition in front of us meets the rule's semantic description of the minor premiss, namely that it postulates the existence of a subclass of B, and we have to do the work of coming up with a proposition (using the syllogistic relations of a, e, i, and o) which meets the rule's semantic description of the conclusion, namely that it expresses that A holds of that subclass.

4. Why does the *dictum* not work with the other syllogisms?

Before discussing some further difficulties with my interpretation, I want to show briefly how it is that the *dictum* cannot be applied to the imperfect syllogisms. Let us take the very first imperfect syllogism in the second figure, Cesare: AeB; AaC; therefore BeC. Now, you might think that we are in good shape to be able to apply the *dictum* to the premisses, since the major premiss, AeB, is an a- or e-predication. But the minor premiss, AaC, does not postulate a subclass of the subject of the major premiss (B). In fact, it tells us nothing about B at all! So we cannot apply the *dictum*. To do so, you would have to convert the major premiss AeB to BeA. Then the subject term of the major premiss is A, and our minor premiss, AaC, *does* tell us something about that subject: it tells us that the

[62] For some other examples of Aristotle's tendency to do logic by focusing on semantic, not syntactic, form see B. Morison, 'What was Aristotle's Concept of Logical Form?', in B. Morison and K. Ierodiakonou (eds.), *Episteme etc.: Essays in Honour of Jonathan Barnes* (Oxford, 2012), 172–88.

Cs are a subclass of the As (in other words, we have Celarent). But notice that we had to introduce a new proposition (BeA) before we could employ the *dictum*, a proposition which was not one of the premisses of Cesare. Hence Cesare is an imperfect syllogism: for its validity to become clear, we needed one or more things which had not been assumed in the initial premisses (cf. the definition of imperfection at 1. 1, $24^{b}24$–6).

Let us take another example, Datisi in the third figure: AaB; CiB; therefore AiC. Here, the major premiss is AaB, so once again, it might look as though we are in good shape for applying the *dictum*. However, the minor premiss, CiB, does not postulate any subclass of the subject term of that major premiss (B). It tells us what C belongs to, but not what B belongs to; for that, we have to convert it to BiC, thereby introducing a new proposition which was not one of the premisses, and thereby revealing Datisi to be imperfect (and perfected through Darii). Now, the minor premiss of Datisi is CiB, and I said that this premiss does not postulate a subclass of B. It is crucial for this to work that we do not say something like this: 'CiB means the same as BiC, and yet BiC postulates the existence of a subclass of B; therefore CiB postulates the existence of a subclass of B.' Luckily, we know that we can block this sort of move by appealing to the fact that Aristotle thinks AiB and BiA express different propositions; if they did not, there would be no sense in having i-conversion.

It should be clear from these explanations of why the *dictum* cannot be applied to Cesare and Datisi that only a syllogism in the first figure could be perfect. For if the premisses of a syllogism are going to be related in such a way that the *dictum* alone will deliver a conclusion, then the minor premiss has to postulate a subclass of the subject term of the major premiss; in other words, if we write the major premiss in the form AxB, the minor premiss has to be of the form BaC or BiC (because only BaC and BiC postulate the existence of a subclass of the subject term of the major premiss, B). So only a syllogism where the subject of one premiss is predicate in the other could be perfect. So only a first-figure syllogism could be perfect.

It seems to me a particularly attractive feature of the interpretation I am proposing that the *dictum* can be applied only to first-figure syllogisms. One of the major stumbling-blocks with Barnes's and Malink's interpretations is that one could easily apply the *dictum*, in its role as a paraphrase or elucidation of a- and

What is a Perfect Syllogism? 147

e-predications, to the premises of second- and third-figure syllogisms. So, for instance, one could take the premises of Darapti and apply the *dictum* to its two premises, and then wheel in the apparatus of modern logic and derive the conclusion. Both Barnes and Malink are uneasy about this, since they recognize that it then becomes hard, on their interpretations, to make a principled distinction between the way in which Barbara is valid and the way in which Darapti is valid. On my interpretation, Barbara can be validated by a single application of the *dictum*, whereas it is impossible even to apply the *dictum* to Darapti.

On my interpretation, then, only first-figure syllogisms can be perfect. Does this mean that *all* the first-figure syllogisms come out perfect? Well, certainly not in the case of modal syllogistic; uncontroversially, all the first-figure XQM syllogisms (proven in 1. 15), NQM syllogisms (proven in 1. 16), and NQX syllogisms (also proven in 1. 16) are imperfect, and some of the QQQ ones (proven in 1. 14)—we know this because Aristotle tells us so in most of those cases,[63] and in any case, they are all proven through conversion or reductio. What then about assertoric Fapesmo, whose validity is proved at 1. 7, 29^{a}23–6? Its premises are AaB and BeC. Here, whichever premiss you take to be the major premiss, you will not be able to apply the *dictum*. If you take AaB as major, then the problem is that the other premiss does not postulate the existence of a subclass of B (since it is BeC, and not BaC or BiC). If you take BeC as the major premiss, then the other premiss does not postulate the existence of a subclass of the subject (C), since it does not even mention C. By this reasoning, then, Fapesmo is imperfect—which is what one would expect anyway, since Aristotle proves it not by an appeal to the *dictum* alone, but by converting both premises to get Ferio. So on this line of reasoning, Fapesmo is a first-figure assertoric syllogism which is imperfect.[64]

(There is only one text which would seem to suggest that Fapesmo is not an imperfect first-figure syllogism. At the end of

---

[63] First-figure aea-QQQ and eee-QQQ are said to be imperfect at 1. 14, 33^{a}17–20; first-figure aoi-QQQ at 33^{a}27–34 (for discussion of this case see below, sect. 6: 'Objection: texts which suggest the prevailing interpretation of what a perfect syllogism is'). The first-figure QXM syllogisms are said to be imperfect at 1. 15, 33^{b}28–9. Barbara NQM is said to be imperfect at 1. 16, 35^{b}38, so presumably the other first-figure NQM syllogisms are too, although Aristotle never says so. He does not say whether the NQX syllogisms are perfect (but no commentator thinks they are).

[64] This is also Patzig's view (*Theory*, 56).

1. 4, when Aristotle has described the first figure and produced Barbara, Celarent, Darii, and Ferio as syllogisms within it, he says: 'It is also clear that all the syllogisms in this figure [πάντες οἱ ἐν αὐτῷ συλλογισμοί] are perfect, for they all reach their conclusion through the initial assumptions' (26^b28–30). So, the thought goes, if all the syllogisms in the first figure are meant to be perfect, and Fapesmo is not, then Fapesmo cannot have been intended by Aristotle to be in the first figure. *A fortiori*, it is not an imperfect first-figure syllogism. However, against this, it seems to me that at 26^b28–30 Aristotle could easily be saying that all the syllogisms *we have found so far* in this figure are perfect. The definite article in the expression 'all the syllogisms in this figure' (πάντες οἱ ἐν αὐτῷ συλλογισμοί) might serve to restrict the domain of discourse to a group of pertinent syllogisms, i.e. the ones that Aristotle has mentioned in that chapter. If that is right, then Fapesmo and for that matter Frisesomorum, also proven in 1. 7, 26^a23–6, should be classed as first-figure, imperfect, syllogisms.)

SUMMARY OF THE POSITION

Before turning to consider further objections to my interpretation, I shall summarize the interpretation I am offering.[65]

- Perfect syllogisms are not self-evident, but become evident after an explanation (based on the fact that Aristotle virtually always offers explanations for perfect syllogisms).
- Imperfect syllogisms also become evident after an explanation (as the definition of imperfection suggests, and as is clear from 1. 5, 27^a16).
- The difference between them is *what it takes* to make them evident (again, as the definitions of perfection and imperfection suggest).

[65] The closest view to mine in the literature as regards the role of the *dictum* is discussed (and rejected) by Barnes: 'Aristotle will appeal to the *dictum de omni et nullo* in the case of all the syllogisms which he recognizes to be perfect, and only in their cases' (*Truth*, 397). But even this is not quite my view, for I think the *dictum* will be appealed to in a *complete* explanation of the validity of even the imperfect syllogisms, since the explanation of their validity will make reference to the perfect syllogisms, whose validity is in turn to be explained by reference to the *dictum*. (See the next section for plentiful examples of this.) So Barnes should not have said 'and only in their cases', but rather 'and, in the case of these syllogisms alone, only the *dictum*'. That might be what he meant anyway.

What is a Perfect Syllogism? 149

- For perfect syllogisms, the explanation appeals to the *dictum de omni et nullo* alone (following Aristotle's tactic in 1. 4), and hence makes reference only to the premisses as they are taken in the syllogism and not any other proposition (cf. μόνον at 1. 5, 27ª17).
- For imperfect syllogisms, you need to bring in other propositions in order to explain their validity, for instance propositions obtained by conversion from the original premisses, or by hypothesis (in the case of reductio).
- The *dictum de omni et nullo* is a rule of inference, stating an inferential property of a- and e-predications when they are accompanied by a minor premiss of a certain kind (viz. one which posits the existence of a subclass of the subject term of the a- or e-predication). (That the *dictum* is a rule of inference respects the fact that there is a modality in the *dictum*, and its use in generating a conclusion from arguments where a- and e-predications are the major premisses explains why Aristotle never employs or appeals to a *dictum de aliquo* or a *dictum de aliquo non*.)
- The *dictum de omni* is this: *Given as a premiss AaB, whenever you have another premiss which postulates a subclass of B, it necessarily follows that A is said of that subclass.*
- The *dictum de nullo* is this: *Given as a premiss AeB, whenever you have another premiss which postulates a subclass of B, it necessarily follows that A is not said of that subclass.*

5. The lack of quantifiers in the *dictum*

I noted above that Aristotle does not use quantifiers in the *dictum* when he is describing the content of the minor premiss and the conclusion. Or more precisely, that Aristotle does not tell you straightforwardly what form the minor premiss must have, or what form the conclusion will have. He simply says that 'it is impossible to take something of the subject [minor premiss] of which the other will not be said [conclusion]'. I have exploited this indeterminacy to argue that Aristotle is abstractly describing minor premisses of *two* forms, a- and i-predications, both of which postulate a subclass of the subject of the major premiss.

This is worth spending some time on. In all four assertoric perfect syllogisms, the minor premiss is either the a-predication BaC or the i-predication BiC. Both, I have claimed, involve postulating a subclass of B—in the first case, the Cs quite generally, and in the second, only part of C, namely those Cs which are B. It would be nice to have some other evidence that Aristotle thought of these two types of predications, a- and i-predication, as having a *common* semantic description. And in fact there is such evidence. For at several points in the presentation of the modal syllogistic Aristotle employs a strange locution, 'C is under B' (τὸ Γ ὑπὸ τὸ Β ἐστι), which, in each case, describes *either* the proposition Ba_XC *or* Bi_XC when they occur as the minor premiss *in a perfect syllogism*, and always in a *justificatory* context. Sometimes Aristotle employs the formula when justifying a perfect syllogistic form (1. 9, 30^{a}40: Darii NXN; 1. 15, 33^{b}34: Barbara QXQ), and sometimes when he has converted the premisses of an imperfect syllogism and justifies why those new premisses will entail a conclusion (1. 10, 30^{b}13: Cesare NXN; 1. 11, 31^{a}30: Darapti NXN; 31^{a}37: Felapton NXN; 31^{b}17: Disamis XNN; 31^{b}20: Datisi NXN). Let us look at both sets of cases.

(a) Darii NXN and Barbara QXQ

Darii NXN is a perfect syllogism. Here is Aristotle's explanation: 'Let the universal premiss be necessary, and let A belong to B of necessity and B merely belong to some C. Then it is necessary that A belong to some C of necessity, for C is under B [τὸ γὰρ Γ ὑπὸ τὸ Β ἐστι], and A belonged to every B of necessity' (1. 9, 30^{a}37–^{b}1). Here we have the classic structure that we have seen Aristotle adopting elsewhere: the statement of the conclusion that follows of necessity from the premisses, followed by an explanation (signalled by γάρ, ^{a}40). That explanation involves pointing out that C is under B, derived from the minor premiss 'B merely belong[s] to some C' (Bi_XC). I submit that the description of C being under B is supposed to recall for us that we are postulating a *subclass* of B, in this case part of C, and that is why *rephrasing* Bi_XC as 'C is under B' has explanatory value. We are, after all, being offered an explanation for why the conclusion follows from the premisses, so the locution 'C is under B' must be doing some work.

Let us test this interpretation by looking at the other case: Barbara QXQ, which is also perfect. Aristotle's explanation for it runs

What is a Perfect Syllogism? 151

as follows: 'For let A possibly belong to every B and let B be posited to belong to every C. Now since C is under B and A possibly belongs to every B, it is evident that it also possibly belongs to every C; so a perfect syllogism comes about' (1. 15, 33^{b}33–6). Here, we can see the locution 'C is under B' being used to describe the minor premiss, Ba$_X$C. We are *explaining* why (ἐπεί, ^{b}34) there is a conclusion for the two premisses Aa$_Q$B and Ba$_X$C. The *reason* is that C is under B and A possibly belongs to every B. Again, the locution 'C is under B' occurs in an explanation of why a conclusion follows, and I submit that it is supposed to signal the application of the *dictum de omni*—we are postulating a subclass of the Bs, namely, in this case, the Cs.

Given these two cases, we must ask: what does 'C is under B' *mean*? We have to give it a meaning that will allow us to see how it can cover the two cases, BiC and BaC. Well, if you think about what it means to say that something is under something else, e.g. that a car is under a bridge, then it seems to me that this describes both a case where the car is under the bridge and covered completely by the bridge (the bridge is big enough to cover it) and a case where the car is under the bridge but the bridge does not cover all of it (perhaps because the bridge is not wide enough). So 'C is under B' captures both the case where B is wide enough to cover all of C (BaC) and the case where it is not wide enough to cover all of C (BiC). In each of the cases above, when Aristotle describes the minor premiss as a case where C is under B, he is reminding us that B does cover C (albeit perhaps only part of C). And that is supposed to trigger the application of the *dictum*: the major premiss states that AaB, and the *dictum* states that if the minor premiss postulates a subclass of B, then A must apply to that subclass. So since our minor premiss puts C under B, it does postulate a subclass of B (in one case, some of the Cs, in the other, all of the Cs).

Since 'C is under B' covers two different cases (BaC and BiC), it is not possible to have a version of the *dictum* which uses the 'under' locution alone. The best one could do would be this:

> Given as a premiss AaB, whenever you have another premiss which postulates something as being under B, it necessarily follows that A is said of *that thing* under B.

But since we know from the text we have just looked at that Aristotle is happy to say that C is under B when BiC (not that *part* of

C is under B, but C *itself* is under B), then the thing you would be inferring using this version of the *dictum* would be that A is said of C. But that does not give the right result. (The conclusion of Darii is not 'A is said of C', but rather 'A is said of part of C'.) For this reason, I think it is safest to take the locution 'C is under B' to *indicate* that we are postulating a subclass of B, and hence that we *can* apply the official *dictum*; the locution by itself does not tell us what the subclass in question of B is: it could be C as a whole, or just a part of C.

So, in the case of Darii NXN and in the case of Barbara QXQ, Aristotle uses the locution 'C is under B' to indicate that the minor premiss posits a subclass of B (the locution is neutral as to what that subclass is), and hence that the *dictum de omni* can be applied in order to *justify* the perfect syllogism.

(*b*) *The remaining cases*

Let us take as representative examples Cesare NXN and Darapti NXN. The premisses of Cesare NXN are Ae$_N$B and Aa$_X$C. 'Now since the privative proposition converts, it is also not possible for B to belong to any A; but A belongs to every C, so that it is not possible for B to belong to any C, for C is under A [τὸ γὰρ Γ ὑπὸ τὸ A ἐστι]' (1. 10, 30^{b}11–13). This is Aristotle's first example of a fully worked-out proof for an imperfect modal syllogism, and he is keen to show his method fully. He converts the privative proposition Ae$_N$B to get Be$_N$A and then states that the conclusion will follow, because 'C is under A'. Why does he do that? He could have just said 'then we use Celarent NXN, which has already been shown' (as indeed it was at 1. 9, 30^{a}21–3); then he could have kept the minor premiss of Cesare NXN as Aa$_X$C without rewriting it as 'C is under A'. But he does not do this, because he wants to show that once you have converted the major premiss of Cesare NXN, you can apply the *dictum* (in this case the *dictum de nullo*) to validate the syllogism. So he states that once we have converted Ae$_N$B to get Be$_N$A, we can get the conclusion, Be$_N$C, *since* the minor premiss posits that 'C is under A'. If the rephrasing of Aa$_X$C as 'C is under A' has explanatory value, then that is because it indicates that a subclass of the subject term (A) of the major premiss is in the offing, and the conditions are ripe for the *dictum de nullo* to be applied.

As our second example, let us look at Darapti NXN. Its

What is a Perfect Syllogism? 153

premisses are Aa$_N$C and Ba$_X$C. 'Now since B belongs to every C, C will also belong to some B, since the universal premiss converts to the particular. Hence if A belongs to every C of necessity and C belongs to some B, it is also necessary for A to belong to some B, for B is under C, so the first figure comes about' (1. 11, 30^{b}26–30). Aristotle converts Ba$_X$C to Ci$_X$B and then states that the conclusion, Ai$_N$B, will follow *since* B is under C. Once again, if the rephrasing of Ci$_X$B as 'B is under C' is to help explain why Ai$_N$B follows, that can only be because it indicates that we can apply the *dictum de omni* to the premisses that we have before us.

The upshot, then, is that Aristotle uses the locution 'C is under B' (or whatever the appropriate letters are) to indicate when the *dictum de omni et nullo* can be applied. It is a justificatory device; in rewriting the relevant premiss using this locution, Aristotle is *explaining* that a conclusion follows from a pair of premisses because they fit the conditions of the *dictum de omni et nullo*. He uses this device both when directly verifying that the premisses of perfect syllogisms entail their conclusion, and when verifying that the converted premisses of an imperfect syllogism entail the target conclusion (also through a perfect syllogism). In other words, Aristotle only ever employs the locution 'C is under B' when justifying why the premisses of a perfect syllogism entail their conclusion, and I have hypothesized that the locution is supposed to call to mind the *dictum de omni et nullo*. The locution is supposed to cover cases of both Ba$_X$C and Bi$_X$C, thus confirming my contention that Aristotle thought of the *dictum* as applicable both in the case where the minor premiss is an a-proposition and in the case where the minor premiss is an i-proposition.

So far, I have told a story about why the *dictum* does not use quantificational vocabulary in describing the minor premiss of a syllogism: the answer is that it needs to describe with sufficient generality two different cases where a subclass of the subject has been posited, namely the cases where the minor premiss is expressed using a-predication and i-predication. A similar explanation holds for why Aristotle does not describe the conclusion of the inference in the *dictum* with quantificational vocabulary: he needs to keep the description of the conclusion general enough to cover a- and i-predication in the case of the *dictum de omni*, and e- and o-predication in the case of the *dictum de nullo*. The important point concerns the *generality* of the descriptions: the *dictum* gets its explanatory force from the fact that it enshrines a *general* principle concerning a-predication and its interaction with a- and i-predications, and a *general* principle concerning e-predication and its interaction with a- and i-predications.

6. Objection: texts which suggest the prevailing interpretation of what a perfect syllogism is

Patzig, you will recall, thought that perfect syllogisms were just the evident ones, the ones for which it is clear that the conclusion follows from the premisses (or, if you prefer, ones such that if the premisses hold, it is clear that the conclusion must hold). He cites two texts as evidence for this;[66] both are in the modal syllogistic. I shall look at them both, and also examine another text which seems to support the same view. All are relatively easy to deal with.

(1) At 1. 15, $33^{b}33$–6, Aristotle explains why it is that there are perfect QXQ syllogisms:

For let A possibly belong to every B and let B be posited to belong to every C. Now since [ἐπεί] C is under B and A possibly belongs to every B, it is evident [φανερόν] that it also possibly belongs to every C; so [δή] a perfect syllogism comes about.

This is the justification of Barbara QXQ, which we have already looked at above (it contains the 'under' locution). Now, it is true that Aristotle produces some reasoning of the form 'since X and Y, it is clear that Z' (where Z is the conclusion of the syllogism with X and Y as premisses), and immediately goes on to infer that the syllogism is perfect. This has given the impression that the basis for Aristotle's inference that the syllogism is perfect is that the conclusion of the syllogism has just been said to follow *clearly* from the premisses.[67] And this is not the only text where Aristotle seems to do this:

(2) 1. 9, $30^{a}15$–23

συμβαίνει δέ ποτε καὶ τῆς ἑτέρας προτάσεως ἀναγ- $30^{a}15$
καίας οὔσης ἀναγκαῖον γίνεσθαι τὸν συλλογισμόν, πλὴν οὐχ

---

[66] Patzig, *Theory*, 84 n. 6. His two texts are texts (1) and (3) below.
[67] See also Ebert and Nortmann, *Buch I*, 293–4.

What is a Perfect Syllogism? 155

ὁποτέρας ἔτυχεν, ἀλλὰ τῆς πρὸς τὸ μεῖζον ἄκρον, οἷον εἰ τὸ
μὲν A τῷ B ἐξ ἀνάγκης εἴληπται ὑπάρχον ἢ μὴ ὑπάρχον,
τὸ δὲ B τῷ Γ ὑπάρχον μόνον· οὕτως γὰρ εἰλημμένων τῶν
προτάσεων ἐξ ἀνάγκης τὸ A τῷ Γ ὑπάρξει ἢ οὐχ ὑπάρξει.   30ᵃ20
ἐπεὶ γὰρ παντὶ τῷ B ἐξ ἀνάγκης ὑπάρχει ἢ οὐχ ὑπάρχει
τὸ A, τὸ δὲ Γ τι τῶν B ἐστί, φανερὸν ὅτι καὶ τῷ Γ ἐξ ἀνάγκης ἔσται θάτερον τούτων.

It sometimes results that the syllogism becomes necessary when only one of the propositions is necessary (not whatever proposition it might be, however, but only the proposition in relation to the major extreme). For instance, if A has been taken to belong or not to belong of necessity in this way, then A will belong or not belong to C of necessity. For since A belongs or does not belong to all of B of necessity, but C is something of the Bs, it is clear that one or the other of these will also apply to C of necessity. (trans. Striker, lightly adapted)

This is also a text we have seen previously (it is the justification of Barbara NXN): the feature of this text that caught my attention above and which became the basis of my interpretation of Aristotle's employment of the *dictum de omni et nullo* is the locution 'C is something of the Bs'. But the feature of this text that will catch the eye of the interpreter who thinks that self-evidence is the criterion for perfection is that in the last sentence Aristotle once again produces a phrase of the form 'since X and Y, it is clear that Z', where X and Y are the premisses and Z the conclusion of a syllogism. Those who espouse the orthodox view will conclude that Aristotle is telling us that the conclusion *clearly* follows from the premisses in order that we see that the syllogism is evident and therefore perfect.[68]

But texts (1) and (2) do not seem to me decisive. For a start, in both cases Aristotle is explaining why the conclusion follows from the premisses—that is the force of the 'since' in both cases. And in *both* those explanations Aristotle employs tell-tale locutions signalling application of the *dictum*: τὸ δὲ Γ τι τῶν B ἐστι at 1. 9, 30ᵃ22, and ὑπὸ τὸ B ἐστι τὸ Γ at 1. 15, 33ᵇ34–5. Second, as we have already seen, Aristotle does not consider it a sufficient condition for a syllogism to be perfect that it is clear its conclusion follows from its premisses. We looked above in detail (Section 1(*c*): '*What about imperfect syllogisms?*') at the case of Camestres at 1. 5, 27ᵃ15–16, where Aristotle finishes his discussion by saying expli-

[68] So, for instance, Striker: 'Barbara NXN and Celarent NXN are evidently valid and therefore perfect moods' (*Book I*, 116).

citly that although it is clear that Camestres' conclusion follows from its premises, that does not make it *perfect*. But in these two texts, just as with Camestres, Aristotle engages in an explanation of why the conclusion follows from the premises, and states that it is clear that the conclusion is such-and-such. In other words, we have in texts (1) and (2) a standard case of *conditional* clarity: something becomes clear *in the light of* an explanation. The reason why Aristotle concludes that Barbara QXQ is perfect in text (1), and the reason why Barbara NXN, described in text (2), is perfect, is that *what it took* to make it clear that their conclusions follow from their premises—*what it took* to explain why their conclusions follow from their premises—is an application of the *dictum de omni et nullo* alone, signalled by the locutions 'C is something of the Bs' and 'C is under B'. So it is easy enough to explain why Aristotle says what he says in texts (1) and (2) without having recourse to the orthodox view.

(3) The third text is 1. 14, 33^a27–34:

And when the particular premiss is taken as privative, the universal one as affirmative, and they are in the same position (that is, it is possible for A to belong to every B and for B not to belong to some C), then an evident syllogism does not come about through the premises as taken, but when the particular premiss is converted and it is assumed that B possibly belongs to some C, there will be the same conclusion as before, just as in the cases with which we began.

The logical result referred to here is the validity of the first-figure syllogism aoi-QQQ. (It does not have a name because the corresponding assertoric version is not a syllogism.) This syllogism is one of those interesting cases of a first-figure (modal) syllogism which is *not* perfect. Aristotle tells us that with our premises Aa_QB and Bo_QC 'an evident syllogism does not come about through the premises as taken'. Rather, to prove it, one must 'convert'[69] the particular premiss Bo_QC to Bi_QC to get Darii-QQQ. The implication is that this syllogism is not perfect, in contrast to the perfect syllogisms which Aristotle had outlined in the immediately preceding lines, 33^a21–7 (Darii-QQQ and Ferio-QQQ).

Now, defenders of the orthodox interpretation of perfection leap

[69] As Ross points out ad loc., this is not a reference to conversion 'in the ordinary sense' but to a kind of conversion not involving the reversal of the order of the terms, described at 1. 13, 32^a29–$^b1$.

What is a Perfect Syllogism? 157

upon Aristotle's reference to an 'evident syllogism' (φανερὸς συλλογισμός) as evidence that Aristotle did indeed recognize a class of syllogisms as 'evident', and claim that these are the perfect syllogisms. Needless to say, I think this is too hasty. We need to pay attention to the whole phrase that Aristotle uses: he says that when we look at the premisses of aoi-QQQ, 'an evident syllogism *does not come about through the premisses as taken*' (διὰ μὲν τῶν εἰλημμένων προτάσεων οὐ γίνεται φανερὸς συλλογισμός). In other words, the key for Aristotle is that those premisses *alone* cannot serve to make evident the necessity of the conclusion. He is not merely saying that a clear syllogism does not come about; he is saying that a clear syllogism does not come about *through the premisses alone*. Aristotle seems to be deliberately recalling the wording of his definition of a perfect syllogism, where he says that a perfect syllogism is one which needs nothing in addition to the premisses (παρὰ τὰ εἰλημμένα) for the necessity (of the conclusion's following from the premisses) to become clear (πρὸς τὸ φανῆναι τὸ ἀναγκαῖον). So in other words, this text actually goes some way towards *validating* the hypothesis of this paper, that a perfect syllogism is one whose necessity becomes clear through an explanation making reference only to the premisses of the argument, i.e. through a single application of the logical principles enshrined in the *dictum de omni et nullo*.

7. What does *teleios* mean, and why designate a class of *teleioi* syllogisms?

Why does Aristotle have perfect syllogisms in his logic? What role do they play? And what does it really mean to call them *teleios*— how should we translate the term? I have already claimed that perfect syllogisms are the basic syllogisms of the system, the ones with reference to which the validity of all other syllogisms will be explained. I acknowledged that they are *in some ways* like principles or axioms of the syllogistic system (with the proviso that since syllogisms are arguments, not statements, they cannot be axioms or principles in the strict sense of the term). So much is scholarly orthodoxy about the role of the perfect syllogisms. In the systems of

Corcoran,[70] Smiley,[71] and Smith,[72] the four perfect assertoric syllogisms are taken as primitive rules of inference (and are therefore like axioms in being taken as part of the basic description of the system). The other logical machinery postulated by Aristotle would be the conversion rules, and reductio.

In the light of the interpretation that I have proposed in this paper, it is no longer true to say that the perfect syllogisms are like the axioms of the system. First, they are derivable from the *dictum de omni et nullo*, which is one of the inference rules of the system, so they receive a proof within the system, and hence are not axioms. (So in this sense, there is something prior to them within the system, and hence they are not primary explanatory items.) Second, we should have been suspicious anyway of the claim that the perfect syllogisms are like axioms, because if Aristotle's desire in carving out the class of perfect syllogisms was to isolate the basic assumptions of the system, we need to confront the fact that in 1. 7 he actually shows that one can *derive* assertoric Darii and Ferio from the set consisting of Barbara and Celarent (together with the apparatus of reductio and conversion). Aristotle nonetheless still affirms that Darii and Ferio are perfect, for after showing that the second figure can be derived from Barbara and Celarent, he says that 'those in the first figure—the particular ones [i.e. Darii and Ferio]—are perfected even through themselves [ἐπιτελοῦνται μὲν καὶ δι' αὑτῶν], but one can also prove them through the second figure by reduction to the impossible' (1. 7, 29^{b}6–8, trans. Striker). The reference to perfecting Darii and Ferio through themselves echoes what Aristotle said at the end of 1. 4 and his presentation of the four perfect syllogisms of the first figure: they are all perfect, 'for they are all perfected through the initial assumptions' (πάντες γὰρ ἐπιτελοῦνται διὰ τῶν ἐξ ἀρχῆς ληφθέντων, 1. 4, 26^{b}30). That text from 1. 4 tells us that being perfected through the initial assumptions is sufficient for being perfect, so in 1. 7 Aristotle is not dropping the idea that Darii and Ferio are perfect, even though they are derivable from Barbara and Celarent. The fact that Aristotle persists in thinking of Darii and Ferio as perfect, despite this derivability from the other two perfect syllogisms, shows that if he was interested in identifying the perfect

---

[70] J. Corcoran, 'Completeness of an Ancient Logic', *Journal of Symbolic Logic*, 37 (1972), 696–702.
[71] T. Smiley, 'What is a Syllogism?', *Journal of Philosophical Logic*, 2 (1973), 136–54.   [72] Smith, *Prior*, xx.

syllogisms as the minimal axiomatic base of the system, he did a pretty bad job, since he himself knew that one could take just two of the four perfect syllogisms and derive all the other syllogisms from them. In other words, there is more to being perfect than being a member of the minimal logical base from which to develop the entire system. I have tried to isolate what that missing ingredient is: it is that perfect syllogisms are directly validated by the *dictum de omni et nullo*.

There is a parallel result in the modal syllogistic: the NNN perfect syllogisms could have been proven on the basis of the NXN perfect syllogisms, and the QNQ ones on the basis of the QXQ (since N propositions entail their assertoric counterparts). But again, Aristotle does not want to *downgrade* the derivable perfect syllogisms; he is quite clear that Barbara, Celarent, Darii, and Ferio QNQ are all perfect (1. 16, 35^{b}23–6), and all commentators agree that those same four NNN forms are perfect too, despite Aristotle's silence on the matter (see n. 26 above). So again, this suggests that he has something else in mind when calling syllogisms perfect other than their aptness for being a *minimal* base for a logical system.

What, then, *is* the logical property that Aristotle is aiming at in calling these syllogisms perfect? He does not mean that they are the minimal (quasi-)axiomatic base. This paper has put forward a different view. I have argued that the *dictum de omni et nullo* is a pair of rules of inference:

> (*Dictum de omni*) Given as a premiss AaB, whenever you have another premiss which postulates a subclass of B, it necessarily follows that A is said of that subclass.

> (*Dictum de nullo*) Given as a premiss AeB, whenever you have another premiss which postulates a subclass of B, it necessarily follows that A is not said of that subclass.

These rules immediately validate Barbara, Celarent, Darii, and Ferio. So those syllogisms (or better: arguments of those forms) are immediately validated by the *dictum*. Arguments of those forms are shown to be valid by a single application of the *dictum*. Nothing else is needed to show their validity. They are the primitive valid *arguments* delivered by the system. So in my understanding of Aristotle's system, arguments in those forms are not *presupposed* to be valid; the system *shows* them to be valid by appealing to the *dictum*. Those primitive valid arguments then become fodder, so to speak, for proving any other argument to be valid, which we do using the tools of conversion and reductio. So the perfect syllogisms are the basic or primitive *syllogisms*, without being primitives of the system *tout court*.

The importance of the perfect syllogisms can be brought out in another way. On the interpretation I have been pressing, the rules of inference in the system of Aristotelian logic are the *dictum de omni et nullo*, conversion, and reductio. But the tools of conversion and reductio are used to show an argument to be valid *only if you can refer to some other valid argument in the course of using them*. The rule underwriting Aristotle's conversion proofs is something like this: 'If W converts to X, then *if* "{X, Y} therefore Z" is a syllogism, "{W, Y} therefore Z" is a syllogism.' The rule underwriting Aristotle's reductio proofs goes something like this (where 'ϕ^*' means 'the contradictory proposition to ϕ': '*If* "{Y, Z} therefore X*" is a syllogism, then "{X, Y} therefore Z*" is a syllogism.' I have italicized the conditions showing that these two rules can be applied only if one has *antecedently* identified some syllogisms. The *dictum*, on the other hand, unlike conversion and reductio, actually delivers you a conclusion when presented only with *propositions*. So the arguments validated immediately by the *dictum* have a special status: they are the arguments pronounced to be valid by the only rule in the system which validates an argument by looking only at the relationship between its premises and its conclusion (rather than by looking at the relationship between that argument *and some other argument*). This, I want to say, is what it is for a syllogism to be perfect: it is for it to be immediately or primitively validated by those rules of inference which actually generate syllogisms out of premises alone, i.e. (in this system) the *dictum de omni et nullo*.

Does this mean that different syllogisms would be ruled perfect if the system had been configured differently?[73] The answer is yes. This is not surprising if one reflects on the way the definitions of perfection and imperfection are set out: a perfect syllogism is one the explanation of whose validity uses only its premises, whereas an imperfect syllogism is one the explanation of whose validity uses its premises plus other propositions which feature as premises in

[73] I am grateful to Christopher Roser for raising this question.

other syllogisms. Explanation is relative to a system; an explanation or proof of validity in a logical system uses as its constituents the basic rules and assumptions of that system. But does that mean that it is *arbitrary* which syllogisms count as perfect for Aristotle? That will depend on whether one thinks it is arbitrary which principles Aristotle chose for his logic. I can only touch on this subject here, but there are certainly reasons for thinking his choice is not arbitrary. For Aristotle obviously did think that the *dictum de omni et nullo* answers the question 'What is a- and e-predication?', since he announces at the start of *Prior Analytics* 1. 1 that he will be telling us what a- and e-predication are ($24^a 11$–15), and he presumably takes himself to be telling us just those logical properties of those predications sufficient for the kind of logic that he wants to construct, namely a logic suitable for scientific demonstration (*Pr. An.* 1. 1, $24^a 10$–11). And it stands to reason that Aristotle wanted a pair of principles governing the logical behaviour of *predications*, since (or so he thinks) propositions are a matter of one thing being predicated of another (*Pr. An.* 1. 1, $24^a 16$–17), and since the suitability of a proposition's inclusion in a science will be determined by the relation its subject and predicate bear to one another, viz. whether the predicate is predicated of the subject 'in itself' (*Post. An.* 1. 4). So one can come up with reasons why Aristotle chose to construct his system in just the way he did, with a pair of principles governing the logical behaviour of a- and e-predications. As for why he chose those two principles about a- and e-predication, it is important to observe that he structured them in an entirely parallel way to each other, so that Aristotle does not even feel the need to spell out the *dictum de nullo*, just writing instead 'similarly for predicated of none' ($24^a 30$) after giving the *dictum de omni*. (We saw before that this involves dropping a negation from the *dictum de omni*.) The structural similarity of the two principles certainly contributes to the impression that we are at the most basic of explanatory levels for these two predications.

In the light of this investigation, what would be a good translation of *teleios*? The usual translation is 'perfect' (to contrast with 'imperfect'), although some translators prefer 'complete' (to contrast with 'incomplete'). Both translations suffer from the same problem. 'Perfect' and 'complete' are attributive adjectives; to be perfect or to be complete is to be a perfect *such-and-such*, or a complete *such-and-such*. But in our case, the noun to supply with 'perfect' must be 'syllogism'; it is *syllogisms* which are said to be perfect (cf. 1. 4, 24^{b}22–3: 'I call a syllogism perfect when . . .'). The problem, though, is that syllogisms which are not *teleios* have nothing imperfect or incomplete about them *as far as being a syllogism goes*. As we have seen, Aristotle understands the property of being *teleios* as being a property which tells us something about the *explanation* of why a given argument (*logos*) counts as a syllogism, rather than whether the argument (*logos*) is a syllogism.[74]

So what might a better translation of *teleios* be? An instructive analogy can be made with Aristotle's description of certain actions or goods as *teleios*. Cooper glosses the notion thus: 'a good that is unqualifiedly τέλειον is such that it really is in the strongest possible way an *end* of action: it is always choiceworthy for itself, as ends must be, *and* in being choiceworthy it is never referred in any way to anything else'.[75] So a good is *teleios* when it most fully meets the description of being an end, namely by not also being for the sake of something *else*. It is the reference here to something *else* in the gloss of *teleios* that is suggestive for us. For when we bear in mind that the 'for the sake of' relation is an explanatory relation, we could generalize Cooper's gloss as follows: for something to be a *teleios* F is for the explanation of why it is an F not to refer to something else's being F. In explaining why a *teleios* good is good, we do not need to make reference to any good other than it: it is something which is done or sought for its own sake and not for the sake of anything else. Similarly, it seems to me, a *teleios* syllogism is one where the explanation of why it counts as a syllogism (why its conclusion follows of necessity from its premisses because of their being so) makes no reference to any syllogism other than it; or to put it another way, even closer to the way Aristotle actually puts it: the explanation for why it is a syllogism does not need to make a detour through any other proposition serving as a premiss for a *different* syllogism. So, the feature of the meaning of the word *teleios* which Aristotle seizes upon in using the term for perfect syllogisms is that for something

---

[74] In a recent paper, Barnes translates the terms as 'finished' and 'unfinished' (J. Barnes, 'Boethus and Finished Syllogisms', in Mi-Kyoung Lee (ed.), *Strategies of Argument: Essays in Ancient Ethics, Epistemology, and Logic* (New York, 2014), 175–98); these translations suffer from the same problem.

[75] J. M. Cooper, 'Plato and Aristotle on "Finality" and "(Self-)Sufficiency"', in R. Heinaman (ed.), *Plato and Aristotle's Ethics* (London, 2003), 117–47; repr. in Cooper, *Knowledge, Nature, and the Good* (Princeton, 2004), 270–308. The quotation in the text comes from p. 280 of the reprint.

What is a Perfect Syllogism? 163

to be a *teleios* F is for the explanation of why it is an F not to refer to something else's being F.[76]

To capture the idea that being a *teleios* good or a *teleios* syllogism is a matter of having an explanation of a certain sort, one might think of rendering *teleios* as 'self-explanatory' or 'self-supporting' or 'self-dependent'. ('Self-sufficient' will not do, because we already have an Aristotelian word in the *Ethics* for that, namely *autarkēs*, which denotes a different property.)[77] But there is still something unsatisfactory about the translation 'self-explanatory', semantically speaking: the word *teleios* does not have (as, for instance, *autarkēs* does) a part corresponding to the prefix 'self-'. So one could bite the bullet and translate *teleios*, as Cooper does, by 'final'. *Final* syllogisms would be those which are explanatorily final: they do not need any syllogism outside of themselves for their validity to be explained. The explanation of why they are syllogisms makes no reference to any other syllogism. Non-final syllogisms, on the other hand, require reference to other syllogisms when they have their validity explained.[78]

In the light of this translation, we can revisit the question of what to make of Aristotle's frequent employment of verbs usually translated 'to perfect', *teleioun* and *epitelein*. When Aristotle talks of 'perfecting' a syllogism, it is sometimes in the context of talking of perfecting a syllogism which is already perfect (we have seen a couple of those texts already), and sometimes of perfecting a syllogism which is not perfect. Both uses can strike one as odd. The perfect syllogisms are already perfect and so it makes little sense that there should be such a thing as *perfecting* them, whereas the imperfect syllogisms are imperfect once and for all, so it makes little sense that there should be such a thing as perfecting *them*. Now, perfecting is not the focus of this paper,[79] but the translation I have just offered

---

[76] I am grateful to Emily Perry for help with some of the formulations of this paragraph.

[77] εὐδαιμονία is self-sufficient because its presence alone in a life suffices to explain why that life is choiceworthy.

[78] Gabriel Richardson Lear points out to me one important disanalogy between Aristotle's use of the word *teleios* in relation to actions and in relation to syllogisms. As applied to actions, the adjective *teleios* is clearly supposed to be cognate with the noun τέλος ('end' or 'goal'): as Cooper put it in the passage I quoted in the text, 'a good that is unqualifiedly τέλειον is such that it really is in the strongest possible way an *end* of action' (his emphasis). There is no such connection with the noun in the case of syllogisms, at least not on my interpretation.

[79] G. Striker, 'Perfection and Reduction in Aristotle's *Prior Analytics*', in M.

for *teleios* makes available for those verbs the neat translation 'to finalize'. To *finalize* a syllogism means to make its validity evident, to explain why it counts as a syllogism—the very activity which is put front and centre in the definitions of finality and non-finality (perfection and imperfection). In those cases where you can finalize a syllogism using only its premisses (i.e. by an application of the *dictum de omni et nullo* alone), you have a final syllogism. In those cases where you need to bring in other propositions, and hence other syllogisms, you have a non-final syllogism.

The thesis of this paper does not stand or fall with one's acceptance of this or that translation of *teleios*. Rather, the thesis of this paper is that the *final* or *perfect* syllogisms were not conceived of by Aristotle as being the evident or obvious syllogisms, but rather the ones which were immediately delivered by the only rule of inference of his system which generates syllogisms out of propositions alone, namely the *dictum de omni et nullo*.

Princeton University
Humboldt-Universität zu Berlin

BIBLIOGRAPHY

Barnes, J., *Aristotle:* Posterior Analytics, translated with an introduction and commentary, 2nd edn. (Clarendon Aristotle Series; Oxford, 1994).
Barnes, J., 'Boethus and Finished Syllogisms', in Mi-Kyoung Lee (ed.), *Strategies of Argument: Essays in Ancient Ethics, Epistemology, and Logic* (New York, 2014), 175–98.
Barnes, J., 'Proof Destroyed', in Schofield, Burnyeat, and Barnes (eds.), *Doubt and Dogmatism*, 161–81.
Barnes, J., *Truth etc.* [*Truth*] (Oxford, 2007).
Barnes, J., et al. (trans.), *Alexander of Aphrodisias: On Aristotle,* Prior Analytics *1. 1–7* (Ancient Commentators on Aristotle; London, 1991).
Brunschwig, J., 'Proof Defined', in Schofield, Burnyeat, and Barnes (eds.), *Doubt and Dogmatism*, 125–60.
Cooper, J. M., 'Plato and Aristotle on "Finality" and "(Self-)Sufficiency"', in R. Heinaman (ed.), *Plato and Aristotle's Ethics* (London, 2003), 117–47; repr. in Cooper, *Knowledge, Nature, and the Good* (Princeton, 2004), 270–308 [references are to the reprint].
Frede and G. Striker (eds.), *Rationality in Greek Thought* (Oxford, 1996), 203–19, is a recent classic text on the issue.

Cooper, J. M., with Hutchinson, D. H. (ed.), *Plato: Complete Works* (Indianapolis and Cambridge, 1997).

Corcoran, J., 'Completeness of an Ancient Logic', *Journal of Symbolic Logic*, 37 (1972), 696–702.

Crivelli, P., and Charles, D., '"Πρότασις" in Aristotle's *Prior Analytics*', *Phronesis*, 56 (2011), 193–203.

Ebert, T., 'Was ist ein vollkommener Syllogismus des Aristoteles?', *Archiv für Geschichte der Philosophie*, 77 (1995), 221–47.

Ebert, T., and Nortmann, U., *Aristoteles: Analytica Priora Buch I*, übersetzt und erläutert [*Buch I*] (Aristoteles: Werke in deutscher Übersetzung, 3.I/1; Berlin, 2007).

Enderton, H. B., *A Mathematical Introduction to Logic* (San Diego, 1972).

Joachim, H. H., *Aristotle: On Coming-to-Be and Passing-Away* (De generatione et corruptione), a revised text with introduction and commentary (Oxford, 1922).

Lear, J., *Aristotle and Logical Theory* [*Logical*] (Cambridge, 1980).

Łukasiewicz, J., *Aristotle's Syllogistic from the Standpoint of Modern Formal Logic* [*Syllogistic*] (Oxford, 1951).

Malink, M., *Aristotle's Modal Syllogistic* [*Modal*] (Cambridge, Mass., 2013).

Malink, M., 'Τῷ vs. τῶν in *Prior Analytics* 1. 1–22' ['Text'], *Classical Quarterly*, NS 58 (2008), 519–36.

Malink, M., and Rosen, J., 'Proof by Assumption of the Possible in *Prior Analytics* I. 15', *Mind* (forthcoming).

Mignucci, M., 'Syllogism and Deduction in Aristotle's Logic', in M. Canto-Sperber and P. Pellegrin (eds.), *Le Style de la pensée: recueil de textes en hommage à J. Brunschwig* (Paris, 2002), 244–66.

Morison, B., 'Aristotle etc.' ['Notes'], *Phronesis*, 53 (2008), 209–22.

Morison, B., 'What was Aristotle's Concept of Logical Form?', in B. Morison and K. Ierodiakonou (eds.), *Episteme etc.: Essays in Honour of Jonathan Barnes* (Oxford, 2012), 172–88.

Mueller, I., and Gould, J. (trans.), *Alexander of Aphrodisias: On Aristotle, Prior Analytics 1. 8–13* (Ancient Commentators on Aristotle; London, 1999).

Patzig, G., *Die Aristotelische Syllogistik: Logisch-philologische Untersuchungen über das Buch A der 'Ersten Analytiken'*, 2nd edn. (Göttingen, 1963); trans. J. Barnes as *Aristotle's Theory of the Syllogism: A Logico-Philological Study of Book A of the Prior Analytics* [*Theory*] (Dordrecht, 1968).

Ross, W. D., *Aristotle's Prior and Posterior Analytics: A Revised Text with Introduction and Commentary* (Oxford, 1949).

Schofield, M., Burnyeat, M., and Barnes, J. (eds.), *Doubt and Dogmatism: Studies in Hellenistic Epistemology* (Oxford, 1980).

Smiley, T., 'What is a Syllogism?', *Journal of Philosophical Logic*, 2 (1973), 136–54.
Smith, R., *Aristotle:* Prior Analytics [*Prior*] (Indianapolis, 1989).
Striker, G., *Aristotle:* Prior Analytics *Book I* [*Book I*], translated with an introduction and commentary (Clarendon Aristotle Series; Oxford, 2009).
Striker, G., 'Perfection and Reduction in Aristotle's *Prior Analytics*', in M. Frede and G. Striker (eds.), *Rationality in Greek Thought* (Oxford, 1996), 203–19.

TRUTH IN *METAPHYSICS* E 4

PAOLO CRIVELLI

Two chapters of Aristotle's *Metaphysics*, E 4 and Θ 10, discuss truth and a use of the verb 'to be' associated with it. The relationship between these two chapters is problematic because despite an apparent cross-reference connecting them, they seem to put forward incompatible views.

This study argues that (contrary to appearances and to what some commentators believe) E 4 agrees with Θ 10. One of the assumptions on which the reconciliation relies is that when 'to be' is employed in accordance with the use associated with truth, it applies to external things but neither to thoughts nor to sentences (to both of which, however, 'true' applies). This sheds a novel light on E 4, which turns out to make claims rather different from those which commentators have taken it to defend.

1. Background

Metaphysics E 4 in its context

In *Metaphysics* E 1 Aristotle announces an investigation of 'the principles and the causes of beings . . . *qua* beings' (1025^b3–4). At the beginning of E 2 (1026^a33–$^b2$) he distinguishes four uses[1] or groups of uses of 'to be': (1) the accidental use, (2) a use associated with truth, (3) the uses that correspond to the categories, and (4) the uses corresponding to potentiality and actuality.[2] He wants to show

© Paolo Crivelli 2015

I would like to thank Oliver Primavesi for allowing me to inspect the provisional and as yet unpublished collation of *Metaphysics* E 4 and Θ 10 prepared by the team directed by him: this enabled me to take account of the readings of C (Taurinensis B. VII. 23), M (Ambrosianus F 113 sup.), E^s (Escorialensis Y. III. 18), and V^d (Vaticanus gr. 255). Drafts of this study were presented in Neuchâtel, Paris, Lisbon, Oxford, and Geneva. I am grateful to the audiences for many useful questions and comments. The responsibility for the remaining deficiencies is mine alone.

[1] I employ 'use' in a deliberately vague way. I take no position on the question whether the uses singled out by Aristotle fix corresponding senses or meanings.

[2] Cf. *Metaph*. Δ 7, 1017^a7–$^b9$. Elsewhere Aristotle distinguishes three (groups of) uses of 'to be': cf. *Metaph*. Θ 10, 1051^a34–$^b2$; Λ 2, 1069^b26–8; N 2, 1089^a26–

that the first two uses may be left aside. He turns immediately to establishing this result: the rest of *E* 2 and the whole of *E* 3 deal with the accidental use, while *E* 4 addresses the use associated with truth. Here is *E* 4:

[T1] περὶ μὲν οὖν τοῦ κατὰ συμβεβηκὸς ὄντος ἀφείσθω 1027[b]17
(διώρισται γὰρ ἱκανῶς)· τὸ δὲ ὡς ἀληθὲς ὄν, καὶ μὴ ὂν ὡς
ψεῦδος, ἐπειδὴ παρὰ σύνθεσίν[3] ἐστι καὶ διαίρεσιν, τὸ δὲ σύνο-
λον περὶ μερισμὸν ἀντιφάσεως, τὸ μὲν γὰρ ἀληθὲς τὴν [b]20
κατάφασιν ἐπὶ τῷ συγκειμένῳ ἔχει τὴν δ' ἀπόφασιν ἐπὶ
τῷ διῃρημένῳ, τὸ δὲ ψεῦδος τούτου τοῦ μερισμοῦ τὴν ἀντίφα-
σιν (πῶς δὲ τὸ ἅμα ἢ τὸ χωρὶς νοεῖν συμβαίνει, ἄλλος
λόγος, λέγω δὲ τὸ ἅμα καὶ τὸ χωρὶς ὥστε μὴ τὸ ἐφεξῆς
ἀλλ' ἕν τι γίγνεσθαι), οὐ γάρ ἐστι τὸ ψεῦδος καὶ τὸ ἀληθὲς [b]25
ἐν τοῖς πράγμασιν,[4] οἷον τὸ μὲν ἀγαθὸν ἀληθὲς τὸ δὲ κα-
κὸν εὐθὺς ψεῦδος, ἀλλ' ἐν διανοίᾳ, περὶ δὲ τὰ ἁπλᾶ καὶ
τὰ τί ἐστιν οὐδ' ἐν διανοίᾳ—ὅσα μὲν οὖν δεῖ θεωρῆσαι περὶ
τὸ οὕτως ὂν καὶ μὴ ὄν, ὕστερον ἐπισκεπτέον· ἐπεὶ δὲ ἡ συμ-
πλοκή ἐστιν καὶ ἡ διαίρεσις ἐν διανοίᾳ ἀλλ' οὐκ ἐν τοῖς [b]30
πράγμασι, τὸ δ' οὕτως ὂν ἕτερον ὂν τῶν κυρίως[5] (ἢ γὰρ τὸ
τί ἐστιν ἢ ὅτι ποιὸν ἢ ὅτι ποσὸν ἢ εἴ τι ἄλλο[6] συνάπτει ἢ
ἀφαιρεῖ ἡ διάνοια),[7] τὸ μὲν ὡς συμβεβηκὸς καὶ τὸ ὡς ἀληθὲς ὂν ἀφετέον. τὸ γὰρ αἴτιον τοῦ μὲν ἀόριστον τοῦ δὲ τῆς
διανοίας τι πάθος, καὶ ἀμφότερα περὶ τὸ λοιπὸν γένος τοῦ 1028[a]1
ὄντος, καὶ οὐκ ἔξω δηλοῦσιν οὐσάν τινα φύσιν τοῦ ὄντος. διὸ
ταῦτα μὲν ἀφείσθω, σκεπτέον δὲ τοῦ ὄντος αὐτοῦ τὰ αἴτια
καὶ τὰς ἀρχὰς ᾗ ὄν.[8] [a]4

8. Other passages introduce different classifications: cf. *Metaph. Z* 1, 1028[a]10–14; Θ 1, 1045[b]32–4.

[3] I read 'παρὰ σύνθεσιν' with the main manuscripts, ps.-Alexander (*In Metaph.* 456. 31; 457. 20–1, 22, 25–6, 27, 38–9; 458. 4–5 Hayduck), William of Moerbeke, the Aldine edition, Weise, Ross, and Tredennick. Asclepius (*In Metaph.* 373. 32 Hayduck) and more recent manuscripts have 'περὶ σύνθεσιν', the reading printed by Jaeger and other editors.

[4] At 1027[b]19–26 my punctuation differs from those of the editions I consulted.

[5] 'τῶν κυρίως' is the reading of A[b] and M, while J, E, E[s], V[d], and C have 'τῶν κυρίων'. Most editors print 'τῶν κυρίως', whereas the Aldine edition and Weise choose 'τῶν κυρίων'.

[6] I read 'ἢ εἴ τι ἄλλο' with J, E, E[s], William of Moerbeke, and most editions (cf. *E* 2, 1026[a]37); A[b], M, C, Brandis, and Ross read 'ἤ τι ἄλλο'; V[d] reports 'ἢ ὅτι ἄλλο'.

[7] I adopt the reading 'ἀφαιρεῖ ἡ διάνοια', attested unanimously by the main manuscripts and printed by the Aldine edition, Brandis, Bekker, Weise, Schwegler, Ross, and Tredennick. Bonitz, Dübner, Christ, and Jaeger read 'διαιρεῖ ἡ διάνοια' with William of Moerbeke and ps.-Alexander (*In Metaph.* 458. 8–9 Hayduck).

[8] Following recent editors, I omit lines 1028[a]4–6, which are repeated almost literally in their immediate sequel, at the beginning of book *Z* (1028[a]10–11).

Truth in Metaphysics E 4   169

Let us then leave aside what 'is' accidentally: for it has been sufficiently determined. As for what 'is' as true and what 'is not' as false, since they depend on composition and division and together they are concerned with the apportionment of a contradiction, for truth has the affirmation in the case of what is combined and the negation in the case of what is divided, whereas falsehood has the contradiction of this apportionment (how thinking together or separately come about is another question,[9] but I use 'together' and 'separately' in such a way that what comes to be is not a contiguity but a single thing), for falsehood and truth are not in objects, as if the good were true and the bad were immediately false, but in thought, and with regard to simples and essences they are not even in thought—then[10] what needs to be considered about what 'is' and what 'is not' in this way must be investigated later, but since the interweaving and the division are in thought, not in objects, and what 'is' in this way is a different thing that 'is' from those that 'are' strictly (because thought joins or subtracts either the 'what it is' or that it is such-and-such or that it is thus much or something else, whatever it may be), we must leave aside what 'is' accidentally as well as what 'is' as true: for the cause of the former is indeterminate, whereas that of the latter is an affection of thought, and both are about the remaining genus of being and do not reveal an outside nature of being. Given that things are so, let these be left aside and let us consider the causes and the principles of being itself, *qua* being. (*Metaph. E* 4, 1027^{b}17–1028^{a}4)

Truth and falsehood: some Aristotelian tenets

In various works Aristotle ascribes truth and falsehood both to linguistic expressions (specifically, to certain sentences)[11] and to mental states or acts (specifically, to certain thoughts, perceptions, and

[9] Cf. *DA* 1. 3, 407^{a}6–10; 3. 6, 430^{a}26–^{b}6.
[10] The apodosis of the long 'since . . . then' period begins here: cf. [Alex. Aphr.] *In Metaph.* 457. 36–458. 1 Hayduck; *Schol. in Arist.* 739^{a}1–2 Brandis; H. Bonitz, *Observationes criticae in Aristotelis libros metaphysicos* (Berlin, 1842), 33; H. Bonitz (ed. and comm.), *Aristotelis Metaphysica* [*Metaphysica*] (Bonn, 1848–9), ii. 293–4; W. W. Jaeger, *Studien zur Entstehungsgeschichte der Metaphysik des Aristoteles* [*Studien*] (Berlin, 1912), 23; W. D. Ross (ed. and comm.), *Aristotle:* Metaphysics [*Metaphysics*] (Oxford, 1924), i. 365. For οὖν at the beginning of an apodosis see H. Bonitz, *Index Aristotelicus* [*Index*] (Berlin, 1870), 540^{b}12–25. For a long parenthetical passage separating protasis from apodosis see *De int.* 9, 19^{a}7–22. According to A. Schwegler (ed., trans., and comm.), *Aristoteles: Die Metaphysik* [*Metaphysik*] (Tübingen, 1847–8), iv. 29–30, and E. Martineau, 'De l'inauthenticité du livre *E* de la *Métaphysique* d'Aristote' ['Inauthenticité'], *Conférence*, 5 (1997), 443–509 at 493, Aristotle forgets the apodosis (Schwegler suggests that 'ἐπεὶ δέ . . . ἡ διάνοια' at 1027^{b}29–33 is a new protasis with the same meaning as the one whose apodosis is forgotten).

[11] Cf. *Cat.* 5, 4^{a}23–6, 4^{b}8–10; 12, 14^{b}14–22; *De int.* 1, 16^{a}9–18; 4, 17^{a}1–5; 9, 19^{a}33; *SE* 22, 178^{b}24–9; *Metaph.* Θ 10, 1051^{b}13–14.

imaginations).[12] In *Metaphysics* E 4 he says that 'falsehood and truth are . . . in thought' ($1027^{b}25$–7). Thus in E 4 he focuses on truth and falsehood as attributes of thoughts.

In *De interpretatione* Aristotle lays down some theses about true and false linguistic expressions. The main ones are: as far as linguistic expressions are concerned, only sentences (*logoi*) are ever either true or false;[13] sentences of certain kinds (e.g. prayers) are always neither true nor false; every sentence that at any time is either true or false is a declarative sentence (*logos apophantikos*), or (as Aristotle often calls it) a declaration (*apophansis*); declarations of the most important type have a predicative structure and consist of a subject-component (*onoma*) and a predicate-component (*rhēma*); there are two main types of predicative declaration, namely affirmative predicative declaration, or affirmation (*kataphasis*), and negative predicative declaration, or negation (*apophasis*).[14]

Some remarks of Aristotle's imply that there is a kind of thought that plays in the mental sphere a role analogous to that of declaration in the linguistic sphere.[15] Some passages from the *Categories* and *De interpretatione* suggest that he identifies this kind of thought that corresponds to declaration with judgement[16] (*doxa* or *hupolēp-*

[12] For thoughts, cf. *Cat.* 5, $4^{a}26$–8; *De int.* 14, $23^{a}38$; *Post. An.* 1. 33, $88^{b}32$–$89^{a}4$; 2. 19, $100^{b}5$–9; *Top.* 4. 2, $123^{a}15$–19; *SE* 22, $178^{b}24$–9; *DA* 3. 3, $427^{b}20$–1, $428^{a}3$–5, 16–19, $^{b}2$–9; *Metaph.* Θ 10, $1051^{b}13$–14; *NE* 3. 4, $1111^{b}31$–4; 4. 8, $1124^{b}6$; 6. 3, $1139^{b}15$–18; 6. 10, $1142^{b}11$; 7. 10, $1151^{b}3$–4; *EE* 2. 10, $1226^{a}1$–4. For perceptions, cf. *Top.* 2. 4, $111^{a}14$–20; *DA* 2. 6, $418^{a}11$–16; 3. 3, $427^{b}11$–14, $428^{a}3$–4, 11, $^{b}18$–30; 3. 6, $430^{b}29$–30; *De sensu* 4, $442^{b}8$–10; *Metaph.* Γ 5, $1010^{b}2$–3, 14–26. For imaginations, cf. *DA* 3. 3, $428^{a}1$–4, 12, 16–18, $^{b}10$–17.

[13] The English 'sentence' does not match the Greek 'λόγος' as Aristotle uses it in *De interpretatione* because in this work Aristotle sometimes applies 'λόγος' to the *definientia* of definitions (cf. 5, $17^{a}11$–12) and to phrases such as 'beautiful horse' (cf. 2, $16^{a}22$), which are not denoted by 'sentence'. 'Phrase' does not fare better because Aristotle in *De interpretatione* sometimes applies 'λόγος' to sentences (cf. 14, $23^{a}27$–30), which are not denoted by 'phrase'. 'Formula' would perhaps match 'λόγος', but its systematic adoption would sound odd. Despite the mismatch I settle for 'sentence', for two reasons: first, in most cases it yields a translation with the same truth value as the original Greek; secondly, on various occasions Aristotle appears to employ 'λόγος' in a way whereby it refers exclusively to sentences.

[14] Cf. *De int.* 1, $16^{b}9$–18; 2, $16^{a}19$–20; 3, $16^{b}6$–8; 4, $16^{b}33$–$17^{a}4$; 5, $17^{a}8$–12.

[15] Cf. *De insomn.* 1, $458^{b}10$–13; *NE* 6. 10, $1142^{b}12$–15; F. D. Miller, Jr., 'Aristotle on Belief and Knowledge' ['Belief'], in G. Anagnostopoulos and F. D. Miller, Jr. (eds.), *Reason and Analysis in Ancient Greek Philosophy: Essays in Honor of David Keyt* (Dordrecht, 2013), 285–307 at 288.

[16] In *Categories* 5 ($4^{a}23$–8, $^{a}36$–$^{b}2$) Aristotle discusses in parallel sentence (λόγος) and judgement (δόξα) as bearers of truth and falsehood. In *De int.* 14 ($23^{a}27$–39 and $24^{b}1$–7) he treats δόξα as the analogue in the mental sphere of κατάφασις and ἀπόφα-

Truth in Metaphysics *E* 4   171

sis).¹⁷ Since he regards the mental sphere and the linguistic one as isomorphic,¹⁸ one may speculate that Aristotle would aver theses concerning thoughts and judgements that parallel those he accepts for linguistic expressions and declarations: as far as thoughts are concerned, only composite thoughts are ever either true or false (here I use 'composite thought' for whatever thoughts correspond to sentences, which are composite linguistic expressions);¹⁹ composite thoughts of certain kinds (e.g. desires) are always neither true nor false; every composite thought that at any time is either true or false is a judgement; judgements of the most important type have a predicative structure and consist of a subject-component and a predicate-component; there are two main types of predicative judgement, namely affirmative predicative judgement and negative predicative judgement.²⁰

The veridical use of 'to be'

In *E* 4 Aristotle discusses a use of 'to be' associated with truth.²¹ Such a use of 'to be' is attested in Greek. Constructions of two types deserve special mention. First, noun-phrases based on the participles of 'to be' and 'not to be' occur as complements of verbs of saying or thinking, in constructions such as 'to say the things that are', 'to say the things that are not', 'to judge the things that are', 'to judge the things that are not', etc.²² In many such cases, 'to be' is naturally regarded as associated with truth. Secondly, in the literature of the fifth and fourth centuries BC there are dozens of occurrences of the sentence 'These things are' signalling the endorsement of a

---

σις in the linguistic sphere (cf. *NE* 6. 3, 1139ᵇ15–18). Earlier in the same work (5, 17ᵃ8–9) he introduced κατάφασις and ἀπόφασις as two types of λόγος ἀποφαντικός.

¹⁷ In one passage (*DA* 3. 3, 427ᵇ24–6) Aristotle describes δόξα as a special type of ὑπόληψις; in others he uses 'δόξα' and 'ὑπόληψις' as if they were equivalent expressions (cf. Bonitz, *Index*, 800ᵇ5–7; Miller, 'Belief', 302, 305–6).

¹⁸ Cf. B. Hestir, 'Aristotle's Conception of Truth: An Alternative View', *Journal of the History of Philosophy*, 51 (2013), 193–222 at 194–5 and 204–7.

¹⁹ Cf. *De int.* 1, 16ᵃ9–18. On 'sentence' as a rendering of 'λόγος', cf. n. 13 above.

²⁰ Cf. *De int.* 14, 24ᵇ1–2; *NE* 6. 3, 1139ᵇ15–18.

²¹ Cf. *Metaph. Δ* 7, 1017ᵃ31–2. Here and elsewhere I mention English expressions where Greek ones would be appropriate.

²² Cf. Hdt. 5. 50. 2; 5. 106. 4; 7. 209. 1; 9. 11. 3; Plato, *Euthd.* 284 A 5–8, C 2–6; 286 A 2–3; *Crat.* 385 B 10; 429 D 5–6; *Rep.* 3, 389 C 4–5; 413 A 7–8; *Phdr.* 262 B 2–3; *Parm.* 161 E 5–162 A 1; *Theaet.* 167 A 7–8; 171 A 9; 188 D 3–4, 8–10; 189 A 10–B 6; 199 B 8–9; *Soph.* 240 D 9–10; 260 C 3–4; C. H. Kahn, *The Verb 'Be' in Ancient Greek* [*Verb*], 2nd edn. (Indianapolis and Cambridge, Mass., 2003), 349–55.

previous remark,[23] and a few occurrences of 'These things are not' indicating rejection.[24] Within such contexts, 'to be' again seems associated with truth.[25]

In constructions of the first type, the noun-phrases based on the participles of 'to be' and 'not to be' cannot easily be taken to refer to linguistic expressions or mental states or acts. For the position occupied by these noun-phrases is often taken by 'that'-clauses: compare 'to say the things that are' and 'to say the things that are not' with 'to say that the earth is round' and 'to say that the earth is flat'. Although 'that the earth is round', 'that the earth is flat', 'the things that are', and 'the things that are not' are linguistic expressions, they cannot easily be taken to refer to linguistic expressions or mental states or acts when they occur as complements of verbs of saying or thinking: 'Galileo said that the earth is round' and 'Galileo said the things that are' are true, but 'Galileo said a linguistic expression', 'Galileo said a mental state', and 'Galileo said a mental act' are either false or ill-formed (unless 'to say' shifts its meaning and acquires the sense of 'to utter'); similarly, 'Galileo judged that the earth is round' and 'Galileo judged the things that are' are true, but 'Galileo judged a linguistic expression', 'Galileo judged a mental state', and 'Galileo judged a mental act' are either false or ill-formed (unless 'to judge' acquires the sense of 'to pass judgement on').[26] Hence, if the noun-phrases based on the participles of 'to be' and 'not to be' refer to something when they occur as complements of verbs of saying or thinking, what they refer to in such contexts is neither a linguistic expression nor a mental state nor a mental act.

In constructions of the second type, i.e. with the sentences 'These things are' and 'These things are not' expressing endorsement and rejection, the items to which 'to be' and 'not to be' are applied might

---

[23] Cf. And. 1. 14; Plato, *Euthphr.* 7 C 6; *Crito* 43 C 4; 47 B 12; *Phaedo* 65 C 10; 68 D 10; etc.

[24] Cf. Antiphanes fr. 56. 1 Koch; Aristophon fr. 9. 4 Koch; Xen. *Oec.* 19. 17; Isaeus 10. 17; Dem. 8. 45; S. Benardete, 'The Grammar of Being', *Review of Metaphysics*, 30 (1976–7), 486–96 at 487.

[25] According to S. Maurus (trans. and comm.), *Aristotelis opera quae extant omnia* [*Aristotelis opera*] (repr. Paris, 1885–6), iv. 404, the use of 'to be' and 'not to be' associated with truth and falsehood is exemplified in the sentences 'It is' and 'It is not' uttered in answering the question 'Is man an animal or not?'

[26] Cf. M. R. Wheeler, 'A Deflationary Reading of Aristotle's Definitions of Truth and Falsehood at *Metaphysics* 1011^{b}26–7' ['Reading'], *Apeiron*, 44 (2011), 67–90 at 75–83.

be sentences: speakers might be referring to earlier utterances produced by their interlocutors.[27] But such a reading of these constructions is counter-intuitive: speakers are more naturally understood as referring to what has been said by their interlocutors' earlier utterances (rather than the utterances themselves).[28]

E4's promise

In the middle of *Metaphysics* E 4 Aristotle promises to discuss later certain questions about 'what "is" and what "is not" in this way [*to houtōs on kai mē on*]' ($1027^{b}29$). The occurrence of the phrase 'what "is" and what "is not" in this way' at $1027^{b}29$ can be understood in two ways. According to the first exegesis, it means 'what "is" as true and what "is not" as false'.[29] This interpretation is supported by the fact that shortly later (two lines down in the text) we find an occurrence of the phrase 'what "is" in this way [*to houtōs on*]' ($1027^{b}31$) meaning 'what "is" as true'. If this exegesis is correct, Aristotle is promising to discuss later certain questions about what 'is' as true and what 'is not' as false. According to the second exegesis, the occurrence of the phrase 'what "is" and what "is not" in this way' at $1027^{b}29$ means 'what "is" as true in the way appropriate to simples and essences and "what is not" as false in the way appropriate to simples and essences'.[30] This interpretation is sup-

---

[27] Cf. Aquinas, *In Metaph.* 1223 Cathala–Spiazzi; F. Brentano, *Von der mannigfachen Bedeutung des Seienden nach Aristoteles* [*Bedeutung*] (Freiburg i.B., 1862), 34.
[28] Cf. C. H. Kahn, 'The Greek Verb "To Be" and the Concept of Being', *Foundations of Language*, 2 (1966), 245–65 at 252–3; Kahn, *Verb*, 335–9. There are examples where 'to be' and 'not to be' are associated with truth and falsehood and are applied directly to items referred to by 'λόγος' (Hdt. 1. 95. 1; 1. 116. 5; Ar. *Ran.* 1052), 'σκῆψις' (Soph. *El.* 584), 'ἔπος' (*Il.* 24. 56), or 'μῦθος' (Eur. *El.* 346) (cf. Kahn, *Verb*, 346, 354–5, 366–7). It is not, however, clear whether in these examples 'λόγος', 'σκῆψις', 'ἔπος', and 'μῦθος' refer to linguistic expressions or to their contents.
[29] Cf. [Alex. Aphr.] *In Metaph.* 457. 36–458. 1 Hayduck; Aquinas, *In Metaph.* 1233 Cathala–Spiazzi; Bonitz, *Metaphysica*, ii. 294; Ross, *Metaphysics*, i. 365; L. M. de Rijk, *The Place of the Categories of Being in Aristotle's Philosophy* [*Categories*] (Assen, 1952), 8.
[30] Cf. Schwegler, *Metaphysik*, iv. 32; A. Bullinger, *Aristoteles' Metaphysik in Bezug auf Entstehungsweise, Text und Gedanken* (Munich, 1892), 150–1; W. Christ (ed.), *Aristotelis Metaphysica* [*Metaphysica*], 2nd edn. (Leipzig, 1906), 131; P. Gohlke (trans. and comm.), *Aristoteles: Metaphysik* [*Metaphysik*], 2nd edn. (Paderborn, 1961), 197; K. Oehler, *Die Lehre vom noetischen und dianoetischen Denken bei Platon und Aristoteles* [*Lehre*], 2nd edn. (Hamburg, 1985), 171; W. Luther, 'Wahrheit, Licht und Erkenntnis in der griechischen Philosophie bis Demokrit' ['Wahrheit'], *Archiv für Begriffsgeschichte*, 10 (1966), 1–240 at 180; J. Tricot (trans. and comm.), *Aristote: la Métaphysique* [*Métaphysique*], 2nd edn. (Paris, 1966), i. 344; L. M. de Rijk, 'The

ported by the fact that immediately before his promise Aristotle mentions 'simples and essences [*ta hapla kai ta ti estin*]' (1027^{b}27–8). If this exegesis is correct, Aristotle is promising to discuss later certain questions concerning the 'being' as truth and the 'not being' as falsehood of simples and essences.

Three considerations lead me to prefer the second interpretation.[31] (1) The meaning of the occurrence of 'what "is" and what "is not" in this way' at 1027^{b}29 is naturally taken to be fixed by what immediately precedes it. Although the occurrence of 'what "is" in this way' two lines later (1027^{b}31) means 'what "is" as true', the meaning of occurrences of phrases containing 'in this way' can easily vary from one sentence to the next. (2) What most strikingly distinguishes Θ 10's discussion of matters pertaining to 'being' as truth and 'not being' as falsehood from that of *E* 4 is the focus on incomposites and essences. (3) If the first interpretation were correct, Aristotle in the middle of *Metaphysics E* 4 would be promising to discuss later certain questions about what 'is' as true and what 'is not' as false. This promise would sit uneasily with the claim which the chapter as a whole strives to establish, i.e. that the study of what 'is' as true may be left aside.[32]

Whatever interpretation one adopts, Aristotle seems to fulfil his promise of a later treatment of issues pertaining to 'what "is" and what "is not" in this way' (1027^{b}29) in *Metaphysics* Θ 10. Hence Θ 10 probably expands on *E* 4.

Anatomy of the Proposition: Logos and Pragma in Plato and Aristotle' ['Anatomy'], in L. M. de Rijk and H. A. G. Braakhuis (eds.), *Logos and Pragma: Essays on the Philosophy of Language in Honour of Professor Gabriel Nuchelmans* (Nijmegen, 1987), 27–61 at 51; E. C. Halper, *One and Many in Aristotle's* Metaphysics*: The Central Books* [*Metaphysics*] (Columbus, Ohio, 1989), 217; Martineau, 'Inauthenticité', 494; L. M. de Rijk, *Aristotle: Semantics and Ontology* [*Semantics*] (Leiden, Boston, and Cologne, 2002), ii. 146, 325; G. Pearson, 'Aristotle on Being-as-Truth' ['Being'], *Oxford Studies in Ancient Philosophy*, 28 (2005), 201–31 at 207, 210, and 211.

[31] On this point I have changed my mind with respect to my *Aristotle on Truth* [*Truth*] (Cambridge, 2004), 63–4.

[32] Some advocates of the first exegesis take the inconsistency to indicate that lines 1027^{b}25–9 were inserted by Aristotle in a revised edition of the *Metaphysics*: cf. Jaeger, *Studien*, 24–5; W. W. Jaeger, *Aristoteles: Grundlegung einer Geschichte seiner Entwicklung* [*Aristoteles*] (Berlin, 1923), 212; Ross, *Metaphysics*, i, pp. xxx, 365; W. W. Jaeger (ed.), *Aristotelis Metaphysica* (Oxford, 1957), 127; Gohlke, *Metaphysik*, 197, 451. Other advocates of this exegesis argue that the inconsistency is merely apparent: cf. [Alex. Aphr.] *In Metaph.* 458. 10–15 Hayduck; W. Leszl, *Aristotle's Conception of Ontology* [*Ontology*] (Padua, 1975), 216.

Apparent inconsistencies in Aristotle's text

Chapters *E* 4 and Θ 10 of the *Metaphysics* seem to clash (I discuss the apparent clashes in the next section). The situation is disturbing because the two chapters belong to a single work and are linked by a cross-reference.

Two opposite reactions to such an apparent clash are possible. One may assume that the apparent clash is real and that there is a tension in the views about what 'is' as true presented in the *Metaphysics*,[33] a tension that might be due to the fact that the passages concerned belong to different phases of Aristotle's reflection and were put together in their present positions either by Aristotle himself[34] or by an editor responsible for the version of the *Metaphysics* we now read.[35] Alternatively, one may try to show that the apparent clash is merely apparent.

Both responses are reasonable.[36] The choice of one of them depends on general exegetical strategies which one may adopt in addressing Aristotle's work. In what follows I pursue the second approach and endeavour to establish that the apparent clash between *E* 4 and Θ 10 is merely apparent.

2. Three apparent clashes between *Metaphysics E* 4 and Θ 10

First apparent clash: true thoughts concerning simples

The first apparent clash between *E* 4 and Θ 10 arises because in *E* 4 Aristotle says that 'with regard to simples and essences they [*sc.* truth and falsehood] are not even in thought' ($1027^{b}27$–8) while in the central section of Θ 10 ($1051^{b}17$–$1052^{a}4$) he commits himself to the claim that thoughts and linguistic expressions concerning incomposites are true (and cannot be false). The tension is increased by the circumstance that in *De anima* 3. 6 ($430^{b}26$–31) Aristotle claims that the intellection of essence is true.

There are two ways of showing that the first apparent clash is

---

[33] Cf. S. Makin (trans. and comm.), *Aristotle: Metaphysics Book* Θ [*Theta*] (Oxford, 2006), 252; J. Szaif, 'Die Geschichte des Wahrheitsbegriffs in der klassischen Antike' ['Geschichte'], in M. Enders and J. Szaif (eds.), *Die Geschichte des philosophischen Begriffs der Wahrheit* (Berlin and New York, 2006), 1–32 at 21.

[34] Cf. Jaeger, *Studien*, 25, 53.

[35] Cf. Schwegler, *Metaphysik*, iv. 186; Christ, *Metaphysica*, 196.

[36] What strikes me as unreasonable is to assert that Aristotle is not the author of *E* 4 (cf. Martineau, 'Inauthenticité', 500–1) or of Θ 10 (cf. F. Grayeff, *Aristotle and his School: An Inquiry into the History of the Peripatos with a Commentary on* Metaphysics *Z, H, Λ, and* Θ (London, 1974), 206, 210).

merely apparent. First, in E 4 Aristotle might be saying that truth and falsehood are not *both* present in thoughts concerning simples and essences, the ground for this being that thoughts concerning simples and essences are only true and cannot be false—precisely the contention of Θ 10 and *De anima* 3 .6. This solution gains some support from *De anima* 3. 6, where Aristotle says that 'the thinking of indivisibles concerns things about which there is no falsehood, while where both falsehood and truth are present there is already some sort of composition of thoughts as if they were a single one' (430^a26–8).[37]

Secondly, in E 4 Aristotle might be using 'thought' (*'dianoia'*) to mean something like 'discursive thought' and to refer to predicative judgements, which involve a passage (suggested by the *'dia'* within *'dianoia'*) from the entities thought about through their subject-components to those thought about through their predicate-components.[38] He would then be saying that truth and falsehood concerning simples and essences are not present in predicative judgements but in thoughts of a different sort.[39] According

[37] Cf. Ross, *Metaphysics*, i. 365; M. Heidegger, *Logik: Die Frage nach der Wahrheit*, ed. by W. Biemel, 2nd edn. (Frankfurt a.M., 1995) , 129, 135–6; P. J. Harvey, 'Aristotle on Truth and Falsity in *De anima* 3. 6', *Journal of the History of Philosophy*, 16 (1978), 219–20 at 220; K. Pritzl, 'Being True in Aristotle's Thinking' ['True'], *Proceedings of the Boston Area Colloquium in Ancient Philosophy*, 14 (1998), 177–201 at 187–8; Crivelli, *Truth*, 64.

[38] Cf. *Metaph. A* 9, 1075^a5–10; I. Schüssler, *La Question de la vérité: Thomas d'Aquin – Nietzsche – Kant – Aristote – Heidegger [Vérité]* (Lausanne, 2001), 129–30. In our passage's sequel (1027^b29–30, 31–3) 'διάνοια' denotes the faculty responsible for the operations of joining and separating characteristic of affirmative and negative predicative judgements.

[39] Cf. Ascl. *In Metaph.* 374. 7–8 Hayduck; Bonitz, *Metaphysica*, ii. 293–4; Bonitz, *Index*, 186^a52–60; Jaeger, *Studien*, 23; Jaeger, *Aristoteles*, 212; de Rijk, *Categories*, 16, 24; Luther, 'Wahrheit', 180; G. Sillitti, 'I "Fondamenti della logica aristotelica" e la critica di Emanuele Severino', in G. Calogero, *I fondamenti della logica aristotelica*, 2nd edn. (Florence, 1968), 313–25 at 320–1; H. Seidl, *Der Begriff des Intellekts (νοῦς) bei Aristoteles im philosophischen Zusammenhang seiner Hauptschriften* (Meisenheim am Glan, 1971), 181; K.-H. Volkmann-Schluck, *Die Metaphysik des Aristoteles* (Frankfurt a.M., 1979), 262; K. Pritzl, 'The Cognition of Indivisibles and the Argument of *De anima* 3. 4–8', *Proceedings of the American Catholic Philosophical Association*, 58 (1984), 140–50 at 144; de Rijk, 'Anatomy', 39, 45, 51; E. Berti, 'Heidegger e il concetto aristotelico di verità' ['Verità'], in R. Brague and F. Courtine (eds.), *Herméneutique et ontologie: mélanges en hommage à Pierre Aubenque* (Paris, 1990), 97–120 at 113; C. Segura, 'El ser de la verdad en la *Metafísica* de Aristóteles' ['Ser'], *Tópicos*, 4 (1994), 89–115 at 115; F. Fiorentino, 'Il problema della verità in Aristotele', *Sapienza*, 54 (2001), 257–302 at 282; D. K. W. Modrak, *Aristotle's Theory of Language and Meaning* (Cambridge, 2001), 65; Schüssler, *Vérité*, 144; de Rijk, *Semantics*, ii. 146; E. Sonderegger, 'La vérité chez Aristote', in J.-F.

to most proponents of this solution, the thoughts of a different sort concerning simples and essences to which Aristotle alludes are thoughts of a non-propositional nature which are necessarily true in that they must grasp the entities they are about (because if they failed to grasp these entities then they would lack a characteristic essential to them).[40] Alternatively, the thoughts of a different sort concerning simples and essences to which Aristotle alludes could be thoughts that are propositional albeit non-predicative, e.g. existential judgements (because an attribution of existence is not an attribution of a universal such as occurs in a predicative judgement).[41]

Both solutions are plausible. I prefer the second because the first strains the text. For, the first solution requires that Aristotle's words, 'With regard to simples and essences they [*sc.* truth and falsehood] are not even in thought' ($1027^{b}27$–8), mean that truth and falsehood are not *both* present in thoughts concerning simples and essences. But such a meaning cannot be easily given to the Greek sentence corresponding to my English translation: in the Greek, the subject for '*oud' en dianoiāi*' ('are not even in thought', $1027^{b}28$) is understood (there is no Greek expression corresponding to the 'they' of my English translation). Had Aristotle intended to say that truth and falsehood are not both present in thoughts concerning simples and essences, he would probably have placed words corresponding to 'both truth and falsehood' in an emphatic position.

Second apparent clash: is the veridical use of 'to be' fundamental?

E 4 appears to clash with Θ 10 also on whether the use of 'to be' and 'not to be' associated with truth and falsehood is fundamental. Consider the beginning of Θ 10:

Aenishanslin, D. O'Meara, and I. Schüssler (eds.), *La Vérité: antiquité – modernité* (Lausanne, 2004), 47–63 at 53; Pearson, 'Being', 226.

[40] For the distinction between discursive and intuitive thought in connection with truth and falsehood see *Metaph.* Γ 7, $1012^{a}2$–5, with H. Maier, *Die Syllogistik des Aristoteles* [*Syllogistik*], 2nd edn. (repr. Hildesheim, 1969), i. 21, 79; Wheeler, 'Reading', 71.

[41] I discussed the interpretations of Aristotle's views on thoughts concerning simples and essences in my *Truth*, 99–116. Some commentators (e.g. [Alex. Aphr.] *In Metaph.* 457. 33–6 Hayduck; Maurus, *Aristotelis opera*, iv. 405; Schwegler, *Metaphysik*, iv. 30) suggest that when in E 4 Aristotle says that 'with regard to simples and essences they [*sc.* truth and falsehood] are not even in thought' ($1027^{b}27$–8), he has in mind (not the incomposites of Θ 10, but) the 'things said with no combination' of the *Categories* (4, $2^{a}7$–10) and *De interpretatione* (1, $16^{a}9$–18). This is unlikely because the passages from the *Categories* and *De interpretatione* do not mention essences, which instead appear in Θ 10 (at $1051^{b}32$).

[T2] ἐπεὶ δὲ τὸ ὂν λέγεται καὶ τὸ μὴ ὂν τὸ μὲν κατὰ 1051ᵃ34
τὰ σχήματα τῶν κατηγοριῶν, τὸ δὲ κατὰ δύναμιν ἢ ἐνέρ- ᵃ35
γειαν τούτων ἢ τἀναντία, τὸ δὲ κυριώτατα ὄν⁴² ἀληθὲς ἢ⁴³ 1051ᵇ1
ψεῦδος, τοῦτο δ' ἐπὶ τῶν πραγμάτων ἐστὶ τὸ⁴⁴ συγκεῖσθαι ἢ
διῃρῆσθαι,⁴⁵ ὥστε⁴⁶ ἀληθεύει⁴⁷ μὲν ὁ τὸ διῃρημένον οἰόμενος διῃ-
ρῆσθαι⁴⁸ καὶ τὸ συγκείμενον συγκεῖσθαι, ἔψευσται δὲ ὁ ἐναν-
τίως ἔχων ἢ⁴⁹ τὰ πράγματα, πότ' ἔστιν ἢ οὐκ ἔστι τὸ ὡς⁵⁰ ἀληθὲς ᵇ5

⁴² The main witnesses present various readings: Aᵇ, M, and (probably) ps.-Alexander (*In Metaph.* 598. 1–4 Hayduck) have 'κυριώτατα ὄν'; the first hand of E has 'κυριώτατον εἰ̓'; J and the second hand of E have 'κυριώτατα εἰ̓'; Eˢ and C have 'κυριώτατα ἢ', presupposed also by William of Moerbeke's translation; Vᵈ has 'κυριώτατ~ εἰ̓'. The Aldine edition has 'κυριώτατον ὄν'. Brandis, Bekker, Weise, Schwegler, Bonitz, Dübner, Christ, and Jaeger print 'κυριώτατα ὄν'. Ross, followed by Tredennick, Reale, Zanatta, and various commentators (e.g. Oehler, *Lehre*, 179, and K. Bormann, 'Wahrheitsbegriff und νοῦς-Lehre bei Aristoteles und einigen seiner Kommentatoren', *Miscellanea mediaevalia*, 12 (1982), 1–24 at 3), excises 'κυριώτατα ὄν' (he also contemplates transposing it after 'τὸ μὲν' at 1051ᵃ34). Jaeger suspects a lacuna between 'κυριώτατα ὄν' and 'ἀληθὲς ἢ ψεῦδος': he suggests 'κυριώτατα ὄν ⟨ἡ οὐσία, λείπεται δὲ ἐπισκοπεῖν τὸ ὄν⟩ ἀληθὲς ἢ ψεῦδος'.
⁴³ All the main witnesses read 'ἢ' except J, which has 'ἡ̓'.
⁴⁴ J, E, Eˢ, and Vᵈ read 'τοῦτο δ' ἐπὶ τῶν πραγμάτων ἐστὶ τὸ', while C has 'τοῦτο δὲ ἐπὶ τῶν πραγμάτων ἐστὶ τὸ'. Either of these readings is presupposed by William of Moerbeke's translation and was perhaps the basis for the commentary of ps.-Alexander (*In Metaph.* 598. 4–6 Hayduck): the phrase 'ἐπὶ τῶν πραγμάτων' is reproduced (598. 4) and the words 'ἔστι τὸ τοιοῦτον ἀληθὲς καὶ ὂν ἐπὶ τοῦ πράγματος' (598. 5–6) suggest a statement of identity corresponding to 'ἐστὶ τὸ'. Aᵇ has instead 'τοῦτο δὴ ἔτι τῶν πραγμάτων ἐστὶ τῷ', while M has 'τοῦτο δὴ ἐπὶ τῶν πραγμάτων ἐστὶ τῷ'. I follow the reading of J, E, Eˢ, and Vᵈ, which is printed by Brandis. The Aldine edition and Weise print 'τούτων δ' ἐπὶ τῶν πραγμάτων ἐστὶ τὸ'. Most modern editors (Bekker, Schwegler, Bonitz, Dübner, Christ, Ross, Tredennick, and Jaeger) print 'τοῦτο δ' ἐπὶ τῶν πραγμάτων ἐστὶ τῷ'.
⁴⁵ I follow the reading of the main manuscripts, 'διῃρῆσθαι', printed by Brandis, Bekker, Schwegler, Bonitz, Dübner, Christ, Ross, Tredennick, and Jaeger. William of Moerbeke's translation presupposes instead 'διαιρεῖσθαι', which is printed by the Aldine edition and Weise.
⁴⁶ Vᵈ omits the whole of 'ὥστε ἀληθεύει μὲν ὁ τὸ διῃρημένον οἰόμενος διῃρῆσθαι', but a later hand adds it in the margin (with 'ἀληθεύειν' instead of 'ἀληθεύει').
⁴⁷ I read 'ἀληθεύει' with J, E, Eˢ, and C; Aᵇ and M have 'ἀληθεύειν'.
⁴⁸ I follow the reading of J, E, and Eˢ, 'διῃρῆσθαι', printed by Bonitz, Dübner, Christ, Ross, Tredennick, and Jaeger. Aᵇ, M, and C read instead 'διαιρεῖσθαι', which is presupposed by William of Moerbeke's translation and is printed by the Aldine ed., Brandis, Bekker, Weise, and Schwegler.
⁴⁹ Three of the main manuscripts (J, E, and Vᵈ) omit 'ἢ', whose absence is also presupposed by William of Moerbeke's translation. 'ἢ' is present in Aᵇ, M, C, and Eˢ, it is added by the second hand of E, and it is printed by all the editions I consulted. The reading without 'ἢ' should not, however, be discarded lightly. Its translation would be: '. . . whereas he who has the objects contrariwise is wrong . . .'. The verb 'has' ('ἔχων', 1051ᵇ5) should then be understood as expressing 'assignment', as it does in the parallel passage in E 4 (cf. 'ἔχει' at 1027ᵇ21).
⁵⁰ The main manuscripts report different readings: 'ὡς τὸ' (E, Eˢ, Vᵈ, and C),

Truth in Metaphysics *E 4* 179

λεγόμενον ἢ ψεῦδος; τοῦτο γὰρ σκεπτέον τί λέγομεν. οὐ
γὰρ διὰ τὸ ἡμᾶς οἴεσθαι ἀληθῶς σε λευκὸν εἶναι εἶ σὺ
λευκός, ἀλλὰ διὰ τὸ σὲ εἶναι λευκὸν ἡμεῖς οἱ φάντες τοῦτο
ἀληθεύομεν.   1051ᵇ9

Given that 'being' and 'not being' are spoken of in some cases with reference to the figures of predication, in others with reference to the potentiality or the actuality of these or to their opposites,[51] in others by being most strictly true or false,[52] and this [*sc.* 'being' by being most strictly true and 'not being' by being most strictly false], in the case of objects, is to be combined or to be divided, so that he who thinks of what is divided that it is divided and of what is combined that it is combined is right, whereas he who is in a state contrary to that of the objects is wrong,[53] when is it that what is spoken of as true or false 'is' or 'is not'? For what we say on this must be investigated. For it is not because we truly think that you are white that you are white, but it is because of your being white that we who say this are right. (*Metaph. Θ* 10, 1051ᵃ34–ᵇ9)

Most translators and commentators render the words '... *to de kuriōtata on alēthes ē pseudos*' (1051ᵇ1–2) by something like '... while what "is" most strictly ⟨is⟩ true or false'. They then find that the claim thereby made clashes with *E* 4's claim that 'what "is" in this way [*sc.* as true] is a different thing that "is" from those that "are" strictly' (1027ᵇ31). The fact that *E* 4, at 1027ᵇ28–9, contains a forward reference to *Θ* 10 makes such a clash particularly unpalatable.

In order to get rid of this second alleged inconsistency between *E* 4 and *Θ* 10, some scholars emend the text.[54] One feels uneasy,

---

'ὥστε τὸ' (J), and simply 'τὸ' (Aᵇ and M, which, however, added 'ὡς'). Most modern editions follow Aᵇ, whereas the Aldine edition and Weise opt for 'ὥστε τὸ'. Jaeger (implementing a suggestion in Christ's apparatus, which in fact is already mentioned by Du Val) prints 'τὸ ὡς'. I follow Jaeger.

[51] The words 'their opposites' mean 'the opposites of the potentiality or the actuality of the figures of predication' ('τἀναντία' at 1051ᵇ1 must be construed with 'κατὰ' at 1051ᵃ35, and is therefore co-ordinate with 'δύναμιν ἢ ἐνέργειαν' at 1051ᵃ35–ᵇ1). They allude either to the lack of potentiality and the lack of actuality (cf. *Δ* 15, 1021ᵃ25–6; E. Rolfes (trans. and comm.), *Aristoteles: Metaphysik*, 3rd edn. (Leipzig, 1928), ii. 239; Tricot, *Métaphysique*, ii. 521–2) or to the potentiality and the actuality of not being a certain substance (e.g. a man), the potentiality and the actuality of not being of a certain quality (e.g. white), etc. (cf. *Θ* 8, 1050ᵇ8–34; Oehler, *Lehre*, 175).

[52] My translation here gives away my preferred solution for the second apparent clash.

[53] No English verb-phrase renders adequately 'ἀληθεύειν': some occurrences of 'ἀληθεύειν' require 'to be right', others 'to speak truly'. Similarly, no English verb-phrase renders adequately 'ψεύδεσθαι': some occurrences of 'ψεύδεσθαι' require 'to be wrong', others 'to speak falsely'.

[54] Cf. above, n. 42.

however, at ironing the inconsistency away by editorial intervention.

Some commentators[55] try to resolve the second alleged inconsistency between *E* 4 and *Θ* 10 by taking 'kuriōtata' to mean something like 'on the most common or widespread use'. So: in *E* 4 Aristotle would be saying that what 'is' as true is different from what 'is' strictly; in *Θ* 10 he would be saying that what 'is' as true is what 'is' in accordance with the most common or widespread use of 'to be'. The inconsistency between *E* 4 and *Θ* 10 would then be merely apparent. This solution is unconvincing because when in the course of a discussion of the various uses of an expression Aristotle employs a sentence roughly equivalent to 'This is how things are called so-and-so *kuriōtata*', '*kuriōtata*' normally means (not 'on the most common or widespread use', but) 'most properly' or 'most strictly'.[56]

Heidegger[57] attempts to resolve the second alleged inconsistency between *E* 4 and *Θ* 10 by assuming that the two chapters address different topics. In his view, *E* 4 examines the 'being' as truth which is an attribute of thoughts; *Θ* 10 instead studies the 'being' as truth

[55] See Jaeger, *Studien*, 51–2; cf. P. Wilpert, 'Zum aristotelischen Wahrheitsbegriff' ['Wahrheitsbegriff'], *Philosophisches Jahrbuch der Görres-Gesellschaft*, 53 (1940), 3–16 at 9; J. Owens, *The Doctrine of Being in the Aristotelian Metaphysics* [*Doctrine*], 3rd edn. (Toronto, 1978), 411–12; E. Tugendhat, review of Oehler, *Lehre* ['Oehler'], in E. Tugendhat, *Philosophische Aufsätze* (Frankfurt a.M., 1992), 402–13 at 408; Berti, 'Verità', 111–13; Pritzl, 'True', 178; E. Berti, 'I luoghi della verità secondo Aristotele: un confronto con Heidegger', in V. Melchiorre (ed.), *I luoghi del comprendere* (Milan, 2000), 3–27 at 6–7.

[56] Cf. Ross, *Metaphysics*, ii. 275; M. Heidegger, *Vom Wesen der menschlichen Freiheit: Einleitung in die Philosophie* [*Freiheit*], ed. by H. Tietjen (Frankfurt a.M., 1982), 83–5. Jaeger, the first to propose the solution under consideration (cf. n. 55 above), abandoned it later: for in his 1957 edition of the *Metaphysics* he resorted to textual emendation (cf. n. 42 above). At *Metaph. Θ* 1, 1045^{b}36, Aristotle uses 'μάλιστα κυρίως' to describe one of the uses of 'potentiality'. Some commentators take the expression here to mean 'in the most common or widespread way', but it is not clear that it should be thus understood. In *Categories* 13, a chapter dedicated to the uses of 'together', Aristotle implicitly equates 'κυριώτατα' with 'ἁπλῶς' (cf. 14^{b}24 and 15^{a}11). Cf. *DA* I. 4, 408^{a}6 ('κυριώτατα' with 'ἐντεῦθεν' at 408^{a}9); *Metaph. I* 1, 1052^{b}19 ('κυριώτατα' with 'ἐντεῦθεν' on the same line); 1053^{b}5 ('κυριώτατα' with 'εἶτα' on the same line). In *Metaphysics Δ*, the book dedicated to distinguishing uses of expressions, there are no occurrences of 'κυριώτατα' and two occurrences of 'κυρίως': 4, 1015^{a}14, and 5, 1015^{b}12. In both cases the adverb is paired with some form of 'πρῶτος' and seems to mean something like 'in the primary way' or 'strictly'. On Aristotle's use of 'κυριώτατα' cf. also below, paragraph to n. 74.

[57] Cf. M. Heidegger, *Die Grundbegriffe der antiken Philosophie* [*Grundbegriffe*], ed. by F.-K. Bust (Frankfurt a.M., 1993), 168, 305–6; Heidegger, *Freiheit*, 87–91; C. P. Long, *Aristotle on the Nature of Truth* (New York, 2011), 172–3.

which is an attribute of external things.[58] Aristotle could consistently say, on the one hand, that the 'being' as truth which is an attribute of thoughts is different from the 'being' of what 'is' strictly, and, on the other, that the 'being' as truth which is an attribute of external things is the 'being' of what 'is' most strictly.[59] Some of the claims made by Heidegger in his attempt to resolve the alleged inconsistency between E 4 and Θ 10 are correct and important: he is right in claiming that E 4 and Θ 10 focus on different attributes, and, specifically, that E 4 concentrates on an attribute of thoughts while Θ 10 concentrates on an attribute of external things. But Heidegger's solution cannot stand as it is. For it requires that this change of attributes should not be reflected in any change in terminology nor indicated by any warning: in the two chapters Aristotle would be using the same keyword, 'true', in different ways without giving any indication that this is what he is doing. This would be poor practice, particularly in view of the fact that the chapters are linked (by the promise of E 4, 1027^{b}28–9).

Other commentators[60] have a better solution for the second alleged inconsistency between E 4 and Θ 10. They take the words '*kuriōtata on alēthes ē pseudos*' to mean 'by being most strictly true or false': the adverb '*kuriōtata*' modifies the immediately following '*on*', which in turn takes '*alēthes ē pseudos*' as its complement. On this reading, '*to de*' at 1051^{b}1 is co-ordinate with '*to men*' at 1051^{a}34

---

[58] I use 'external thing' to mean 'entity that is neither a linguistic expression nor a mental state nor a mental act'.
[59] Elsewhere (in *Platon: Sophistes*, ed. by I. Schüssler (Frankfurt a.M., 1992), 187–8) Heidegger insists that the 'being' as truth discussed in E 4 is an attribute of external things.
[60] Cf. C. A. Brandis, *Handbuch der Geschichte der griechisch-römischen Philosophie* (Berlin, 1835–66), ii/2.1. 519–20; C. Prantl, *Geschichte der Logik im Abenlande*, i (Leipzig, 1855), 185; G. Grote, *Aristotle*, ed. by A. Bain and G. C. Robertson, 2nd edn. (London, 1880), 618; W. D. Ross (trans.), *Aristotle: Metaphysica* [*Metaphysica*] (Oxford, 1908), ad loc.; Ross, *Metaphysics*, ii. 275; J. G. Deninger, '*Wahres Sein' in der Philosophie des Aristoteles* (Meisenheim am Glan, 1961), 140–1; Tricot, *Métaphysique*, ii 522; A. Russo (trans.), *Aristotele: Metafisica*, 2nd edn. (Rome and Bari, 1982), 273; H. Seidl (trans. and comm.), *Aristoteles' Metaphysik*, 3rd edn. (Hamburg, 1991), ii. 491; M. Burnyeat *et al*., *Notes on Eta and Theta of Aristotle's Metaphysics* [*Notes*] (Oxford, 1984), 156; G. Salmeri (trans. and comm.), *Aristotele: Discorsi sull'esistenza. Libri 7–8–9 della Metafisica* (Cinisello Balsamo, 1996), 243, 306; Crivelli, *Truth*, 234–7; Pearson, 'Being', 211; Makin, *Theta*, 14, 248; M.-P. Duminil and A. Jaulin (trans.), *Aristote: Métaphysique* [*Métaphysique*] (Paris, 2008), 315. Schüssler, *Vérité*, 136–7, argues that the two translations should be run together and presupposes a conscious deployment of an ambiguous formulation: Aristotle would be talking of what is in the strictest way by being true in the strictest way.

and 'to de' at 1051ᵃ35, so the clause 'kuriōtata on alēthes ē pseudos' explains the third way in which 'being' and 'not being' are spoken of (in the immediately preceding portion of text this role is played by the clauses 'kata ta schēmata tōn katēgoriōn' and 'kata dunamin ē energeian toutōn ē tanantia'). There are examples of a single occurrence of 'men' correlated with two of 'de' in a list of three items.[61] In particular, at *Metaph. Δ* 28, 1024ᵇ6–8, there is an example of a distinction of linguistic uses where 'to men' followed by 'kata' construed with the accusative is linked to a first 'to de' also followed by 'kata' with the accusative and to a second 'to de' followed, however, by 'hōs' construed with the nominative: the change of construction with the second 'to de' has therefore a parallel. So at 1051ᵃ34–ᵇ2 Aristotle is saying that 'being' and 'not being' are spoken of, first, with reference to the categories, secondly, with reference to the potentiality or the actuality of the categories or to their opposites, and, thirdly, 'by *being* most strictly *true or false*'. Note that on the usual way of rendering the beginning of Θ 10, the words 'to de kuriōtata on alēthes ē pseudos' constitute a single independent sentence, to be translated by something like '. . . while what "is" most strictly is true or false': this is awkward because it saddles Aristotle with a use of 'to be' associated not only with truth but also with falsehood. Although Aristotle's telegraphic style can tolerate such quirks, the situation does tell against the usual rendering of the beginning of Θ 10. One might object that since Aristotle is offering a classification of the uses of 'to be', the adverb '*kuriōtata*' ('most strictly') is naturally understood as introducing the strictest use of 'to be'.[62] This objection is answered by pointing out that since Θ 10 discusses truth and falsehood, it is just as natural to understand '*kuriōtata*' ('most strictly') as introducing the strictest way of being true or false.

I therefore endorse the last solution for the second apparent inconsistency between *E* 4 and Θ 10. In Θ 10 there is no question of 'what "is" most strictly': the text speaks only of 'being' and 'not being' that 'are spoken of . . . by being most strictly true or false'. Since Θ 10 does not contain the claim that what 'is' as true 'is' most strictly, the second apparent inconsistency between *E* 4 and Θ 10 evaporates.

[61] Cf. *Pr. An.* 1. 2, 25ᵃ4–5; 9, 30ᵃ29–30; 11, 31ᵇ28–9; *Metaph. Z* 4, 1030ᵇ11–12; 7, 1032ᵃ12–13; etc.
[62] Cf. Burnyeat *et al.*, *Notes*, 156.

Truth in Metaphysics *E* 4

Third apparent clash: what do truth and falsehood hold of?

There seems to be a third clash between *E* 4 and *Θ* 10. According to some commentators,[63] *E* 4's remark that 'falsehood and truth are not in objects . . . but in thought' ($1027^{b}25$–7) clashes with *Θ* 10's remark that 'being' by being most strictly true and 'not being' by being most strictly false, 'in the case of objects, is to be combined or to be divided' ($1051^{b}1$–3). For *E* 4's remark seems to entail

[a] All objects are neither true nor false,

whereas *Θ* 10's remark seems to entail

[b] All objects are either true or false.

Claims [a] and [b] appear to clash, given the uncontroversial assumption that there are objects.

There are two ways of showing that the third apparent clash between *E* 4 and *Θ* 10 is merely apparent. The first assumes that the two claims are consistent because of different uses of the expression 'object' in the sentences employed to formulate them, the second assumes that they are consistent because of different uses of the expressions 'true' and 'false' in the relevant sentences.

First solution for the third apparent clash   Perhaps Aristotle's use of 'object' (*'pragma'*) in *E* 4 is different from his use in *Θ* 10. Specifically, it could be the case that in *E* 4 Aristotle uses 'object' to refer only to universals and individuals while in *Θ* 10 he uses it to refer only to composite external things. Then the remark of *E* 4 commits Aristotle to

[c] All objects are neither true nor false, where objects comprise only universals and individuals,

whereas the remark of *Θ* 10 commits Aristotle to

[d] All objects are either true or false, where objects comprise only composite external things.

Claims [c] and [d] are compatible (they could both be true if no universals and no individuals are composite external things).

[63] Cf. G. E. Vollrath, *Studien zur Kategorienlehre des Aristoteles*. (diss. University of Cologne, 1959), 177; Tugendhat, 'Oehler', 405; M. Fleischer, *Wahrheit und Wahrheitsgrund: Zum Wahrheitsproblem und zu seiner Geschichte* (Berlin and New York, 1984), 27; H. Schmitz, *Die Ideenlehre des Aristoteles*, i/2 (Bonn, 1985), 116–17.

The cost of this first solution is the change in the use of 'object' between E 4 and Θ 10. This cost is not unbearable because such a change in the use of 'object' is attested in Aristotle's works.[64]

Second solution for the third apparent clash   It could be the case that Θ 10's remark commits Aristotle merely to

[e] All objects either 'are' by being most strictly true or 'are not' by being most strictly false.

This reconciliation relies on two claims: first, that something's 'being' by being most strictly true does not entail its being true; secondly, that something's 'not being' by being most strictly false does not entail its being false. These two claims, which may be reasonably regarded as standing or falling together, are required by the second reconciliation's viability. For, suppose the two claims were to fail. It would then follow that something's 'being' by being most strictly true entails its being true and that something's 'not being' by being most strictly false entails its being false. Since all objects either 'are' by being most strictly true or 'are not' by being most strictly false (cf. [e] above), it would then follow that all objects are either true or false (cf. [b] above). Since E 4 commits Aristotle to the claim that all objects are neither true nor false (cf. [a] above), the second reconciliation would not achieve its goal of resolving the third apparent clash between E 4 and Θ 10.

The second solution for the third apparent clash has textual support. To begin with, note that in Θ 10 Aristotle treats 'being'-by-being-most-strictly-true, 'being', and 'being'-as-truth as one and the same attribute (I sometimes add hyphens to ease the identification of attributes): for he equates each of them with combination (at least as far as objects or composites are concerned). Specifically, at $1051^{b}2$ he says that in the case of objects 'being'-by-being-most-strictly-true is combination; at $1051^{b}11$–12 he says that in the case of objects 'being' is combination; at $1051^{b}19$ he says that in the case of composites 'being' is combination; and at $1051^{b}33$–4 he equates 'being'-as-truth with combination in the case of composites. Similarly, Aristotle treats 'not-being'-by-being-most-strictly-false, 'not-being', and 'not-being'-as-falsehood as one and the same attribute: for he equates each one of them with division (at least as far as objects or composites are concerned). Specifically, at

[64] Cf. below, pp. 193–5.

Truth in Metaphysics E 4   185

$1051^{b}2$–3 he says that in the case of objects 'not-being'-by-being-most-strictly-false is division; at $1051^{b}12$–13 he says that in the case of objects 'not-being' is division; at $1051^{b}19$–20 he says that in the case of composites 'not-being' is division; and at $1051^{b}33$–5 he equates 'not-being'-as-falsehood with division in the case of composites.

Now, in Θ 10 Aristotle tends to ascribe 'being', i.e. 'being'-by-being-most-strictly-true, and 'not-being', i.e. 'not-being'-by-being-most-strictly-false, to objects while reserving truth and falsehood for thoughts and sentences. Consider, for instance, $1051^{b}9$–17: Aristotle first distinguishes three situations, namely that where objects are always combined, that where objects are always divided, and that where objects are sometimes combined and sometimes divided ($1051^{b}9$–11);[65] he then says that 'being' is to be combined and 'not-being' is to be divided ($1051^{b}11$–13); and he concludes that in the first two situations (namely that where objects are always combined and that where they are always divided) the same judgements and the same sentences are always true or always false, while in the third situation (namely that where objects are sometimes combined and sometimes divided) the same judgements and the same sentences are true at one time and false at another ($1051^{b}13$–17). There is a clear distribution of roles: 'being', i.e. 'being'-by-being-most-strictly-true, and 'not-being', i.e. 'not-being'-by-being-most-strictly-false, hold of objects, whereas truth and falsehood hold of thoughts and sentences. The pattern is preserved in the passage's sequel, at $1051^{b}17$–22: here Aristotle says that for composites 'being' is to be combined and 'not-being' is to be divided ($1051^{b}19$–20); he offers the log's being white and the diagonal's being incommensurable as examples of composites ($1051^{b}20$–1); and he goes on to mention truth and falsehood as if they were attributes different from 'being' and 'not-being' ($1051^{b}21$–2). On the plausible assumption that composites coincide with objects,[66] Aristotle is thus committing himself to the claim that objects enjoy 'being', i.e. 'being'-by-being-most-strictly-true, or 'not-being', i.e. 'not-being'-by-being-most-strictly-false, and suggests (by implication) that truth and falsehood are enjoyed by other things. An analogous allocation of roles appears in the

[65] The expressions 'τὰ μὲν' ($1051^{b}9$), 'τὰ δ'' ($1051^{b}10$), and 'τὰ δ'' (again $1051^{b}10$) are to be integrated with a 'πράγματα' supplied from a preceding line ($1051^{b}5$).
[66] Cf. below, paragraph to n. 92.

186   *Paolo Crivelli*

passage's sequel (1051ᵇ22–1052ᵃ4), which concerns incomposites. Composition and division cannot be invoked to explain 'being'-as-truth and 'not-being'-as-falsehood for incomposites. Nevertheless, after saying that 'just as truth in the case of these [*sc.* incomposites] is not the same, so also "being"' (1051ᵇ22–3), Aristotle goes on to offer an account in which 'true' is reserved for linguistic expressions and thoughts.⁶⁷ So, there is textual support for the two claims on which the second reconciliation relies: that something's 'being' by being most strictly true does not entail its being true and that something's 'not being' by being most strictly false does not entail its being false.

These two claims on which the second reconciliation relies nevertheless invite an objection. 'If something "is" by being most strictly true, how can it not be true? If something "is not" by being most strictly false, how can it not be false? The two claims on which the second reconciliation relies fly in the face of our intuitions!'

This objection may be strengthened by adducing a later passage from Θ 10:

[T3]   ... τὸ δὲ εἶναι τὸ ὡς⁶⁸ ἀληθές, καὶ τὸ μὴ   1051ᵇ33
εἶναι τὸ ὡς⁶⁹ ψεῦδος, ἕν μέν ἐστιν, εἰ σύγκειται, ἀληθές, τὸ
δ᾽ εἰ μὴ σύγκειται, ψεῦδος· τὸ δὲ ἕν ...   ᵇ35

... with 'being' as truth and 'not being' as falsehood, one unity [*sc.* a composite] is true if it is combined, while it is false if it is not combined, whereas the other unity [*sc.* an incomposite] ... (*Metaph.* Θ 10, 1051ᵇ33–5)

In [T3] Aristotle appears to commit himself to the view that some composites, i.e. objects,⁷⁰ not only 'are' as true, i.e. 'are' by being most strictly true,⁷¹ but also are true, and that some composites, i.e.

⁶⁷ It is interesting to observe that A. Reinach, 'Zur Theorie des negativen Urteils', in A. Pfänder (ed.), *Münchener philosophische Abhandlungen: Festschrift für Theodor Lipps* (Leipzig, 1911), 196–254 at 224, uses 'true' ('*wahr*') and 'false' ('*falsch*') for sentences (*Sätze*) and reserves 'to subsist' ('*bestehen*') and 'not to subsist' ('*nicht bestehen*') for states of affairs (*Sachverhalte*).

⁶⁸ The main manuscripts record 'ὡς τό', which is adopted by all editions I consulted except Jaeger, who prints 'τὸ ὡς', the reading presupposed by the paraphrase of [Alex. Aphr.] *In Metaph.* 600. 39 Hayduck.

⁶⁹ The reading 'τὸ ὡς', recorded by Aᵇ, M, and C, is printed by Jaeger. J has 'τὸ ὡς τό'. This reading, also presupposed by the paraphrase of [Alex. Aphr.] *In Metaph.* 600. 39 Hayduck, is printed by Ross. The scribe of E modified his text so as to obtain 'ὡς τό', the reading recorded also by Eˢ and Vᵈ and printed by the Aldine edition, Brandis, Bekker, Weise, Schwegler, Bonitz, Dübner, Christ, and Tredennick.

⁷⁰ Cf. above, text to n. 66, and below, paragraph to n. 92.

⁷¹ Recall that the second reconciliation owes its plausibility to the fact that

objects, not only 'are not' as false, i.e. 'are not' by being most strictly false, but also are false. This is what the last paragraph's objection predicted.

However, reflection on passage [T3] in the context of Θ 10 provides the starting-point for a reply to the objection. It can hardly be denied that in [T3] Aristotle not only says that composites, i.e. objects, 'are' as true or 'are not' as false, but also that they are true or false. But it is just as undeniable that in the rest of Θ 10 he ascribes 'being'-as-truth and 'not-being'-as-falsehood only to objects and refrains from describing objects as true or false, descriptions which he reserves for thoughts and sentences. Thus, [T3] brings to the fore a tension in Θ 10. The most plausible solution to this tension is to admit that there is an ambiguity in Aristotle's use of 'true' and 'false'.[72] Such an ambiguity would spell disaster for Aristotle's treatment in Θ 10 if it remained unacknowledged. Luckily, however, Aristotle signals the ambiguity's existence. For, at the beginning of the chapter, he identifies the use of 'being' and 'not being' which will be at the centre of its analysis by saying that in some cases '"being" and "not being" are spoken of . . . by being *most strictly* true or false' ($1051^a34^-{}^b2$). This talk of 'being most strictly true or false' suggests a contrast with 'being true or false in the ordinary way'. Aristotle's position could then be that 'true' and 'false' can be employed both in an ordinary way, whereby they apply to thoughts and sentences but not to objects, and in an extremely strict way, whereby they apply to objects but neither to thoughts nor to sentences.

Note that [T3] opens with an explicit mention of 'being'-as-truth and 'not-being'-as-falsehood, namely the attributes which have been hitherto distinguished from truth and falsehood. Aristotle may then expect his readers to realize that when in [T3]'s sequel he goes on to describe composites, i.e. objects, as true or false, he is using 'true' and 'false' in the extremely strict way, that whereby they express the attributes that hold only of objects (and therefore hold neither of thoughts nor of sentences).

To summarize, the reply to the objection under consideration is that in Θ 10 the expressions 'true' and 'false' are used in two

---

'being'-by-being-most-strictly-true and 'not-being'-by-being-most-strictly-false are identical, respectively, to 'being'-as-truth and 'not-being'-as-falsehood.

[72] Cf. Brentano, *Bedeutung*, 25.

ways and Aristotle is conscious of this ambiguity and flags its existence. Specifically, the expressions 'true' and 'false' are used both in an ordinary way and in an extremely strict way. On their ordinary use, 'true' and 'false' express attributes that hold only of thoughts and sentences (and therefore do not hold of objects). On their extremely strict use, 'true' and 'false' express attributes that hold only of objects (and therefore hold neither of thoughts nor of sentences). On its ordinary use, 'true' expresses the attribute we typically have in mind when we describe a thought or a sentence as true; on its extremely strict use, 'true' expresses instead the attribute 'being'-by-being-most-strictly-true, which is identical both to 'being'-as-truth and to 'being'. In parallel fashion, on its ordinary use, 'false' expresses the attribute we typically have in mind when we describe a thought or a sentence as false; on its extremely strict use, 'false' expresses instead the attribute 'not-being'-by-being-most-strictly-false, which is identical both to 'not-being'-as-falsehood and to 'not-being'. When 'true' and 'false' are used in the ordinary way, Aristotle endorses the claim made by the sentence 'All objects are neither true nor false' and rejects the claim made by the sentence 'All objects are either true or false'. When 'true' and 'false' are used in the extremely strict way, Aristotle takes the opposite stance: he rejects the claim made by the sentence 'All objects are neither true nor false' and he endorses the claim made by the sentence 'All objects are either true or false'. The claim to which one should concede Aristotle to be committed in E 4 is the first one, namely the claim made by the sentence 'All objects are neither true nor false' with 'true' and 'false' used in the ordinary way (this is what claim [a] amounts to). The claim to which one should concede Aristotle to be committed in Θ 10 is the fourth one, namely the claim made by the sentence 'All objects are either true or false' with 'true' and 'false' used in the extremely strict way (this is what claim [b] amounts to). On the ordinary use of 'true' and 'false', something's 'being' by being most strictly true does not entail its being true and something's 'not being' by being most strictly false does not entail its being false; on the extremely strict use of 'true' and 'false', both entailments hold. Thus, an advocate of the second solution for the third apparent clash between E 4 and Θ 10 must concede something to the objection under consideration: he or she must concede that the objection is right in so far as something's 'being' by being most strictly true does entail its being true when 'true' is used in the ex-

Truth in Metaphysics *E 4*   189

tremely strict way, and, in parallel fashion, something's 'not being' by being most strictly false does entail its being false when 'false' is used in the extremely strict way. The advocate of the second solution may, however, hold on to the solution's basic intuition: that something's 'being' by being most strictly true does not entail its being true when 'true' is used in the ordinary way, and, in parallel fashion, something's 'not being' by being most strictly false does not entail its being false when 'false' is used in the ordinary way.

A similar approach provides a reply to an objection that someone might raise by appealing to *Metaphysics Δ* 29. In this chapter Aristotle lists the uses of 'false': on its first two uses 'false' applies to objects, on the third to phrases, on the fourth to people. The objector might use this evidence to insist that for Aristotle there are false objects. However, on reflection, *Δ* 29 corroborates the interpretation of *Θ* 10 developed in the last paragraphs because it shows that Aristotle distinguishes uses of 'false'. In particular, the first use of 'false' mentioned in *Δ* 29 (at 1024^{b}17–21 = [T5]) seems identical to what in *Θ* 10 is considered its extremely strict use[73] (its position at the head of *Δ* 29 also fits well with its being the strictest use of 'false'). Although no chapter of *Metaphysics Δ* is dedicated to the uses of 'true', it is reasonable to assume that in Aristotle's view they match those of 'false' distinguished in *Δ* 29.

One might be worried by the assumption that something can be called 'true' (or 'false') in accordance with the strictest use of the expression but cannot be so called in accordance with its ordinary use. Could Aristotle commit himself to an instance of 'Although σ may be called "Φ" in accordance with the strictest use of "Φ", σ cannot be called "Φ" in accordance with the ordinary use of "Φ"'?[74] In fact, he does. For instance, in *De caelo* (1. 11, 280^{b}25–281^{a}1) Aristotle distinguishes several uses of '*aphthartos*'[75] and singles out one as extremely strict (he employs '*malista kuriōs*' at 280^{b}31–2 and '*kuriōtata*' at 281^{a}3): '*aphthartos*' applies to (1) what exists at one time and not at a later one without undergoing any process of destruction (e.g. contacts), (2) that which now exists but either could fail to exist or will later not exist (e.g. you or contacts), (3) what has not

---

[73] More on this in the subsection corresponding to n. 93 below.
[74] Cf. U. Coope, review of Crivelli, *Truth*, in *Notre Dame Philosophical Reviews* (2005), 11.12 ⟨https://ndpr.nd.edu/news/24902-aristotle-on-truth/⟩.
[75] I do not translate '*ἄφθαρτος*' because the most obvious renderings, i.e. 'undestroyed' and 'indestructible', are both inadequate in that they fail to cover the spectrum of uses envisaged by Aristotle.

yet been destroyed and exists now but can fail to exist later, and (4) what is destroyed only with difficulty (e.g. the pyramids); in its extremely strict use, however, '*aphthartos*' applies to (5) what exists and cannot be destroyed by existing at one time and not at a later one. Clearly, '*aphthartos*' on its extremely strict use (5) does not apply to anything to which it applies according to uses (1), (2), (3), and (4).[76] Again, in *Categories* 12 Aristotle distinguishes five uses of 'prior'. (1) When it is used 'most strictly [*kuriōtata*]' ($14^{a}27$), 'prior' applies to what is older or more ancient than other things. 'Prior' applies also to (2) that whose being is implied by another thing's being but does not imply it, (3) what precedes in any order (as in speeches, where the introduction is called 'prior' to the exposition), (4) what is better and more valued, and (5) that which reciprocates as to implication of being with another thing but whose being is somehow an explanation or cause of that of the other thing. 'Prior' in its extremely strict use (1) need not apply to what it applies to in uses (2), (3), (4), or (5).[77]

The reconciliation under consideration becomes more palatable once one realizes that in Θ 10 the attributes expressed by 'true' and 'false' on their strictest use play a foundational and explanatory role with respect to the attributes expressed by 'true' and 'false' on their ordinary use. For, as we shall see,[78] the attributes expressed by 'true' and 'false' on their strictest use, i.e. 'being'-as-truth and 'not-being'-as-falsehood, are appealed to in definitions that fix when it is that the attributes expressed by 'true' and 'false' on their ordinary use, i.e. truth and falsehood, hold of declarations and judgements. Indeed, the reason why the use of 'true' and 'false' whereby they express the first two attributes is called 'extremely strict' is probably that these attributes play such a foundational and explanatory role with respect to those expressed by 'true' and 'false' on their ordinary use. But now, when a certain attribute P plays a foundational and explanatory role with respect to an attribute Q, P is usually expected not to entail Q: otherwise a situation of circularity or regress

---

[76] I take it that according to the extremely strict use (5) 'ἄφθαρτος' applies to x now just if x exists now and it is not possible for there to be a time t and a later time t' such that x exists at t but not at t'. I owe to Marwan Rashed the reference to the passage from *De caelo*.

[77] Something similar happens with the uses of 'together' ('ἅμα') in *Categories* 13 ('κυριώτατα' occurs at $14^{b}24$).

[78] Cf. below, propositions [1] and [2] within the paragraph to n. 108.

could be deemed to arise.[79] In several passages Aristotle uses the adverb '*kuriōtata*' to describe a use that is fundamental and distinct from uses that are somehow derived from it.[80]

Which of the two reconciliations of the third apparent clash between E 4 and Θ 10 is preferable? In earlier subsections I examined two possible reconciliations of the third apparent clash between E 4 and $Θ$ 10. They both require saddling Aristotle with an ambiguous use of expressions: according to the first reconciliation, the ambiguity concerns 'object'; according to the second, it concerns 'true' and 'false'. Which of these reconciliations should be preferred?

The second reconciliation has an advantage over the first in that the ambiguity it imputes to Aristotle is one that he may be plausibly taken to acknowledge: when in $Θ$ 10 he announces that in some cases '"being" and "not being" are spoken of . . . by being *most strictly* true or false' (1051^a34-^b2), Aristotle is probably implying that 'true' and 'false' are used in various ways. Another advantage of the second reconciliation over the first is the textual support it gets from $Θ$ 10 as a whole.[81] In view of these strengths, the second reconciliation of the third apparent clash between E 4 and $Θ$ 10 is superior to the first. I conclude that the third apparent clash between E 4 and $Θ$ 10 is merely apparent and that in $Θ$ 10 Aristotle assigns 'being'-as-truth and 'not-being'-as-falsehood (i.e. 'being'-by-being-most-strictly-true and 'not-being'-by-being-most-strictly-false) to objects while reserving truth and falsehood (i.e. the attributes expressed by 'true' and 'false' on their ordinary use) for thoughts and sentences.[82]

3. Objects and states of affairs

Composites

A few lines after passage [T2] Aristotle says:

[79] Here I am indebted to Richard Glauser.
[80] Cf. above, n. 56.
[81] Cf. above, paragraph to n. 65.
[82] For different attempts to solve the third apparent clash between E 4 and $Θ$ 10 see Aquinas, *In Metaph.* 1230–40 Cathala–Spiazzi; W. Wieland, *Die aristotelische Physik* (Göttingen, 1962), 194; Luther, 'Wahrheit', 183; A. Graeser, 'Aristotle and Aquinas on Being as Being True', in C. Gagnebin (ed.), *Métaphysique: histoire de la philosophie. Recueil d'études offert à F. Brunner* (Neuchâtel, 1981), 85–97 at 88; Halper, *Metaphysics*, 217.

[T4]   περὶ δὲ δὴ τὰ ἀσύνθετα τί   1051ᵇ17
τὸ εἶναι ἢ μὴ εἶναι καὶ τὸ ἀληθές καὶ τὸ ψεῦδος; οὐ γάρ
ἐστι σύνθετον, ὥστε εἶναι μὲν ὅταν συγκέηται, μὴ εἶναι δὲ
ἐὰν διῃρημένον ᾖ, ὥσπερ τὸ λευκὸν ⟨τὸ⟩ ξύλον⁸³ ἢ τὸ ἀσύμμετρον   ᵇ20
τὴν διάμετρον· οὐδὲ τὸ ἀληθὲς καὶ τὸ ψεῦδος ὁμοίως ἔτι ὑπάρξει καὶ ἐπ' ἐκείνων.   ᵇ22

But then, with regard to incomposites, what are 'to be' or 'not to be' and truth and falsehood? For they are not composite, so as 'to be' when they are combined and 'not to be' if they are divided, like the log's being white and the diagonal's being incommensurable, nor will truth and falsehood hold still in the same way as⁸⁴ in the case of those. (*Metaph.* Θ 10, 1051ᵇ17–22)

Passage [T4] relies on a distinction between incomposites and composites.⁸⁵ It mentions 'the log's being white' (1051ᵇ20) and 'the diagonal's being incommensurable' (1051ᵇ20–1) as examples of composites. The log and whiteness are components of the first of these composites whereas the diagonal and incommensurability are components of the second. The log is an individual. Whiteness, the diagonal, and incommensurability are universals.⁸⁶ A conclusion that may therefore be plausibly drawn is that both individuals and universals are components of composites.⁸⁷

The log, whiteness, the diagonal, and incommensurability seem

⁸³ The witnesses and the earlier editions read 'τὸ λευκὸν ξύλον'. I adopt the emendation 'τὸ λευκὸν ⟨τὸ⟩ ξύλον', originally proposed by I. Bywater, 'Aristotelia V', *Journal of Philology*, 32 (1913), 107–22 at 110, and printed by Ross, Tredennick, and Jaeger.   ⁸⁴ For the use of 'καί' in comparisons cf. LSJ s.v. καί A III 2.

⁸⁵ The expressions 'incomposite' and 'composite' may be understood in two ways: they may indicate either the absence or presence of composition *with* other things, i.e. isolation or non-isolation, or the absence or presence of composition *of* other things, i.e. simplicity or non-simplicity. The second way of understanding 'incomposite' and 'composite' is the right one in the context of Θ 10 because in the passage of *E* 4 that alludes to the theories more fully developed in Θ 10, Aristotle speaks of 'simples' (1027ᵇ27).

⁸⁶ I cannot address here Aristotle's conception of universals. I take it that it is characterized by three theses: first, every universal is an external thing (it is neither a linguistic expression nor a mental state nor a mental act) and does not depend for its existence on someone's thinking of it; secondly, every universal can (at least in principle) be instantiated by two or more individuals; thirdly, every universal exists just when it is instantiated by at least one individual. Cf. *De int.* 7, 17ᵃ38–ᵇ1; *Pr. An.* 1. 27, 43ᵃ25–32; *Post. An.* 1. 1, 71ᵃ23–4; *SE* 22, 178ᵇ37–9, 179ᵃ8–10; *PA* 1. 4, 644ᵃ27–8; *Metaph.* B 4, 999ᵇ33–1000ᵃ1; Δ 9, 1018ᵃ1–4; Δ 26, 1023ᵇ29–32; Z 13, 1038ᵇ11–12, 16; Z 16, 1040ᵇ25–6; Crivelli, *Truth*, 78–82; M. J. Loux, 'Aristotle on Universals', in G. Anagnostopoulos (ed.), *A Companion to Aristotle* (Chichester, 2009), 186–196 at 190.

⁸⁷ Someone might object that the log which is a component of the log's being white is not an individual and that there is therefore no evidence that some individuals are components of composites. I disagree with the assumption that constitutes

Truth in Metaphysics E 4   193

not to enjoy the type of complexity that is present in the log's being white and the diagonal's being incommensurable, the composites furnished as examples. Hence another conclusion that may be plausibly drawn is that individuals and universals are not composites.

Objects[88]

When he discusses matters of philosophy of language or philosophy of mind, Aristotle normally uses 'object' ('*pragma*') for worldly entities which in some way or other correspond to linguistic expressions or thoughts. Thus, in a philosophy of language environment, 'object' is applied either to worldly entities signified by linguistic expressions, or to worldly entities of which linguistic expressions are true or false, or to worldly entities to which linguistic expressions are related in some other way;[89] similarly, in a philosophy of mind environment, 'object' is applied to worldly entities which in some way or other correspond to thoughts.[90] This Aristotelian use

the starting-point of this objection, i.e. the assumption that the log which is a component of the log's being white is not an individual. However, even if one were to grant it, there is further evidence that some individuals are components of composites. For, at the beginning of *Metaphysics Δ* 29 Aristotle mentions 'your being seated' (1024^b20) as an example of a 'false object' (1024^b17–18). Given that the position put forward at the beginning $Δ$ 29 is very close to that of $Θ$ 10 (as I shall argue later: cf. below, paragraph to n. 93), it may be plausibly inferred that your being seated is a composite. Since you are a component of your being seated (just as the log is a component of the log's being white), it may be plausibly inferred that you are a component of some composite. If this is right, then some individuals are components of composites (because you are an individual).

[88] Discussions of Aristotle's use of 'object' ('πρᾶγμα') may be found in P. Hadot, 'Sur divers sens du mot *pragma* dans la tradition philosophique grecque', in P. Aubenque (ed.), *Concepts et catégories dans la pensée antique* (Paris, 1980), 309–19 at 309–13, and de Rijk, 'Anatomy', 36–9.

[89] For instance, in the *Categories* (10, 12^b6–15) Aristotle says that just as an affirmative sentence is opposed to a negative sentence, so also 'under [ὑπό]' the affirmative sentence there is an 'object [πρᾶγμα]' opposed to one under the negative sentence. In chapter 1 of *De interpretatione* he says that 'affections of the soul, which are the first items of which these [sc. utterances] are signs, are the same for all, and the objects [πράγματα] of which these are likenesses are also the same' (16^a6–8). In chapter 9 he says that 'sentences are true in the same way as the objects [πράγματα]' (19^a33). In the *Topics* (1. 7, 103^a9–10) he declares that numerical identity obtains where 'the names are many but the object [πρᾶγμα] one'. In *Sophistici elenchi* he says that 'it is not possible to converse by bringing in the objects themselves [αὐτὰ τὰ πράγματα], but instead of the objects we use words as tokens' (1, 165^a6–8; cf. 16, 175^a8–9; 19, 177^a31–2; 22, 178^a25–7).

[90] For instance, in chapter 1 of *De interpretatione* Aristotle describes 'affections of the soul' as 'likenesses' of 'objects [πράγματα]' (cf. the quotation in the previous

of 'object' is rather generic. It is narrowed down in different ways in different contexts.

On the one hand, in a passage at the beginning of *De interpretatione* 7 Aristotle says that 'of objects some are universal, others individual (and I call "universal" what is of such a nature as to be predicated of more things while I call "individual" what is not such, e.g. man is one of the universals whereas Callias is one of the individuals)' ($17^{a}38$–$^{b}1$). This passage displays a narrow Aristotelian use of 'object' whereby the noun is applied to all universals and all individuals and nothing else.

On the other hand, in [T2] Aristotle says that 'this [*sc.* "being" by being most strictly true and "not being" by being most strictly false], in the case of *objects*, is to be combined or to be divided' ($1051^{b}1$–3). In [T4] he says about incomposites that they 'are not *composite*, so as "to be" when they are combined and "not to be" if they are divided' ($1051^{b}19$–20). The way in which the two passages are embedded in Θ 10 makes it plausible to assume that in them Aristotle makes the same claim about the same entities by using somewhat different words. In particular, it looks as if the noun 'object' as it is used in [T2] applies to all and only the entities to which the adjective 'composite' applies as it is used in T4. Since composites are precisely the entities to which the adjective 'composite' applies as it is used in [T4], there is a second narrow Aristotelian use of 'object', one whereby the noun is applied to all composites and nothing else.

On its first narrow Aristotelian use, 'object' is applied to all universals and all individuals and nothing else; on its second narrow Aristotelian use, 'object' is applied to all composites and nothing else. If, as I suggested at the end of the last subsection, individuals and universals are not composites, then on its first narrow Aristotelian use 'object' is applied to entities to which it is not applied on its second narrow Aristotelian use. The two uses are therefore different.

We therefore seem to be confronted with three Aristotelian uses of 'object': a generic use whereby the noun is applied to all worldly entities which in some way or other correspond to linguistic expressions or thoughts, a first narrow use whereby it is applied to all universals and all individuals and nothing else, and a second nar-

note). In *Phys.* 3. 8, $208^{a}14$–16, he uses 'object [πρᾶγμα]' and 'thought [νόησις]' to express the contrast between how things really are and how they are thought to be.

row use whereby it is applied to all composites and nothing else. These three Aristotelian uses of 'object' need not be regarded as constituting a case of full-blown ambiguity, i.e. of a single linguistic expression with three different senses. I think it is more plausible to understand them in terms of an expression being employed in a single sense (corresponding to the generic use) but having its range of application restricted by contextual factors in two different ways (which correspond to the two narrow uses). Consider, by way of analogy, how 'man' is used in 'England expects that every man will do his duty': although an utterance of this sentence at Trafalgar did not commit its speaker to the claim that England expects the men on the French ships (let alone men in other parts of the earth) also to do their duty, no special sense of 'man' was involved whereby the noun would denote only English men.[91] In this study, my own use of 'object' coincides with the second narrow Aristotelian one, namely the use whereby 'object' is applied to all composites and nothing else. Thus, objects coincide with composites.[92]

True and false judgements concerning objects

In passage [T2] Aristotle discusses true and false judgements concerning objects, i.e. composites (1051^b3-5). He describes a true judgement concerning an object as one where the thinker 'thinks of what is divided that it is divided and of what is combined that it is combined' (1051^b3-4). Since in his view for an object 'to be' as true is to be combined whereas 'not to be' as false is to be divided, it may be plausibly inferred that in his description Aristotle is committing himself to the view that in a true judgement concerning an object, the thinker either judges with regard to an object which 'is not' as false (i.e. 'of what is divided') that it 'is not' as false (i.e. 'that it is divided') or judges with regard to an object which 'is' as true (i.e. 'of what is combined') that it 'is' as true (i.e. 'that it is combined').

Aristotle briefly describes a false judgement concerning an object as one where the thinker 'is in a state contrary to that of the objects' (1051^b4-5). This brief description may be expanded by using the earlier and longer one as a model. Aristotle may then be plausibly regarded as committing himself to the view that in a false judge-

---

[91] Cf. P. Crivelli and D. Charles, '"Πρότασις" in Aristotle's *Prior Analytics*', *Phronesis*, 56 (2011), 193–203 at 199–200.   [92] Cf. above, text to n. 66.

ment concerning an object, the thinker either judges with regard to an object which 'is not' as false (i.e. 'of what is divided') that it 'is' as true (i.e. 'that it is combined') or judges with regard to an object which 'is' as true (i.e. 'of what is combined') that it 'is not' as false (i.e. 'that it is divided'). The thinker's state may be described as 'contrary to that of the objects' ($1051^{b}4$–5) because the attributes judged by the thinker to hold of the object are the contraries of those actually enjoyed by the object: the attribute judged by the thinker to hold of the object is either combination when the object actually enjoys division, or division when the object actually enjoys combination.

States of affairs

What are the objects of which Aristotle speaks (explicitly) in [T2] and (implicitly) in [T4]? Some light is thrown on this issue by two passages at the beginning of *Metaphysics* Δ 29:

[T5] τὸ ψεῦδος λέγεται ἄλλον μὲν τρόπον ὡς πρᾶγμα $1024^{b}17$
ψεῦδος, καὶ τούτου τὸ μὲν τῷ μὴ συγκεῖσθαι ἢ ἀδύνατον
εἶναι συντεθῆναι (ὥσπερ λέγεται τὸ τὴν διάμετρον εἶναι
σύμμετρον ἢ τὸ σὲ καθῆσθαι· τούτων γὰρ ψεῦδος τὸ μὲν $^{b}20$
ἀεὶ τὸ δὲ ποτέ· οὕτω γὰρ οὐκ ὄντα ταῦτα), τὰ δὲ . . . $^{b}21$

One way in which what is false is spoken of is as a false object. This can happen, on the one hand, because it is not combined or it is impossible for it to be composed (the diagonal's being commensurable and your being seated are spoken of in this way, for one of these is false always and the other sometimes, for it is in this way [sc. as false] that these are non-beings), and, on the other hand, in the case of such items that . . . (*Metaph.* Δ 29, $1024^{b}17$–21)

[T6]   πράγματα $1024^{b}24$
μὲν οὖν ψευδῆ οὕτω λέγεται, ἢ τῷ μὴ εἶναι αὐτὰ ἢ . . . $^{b}25$

Objects are then called 'false' in this way, either because they themselves are not [sc. as false] or . . . (*Metaph.* Δ 29, $1024^{b}24$–5)

Passages [T5] and [T6] are close to [T2] and [T4]. For, Aristotle's use of 'object' in [T5] in the phrase 'false object' recalls his use of 'object' in [T2] in the context of a discussion of truth and falsehood. Moreover, in [T5] the items to which 'object' is applied are said to be false because they are not combined and are characterized as 'non-beings' (presumably, as I suggested in my glosses, as false).

Truth in Metaphysics E 4   197

This matches rather closely some remarks made in [T2], [T4], and [T3]. Finally, the examples of [T5] (the diagonal's being commensurable and your being seated) recall those of [T4] (the log's being white and the diagonal's being incommensurable). I therefore assume that the items to which Aristotle in [T5] applies 'false object' are a subset of the objects discussed in Θ 10. I also assume that they are called 'false' in accordance with the 'extremely strict' use of the expression introduced in Θ 10.[93]

As I said earlier,[94] when he discusses issues of philosophy of language or philosophy of mind, Aristotle normally uses 'object' (*'pragma'*) for worldly entities which in some way or other correspond to linguistic expressions or for worldly entities which in some way or other correspond to thoughts. It is therefore probable that the word 'object' (*'pragma'*) within Aristotle's phrase 'false object' (*'pragma pseudos'*) indicates that what Aristotle is talking about is an external thing, i.e. an entity that is neither a linguistic expression nor a mental state nor a mental act.[95]

It is tempting to suggest that the items to which Aristotle in [T5] applies 'false object' exist sometimes (namely when their components are reciprocally combined) but do not exist at other times (namely when their components are not reciprocally combined), and that the fact that they exist sometimes is what earns them the title 'object'. The status of the items to which Aristotle in [T5] applies 'false object' would then be similar to that of thresholds: a certain particular threshold exists sometimes (namely when a certain particular stone is combined with the attribute of being in such-and-such a position) but does not exist at other times (namely when that stone is not combined with that attribute), and the fact that the threshold exists sometimes is what earns it the epithet

---

[93] Pearson, 'Being', 215, downplays the relevance of *Metaphysics Δ* 29. First, he maintains that in this passage Aristotle 'is providing accounts of different ways *false* can be used, not *being*'. However, although *Metaphysics Δ* 29 is dedicated to the uses of 'false' and not to those of 'being', at the beginning of the chapter (at 1024^{b}21 and 1024^{b}25) Aristotle describes falsehoods as non-beings. Secondly, Pearson points out that 'we should not assume that he [*sc.* Aristotle] would endorse the uses he mentions as good philosophical practice'. However, although one cannot automatically accept that the uses singled out in a chapter of *Metaphysics Δ* are taken on board by Aristotle as 'good philosophical practice', when these uses fit well with what Aristotle says elsewhere one may safely regard them as tools of Aristotelian philosophical analysis.

[94] Cf. above, paragraph to n. 88.

[95] Cf. above, n. 58.

'object'.⁹⁶ This suggestion, however, cannot be right. For one of the examples furnished in [T5] to explain the use of 'false object', namely the diagonal's being commensurable, is *always* false because its components are *always* reciprocally separated. If the suggestion under examination were correct, then the diagonal's being commensurable would never exist and would therefore not deserve the epithet 'object' because it exists sometimes. [T5]'s example of the diagonal's being commensurable requires that the items to which 'false object' is there applied be worthy of the title 'object' even if they are never combined.

At the end of [T5] Aristotle says: '... it is in this way that these [*sc*. the false objects in question] are non-beings' ($1024^b 21$). Some commentators take this clause to allude to a theory whereby for the items to which Aristotle in [T5] applies 'false object', to exist is to be combined and not to exist is not to be combined.⁹⁷ If this were the point made by this clause, Aristotle would be committed to the claim that it is impossible for the diagonal's being commensurable to exist (for he says that 'it is impossible for it to be composed', $1024^b 18-19$). But it would be extremely strange for Aristotle to apply the word 'object' to something when, in his view, it is impossible for it to exist. So, the clause at the end of [T5], '... it is in this way that these [*sc*. the false objects in question] are non-beings' ($1024^b 21$), is probably not alluding to a theory whereby to exist is to be combined and not to exist is not to be combined. A more plausible interpretation of the clause is that according to which it means that the items to which 'false object' is applied in [T5] are 'non-beings' as false,⁹⁸ where to be a 'non-being' as false is compatible with (indeed, requires) existence.⁹⁹

⁹⁶ Cf. *Metaph*. H 2, $1042^b 26-7$.
⁹⁷ Cf. L. Keeler, 'Aristotle on the Problem of Error', *Gregorianum*, 13 (1932), 241–60 at 244; E. Tugendhat, 'Der Wahrheitsbegriff bei Aristoteles', in E. Tugendhat, *Philosophische Aufsätze* (Frankfurt a.M., 1992), 251–60 at 255; C. Kirwan (trans. and comm.), *Aristotle: Metaphysics, Books Γ, Δ, and E [Metaphysics]*, 2nd edn. (Oxford, 1993), 178–9; J. Thorp, 'Aristotle on Being and Truth', *De Philosophia*, 3 (1982), 1–9 at 8; M. Matthen, 'Greek Ontology and the "Is" of Truth', *Phronesis*, 28 (1983), 113–35 at 125–7; M.-P. Duminil and A. Jaulin (trans. and comm.), *Aristote: Métaphysiques, livre Delta* (Toulouse, 1991), 289–90; R. J. Ketchum, 'Being and Existence in Greek Ontology', *Archiv für Geschichte der Philosophie*, 80 (1998), 321–32 at 322–3; A. T. Bäck, *Aristotle's Theory of Predication* (Leiden, Boston, and Cologne, 2000), 84; J. Thorp, 'Aristotle on the Truth of *Things*', unpublished typescript, 7.
⁹⁸ Cf. de Rijk, 'Anatomy', 38, 56. The phrase 'οὕτω . . . οὐκ ὄντα' at $1024^b 21$ recalls 'τὸ . . . οὕτως ὄν' ('what "is" in this way [*sc*. as true]') at *E* 4, $1027^b 31$, and 'τὸ οὕτως ὄν' ('what "is" in this way [*sc*. as true]') at *K* 8, $1065^a 23$. Also cf. 'ὂν οὕτως' at Θ 10, [*See opposite for n. 98 cont. and n. 99*]

A useful analogy for understanding the nature of the items to which Aristotle in [T5] applies 'false object' involves a football team. A football team plays football sometimes (when its members are playing football with one another) and does not play football at other times (when its members are not playing football with one another), but the team itself exists both when it is playing football and when it is not playing. Similarly, some of the items to which Aristotle in [T5] applies 'false object' are combined and true sometimes (when their constituents are reciprocally combined) and are not combined and are false at other times (when their constituents are not reciprocally combined), but they themselves exist both when they are combined and when they are not combined. It follows that the lack of combination which makes these items false does not destroy the combination that makes them composite and is a necessary condition for their existence (similarly, the fact that a team is not playing football at a given time does not destroy the ties that make it a team). The remaining items to which 'false object' is applied in [T5] are always not combined and are always false (because their constituents are never reciprocally combined), but they themselves exist throughout the time they are not combined. One of course expects there to be further items (not mentioned in [T5]) which are combined and true always (because their constituents are always reciprocally combined) and exist throughout the time they are combined.[100]

Thus, the items to which Aristotle in [T5] applies 'false object' are probably states of affairs, which are external things, can (at least in principle) be both true and false at (different) times, and exist not only when they are true but also when they are false.[101] On the basis

---

$1051^{b}35$ (where I adopt Christ's punctuation, with no comma before 'οὕτως' and one after it).

[99] According to S. Rangos, 'Falsity and the False in Aristotle's *Metaphysics Δ*', *Rhizai*, 6 (2009), 7–21 at 9–10, in [T5] Aristotle uses 'πρᾶγμα' to indicate that the non-existence of the combinations he mentions (of the diagonal with commensurability and of you with sitting) is a fact of the world. This suggestion is hard to square with the circumstance that Aristotle describes the πρᾶγμα itself as false and as a non-being. If Aristotle's intention had been to use 'πρᾶγμα' to say that the non-existence of the combinations he mentions is a fact of the world, he would have used sentences such as 'That such-and-such a combination is a non-being is a πρᾶγμα'.

[100] Cf. *Metaph. Θ* 10, $1051^{b}9$–17 (paraphrased above, paragraph to n. 65).

[101] Some philosophers use 'state of affairs' as a synonym of 'fact' (cf. D. Davidson, 'The Folly of Trying to Define Truth', *Journal of Philosophy*, 93 (1996), 263–78 at 266). On my preferred usage, 'state of affairs' and 'fact' apply to different things:

of the closeness of [T5] and [T6] with [T4] and [T2], I assume that not only the items to which Aristotle in [T5] applies 'false object', but also those to which Aristotle applies 'object' in Θ 10, are states of affairs. So, the objects of Θ 10 are states of affairs.[102] Aristotle appears to recognize only 'positive' states of affairs. For, suppose that among the states of affairs he acknowledges there were 'negative' states of affairs (e.g. your not walking). Then, in explaining what it is for a state of affairs to be false, Aristotle would probably have at least suggested that, on the one hand, some states of affairs (i.e. 'positive' ones) are true (or false) just when[103] they are combined (or divided), and, on the other hand, other states of affairs (i.e. 'negative' ones) are true (or false) just when they are divided (or combined). But Aristotle says nothing of this sort. In [T5] he only says that a 'false object', i.e. a false state of affairs, is false 'because it is not combined or it is impossible for it to be composed' (1024^b18-19); and in [T2] he only says that 'being' by being most strictly true and 'not being' by being most strictly false, 'in the case of objects [sc. states of affairs], is to be combined or to be divided' (1051^b2-3).[104]

some of the things to which 'state of affairs' applies are sometimes false, none of those to which 'fact' applies is ever false ('false fact' is an oxymoron).

[102] Cf. G. Nuchelmans, *Theories of the Proposition: Ancient and Medieval Conceptions of the Bearers of Truth and Falsity* (Amsterdam and London, 1973), 33–4; P. J. Harvey, 'Aristotle on Truth with Respect to Incomposites' (diss. University of Michigan, 1975), 108; de Rijk, 'Anatomy', 35–6, 38, 45–7; P. Simons, 'Aristotle's Concept of State of Affairs', in O. Gigon and M. W. Fischer (eds.), *Antike Rechts- und Sozialphilosophie* (Frankfurt a.M., Bern, New York, and Paris, 1988), 97–112 at 112; M. Mignucci, 'Vérité et pensée dans le *De anima*', in G. Romeyer Dherbey and C. Viano (eds.), *Corps et âme: sur le De anima d'Aristote* (Paris, 1996), 405–22 at 417; R. Gaskin, 'Simplicius on the Meaning of Sentences: A Commentary on *In Cat.* 396, 30–397, 28', *Phronesis*, 43 (1998), 42–62 at 44–5; de Rijk, *Semantics*, ii. 126–8; W. Künne, *Conceptions of Truth [Conceptions]* (Oxford, 2003), 96; Crivelli, *Truth*, 46–50; F. A. Lewis, 'Predication, Things, and Kinds in Aristotle's *Metaphysics*' ['Predication'], *Phronesis*, 56 (2011), 350–87 at 358–62.

[103] I use 'just when' to mean 'at all and only the times when'. For Aristotle truth and falsehood are time-relative: declarations and judgements are true or false at times (cf. Crivelli, *Truth*, 183–4).

[104] Cf. 1051^b18-21 (<[T4]); de Rijk, 'Anatomy', 46; Crivelli, *Truth*, 49–50. Aristotle mentions both the diagonal's being commensurable (at *Metaph.* Δ 29, 1024^b19-20<[T5]) and the diagonal's being incommensurable (at *Metaph.* Θ 10, 1051^b20-1<[T4]), which look like a positive state of affairs and the corresponding negative state of affairs. Nevertheless, he treats them both as if they were positive: of the first he says that it is false 'because it is not combined or it is impossible for it to be composed' (1024^b18-19), of the second that it is one of the composites whose nature is '"to be" when they are combined and "not to be" if they are divided' (1051^b19-

Why states of affairs? Why only 'positive' states of affairs?

Why does Aristotle accept states of affairs, awkward entities that exist even when they are false? The most plausible answer appeals to one of the probable linguistic grounds of Aristotle's decision to study 'what "is" as true and what "is not" as false' (1027^b18–19): the employment of noun-phrases based on the participles of 'to be' and 'not to be' as complements of verbs of thinking (or saying), in constructions such as 'to judge (or say) the things that are' and 'to judge (or say) the things that are not'.[105] In a false judgement (or false speech), we judge (or say) the things that are not but there is nevertheless something that we are judging (or saying). This, as Plato pointed out in the *Sophist* (especially at 237 B 7–E 7), suggests that there is something that is not. Aristotle's reaction is, in effect, to accept the existence of something that 'is not' as false (some modern philosophers would be inclined to present the position by drawing a distinction between the existential use of 'to be' and its use associated with truth, but Aristotle never seems to single out an existential use of 'to be').

One might object that if this is the source of Aristotle's acceptance of states of affairs, then he should accept (not only 'positive', but) also 'negative' states of affairs. Specifically, one might object that if I make a false negative judgement (e.g. by judging that the diagonal is not incommensurable), then the existent state of affairs that 'is not' as false must be a 'negative' state of affairs (e.g. the 'negative' state of affairs of the diagonal's not being incommensurable). This objection is met by considering Plato's discussion of the troublesome expression 'to judge the things that are not' in a passage of the *Sophist* (240 D 9–241 A 2) whose examination of falsehood probably lies behind Aristotle's reflections on what 'is' as true and what 'is not' as false. For, at the beginning of the passage in question, Plato characterizes false judgement as a judgement that judges the

---

20). The components of the diagonal's being commensurable must be the diagonal and commensurability, those of the diagonal's being incommensurable must be the diagonal and incommensurability. In this context Aristotle seems to commit himself to negative universals. Aristotle briefly discusses states of affairs also at *Cat.* 10, 12^b6–15, where he describes them as underlying contradictory sentences and as being reciprocally related in the same way as the contradictory sentences they underlie. He probably has in mind situations such as that of the diagonal's being commensurable and the diagonal's being incommensurable (cf. *Metaph.* Δ 7, 1017^a31–5 with n. 142 below).

[105] Cf. above, n. 22, and text thereto.

things which are not. This usual characterization of false judgement then undergoes an unexpected transformation. It gets 'polarized' by the distinction between affirmative and negative judgements: (*a*) a false *affirmative* judgement judges with regard to the things that are not that they are; (*b*) a false *negative* judgement judges with regard to the things that are that they are not. At the end of the passage, the 'polarized' account of falsehood is extended to sentences. If the 'polarized' account of false judgement is translated into the jargon of states of affairs, the result is: (*a**) a false *affirmative* judgement judges with regard to a state of affairs that 'is not' as false that it 'is' as true; (*b**) a false *negative* judgement judges with regard to a state of affairs that 'is' as true that it 'is not' as false. This final account requires only 'positive' states of affairs, as befits Aristotle's conception.

States of affairs and true and false predicative judgements

Objects are states of affairs. In most cases, a state of affairs is composed of two further entities, namely two universals or an individual and a universal. For instance, the state of affairs of the diagonal's being commensurable is composed of the diagonal and commensurability, which are two universals, while the state of affairs of your being seated is composed of you, an individual, and seated, a universal. In a few cases, a state of affairs is composed of a single further entity, a universal: for instance, the state of affairs of a man's being a man is composed only of man, a universal.[106] For a state of affairs to 'be' as true is for it to be combined, which in turn is the same as for its constituents to be reciprocally combined. For a state of affairs 'not to be' as false is for it to be divided, which in turn is the same as for its constituents to be reciprocally divided. A state of affairs exists even when it 'is not' as false. The division whereby a state of affairs 'is not' as false entails that the state of affairs is not combined in such a way as to 'be' as true, but does not entail that the state of affairs is not composed in the way required for its very existence. In other words, the division whereby a state of affairs 'is not' as false does not destroy the composition that makes the state of affairs a composite entity.[107]

We can now return to [T2]. Earlier I argued that in this passage

---

[106] Cf. *Metaph.* Z 17, 1041ª17–18, 1041ª22.
[107] Cf. Lewis, 'Predication', 359–61.

Truth in Metaphysics E 4

Aristotle commits himself, on the one hand, to the view that in a true judgement concerning an object, the thinker either judges with regard to an object which 'is not' as false (i.e. 'of what is divided') that it 'is not' as false (i.e. 'that it is divided') or judges with regard to an object which 'is' as true (i.e. 'of what is combined') that it 'is' as true (i.e. 'that it is combined'), and, on the other hand, to the view that in a false judgement concerning an object, the thinker either judges with regard to an object which 'is not' as false (i.e. 'of what is divided') that it 'is' as true (i.e. 'that it is combined') or judges with regard to an object which 'is' as true (i.e. 'of what is combined') that it 'is not' as false (i.e. 'that it is divided'). Given that objects are states of affairs, and factoring in the uncontroversial idea that the judgements concerning states of affairs are affirmative and negative predicative judgements, the following theses may be plausibly attributed to Aristotle:

[1] In an affirmative predicative judgement, the state of affairs whose constituents are the entity (a universal) thought about through the judgement's predicate-component and the entity (a universal or an individual) thought about through the judgement's subject-component is judged 'to be' as true, i.e. is judged to be combined, i.e. its constituents are judged to be reciprocally combined. The affirmative predicative judgement is true (or false) just when the state of affairs 'is' as true (or 'is not' as false), i.e. just when the state of affairs is combined (or divided), i.e. just when the constituents of the state of affairs (namely the universal thought about through the judgement's predicate-component and the entity thought about through the judgement's subject-component) are reciprocally combined (or divided).

[2] In a negative predicative judgement, the state of affairs whose constituents are the entity thought about through the judgement's predicate-component and the entity thought about through the judgement's subject-component is judged 'not to be' as false, i.e. is judged to be divided, i.e. its constituents are judged to be reciprocally divided. The negative predicative judgement is true (or false) just when the state of affairs 'is not' as false (or 'is' as true), i.e. just when the state of affairs is divided (or combined), i.e. just when the constituents of the state of affairs (namely the universal thought about through

the judgement's predicate-component and the entity thought about through the judgement's subject-component) are reciprocally divided (or combined).

After characterizing 'being'-as-truth and 'not-being'-as-falsehood as combination and division of states of affairs ($1051^a34–^b3$), and after explaining truth and falsehood of affirmative and negative predicative judgements by reference to the 'being'-as-truth and 'not-being'-as-falsehood of states of affairs ($1051^b3–5$), Aristotle asks: 'When is it that what is spoken of as true or false "is" or "is not"?' ($1051^b3–5$). He stresses the importance of the problem by adding: 'What we say on this must be investigated' (1051^b6). He then explains why the problem is important by adding: 'For it is not because we truly think that you are white that you are white, but it is because of your being white that we who say this are right' ($1051^b6–9$).[108] The explanation becomes clear under the natural assumption that your being white is the same thing as the state of affairs of your being white 'being' as true: Aristotle is claiming that the fact that the state of affairs 'is' as true (or 'is not' as false) has explanatory priority over the fact that the judgement concerning it is true (or false). For this reason, to understand the behaviour over time of truth and falsehood with respect to predicative judgements, one must investigate the behaviour over time of 'being'-as-truth and 'not-being'-as-falsehood with respect to states of affairs.[109] This Aristotle proceeds to do in the chapter's sequel (at $1051^b9–17$).[110]

Predicative judgements of different sorts

It is hard to imagine Aristotle maintaining that universal, particular, and singular affirmative (or negative) predicative judgements posit the entity thought about through their predicate-component to be combined *in the same way* with (or divided *in the same way* from) the entity thought about through their subject-component. Perhaps he believes that *universal*, *particular*, and *singular* affirmative (or negative) judgements posit different types of combination (or division). Given his account of universal and particular affirmative and negative predicative declarations in *De interpretatione* 7, and given the isomorphism which in his view obtains between

[108] Cf. *Cat.* 12, $14^b13–22$.
[109] Cf. Crivelli, *Truth*, 57–8; Pearson, 'Being', 212–14; Makin, *Theta*, 250.
[110] Cf. above, paragraph to n. 65.

Truth in Metaphysics E 4   205

the mental and linguistic spheres, Aristotle would probably favour something like the following:

[3] In any universal affirmative predicative judgement, the thinker judges that the universal thought about through the judgement's predicate-component is combined with the universal thought about through its subject-component in such a way as universally to hold of it. Accordingly, a universal affirmative predicative judgement is true (or false) just when the universal thought about through its predicate-component is combined with (or divided from) the universal thought about through its subject-component in such a way as universally to hold of it (or not universally to hold of it).

[4] In any universal negative predicative judgement, the thinker judges that the universal thought about through the judgement's predicate-component is divided from the universal thought about through its subject-component in such a way as universally to fail to hold of it. Accordingly, a universal negative predicative judgement is true (or false) just when the universal thought about through its predicate-component is divided from (or combined with) the universal thought about through its subject-component in such a way as universally to fail to hold of it (or not universally to fail to hold of it).

[5] In any particular affirmative predicative judgement, the thinker judges that the universal thought about through the judgement's predicate-component is combined with the universal thought about through its subject-component in such a way as not universally to fail to hold of it. Accordingly, a particular affirmative predicative judgement is true (or false) just when the universal thought about through its predicate-component is combined with (or divided from) the universal thought about through its subject-component in such a way as not universally to fail to hold of it (or universally to fail to hold of it).

[6] In any particular negative predicative judgement, the thinker judges that the universal thought about through the judgement's predicate-component is divided from the universal thought about through its subject-component in such a way as not universally to hold of it. Accordingly, a particular negative predicative judgement is true (or false) just when

the universal thought about through its predicate-component is divided from (or combined with) the universal thought about through its subject-component in such a way as not universally to hold of it (or universally to hold of it).

[7] In any singular affirmative predicative judgement, the thinker judges that the universal thought about through the judgement's predicate-component is combined with the entity thought about through its subject-component in such a way as to hold of it. Accordingly, a singular affirmative predicative judgement is true (or false) just when the universal thought about through its predicate-component is combined with (or divided from) the entity thought about through its subject-component in such a way as to hold of it (or hold outside it).

[8] In any singular negative predicative judgement, the thinker judges that the universal thought about through the judgement's predicate-component is divided from the entity thought about through its subject-component in such a way as to hold outside it. Accordingly, a singular negative predicative judgement is true (or false) just when the universal thought about through its predicate-component is divided from (or combined with) the entity thought about through its subject-component in such a way as to hold outside it (or hold of it).

To pin down the above, definitions of the relevant relations of combination and division are called for. A universal u is combined with a universal v in such a way as universally to hold of it just when every entity that instantiates v instantiates u. A universal u is divided from a universal v in such a way as universally to fail to hold of it just when every entity that instantiates v is different from every entity that instantiates u. A universal u is combined with a universal v in such a way as not universally to fail to hold of it just when at least one entity that instantiates v instantiates u. A universal u is divided from a universal v in such a way as not universally to hold of it just when at least one entity that instantiates v is different from every entity that instantiates u. A universal u is combined with an entity i in such a way as to hold of it just when i instantiates u. A universal u is divided from an entity i in such a way as to hold outside it just when i is different from every entity that instantiates u.[111]

4. What 'is' as true in E 4

Composition and division

I now present an interpretation of E 4 that relies on the working hypothesis that this chapter agrees with Θ 10. I wish to show that such a hypothesis is plausible and throws light on several difficult passages.

The discussion of what 'is' as true in E 4 opens with the remark that 'what "is" as true and what "is not" as false . . . depend on composition and division' (1027^b18–19). Aristotle could mean either that they depend on the joining and the separating performed by predicative judgements,[112] or that they depend on the actual composition and the actual division of external things.

Two considerations tilt the balance in favour of the second exegesis. (1) The initial sentence, 'What "is" as true and what "is not" as false . . . depend on composition and division' (1027^b18–19), is

---

[111] Cf. F. D. Miller, Jr., 'Aristotle's Account of Being and Truth' (diss. University of Washington, 1971), 29–32; P. Crivelli, 'Notes on Aristotle's Conception of Truth', in M. S. Funghi (ed.), Ὁδοὶ διζήσιος — *Le vie della ricerca: studi in onore di Francesco Adorno* (Florence, 1996), 147–59 at 153–5; Crivelli, *Truth*, 92–5, 258–65; P. Crivelli, 'Aristotle on Signification and Truth', in G. Anagnostopoulos (ed.), *A Companion to Aristotle* (Chichester, 2009), 81–100 at 96–7; Miller, 'Belief', 289. The relations concerning universals described in the main text above and employed in propositions [3]–[8] are based on Aristotle's remarks in *De int.* 7, 17^a38–$^b23$ (in my *Truth*, 239–53, I examined how this passage may be taken to provide evidence for crediting Aristotle with a theory of this sort). A similar theory may be found in the *Prior Analytics*: in my 'Semantiche per la sillogistica di Aristotele', in AA. VV., *Papiri filosofici*, Miscellanea di Studi, VI (Florence, 2011), 297–317 at 304–17, I argued that in the *Prior Analytics* Aristotle puts forward truth conditions for universal and particular affirmative and negative predicative propositions, and these truth conditions are in fact equivalent to those presented in propositions [3]–[6] in the main text above. Two differences between the positions of *De interpretatione* and of the *Prior Analytics* are worth mentioning. First, the truth conditions given in the *Prior Analytics* are formulated by taking existential quantification as fundamental (cf. *Pr. An.* 1. 1, 24^b28–30), while in *De interpretatione* universal quantification is basic (cf. *De int.* 7, 17^a38–$^b23$). Secondly, in the *Prior Analytics* Aristotle concentrates on terms being true of entities rather than on universals (entities signified by terms) holding of entities. This might be due to his desire to have a logic free from controversial ontological assumptions.

[112] Cf. Schwegler, *Metaphysik*, iv. 30; Kirwan, *Metaphysics*, 198–9; de Rijk, *Semantics*, ii. 140.

closely linked to its immediate sequel, '... and together they [sc. what "is" as true and what "is not" as false] are concerned with the apportionment of a contradiction, for truth has the affirmation in the case of what is combined and the negation in the case of what is divided, whereas falsehood has the contradiction of this apportionment' ($1027^{b}20$–3). The combination and the division mentioned in the sequel clearly are the actual combination and the actual division of the external things thought about.[113] The close link between the initial sentence and its sequel makes it plausible to assume that the composition and the division mentioned in the initial sentence are the actual combination and the actual division of external things.[114] (2) In Θ 10 Aristotle clearly claims that what 'is' as true and what 'is not' as false depend on the actual combination and the actual division of external things.[115] The hypothesis that E 4 agrees with Θ 10 makes it desirable to find this claim already at the beginning of E 4's discussion of what 'is' as true.

Apportioning contradictions

Aristotle goes on to speak of the 'apportionment of a contradiction': 'Together they [sc. what "is" as true and what "is not" as false] are concerned with the apportionment of a contradiction, for truth has the affirmation in the case of what is combined and the negation in the case of what is divided, whereas falsehood has the contradiction of this apportionment [sc. falsehood has the negation in the case of what is combined and the affirmation in the case of what is divided]' ($1027^{b}19$–23).[116] The apportionment mentioned by Aristotle is a process of apportioning that consists in dividing up an

[113] Here I differ from S. Maso, 'La verità di Aristotele: intorno a *Epsilon* 4', in L. Cortella, F. Mora, and I. Testa (eds.), *La socialità della ragione: scritti in onore di Luigi Ruggiu* (Milan and Udine, 2011), 89–102 at 95–9. Maso takes '$\dot{\epsilon}\pi\grave{\iota}\ \tau\hat{\wp}\ \sigma\upsilon\gamma\kappa\epsilon\iota\mu\acute{\epsilon}\nu\wp$' ($1027^{b}21$) and '$\dot{\epsilon}\pi\grave{\iota}\ \tau\hat{\wp}\ \delta\iota\eta\rho\eta\mu\acute{\epsilon}\nu\wp$' ($1027^{b}21$–$2$) to refer to mental operations of joining and separating and argues that E 4 presents a coherentist conception of truth.
[114] The oscillation between '$\sigma\acute{\upsilon}\nu\theta\epsilon\sigma\iota\nu$' ($1027^{b}19$) and '$\sigma\upsilon\gamma\kappa\epsilon\iota\mu\acute{\epsilon}\nu\wp$' ($1027^{b}21$) matches that between '$\sigma\upsilon\gamma\kappa\epsilon\hat{\iota}\sigma\theta\alpha\iota$' ($1024^{b}18$) and '$\sigma\upsilon\nu\tau\epsilon\theta\hat{\eta}\nu\alpha\iota$' ($1024^{b}19$) in [T5].
[115] $1051^{b}2$–3, 11–13, 19–20, 33–5.
[116] The phrase 'what "is" as true' ('$\tau\grave{o}\ \ldots\ \dot{\omega}s\ \dot{\alpha}\lambda\eta\theta\grave{\epsilon}s\ \check{o}\nu$', $1027^{b}18$) is picked up by 'in the case of what is combined' ('$\dot{\epsilon}\pi\grave{\iota}\ \tau\hat{\wp}\ \sigma\upsilon\gamma\kappa\epsilon\iota\mu\acute{\epsilon}\nu\wp$', $1027^{b}21$), not by 'truth' ('$\tau\grave{o}\ \ldots\ \dot{\alpha}\lambda\eta\theta\acute{\epsilon}s$', $1027^{b}20$). In parallel fashion, the phrase 'what "is not" as false' ('$\mu\grave{\eta}\ \check{o}\nu\ \dot{\omega}s\ \psi\epsilon\hat{\upsilon}\delta os$', $1027^{b}18$–19) is picked up by 'in the case of what is divided' ('$\dot{\epsilon}\pi\grave{\iota}\ \tau\hat{\wp}\ \delta\iota\eta\rho\eta\mu\acute{\epsilon}\nu\wp$', $1027^{b}21$–2), not by 'falsehood' ('$\tau\grave{o}\ \ldots\ \psi\epsilon\hat{\upsilon}\delta os$', $1027^{b}22$). Commentators often associate 'what "is" as true' ($1027^{b}18$) with 'truth' ($1027^{b}20$) and 'what "is not" as false' ($1027^{b}18$–19) with 'falsehood' ($1027^{b}22$): cf. [Alex. Aphr.] *In Metaph.*

entity, e.g. a prey, and assigning its parts to deserving beneficiaries, e.g. hunters, on the basis of some criterion, e.g. social status. In the case at hand, the apportioned 'prey' is a contradiction, namely a contradictory pair of predicative judgements, the 'hunters' benefiting from the apportionment are the truth values, namely truth and falsehood, and the criterion that determines how the apportionment goes (i.e. which member of the contradictory pair is assigned to which truth value) is the presence of combination or division, i.e. of the actual combination or division of external things. Aristotle has just observed that 'what "is" as true and what "is not" as false . . . depend on composition and division' (1027^b18-19), i.e. on the actual combination or division of external things. Since the actual combination or division of external things determines how the apportionment goes, the claim that 'together they [sc. what "is" as true and what "is not" as false] are concerned with the apportionment of a contradiction' (1027^b19-20) is justified by what immediately follows (note the 'for', '*gar*', which introduces the justification at 1027^b20).[117]

Aristotle then says that 'falsehood and truth are not in objects . . . but in thought' (1027^b25-7). He probably wishes to convey the point that falsehood and truth are attributes that inhere in thought but not in objects,[118] the intended contrast being with 'being'-as-truth and 'not-being'-as-falsehood, attributes that inhere in objects but not in thought. The difference between the behaviour of truth and falsehood and that of 'being'-as-truth and 'not-being'-as-falsehood justifies the role of the latter in the apportionment of a contradictory pair (note the 'for', '*gar*', which introduces the justification at 1027^b25). Recall that according to Θ 10, thoughts and sentences enjoy truth and falsehood whereas 'being'-as-truth and 'not-being'-as-falsehood are reserved for objects.[119] Here in *E* 4, as in Θ 10, objects are composites, i.e.

457. 3–8 Hayduck; Bonitz, *Metaphysica*, ii. 293; Brentano, *Bedeutung*, 33–4; Pearson, 'Being', 204–10.

[117] While 'apportionment' in the phrase 'are concerned with the apportionment of a contradiction' (1027^b20) indicates the *process* of apportioning the 'prey', in the phrase 'the contradiction of this apportionment' (1027^b22-3) it probably indicates the *products of the process* of apportioning the 'prey', i.e. the parts of the 'prey' that are being apportioned.

[118] Aristotle sometimes uses 'in' ('ἐν'+dat.) to express inherence: cf. *Cat.* 2, 1^a20-^b6; *Phys.* 4. 3, 210^a20-1; *Metaph. Δ* 23, 1023^a11-13.

[119] Cf. above, paragraph to n. 65.

states of affairs: 'objects' (1027^b26) are implicitly contrasted with 'simples' (1027^b27).[120]

Truth and falsehood are (1027^b26–7) compared with goodness and badness. On the one hand, there is a similarity: first, truth and falsehood resemble goodness and badness because a true thought achieves its goal whereas a false thought misses it;[121] secondly, as judgements are evaluated by considering truth and falsehood, so choices are evaluated by considering goodness and badness.[122] On the other hand, there is an important difference, which is particularly relevant to the context of *E* 4: while goodness and badness are in external things,[123] truth and falsehood are in thought. For this reason it would be wrong to identify truth with goodness and falsehood with badness.

What 'is' as true and the categories

In the second half of *E* 4, at 1027^b29–1028^a4, Aristotle argues for the chapter's main claim, that the study of being may leave aside the examination of what 'is' as true. The argument starts with the remark that 'the interweaving and the division are in thought, not in objects' (1027^b29–31). Aristotle probably wants to convey the point that the operations of joining and separating are attributes that inhere not in objects but in thought. The motivation is that an affirmative predicative judgement is a thought that joins one entity with one entity whereas a negative predicative judgement is a thought that separates one entity from one entity.[124] It is clear that objects, i.e. states of affairs, do not perform operations of joining or separating.

Aristotle then says that 'what "is" in this way [*sc.* as true] is a different thing that "is" from those that "are" strictly' (1027^b31). He adds that this is 'because thought joins or subtracts either the "what it is" or that it is such-and-such or that it is thus much or something else, whatever it may be' (1027^b31–3). The last remark

[120] Cf. de Rjik, 'Anatomy', 45, 51.
[121] Cf. Crivelli, *Truth*, 63 (with references).
[122] Cf. *DA* 3. 7, 431^a15–16; *NE* 3. 2, 1111^b33–4.
[123] Cf. de Rijk, 'Anatomy', 39. 'Good' is sometimes applied to the inhabitants of the categories: cf. *Top.* 1. 15, 107^a3–12; *NE* 1. 4, 1096^a25–34 (with J. L. Ackrill, 'Aristotle on "Good" and the Categories', in J. L. Ackrill, *Essays on Plato and Aristotle* (Oxford, 1997), 201–11 at 207–11); *EE* 1. 8, 1217^b25–1218^a1.
[124] Cf. *De int.* 1, 16^a9–18. I discuss the operations of joining and separating in the next subsection.

Truth in Metaphysics E 4   211

probably amounts to the claim that the entity which an affirmative (or negative) predicative judgement joins with (or separates from) an entity is one of those that may be properly mentioned in answering the question 'What is it?', or 'What is it like?', or 'How much is it?', or some other similar question. But the entities that may be properly mentioned in answering such questions are the inhabitants of the categories. Aristotle's last remark therefore probably commits him to the claim that the entities which affirmative (or negative) predicative judgements join with (or separate from) entities are inhabitants of the categories. This chimes with the view of the *Categories* (4, 1^{b}25–7) that the inhabitants of the categories are the things signified by 'the things said with no interweaving' (1^{b}25), i.e. by the atomic components of predicative sentences (a difference remains: while *Metaph.* E 4, 1027^{b}31–3, concerns thought, *Cat.* 4, 1^{b}25–7, focuses on language). Since for Aristotle most of the inhabitants of the categories are external things, this passage indicates that according to *E* 4 it is the entities thought about through a predicative judgement's predicate-component and subject-component that are reciprocally joined or separated.[125]

The claim that the joining (or separating) carried out by an affirmative (or negative) predicative judgement is performed on the inhabitants of the categories contributes to justifying the claim that 'what "is" in this way [*sc.* as true] is a different thing that "is" from those that "are" strictly' (1027^{b}31). For, (1) the entities that 'are' as true are states of affairs (simples and essences are left for later consideration), (2) states of affairs are composed of the entities joined (or separated) by affirmative (or negative) predicative judgements targeting them, (3) the entities joined (or separated) by affirmative (or negative) predicative judgements are the inhabitants of the categories, and (4) the inhabitants of the categories are the entities that 'are' strictly. It then follows that the entities that 'are' as true are composed of the entities that 'are' strictly. Hence the entities that 'are' as true are distinct from the entities that 'are' strictly.

[125] Cf. Aquinas, *In Metaph.* 1241 Cathala–Spiazzi. Some commentators believe that according to *E* 4 the items reciprocally joined or separated by a predicative judgement are (not the entities thought about through the judgement's predicate-component and subject-component, but) the judgement's predicate-component and subject-component themselves: cf. M. Kessler, *Aristoteles' Lehre von der Einheit der Definition* (Munich, 1976), 183; Segura, 'Ser', 94, 99–100. In *De anima* Aristotle says that 'where both falsehood and truth are present there is already some sort of composition [σύνθεσίς τις] of thoughts [νοημάτων] as if they were a single one' (3. 6, 430^{a}27–8; cf. 8, 432^{a}11–12). He never says that a thought is divided from a thought.

Joining and separating

What are the joining and the separating performed by affirmative and negative predicative judgements? On the hypothesis that $E\ 4$ agrees with Θ 10, some claims made by Aristotle at the beginning of Θ 10 can guide the search for a plausible answer to this question. Now, at those points of Θ 10 where having read $E\ 4$ one would expect him to say that an affirmative (or negative) predicative judgement joins (or separates) entities, Aristotle says instead that in an affirmative (or negative) predicative judgement the thinker judges a certain state of affairs to be combined (or divided). For a state of affairs to be combined (or divided) is for its constituent entities (individuals or universals) to be reciprocally combined (or divided). This suggests that for a thought to *join* (or *separate*) two entities is for its thinker to *judge* them *to be reciprocally combined* (or *reciprocally divided*).

At 1027^b23 Aristotle speaks of 'thinking together' and 'thinking separately'. The fact that 'thinking together' is paired with 'thinking separately' suggests that they are the joining and the separating of affirmative and negative predicative judgements. If the thought that joins two entities is the same as that whereby a thinker judges the two entities to be reciprocally combined, then this thought may also be described as one whereby the thinker is *thinking* of two entities *together* (take the adverb 'together' in the phrase 'thinking together' as describing the contents of a single episode of thinking, i.e. what one is thinking about things, and avoid understanding 'together' within 'thinking together' as expressing a relation between two episodes of thinking). A similar account may be offered of *thinking* of two entities *separately*.[126]

What 'is' as true eliminated from the rubric of ontology

Aristotle's argument then reaches its conclusion:

[a] The study of being may leave aside what 'is' as true.

Aristotle offers two premisses to justify [a]. Here is the first:

---

[126] Cf. Kirwan, *Metaphysics*, 198–9; K. J. Williams, 'Aristotle's Theory of Truth', *Prudentia*, 10 (1978), 67–76 at 71–2; Schüssler, *Vérité*, 126–8; Künne, *Conceptions*, 99–100; Crivelli, *Truth*, 68–9; Pearson, 'Being', 202–4; Makin, *Theta*, 249; Szaif, 'Geschichte', 19.

Truth in Metaphysics E 4   213

[b] What 'is' as true is 'about the remaining genus of being' (1028ª1-2).

How does [b] help to justify [a]? Premiss [b] perhaps amounts to the claim that the entities that 'are' as true are 'about' entities of a different sort in that they surround or contain them.[127] If this is right, the claim made by [b] is that the entities that 'are' as true are composed of the entities that 'are' strictly. In the subsection at n. 124 above I credited Aristotle with an argument that establishes this claim and uses it to conclude that the entities that 'are' as true are distinct from the entities that 'are' strictly. This conclusion supports [a]: the study of being may leave aside what 'is' as true because it may concentrate on the entities that 'are' strictly.

The second premiss offered to justify [a] is:

[c] What 'is' as true does not 'reveal an outside nature of being' (1028ª2).

On its most natural interpretation, [c] claims that what 'is' as true is not outside the mind, i.e. depends on[128] the mind for its existence.[129] One might object to this exegesis of [c]. For Aristotle actually says that 'both [sc. both what "is" as true and what "is" accidentally] ... do not reveal an outside nature of being' (1028ª1-2). Could he describe what 'is' accidentally as mind-dependent?[130] In fact, an affirmative answer to this question is not unlikely. For in E 2, the

[127] Cf. LSJ s.v. περί C 1. 1.
[128] Glossing 'is not outside' by 'depends on' is warranted by E 4's parallel in K 8 (reported below as [T7]), where 'outside' is paired with 'separate', which can mean 'independent'.
[129] Cf. Aquinas, In Metaph. 1243 Cathala–Spiazzi; Schwegler, Metaphysik, iv. 33; Brentano, Bedeutung, 14, 23, 38, 131; Ross, Metaphysics, i. 366; H. Tredennick (ed. and trans.), Aristotle: The Metaphysics (Cambridge, Mass., and London, 1933), i. 309; Wilpert, 'Wahrheitsbegriff', 7–8; Owens, Doctrine, 310; de Rijk, Categories, 8, 34, 56; G. Reale (trans. and comm.), Aristotele: la Metafisica (Naples, 1968), i. 516; Leszl, Ontology, 215; A. Graeser, 'Sprache und Ontologie bei Aristoteles', Freiburger Zeitschrift für Philosophie und Theologie, 25 (1978), 443–55 at 444; Martineau, 'Inauthenticité', 494–6; A. G. Vigo, 'Der theoretische Wahrheitsbegriff bei Aristoteles: Versuch einer systematischen Rekonstruktion', in N. Öffenberger and A. G. Vigo (eds.), Südamerikanische Beiträge zur modernen Deutung der Aristotelischen Logik (Hildesheim, Zurich, and New York, 1997), 1–48 at 26; Schüssler, Vérité, 123; de Rijk, Semantics, ii. 147; Duminil and Jaulin, Métaphysique, 231.
[130] Some commentators take [c] to mean that accidental 'being' and 'being'-as-truth are not 'external' to the things that 'are' in the ways that correspond to the categories because they mention them in their definitions: cf. [Alex. Aphr.] In Metaph. 458. 18–19 Hayduck; Ascl. In Metaph. 374. 18–21 Hayduck; Bonitz, Metaphysica, ii. 294; P. Natorp, 'Ueber Aristoteles' Metaphysik K 1–8, 1065ª26',

first of the two chapters dedicated to what 'is' accidentally, Aristotle remarks that 'the accidental is like a mere name [*hōsper onoma ti monon*]' (1026^{b}13–14).[131] Given that he can hardly mean that what 'is' accidentally is a mere linguistic expression, Aristotle perhaps means that what 'is' accidentally is language-dependent. If this is right, then, since he regards the mental and the linguistic spheres as isomorphic,[132] Aristotle is probably ready to say that what 'is' accidentally is mind-dependent. The most natural interpretation of [c] is confirmed by an observation made by Aristotle shortly before, when he says that the cause of what 'is' as true 'is an affection of thought' (1027^{b}34–1028^{a}1). The 'affection of thought' in question is most plausibly identified with the joining of affirmative predicative judgements and the separation of negative predicative judgements, which earlier (1027^{b}29–30) were described as being in thought, i.e. as attributes that inhere in thought (Aristotle sometimes uses 'affection' to mean 'attribute').[133]

Since it is states of affairs that 'are' as true, Aristotle's view that what 'is' as true depends for its existence on the mind amounts to the claim that states of affairs depend for their existence on the mind, more specifically on the joining or separating of affirmative or negative predicative judgements targeting them. Thus, a state of affairs exists only so long as there is at least one thinker who either joins (in an affirmative predicative judgement) or separates (in a negative predicative judgement) the entities of which it is composed.[134]

Archiv für Geschichte der Philosophie, 1 (1888), 178–93 at 192; Maier, *Syllogistik*, i. 36; Heidegger, *Grundbegriffe*, 166–7, 304; Kirwan, *Metaphysics*, 200; C. A. Viano (trans. and comm.), *Aristotele: la Metafisica* (Turin, 1974), 351.

[131] Cf. 1026^{b}21; *K* 8, 1064^{b}28–30.   [132] Cf. above, text to n. 18.
[133] Cf. *GC* 1. 4, 319^{b}8–14; *Metaph.* Θ 7, 1049^{a}29–30; *N* 2, 1089^{b}23–4.
[134] My interpretation of Aristotle's remark that 'the cause . . . of the latter [*sc.* of what "is" as true] is an affection of thought' (1027^{b}34–1028^{a}1) differs from those of all commentators I consulted. Some take Aristotle to mean that the cause of what 'is' as true is an affection of thought because truth is an attribute of thought (cf. Kirwan, *Metaphysics*, 200), others that the cause of what 'is' as true is an affection of thought because truth is an attribute of the operations of joining and separating, which in turn are affections of thought (cf. Brentano, *Bedeutung*, 38–9). Neither of these interpretations offers a suitable account of the occurrence of 'cause' in Aristotle's remark. One might be tempted to take Aristotle's remark to mean that affirmation and negation, affections of thought, are (at least part of) the formal cause of 'being'-as-truth and 'not-being'-as-falsehood. This exegesis, however, faces two difficulties: (1) it is not easy to spell out how exactly affirmation and negation could be (at least part of) the formal cause of 'being'-as-truth and 'not-being'-as-falsehood; (2) the mind-

Truth in Metaphysics E 4   215

In the course of the mind-dependent career of certain states of affairs, there are times when they 'are' as true (that is when they are combined, i.e. when their components are reciprocally combined) and other times when they 'are not' as false (that is when they are divided, i.e. when their components are reciprocally divided) (e.g. the state of affairs of your being seated). Other states of affairs 'are' as true throughout their mind-dependent career (e.g. the state of affairs of the diagonal being incommensurable). Yet other states of affairs 'are not' as false throughout their mind-dependent career (e.g. the state of affairs of the diagonal being commensurable). For instance, suppose I now entertain the affirmative predicative judgement that you are seated, but now you are not seated: then the state of affairs of your being seated exists now because it is now the target of my judgement, but it 'is not' now as false because it is now divided in that its components (namely you and being-seated) are now reciprocally divided.[135]

External evidence

Two passages of the *Metaphysics* may be interpreted in ways that corroborate this exegesis. The first is the parallel of *E* 4 in *K* 8:

[T7]   τὸ δ' ὡς ἀληθὲς ὂν καὶ   1065ª21
κατὰ συμβεβηκὸς τὸ μέν ἐστιν ἐν συμπλοκῇ διανοίας
καὶ πάθος ἐν ταύτῃ (διὸ περὶ μὲν τὸ οὕτως ὂν οὐ ζη-
τοῦνται αἱ ἀρχαί, περὶ δὲ τὸ ἔξω ὂν καὶ χωριστόν·) τὸ δ'. . .   ª24

As for what 'is' as true and accidentally, one of them [*sc.* what 'is' as true] is in an interweaving of thought and is an affection in it (for this reason, with regard to what 'is' in this way [*sc.* as true] one does not search for the principles, but one does this with regard to what 'is' outside and separate); the other . . . (*Metaph.* *K* 8, 1065ª21–4)

Despite its uncertain authorship, book *K* constitutes at least evidence of how an ancient reader of Aristotle understood certain parts of his work. On my preferred interpretation, [T7] excludes what 'is'

dependence of what 'is' as true is already indicated by Aristotle when he says that it does not 'reveal an outside nature of being' (1028ª2).

[135] Carl Stumpf, who played a major role in putting states of affairs on the map of modern philosophy, regarded states of affairs as mind-dependent entities (this appears in his 1888 *Leitfaden der Logik*, in manuscript form: cf. L. Cesalli, 'States of Affairs', in J. Marenbon (ed.), *The Oxford Handbook of Medieval Philosophy* (Oxford, 2012), 421–43 at 422 and 433).

as true from the rubric of ontology on the grounds that what 'is' as true is 'in', i.e. depends on,¹³⁶ an interweaving of thought. The passage goes so far as to describe what 'is' as true as an 'affection in' thought, i.e. as an event¹³⁷ dependent on thought. [T7] may therefore be taken to confirm that what 'is' as true is mind-dependent. The second passage introduces the idea that every predicative judgement composes something with something:

[T8] ἔτι πᾶν τὸ διανοητὸν καὶ νοητὸν ἡ διάνοια ἢ κατάφησιν ἢ 1012ᵃ2
ἀπόφησιν—τοῦτο δ᾽ ἐξ ὁρισμοῦ δῆλον—ὅταν ἀληθεύῃ ἢ ψεύδη-
ται· ὅταν μὲν ὡδὶ συνθῇ φᾶσα ἢ ἀποφᾶσα, ἀληθεύει,
ὅταν δὲ ὡδί, ψεύδεται. ᵃ5

Again, whenever thought is right or wrong, it either affirms or denies something thinkable or intelligible—this is clear from the definition: when by its affirming or denying it composes things in this way, it is right, when instead it composes them in this other way, it is wrong. (*Metaph.* Γ 7, 1012ᵃ2–5)

Passage [T8] probably commits Aristotle to the claim that both affirmative and negative predicative judgements compose one entity with one entity (the initial observation that 'thought . . . either affirms or denies something thinkable or intelligible' suggests that the composition is performed on entities). The affirmative or negative composition of entities can be carried out in two ways: in a truth-conferring way and in a falsehood-conferring way.¹³⁸ The precise nature of these two ways of composing is specified in the definition of truth and falsehood at the chapter's beginning (at 1011ᵇ25–7), a definition to which the passage explicitly refers.

The claim that both affirmative and negative predicative judgements compose one entity with one entity might be deemed to clash with another one which Aristotle also appears to endorse: that an affirmative predicative judgement joins one entity with one entity whereas a negative predicative judgement separates one entity from one entity. But the clash is merely apparent. For, the claim that a negative predicative judgement separates one entity from one entity can be taken to imply that a negative predicative judgement com-

¹³⁶ Aristotle sometimes uses 'in' ('ἐν'+dat.) to express dependence: cf. *NE* 1. 6, 1097ᵇ26 (with T. Irwin (trans. and comm.), *Aristotle:* Nicomachean Ethics, 2nd edn. (Indianapolis and Cambridge, Mass., 1999), 183); *MM* 1. 11, 1187ᵇ21; *EE* 2. 10, 1226ᵃ31; *Phys.* 4. 3, 210ᵃ21–3; *Metaph.* Δ 23, 1023ᵃ8–11. For the 'ἐν' at 1065ᵃ22 expressing dependence, cf. Ross, *Metaphysica*, ad loc.; Ross, *Metaphysics*, ii. 322.
¹³⁷ For Aristotle's use of 'affection' ('πάθος') to denote events, cf. *Meteor.* 1. 1, 338ᵇ24, 25, 339ᵃ5; 1. 2, 339ᵃ21; *GA* 5. 1, 779ᵃ3.
¹³⁸ Cf. Ross, *Metaphysics*, i. 285–6; Wheeler, 'Reading', 71.

poses one entity with one entity, albeit in a way different from that of the joining performed by affirmative predicative judgements. What happens in a negative predicative judgement is importantly different from what happens when entities are thought about independently of one another. For example, although the judgement that the diagonal is not commensurable separates commensurability from the diagonal, it does introduce some connection between commensurability and the diagonal: the situation is quite different from that of someone who thinks successively and independently of commensurability and of the diagonal, without connecting them in any predicative judgement. In a nutshell, it is reasonable to assume that there are both a joining-composition and a separating-composition and that the composition involved in both of these amounts simply to the introduction of a predicative tie. Something along these lines might be in Aristotle's mind in E 4 when he says: 'I use "together" and "separately" in such a way that what comes to be is not a contiguity but a single thing' (1027^b24–5).[139]

Now, states of affairs are composite entities and their components are universals and individuals. Since universals and individuals are not (in general) mind-dependent, what makes states of affairs mind-dependent can only be the reciprocal composition of universals and individuals within them. It is reasonable to assume that this is nothing but the composition carried out in all predicative judgements. Note that the composition of universals and individuals within states of affairs is independent of the combination and division which determine the state of affairs' 'being' as true or 'not being' as false (the state of affairs persists in its mind-dependent existence as a composite entity even when its components are reciprocally divided in a way that determines its 'not being' as false).

The mind-dependence of states of affairs

The mind-dependence of states of affairs should assuage the worry that by crediting Aristotle with a commitment to states of affairs one is saddling him with an ontological layer that sits uneasily with

[139] Cf. Crivelli, *Truth*, 70–1. In several passages (*De int.* 8, 18^a13–17; 11, 20^b13–26; *Pr. An.* 1. 1, 24^a16–17, 28–9; 1. 23, 40^b30–1; *Post. An.* 2. 3, 90^b33–4; *SE* 6, 169^a7–8, 10–11, 14; 30, 181^b23–4) Aristotle says that a predicative sentence, be it affirmative or negative, signifies something about ('κατά' +gen.) something. Signifying the relation of aboutness holding between entities is what corresponds, in the linguistic sphere, to the composition performed by all predicative judgements in the mental sphere.

his nominalistic penchant. From a nominalistic point of view, there is something attractive about a position that avoids littering the ontology with countless entities that lie waiting to become the targets of predicative judgements and in some cases never enjoy such a privilege.

The mind-dependence of states of affairs does not amount to idealism because it requires only that a certain sphere of reality depend for its existence on the mind (realists concede that some spheres of reality, e.g. mental states, depend for their existence on the mind). By contrast, the claim that the mind is the cause of a state of affairs having the property of 'being'-as-truth does amount to idealism because it makes the mind responsible for the obtaining of whatever it considers. Such an idealist position would clash with other aspects of Aristotle's thought. In order to avoid saddling Aristotle with such an idealist position, I refrained from interpreting his remark that 'the cause . . . of the latter [*sc.* of what 'is' as true] is an affection of thought' ($1027^{b}34$–$1028^{a}1$) as meaning that an affection of thought is the cause of something's having the property of 'being'-as-truth. What Aristotle means by this remark is probably that an affection of thought is responsible for the existence of the entities that enjoy the property of 'being'-as-truth, i.e. states of affairs. Note, however, that the mind-dependence of states of affairs rules out identifying facts with states of affairs that 'are' as true: there surely are facts which nobody has thought of in the way that would warrant the existence of the corresponding state of affairs. Nevertheless, a state of affairs that 'is' as true or 'is not' as false will be available whenever it is needed in order to make true or false a predicative judgement.[140]

The mind-dependence of states of affairs contrasts with the condition of simples and essences, which do not (in general) depend on minds. This explains why in the middle of *E* 4 Aristotle separates the questions 'about what "is" and what "is not" in this way' ($1027^{b}28$–9), i.e. about what 'is' as true and 'what is not' as false in the way appropriate to simples and essences, from the questions about what 'is' as true and 'what is not' as false in the way appropriate to objects, i.e. states of affairs.[141] The arguments for eliminating what 'is' as true and what 'is not' as false from the rubric of ontology apply only to objects, i.e. states of affairs. They have no bearing on

---

[140] I am indebted to an anonymous referee for raising the issues addressed in this paragraph.   [141] Cf. above, paragraph to n. 30.

simples and essences. The important contribution of Θ 10 lies in its identifying bearers of 'being'-as-truth that are not mind-dependent and explaining what 'being'-as-truth amounts to in their case.

Aristotle's account of the veridical use of 'to be' and natural language

I argued that Aristotle in the *Metaphysics* restricts the use of 'to be' and 'not to be' associated with truth and falsehood to external things, which in the most important case are states of affairs.[142] I also argued that in Greek there is a use of 'to be' and 'not to be' associated with truth and falsehood and that on this use the verb does not apply to linguistic expressions or mental states or acts.[143] It thus turns out that Aristotle's account of the use of 'to be' and 'not to be' associated with truth and falsehood fits in well with the way this use is displayed in natural language. There is no reason to think that Aristotle is creating a strange technical jargon: Aristotle is true to the facts—to the facts of language.

Université de Genève

BIBLIOGRAPHY

Ackrill, J. L., 'Aristotle on "Good" and the Categories', in J. L. Ackrill, *Essays on Plato and Aristotle* (Oxford, 1997), 201–11.
Bäck, A. T., *Aristotle's Theory of Predication* (Leiden, Boston, and Cologne, 2000).
Bekker, I. (ed.), *Aristoteles Graece* (Berlin, 1831).
Benardete, S., 'The Grammar of Being', *Review of Metaphysics*, 30 (1976–7), 486–96.
Berti, E., 'Heidegger e il concetto aristotelico di verità' ['Verità'], in R. Brague and F. Courtine (eds.), *Herméneutique et ontologie: mélanges en hommage à Pierre Aubenque* (Paris, 1990), 97–120.

[142] Space limitations prevent me from discussing Aristotle's examination of the use of 'to be' and 'not to be' associated with truth and falsehood in *Metaphysics* Δ 7 (1017^a31–5). Briefly: when he says that ' "to be" and "is" signify that it is true, and "not to be" that it is not true but false' (1017^a31–2), Aristotle is employing 'true' and 'false' in accordance with their strictest use, whereby they express the attributes of 'being'-as-truth and 'not-being'-as-falsehood; moreover, he analyses the 'is' in 'Socrates is musical' and 'Socrates is not-white' (the 'is not' in 'The diagonal is not commensurable') as attributing 'being'-as-truth ('not-being'-as-falsehood) to the states of affairs of Socrates being musical and of Socrates being not-white (to the state of affairs of the diagonal's being commensurable).
[143] Cf. above, pp. 171–3.

Berti, E., 'I luoghi della verità secondo Aristotele: un confronto con Heidegger', in V. Melchiorre (ed.), *I luoghi del comprendere* (Milan, 2000), 3–27.

Bonitz, H. (ed. and comm.), *Aristotelis Metaphysica* [*Metaphysica*] (Bonn, 1848–9).

Bonitz, H., *Index aristotelicus* [*Index*] (Berlin, 1870).

Bonitz, H., *Observationes criticae in Aristotelis libros metaphysicos* (Berlin, 1842).

Bormann, K., 'Wahrheitsbegriff und νοῦς-Lehre bei Aristoteles und einigen seiner Kommentatoren', *Miscellanea mediaevalia*, 12 (1982), 1–24.

Brandis, C. A. (ed.), *Aristotelis et Theophrasti Metaphysica* (Berlin, 1823).

Brandis, C. A., *Handbuch der Geschichte der griechisch-römischen Philosophie* (Berlin, 1835–66).

Brentano, F., *Von der mannigfachen Bedeutung des Seienden nach Aristoteles* [*Bedeutung*] (Freiburg i.B., 1862).

Bullinger, A., *Aristoteles' Metaphysik in Bezug auf Entstehungsweise, Text und Gedanken* (Munich, 1892).

Burnyeat, M., *et al.*, *Notes on Eta and Theta of Aristotle's* Metaphysics [*Notes*] (Oxford, 1984).

Bussemaker, C., Dübner, F., and Heitz, A. (eds. and trans.), *Aristotelis opera omnia Graece et Latine* (Paris, 1848–74).

Bywater, I., 'Aristotelia V', *Journal of Philology*, 32 (1913), 107–22.

Cathala, M.-R., and Spiazzi, R. M. (eds.), *S. Thomae Aquinatis in duodecim libros Metaphysicorum Aristotelis expositio* (Turin and Rome, 1950).

Cesalli, L., 'States of Affairs', in J. Marenbon (ed.), *The Oxford Handbook of Medieval Philosophy* (Oxford, 2012), 421–43.

Christ, W. (ed.), *Aristotelis Metaphysica* [*Metaphysica*], 2nd edn. (Leipzig, 1906).

Coope, U., review of Crivelli, *Truth*, in *Notre Dame Philosophical Reviews* (2005), 11.12 ⟨https://ndpr.nd.edu/news/24902-aristotle-on-truth/⟩.

Crivelli, P., 'Aristotle on Signification and Truth', in G. Anagnostopoulos (ed.), *A Companion to Aristotle* (Chichester, 2009), 81–100.

Crivelli, P., *Aristotle on Truth* [*Truth*] (Cambridge, 2004).

Crivelli, P., 'Notes on Aristotle's Conception of Truth', in M. S. Funghi (ed.), ʽΟδοὶ διζήσιος — *Le vie della ricerca: studi in onore di Francesco Adorno* (Florence, 1996), 147–59.

Crivelli, P., 'Semantiche per la sillogistica di Aristotele', in AA. VV., *Papiri filosofici*, Miscellanea di Studi, VI (Florence, 2011), 297–317.

Crivelli, P., and Charles, D., '"Πρότασις" in Aristotle's *Prior Analytics*', *Phronesis*, 56 (2011), 193–203.

Davidson, D., 'The Folly of Trying to Define Truth', *Journal of Philosophy*, 93 (1996), 263–78.

de Rijk, L. M., *Aristotle: Semantics and Ontology* [*Semantics*] (Leiden, Boston, and Cologne, 2002).

de Rijk, L. M., 'The Anatomy of the Proposition: Logos and Pragma in Plato and Aristotle' ['Anatomy'], in L. M. de Rijk and H. A. G. Braakhuis (eds.), *Logos and Pragma: Essays on the Philosophy of Language in Honour of Professor Gabriel Nuchelmans* (Nijmegen, 1987), 27–61.

de Rijk, L. M., *The Place of the Categories of Being in Aristotle's Philosophy* [*Categories*] (Assen, 1952).

Deninger, J. G., '*Wahres Sein*' *in der Philosophie des Aristoteles* (Meisenheim am Glan, 1961).

Duminil, M.-P., and Jaulin, A. (trans.), *Aristote: Métaphysique* [*Métaphysique*] (Paris, 2008).

Duminil, M.-P., and Jaulin, A. (trans. and comm.), *Aristote: Métaphysiques, livre Delta* (Toulouse, 1991).

Du Val, G. (ed. and comm.), *Aristotelis opera omnia quae exstant Graece et Latine*, 3rd edn. (Paris, 1654).

Fiorentino, F., 'Il problema della verità in Aristotele', *Sapienza*, 54 (2001), 257–302.

Fleischer, M., *Wahrheit und Wahrheitsgrund: Zum Wahrheitsproblem und zu seiner Geschichte* (Berlin and New York, 1984).

Gaskin, R., 'Simplicius on the Meaning of Sentences: A Commentary on *In Cat.* 396, 30–397, 28', *Phronesis*, 43 (1998), 42–62.

Gohlke, P. (trans. and comm.), *Aristoteles: Metaphysik* [*Metaphysik*], 2nd edn. (Paderborn, 1961).

Graeser, A., 'Aristotle and Aquinas on Being as Being True', in C. Gagnebin (ed.), *Métaphysique: histoire de la philosophie. Recueil d'études offert à F. Brunner* (Neuchâtel, 1981), 85–97.

Graeser, A., 'Sprache und Ontologie bei Aristoteles', *Freiburger Zeitschrift für Philosophie und Theologie*, 25 (1978), 443–55.

Grayeff, F., *Aristotle and his School: An Inquiry into the History of the Peripatos with a Commentary on* Metaphysics *Z, H, Λ, and Θ* (London, 1974).

Grote, G., *Aristotle*, ed. by A. Bain and G. C. Robertson, 2nd edn. (London, 1880).

Hadot, P., 'Sur divers sens du mot *pragma* dans la tradition philosophique grecque', in P. Aubenque (ed.), *Concepts et catégories dans la pensée antique* (Paris, 1980), 309–19.

Halper, E. C., *One and Many in Aristotle's* Metaphysics*: The Central Books* [*Metaphysics*] (Columbus, Ohio, 1989).

Harvey, P. J., 'Aristotle on Truth and Falsity in *De anima* 3. 6', *Journal of the History of Philosophy*, 16 (1978), 219–20.

Harvey, P. J., 'Aristotle on Truth with Respect to Incomposites' (diss. University of Michigan, 1975).

Heidegger, M., *Die Grundbegriffe der antiken Philosophie* [*Grundbegriffe*], ed. by F.-K. Bust (Frankfurt a.M., 1993).
Heidegger, M., *Logik: Die Frage nach der Wahrheit*, ed. by W. Biemel, 2nd edn. (Frankfurt a.M., 1995).
Heidegger, M., *Platon: Sophistes*, ed. by I. Schüssler (Frankfurt a.M., 1992).
Heidegger, M., *Vom Wesen der menschlichen Freiheit: Einleitung in die Philosophie* [*Freiheit*], ed. by H. Tietjen (Frankfurt a.M., 1982).
Hestir, B., 'Aristotle's Conception of Truth: An Alternative View', *Journal of the History of Philosophy*, 51 (2013), 193–222.
Irwin, T. (trans. and comm.), *Aristotle:* Nicomachean Ethics, 2nd edn. (Indianapolis and Cambridge, Mass., 1999).
Jaeger, W. W., *Aristoteles: Grundlegung einer Geschichte seiner Entwicklung* [*Aristoteles*] (Berlin, 1923).
Jaeger, W. W. (ed.), *Aristotelis Metaphysica* (Oxford, 1957).
Jaeger, W. W., *Studien zur Entstehungsgeschichte der Metaphysik des Aristoteles* [*Studien*] (Berlin, 1912).
Kahn, C. H., 'The Greek Verb "To Be" and the Concept of Being', *Foundations of Language*, 2 (1966), 245–65.
Kahn, C. H., *The Verb 'Be' in Ancient Greek* [*Verb*], 2nd edn. (Indianapolis and Cambridge, Mass., 2003).
Keeler, L., 'Aristotle on the Problem of Error', *Gregorianum*, 13 (1932), 241–60.
Kessler, M., *Aristoteles' Lehre von der Einheit der Definition* (Munich, 1976).
Ketchum, R. J., 'Being and Existence in Greek Ontology', *Archiv für Geschichte der Philosophie*, 80 (1998), 321–32.
Kirwan, C. (trans. and comm.), *Aristotle:* Metaphysics, Books Γ, Δ, *and* E [*Metaphysics*], 2nd edn. (Oxford, 1993).
Künne, W., *Conceptions of Truth* [*Conceptions*] (Oxford, 2003).
Leszl, W., *Aristotle's Conception of Ontology* [*Ontology*] (Padua, 1975).
Lewis, F. A., 'Predication, Things, and Kinds in Aristotle's *Metaphysics*' ['Predication'], *Phronesis*, 56 (2011), 350–87.
Long, C. P., *Aristotle on the Nature of Truth* (New York, 2011).
Loux, M. J., 'Aristotle on Universals', in G. Anagnostopoulos (ed.), *A Companion to Aristotle* (Chichester, 2009), 186–96.
Luther, W., 'Wahrheit, Licht und Erkenntnis in der griechischen Philosophie bis Demokrit' ['Wahrheit'], *Archiv für Begriffsgeschichte*, 10 (1966), 1–240.
Maier, H., *Die Syllogistik des Aristoteles* [*Syllogistik*], 2nd edn. (repr. Hildesheim, 1969).
Makin, S. (trans. and comm.), *Aristotle:* Metaphysics Book Θ [*Theta*] (Oxford, 2006).

Martineau, E., 'De l'inauthenticité du livre E de la *Métaphysique* d'Aristote' ['Inauthenticité'], *Conférence*, 5 (1997), 443–509.

Maso, S., 'La verità di Aristotele: intorno a *Epsilon 4*', in L. Cortella, F. Mora, and I. Testa (eds.), *La socialità della ragione: scritti in onore di Luigi Ruggiu* (Milan and Udine, 2011), 89–102.

Matthen, M., 'Greek Ontology and the "Is" of Truth', *Phronesis*, 28 (1983), 113–35.

Maurus, S. (trans. and comm.), *Aristotelis opera quae extant omnia* [*Aristotelis opera*] (repr. Paris 1885–6).

Mignucci, M., 'Vérité et pensée dans le *De anima*', in G. Romeyer Dherbey and C. Viano (eds.), *Corps et âme: sur le De anima d'Aristote* (Paris, 1996), 405–22.

Miller, F. D., Jr., 'Aristotle on Belief and Knowledge' ['Belief'], in G. Anagnostopoulos and F. D. Miller, Jr. (eds.), *Reason and Analysis in Ancient Greek Philosophy: Essays in Honor of David Keyt* (Dordrecht, 2013), 285–307.

Miller, F. D., Jr., 'Aristotle's Account of Being and Truth' (diss. University of Washington, 1971).

Modrak, D. K. W., *Aristotle's Theory of Language and Meaning* (Cambridge, 2001).

Natorp, P., 'Ueber Aristoteles' Metaphysik *K* 1–8, 1065^{a}26', *Archiv für Geschichte der Philosophie*, 1 (1888), 178–93.

Nuchelmans, G., *Theories of the Proposition: Ancient and Medieval Conceptions of the Bearers of Truth and Falsity* (Amsterdam and London, 1973).

Oehler, K., *Die Lehre vom noetischen und dianoetischen Denken bei Platon und Aristoteles* [*Lehre*], 2nd edn. (Hamburg, 1985).

Owens, J., *The Doctrine of Being in the Aristotelian* Metaphysics [*Doctrine*], 3rd edn. (Toronto, 1978).

Pearson, G., 'Aristotle on Being-as-Truth' ['Being'], *Oxford Studies in Ancient Philosophy*, 28 (2005), 201–31.

Prantl, C., *Geschichte der Logik im Abenlande*, vol. i (Leipzig, 1855).

Pritzl, K., 'Being True in Aristotle's Thinking' ['True'], *Proceedings of the Boston Area Colloquium in Ancient Philosophy*, 14 (1998), 177–201.

Pritzl, K., 'The Cognition of Indivisibles and the Argument of *De anima* 3. 4–8', *Proceedings of the American Catholic Philosophical Association*, 58 (1984), 140–50.

Rangos, S., 'Falsity and the False in Aristotle's *Metaphysics Δ*', *Rhizai*, 6 (2009), 7–21.

Reale, G. (trans. and comm.), *Aristotele: la Metafisica* (Naples, 1968).

Reinach, A., 'Zur Theorie des negativen Urteils', in A. Pfänder (ed.), *Münchener philosophische Abhandlungen: Festschrift für Theodor Lipps* (Leipzig, 1911), 196–254.

Rolfes, E. (trans. and comm.), *Aristoteles: Metaphysik*, 3rd edn. (Leipzig, 1928).

Ross, W. D. (trans.), *Aristotle: Metaphysica* [*Metaphysica*] (Oxford, 1908).

Ross, W. D. (ed. and comm.), *Aristotle: Metaphysics* [*Metaphysics*] (Oxford, 1924).

Russo, A. (trans.), *Aristotele: Metafisica*, 2nd edn. (Rome and Bari, 1982).

Salmeri, G. (trans. and comm.), *Aristotele: Discorsi sull'esistenza. Libri 7–8–9 della Metafisica* (Cinisello Balsamo, 1996).

Schmitz, H., *Die Ideenlehre des Aristoteles*, vol. i/2 (Bonn, 1985).

Schüssler, I., *La Question de la vérité: Thomas d'Aquin – Nietzsche – Kant – Aristote – Heidegger* [*Vérité*] (Lausanne, 2001).

Schwegler, A. (ed., trans., and comm.), *Aristoteles: Die Metaphysik* [*Metaphysik*] (Tübingen, 1847–8).

Segura, C., 'El ser de la verdad en la *Metafísica* de Aristóteles' ['Ser'], *Tópicos*, 4 (1994), 89–115.

Seidl, H. (trans. and comm.), *Aristoteles' Metaphysik*, 3rd edn. (Hamburg, 1991).

Seidl, H., *Der Begriff des Intellekts (νοῦς) bei Aristoteles im philosophischen Zusammenhang seiner Hauptschriften* (Meisenheim am Glan, 1971).

Sillitti, G., 'I "Fondamenti della logica aristotelica" e la critica di Emanuele Severino', in G. Calogero, *I fondamenti della logica aristotelica*, 2nd edn. (Florence, 1968), 313–25.

Simons, P., 'Aristotle's Concept of State of Affairs', in O. Gigon and M. W. Fischer (eds.), *Antike Rechts- und Sozialphilosophie* (Frankfurt a.M., Bern, New York, and Paris, 1988), 97–112.

Sonderegger, E., 'La vérité chez Aristote', in J.-F. Aenishanslin, D. O'Meara, and I. Schüssler (eds.), *La Vérité: antiquité – modernité* (Lausanne, 2004), 47–63.

Szaif, J., 'Die Geschichte des Wahrheitsbegriffs in der klassischen Antike' ['Geschichte'], in M. Enders and J. Szaif (eds.), *Die Geschichte des philosophischen Begriffs der Wahrheit* (Berlin and New York, 2006), 1–32.

Thorp, J., 'Aristotle on Being and Truth', *De philosophia*, 3 (1982), 1–9.

Thorp, J., 'Aristotle on the Truth of *Things*', unpublished typescript.

Tredennick, H. (ed. and trans.), *Aristotle: The Metaphysics* (Cambridge, Mass., and London, 1933).

Tricot, J. (trans. and comm.), *Aristote: la Métaphysique* [*Métaphysique*], 2nd edn. (Paris, 1966).

Tugendhat, E., 'Der Wahrheitsbegriff bei Aristoteles', in E. Tugendhat, *Philosophische Aufsätze* (Frankfurt a.M., 1992), 251–60.

Tugendhat, E., review of Oehler, *Lehre* ['Oehler'], in E. Tugendhat, *Philosophische Aufsätze* (Frankfurt a.M., 1992), 402–13.

Viano, C. A. (trans. and comm.), *Aristotele: la Metafisica* (Turin, 1974).

Vigo, A. G., 'Der theoretische Wahrheitsbegriff bei Aristoteles: Versuch einer systematischen Rekonstruktion', in N. Öffenberger and A. G. Vigo (eds.), *Südamerikanische Beiträge zur modernen Deutung der Aristotelischen Logik* (Hildesheim, Zurich, and New York, 1997), 1–48.

Volkmann-Schluck, K.-H., *Die Metaphysik des Aristoteles* (Frankfurt a.M., 1979).

Vollrath, G. E., *Studien zur Kategorienlehre des Aristoteles* (diss. University of Cologne, 1959).

Weise, C. H. (ed.), *Aristotelis opera omnia quae extant* (Leipzig, 1843).

Wheeler, M. R., 'A Deflationary Reading of Aristotle's Definitions of Truth and Falsehood at Metaphysics $1011^{b}26$–7' ['Reading'], *Apeiron*, 44 (2011), 67–90.

Wieland, W., *Die aristotelische Physik* (Göttingen, 1962).

Williams, K. J., 'Aristotle's Theory of Truth', *Prudentia*, 10 (1978), 67–76.

Wilpert, P., 'Zum aristotelischen Wahrheitsbegriff' ['Wahrheitsbegriff'], *Philosophisches Jahrbuch der Görres-Gesellschaft*, 53 (1940), 3–16.

Zanatta, M. (trans. and comm.), *Aristotele: Metafisica* (Milan, 2009).

THE CONCEPT OF *ERGON*: TOWARDS AN ACHIEVEMENT INTERPRETATION OF ARISTOTLE'S 'FUNCTION ARGUMENT'

SAMUEL H. BAKER

1. Introduction

ARISTOTLE thinks that if you want to live well, you should organize your life by reference to the best thing that humans can achieve in action—something he calls 'the human good'. In *NE* 1. 7 he helpfully defines the human good as 'activity of the rational part of the soul on the basis of virtue and if there are more virtues than one, on the basis of the best and most end-like virtue and moreover in an end-like [i.e. complete] life' ($1098^{a}16$–18). This definition is the conclusion of what is known as 'the *ergon* argument' (aka 'the function argument'). In this article I aim to clear the way for a new interpretation of this argument, and I do so by questioning the ubiquitous assumption that the *ergon* of something is always the proper activity of that thing. I argue that though Aristotle has a single concept of an *ergon*, he identifies the *ergon* of any X (that has an *ergon*) as an activity in some cases but a product in others, depending on the sort of thing the X is—for while the *ergon* of the eye is seeing, the *ergon* of a sculptor is not sculpting but a sculpture. This alternative interpretation of Aristotle's concept of an *ergon* allows the key explanatory middle term of the *ergon* argument to be what, I argue, it ought to be: 'the best achievement of a human'. On my interpretation of the argument, Aristotle assumes that the human good is the best achievement of a human, and he uses the concept of

© Samuel H. Baker 2015

For comments on various versions of this article, I would like to thank Brookes Brown, Caleb Cohoe, John Cooper, Sherif Girgis, Brad Inwood, Barry Maguire, Jimmy Martin, Rachel Parsons, Gideon Rosen, David Sedley, Mor Segev, Simon Shogry, and three anonymous referees, as well as audiences at Princeton University and the Humboldt University, Berlin. I especially thank Hendrik Lorenz and Benjamin Morison as they commented on numerous drafts and helped me to develop my ideas from the very beginning.

228   Samuel H. Baker

an *ergon* in order to gain clarity on what this achievement might be. He reasons that just as the best achievement of a sculptor will be a version of his *ergon*, which is a sculpture, so the best achievement of a human will be a version of his *ergon*, which is a certain activity of living. On the basis of this recovered bit of reasoning I close by offering, and briefly discussing, a new reconstruction of the *ergon* argument.

2. *Ergon* in *Nicomachean Ethics* 1. 7: reasons for a reassessment

In *NE* 1. 2 Aristotle introduces the phrase 'the human good' to label what he has explained as the highest, and thus best, of all things achievable in action by humans. To be 'best' (1094ª22) is to be most of all an end: an end that we desire for its own sake and not for the sake of something else, and one for the sake of which we choose everything else (1094ª18–20). Aristotle notes that while the many and the wise agree in naming the best good 'eudaimonia' ('happiness'), they disagree over what exactly this is (1. 4, 1095ª17–22). After briefly considering and critiquing different accounts of what the best good is (1. 5–6), Aristotle gives his own account (1. 7), and he does so by means of an argument that pivots on the concept of an *ergon*. This is 'the *ergon* argument'.

In the lines just before the argument, Aristotle says that while people agree that eudaimonia is 'the best [good]', we still need a clearer idea of what this best good is (1. 7, 1097ᵇ22–4). He then suggests that we might attain this clarity if we grasp the *ergon* of a human. In what I will call 'Section A' of the *ergon* argument, he explains why (cf. *gar* at 1097ᵇ25) doing so might be helpful:

SECTION A

ὥσπερ γὰρ αὐλητῇ καὶ ἀγαλματοποιῷ καὶ παντὶ τεχνίτῃ, καὶ ὅλως ὧν ἔστιν ἔργον τι καὶ πρᾶξις, ἐν τῷ ἔργῳ δοκεῖ τἀγαθὸν εἶναι καὶ τὸ εὖ, οὕτω δόξειεν ἂν καὶ ἀνθρώπῳ, εἴπερ ἔστι τι ἔργον αὐτοῦ.[1]

This is because just as for a flautist, a sculptor, and every artisan, and generally, for whatever has an *ergon* and an action, the good, that is, the well [τὸ εὖ], seems to be [found] in its *ergon*, the same would seem to be so for a human, if he has an *ergon*.[2] (*NE* 1. 7, 1097ᵇ25–8)

---

[1] Unless otherwise noted, I use the Oxford Classical Text edition of Aristotle's Greek.

[2] Unless otherwise noted, all translations are my own, though they do reflect my

The Concept of Ergon 229

This passage supplies us with the fundamental principle upon which the *ergon* argument rests: for anything with an *ergon* and an action, 'the good, that is, the well' is found in its *ergon*. I here translate 'τὸ εὖ' as 'the well', though (as I will later suggest) it is better understood as 'the excellent achievement'. But I give this provisional, literal translation because our understanding of 'τὸ εὖ' turns on our understanding of '*ergon*' since, as is clear from a later part of the argument, Aristotle uses 'τὸ εὖ' to refer to a thing's *ergon* achieved well (1. 7, 1098ª12).

'*Ergon*' in Section A has been translated as 'function',[3] 'characteristic activity',[4] 'activité',[5] 'office' (Fr.),[6] 'eigentümliche Tätigkeit',[7] and so on. Some scholars helpfully explain what they take an *ergon* to be. Barney, for example, says: 'the function of a thing consists in the activity proper to or characteristic of it',[8] noting that 'shoemaking', for example, 'is a function'.[9] In some form or other, this interpretation is ubiquitous,[10] stretching back into the Middle

consultation of published translations, especially T. H. Irwin (trans.), *Aristotle: Nicomachean Ethics, Translated with Introduction, Notes and Glossary* [*Ethics*], 2nd edn. (Indianapolis and Cambridge, 1999); C. D. C. Reeve (trans.), *Plato:* Republic [*Republic*] (Indianapolis and Cambridge, 2004), and the translations found in *The Complete Works of Aristotle*, ed. J. Barnes (Princeton, 1995). (References to editions and translations without page numbers are always to the passage under discussion.)

[3] Irwin, *Ethics*; H. Rackham (trans.), *Aristotle:* Nicomachean Ethics (Cambridge, Mass., 1934); W. D. Ross (trans.), *Nicomachean Ethics*, rev. J. O. Urmson, in *The Complete Works of Aristotle*, ed. Barnes, ii. 1729–1867; S. Broadie (comm.) and C. Rowe (trans.), *Aristotle:* Nicomachean Ethics [*Ethics*] (Oxford, 2002).

[4] R. Crisp (ed. and trans.), *Aristotle:* Nicomachean Ethics (Cambridge, 2000).

[5] P. Destrée, 'Comment démontrer le propre de l'homme? Pour une lecture "dialectique" de *EN* I, 6' in G. R. Dherbey and G. Aubry (eds.), *L'Excellence de la vie* (Paris, 2002), 39–61 at 61.

[6] R. Bodéüs (trans.), *Aristote: l'Éthique à Nicomaque* (Paris, 2004).

[7] O. Gigon (trans.), *Aristoteles: Die Nikomachische Ethik* (Düsseldorf and Zurich, 2001).

[8] R. Barney, 'Aristotle's Argument for a Human Function' ['Human Function'], *Oxford Studies in Ancient Philosophy*, 34 (2008), 293–322 at 293.

[9] Barney, 'Human Function', 304.

[10] The view is truly ubiquitous, but here are a few more quotations in which it is stated or implied: C. Korsgaard, 'Aristotle on Function and Virtue' ['Function and Virtue'], *History of Philosophy Quarterly*, 3 (1986), 259–79 at 259: 'Aristotle reasons that if anything has a function, its good lies in performing that function well'; Irwin, *Ethics*, 183: 'The examples of craftsmen [in Section A] suggest that the function of some kind F is the *goal-directed activity* that is essential to F'; Broadie, *Ethics*, 276: '[P]erhaps the examples [in 1097ᵇ28–33] are meant . . . to illustrate the concept of a *characteristic function* (*ergon*). That the being or essential nature of an individual is expressed through a typifying activity is the central doctrine of [Aristotle's] metaphysics'. G. Lawrence, 'Is Aristotle's Function Argument Fallacious?' ['Fal-

Ages.[11] Several factors have encouraged it. First, the only *erga* explicitly identified in *NE* 1. 7 are activities: the human *ergon* is an 'activity on the basis of reason or not without reason' (1098ᵃ7–8) and the *ergon* of a kitharist is the performance on the kithara (1098ᵃ11–12). Second, while I have said that the claim of Section A is made with reference to 'anything with an *ergon* and an action' (1097ᵇ26), some scholars take the Greek to mean 'anything with an *ergon*, that is, an action'. This would of course imply that the *ergon* of a thing is the same as its proper 'action'. Third, because it is clear that 'the well' (τὸ εὖ, 1097ᵇ27) of a human being is a doing well and that this is 'in' the human *ergon*, which is an activity, scholars assume that 'the well' of every artisan is a doing well and that it must likewise be 'in' their proper activities. We will return to these issues. But for now let us just note that on the basis of the broad scholarly agreement as well as these last considerations, one might draw the not ill-grounded conclusion that Aristotle, in the *ergon* argument of the *Nicomachean Ethics*, understands the *ergon* of a thing to be the proper activity of that thing.

Yet there is reason to be uneasy. First, even if one assumes that Aristotle uses '*ergon*' to mean 'proper activity' in *NE* 1. 7, one must also note that not long before the *ergon* argument (1. 1, 1094ᵃ5), and not long after it (2. 6, 1106ᵇ10), Aristotle uses '*ergon*' in expressions that clearly refer to products. Aristotle would then appear to be switching back and forth between different meanings of the word '*ergon*' without any indication that he is doing so. Second, when Aristotle identifies the *ergon* of a productive artisan, he identifies it as a product, not a proper activity: for example, the *ergon* of a shoemaker is a shoe and the *ergon* of a housebuilder is a house (*NE* 5 (=*EE* 4). 5, 1133ᵃ7–10; cf. *EE* 2. 1, 1219ᵃ14–21). Third and most importantly, if *ergon* means 'proper activity' in *NE* 1. 7, it is unclear how the claim of Section A is supposed to help Aristotle determine the human good, which he considers to be the best thing achievable by a human. Take the example of the sculptor. Even if

---

lacious?'], *Philosophical Inquiry*, 31 (2009), 191–224 at 215, summarizes Section A this way: 'Where the X is something with a function, the X-an good, i.e. *the good of an X*, consists in its doing its function successfully or well.' C. D. C. Reeve, *Action, Contemplation, and Happiness: An Essay on Aristotle* (Cambridge, Mass., 2012), 238, explains that the *ergon* of a carpenter is 'doing woodwork'.

[11] Aquinas, for example, rephrases the claim of Section A this way: 'When a thing has a proper activity [*propriam operationem*], its good and its being well-off consist in its activity [*in eius operatione*]' (*Sententia libri Ethicorum* 1. 10 n. 2 Busa).

'the good, that is, the well' of a sculptor consists in sculpting well, that seems irrelevant to the question of what the best thing achievable by a sculptor is—since this is presumably not sculpting but a *sculpture*. These incongruities should give us pause, and because of them we should be open to reassessing the evidence for what Aristotle's concept of an *ergon* really is.

This article consists in such a reassessment, and as I mentioned earlier, my proposal will be that in *NE* 1. 7 (as elsewhere) Aristotle understands the *ergon* of an X to be an activity in some cases but a product in others, in accordance with the sort of thing the X is—for though Aristotle has a single concept of an *ergon*, he nevertheless identifies the *ergon* of the eye as seeing and the *ergon* of a sculptor as a sculpture. For ease of reference, I will call this the 'alternative concept of an *ergon*'. On my interpretation, the way Aristotle understands 'the *ergon* of an X' is similar to the way he understands 'the limit [πέρας] of an X'. For though Aristotle has a single concept of a limit, he nevertheless identifies the limit of a plane as a line and the limit of a line as a point (cf. *Top.* 4. 4, 141^{b}19–22)—and Aristotle thinks a line (having one dimension) and a point (have zero dimensions) are radically different kinds of things. When Aristotle speaks of 'the *ergon* of a human', that expression does refer to a proper activity, but '*ergon*' does not thereby mean what 'proper activity' means. '*Ergon*' and 'proper activity' express different concepts. Similarly, when Aristotle speaks of 'the limit [πέρας] of a plane', that expression does refer to a line, but 'limit' does not thereby mean what 'line' (or 'γραμμή') means. 'Limit' and 'line' express different concepts.

To argue for this interpretation, I examine passages from Plato's *Republic* and Aristotle's *Protrepticus, Eudemian Ethics, De caelo*, and *Nicomachean Ethics*. Along the way we see that while Plato and Aristotle share the same basic concept of an *ergon*, they nevertheless differ in their accounts of what an *ergon* is. On Aristotle's account (though not on Plato's) the *ergon* of an X is the end for the sake of which an X, *qua* X, has being.

3. Plato's understanding of an *ergon* in the *Republic*

Plato gives an *ergon* argument in *Republic* 1 that scholars rightly take to be a precursor to the *ergon* argument of *NE* 1. 7. They also as-

232   Samuel H. Baker

sume that Plato and Aristotle share the same concept of an *ergon*,[12] and that Plato's concept of an *ergon* is that of a proper activity.[13] Below, for example, is Reeve's translation of the account of an *ergon* that we find at the beginning of Plato's *ergon* argument:

FIRST ACCOUNT

ἆρ' οὖν τοῦτο ἂν θείης καὶ ἵππου καὶ ἄλλου ὁτουοῦν ἔργον, ὃ ἂν ἢ μόνῳ ἐκείνῳ ποιῇ τις ἢ ἄριστα;[14] (*Rep.* 1, 352 E 3–4)

And would you take the function [ἔργον] of a horse or of anything else to be that which one can do [ποιῇ] only with it or best with it?[15]

The translation is representative.[16] The same goes for the second formulation (considered by Plato to be equivalent to the first, 353 A 9):

[12] Scholars who assume that Plato and Aristotle share their concept of an *ergon* include, for example, J. M. Cooper, *Reason and Human Good in Aristotle* [*Human Good*] (Indianapolis and Cambridge, 1986), 145; Irwin, *Ethics*, 183; and Korsgaard, 'Function and Virtue', 260.

[13] However, even if scholars are correct in saying that the concept of an *ergon* in the *ergon* argument of Plato's *Republic* is the concept of a function, that alone would not give us sufficient reason to conclude that the concept of an *ergon* in the *ergon* argument of Aristotle's *Nicomachean Ethics* is that of a function. This is because, as we will see, there is good reason to think that neither in the *Protrepticus* (which certainly comes before the *Nicomachean Ethics*) nor in the *Eudemian Ethics* (which very likely does as well) is Aristotle's concept of an *ergon* the concept of a function.

[14] For citations from the *Republic* I use the OCT edition of S. R. Slings (Oxford, 2003), which is also the text translated in Reeve, *Republic*.

[15] Reeve, *Republic*. These lines may startle a modern reader, for Plato appears to think that the *ergon* of a horse somehow consists in being used by man. On the basis of these lines Barney assumes that Plato's general notion of *ergon* is one of 'instrumentality' ('Human Function', 299). I will not fully address this issue here, but we should note that Socrates considers this first account to be equivalent to his second account (353 A 9), in which the language of a user or instrument is absent. And so it is not obvious that Plato's concept of an *ergon* is inextricably tied to that of a 'user', even if Plato (or Socrates) thinks that the *ergon* of a horse is essentially related to a user.

[16] Cf. R. E. Allen (trans.), *Plato: The Republic* (New Haven and London, 2008); A. Bloom (trans.), *The Republic of Plato*, 2nd edn. (New York, 1991); G. M. A. Grube (trans.), *Republic*, rev. C. D. C. Reeve, in *Plato: Complete Works*, ed. J. M. Cooper with D. H. Hutchinson (Indianapolis and Cambridge, 1997), 971–1223; H. D. P. Lee (trans.), *Plato: Republic* (New York, 2007); A. D. Lindsay (trans.), *Plato: The Republic* (New York, 1976); P. Shorey (trans.), *Plato: Republic, Books I–V* (Cambridge, Mass., 1937); R. Waterfield (trans.), *Plato: Republic* (Oxford, 1993). Allen sometimes translates *ergon* as 'function or work' and sometimes as 'function'. Shorey and Bloom both translate *ergon* as 'work' throughout the *ergon* argument, but their translation of the verbs that take '*ergon*' as their direct object shows that they consider the *ergon* to be a function: for Shorey, 'do' at 352 E 4 and 'perform' at 353 A 11; and for Bloom, 'do' at both 352 E 4 and 353 A 11.

SECOND ACCOUNT

νῦν δὴ οἶμαι ἄμεινον ἂν μάθοις ὃ ἄρτι ἠρώτων, πυνθανόμενος εἰ οὐ τοῦτο ἑκάστου εἴη ἔργον ὃ ἂν ἢ μόνον τι ἢ κάλλιστα τῶν ἄλλων ἀπεργάζηται. (*Rep.* 1, 353 A 10–11)

Now I think you will understand better what I was asking earlier when I asked whether the function [ἔργον] of each thing is what it alone can do [ἀπεργάζηται] or what it can do better than anything else. (trans. Reeve)[17]

Commentators seem to be in agreement with the translators. Irwin, for example, writes: 'Socrates [in *Republic* 1] appeals to the connexion between the virtue of F and the function, or *essential activity* of F: a good knife is good at cutting, a good eye is good at seeing, and so on.'[18]

Despite this consensus, one should note that throughout the *Republic* Plato identifies the *ergon* of a productive art (e.g. the shoemaking art or the housebuilding art) not as its proper activity, but as its proper product. This occurs, for example, in the following passage, which comes shortly before *Republic* 1's *ergon* argument. To distinguish the art (*technē*) of wage-earning from other arts Socrates explains:

This very benefit, receiving wages, doesn't result from [the artisan's] own art. On the contrary, if we are to examine the matter precisely, the doctoring art makes health [ἡ μὲν ἰατρικὴ ὑγίειαν ποιεῖ], and the wage-earning art a wage; the housebuilding art makes a house, and the wage-earning art, which accompanies it, a wage, and the same [οὕτως] goes for all other arts:

---

[17] In the Greek idiom the expression translated as 'better than anything else' actually contains the word 'best' (κάλλιστα), and so the notion of 'best' is used in both accounts.

[18] T. H. Irwin, *Plato's Ethics* (Oxford, 1995), 179 (emphasis added). I here mention a few more scholars who hold that Plato's concept of an *ergon* in the *Republic* is that of a function. G. Vlastos, 'Justice and Happiness in the *Republic*', in G. Vlastos, *Platonic Studies* (Princeton, 1973), 111–39 at 115, writes: 'the ἔργον of anything (of a tool, like a pruning-knife, or of a bodily organ, like an eye or an ear) is that activity which can be "performed either exclusively by that thing or else more excellently [κάλλιστα] by it than by anything else" (353 A)'. Cooper, *Human Good*, 145, notes a claim common to the *ergon* arguments in both the *Nicomachean Ethics* and *Republic* 1: 'a thing's excellence is the essential condition of its performing well its *ergon*'. J. Annas, *An Introduction to Plato's Republic* (Oxford, 1981), 54, writes: '*Ergon* is what a thing does *qua* a thing of that kind.' R. Barney, 'Socrates' Refutation of Thrasymachus', in G. Santas (ed.), *The Blackwell Guide to Plato's Republic* (Oxford, 2006), 44–62 at 55, commenting on what she calls 'the "function" argument', writes: 'the function of anything is "that which one can do only with it or best with it" (352 E 3–4, 353 A 9–11)'.

each achieves its *ergon* [τὸ αὑτῆς ἑκάστη ἔργον ἐργάζεται], and benefits that over which it is placed. (*Rep.* 1, 346 D 1–6)

Socrates here remarks that the doctoring art makes (*poiei*) health, the housebuilding art a house, and the wage-earning art a wage, and then places these examples in parallel structure with the following claim: 'each [art] achieves [*ergazetai*] its *ergon*'. This indicates that we ought to read '*poiei*' as parallel to '*ergazetai*'; and 'health', 'a house', and 'a wage' as parallel to '*ergon*'. Consequently, Plato identifies the *ergon* of each of these particular arts not as their proper activities, but as their products. One should also note that Plato here speaks of *each* art achieving its *ergon*, and there is reason to think that not every art issues in a product. This is because later, in *Republic* 10, Plato implies both that there is an art of flute-playing and that the flute-player (in contrast to the flute-maker) does not make a product (601 D 1–E 2). And so if the flute-player is to have an *ergon*, it will not be a product but an activity, his performance on the flute. If this is so, then when Plato speaks of each art achieving its *ergon*, he would seem to be assuming that while the *ergon* of the housebuilder is a product (a house), the *ergon* of the flute-player is an activity (his performance). Other passages from the *Republic* suggest a similar picture.[19]

But is this the same notion of an *ergon* that occurs in *Republic* 1's *ergon* argument? As far as examples of *erga* within *Republic* 1's *ergon* argument are concerned, nothing prevents it from being so. This is because even though the *erga* explicitly identified there are activities (e.g. seeing, hearing, living), these are the sorts of activities that do not issue in products. And so it is possible that Plato thinks that while the *ergon* of the eye is seeing and the *ergon* of the ear is hear-

---

[19] Consider, for example, *Rep.* 4, 421 D 9–E 5, which pretty clearly implies that the *erga* of potters are pots. In that passage, not only is the verb ἐργάζεται again paired with '*erga*' as its direct object at 421 D 12, just as it was in the *ergon* argument (1, 353 C 6–7; cf. 353 A 10–11), but Socrates also speaks of 'the *erga* of the arts' using the '*ergon*'-plus-genitive construction that, as we note above, regularly signifies the *ergon* proper to a thing. Consider also the famous discussion of art in *Republic* 10, where Socrates clearly identifies the *ergon* of a couch-maker as a couch (not couch-making), and again pairs the same verbs (ποιέω and ἐργάζομαι) with the *erga* as their direct objects (e.g. at 597 A 1–7 and 603 A 9–B 3). Also, in the course of his argument in *Republic* 10 he says that the *ergon* of the rational part of the soul is to deliberate (602 D 6–E 2), echoing a similar claim made in the *ergon* argument of *Republic* 1 (cf. 353 D 3–7), and this strongly suggests that in book 10 Plato assumes that while the *ergon* of a couch-maker is a product (a couch), the *ergon* of the rational part of the soul is an activity (to deliberate).

ing, the *ergon* of a housebuilder is still a house. As for textual indications that the same notion of an *ergon* is present in both places, here are three. First, it is only a few pages after the passage above that Plato gives his *ergon* argument, and in the meantime he gives no indication that his use of the word '*ergon*' has changed. He also explicitly notes that his two accounts of what an *ergon* is are intended to apply to anything with an *ergon* (352 E 3 and 353 A 10). Second, Plato correlates the transitive verbs *poieō* and *ergazomai* with the *erga* as their direct objects both in the passage above and in the two accounts of what an *ergon* is: *poieō* in the first account (352 E 4) and *apergazomai* in the second (353 A 11). And third, in the passage above Plato speaks of 'the *ergon* of the art' (346 D 5) while in the *ergon* argument he speaks of 'the *ergon* of [an X]' (352 D 9–E 3; 353 A 10–11), and in doing so he uses the '*ergon*'-plus-genitive construction that regularly signifies the *ergon* proper to an X.[20]

But what about Plato's two accounts of what an *ergon* is? Current translations suggest that an *ergon* of an X is always an activity: for example, the *ergon* of each thing is 'what it alone can do [*apergazētai*] or what it can do better than anything else' (353 A 10–11, trans. Reeve). But, as we have seen, *apergazomai* and *poieō* do not always indicate a 'doing'. Instead, just as the expression '*ergon* of X' (without changing its meaning) indicated an activity or a product in accordance with the sort of thing the X is, so each of the verbs in question (without changing their meaning) indicated a doing or a making as the case may be. Consequently, we lose the core meaning of these verbs when we translate them as 'do' or 'make'. If we want to retain the core meaning, a few verbs in English may help: 'accomplish', 'achieve', 'execute', etc. We can intelligibly speak of a statue as something that a sculptor has accomplished or achieved, and we can likewise speak of a flute-player's performance as something that the flute-player has accomplished or achieved.[21] Now in certain passages it may not be that important to retain the core meaning of the verbs in question, but in other passages it is important—and Plato's *ergon* argument is one of these passages. I recommend that we translate the two accounts this way:

[20] LSJ s.v. ἔργον, VI.1.a.

[21] Though this use of 'achieve' may seem awkward, note that some languages have verbs that have semantic ranges which are quite similar to those (that I have just drawn attention to) of ποιέω or ἀπεργάζομαι. Consider, for example, French *faire*. One can say 'J'ai fait un gâteau' ('I made a cake') *or* 'J'ai fait une promenade' ('I took a walk').

FIRST ACCOUNT

And would you take the *ergon* of a horse or anything else to be that which one can achieve [ποιῇ] only with it or best with it? (352 E 3–4)

SECOND ACCOUNT

... the *ergon* of each thing is what it alone can achieve [ἀπεργάζηται] or what it can achieve better than anything else. (353 A 10–11)

Later I will make some remarks about how best to translate '*ergon*'. But for the moment, we need only to observe that Plato's two accounts should be translated along these lines if they are to reflect what I am suggesting are the contours of the concept of an *ergon*. Plato, I believe, is trying to give a single account of 'the *ergon* of an X' that can nevertheless pick out different kinds of things (activities or products) just as one might give a single account of 'the limit of an X' that can nevertheless pick out different kinds of things (lines, points, etc.).

If we do understand Plato's accounts in this new way, we are put in a position to appreciate a difficulty—one that Aristotle appears to respond to in the *Eudemian Ethics*. Notice that when Plato in each of his two accounts speaks about achieving something 'best' (κάλλιστα or ἄριστα), he understands 'best' by reference to a comparison class of things that can execute similar *erga* (353 A 1–8). However, as we have seen, he also thinks that, in the cases where the activity of something issues in a product, the product is the *ergon* of that thing and not the activity: for example, the *ergon* of the doctoring art is health, not healing, and the *ergon* of the housebuilding art is a house, not housebuilding (*Rep* 1, 346 D 1–8). The conjunction of these views creates the following gap when it comes to accounting for the *ergon* of any productive art. Taking the doctoring art as an example, we are not given sufficient conditions for picking out health (as opposed to healing) as the *ergon*. For while the doctoring art achieves health best (in comparison with the shoemaking art or any other art), the doctoring art also achieves *healing* best.

4. Aristotle's understanding of an *ergon* in the *Protrepticus*

Before we see how Aristotle in the *Eudemian Ethics* responds to Plato's account, we should look at a telling section of text that forms part of what is probably Aristotle's earliest extant *ergon* argument.

The Concept of Ergon

In fragment B 65 of Aristotle's *Protrepticus*, as recovered from Iamblichus,[22] we read:

If a human is a simple animal and his being is ordered to reason and thought, he has no other *ergon* than the most exact truth, that is, thinking truly about what is [οὐκ ἄλλο ἐστὶν αὐτοῦ ἔργον ἢ μόνη ἡ ἀκριβεστάτη ἀλήθεια καὶ τὸ περὶ τῶν ὄντων ἀληθεύειν]. But if he is naturally composed of several capacities, it is clear that when a thing can achieve several [things], the best of these is always the *ergon* [ἀεὶ τούτων τὸ βέλτιστον ⟨τὸ⟩ ἔργον ἐστίν]: for example, health [is the *ergon*] of a doctor, and safety [is the *ergon*] of a sea captain. Now we can name no better *ergon* of thought or the thinking part of the soul than truth. Truth, therefore, is the supreme *ergon* of the thinking part of the soul.[23]

There are complexities to this passage that I will not now address, but I think we can see here the same basic concept of an *ergon* that we detected in the *Republic*. Aristotle seems to claim that, if a thing can achieve only one thing, then that will be its *ergon*. But if a thing is naturally fit to achieve more than one thing, it is the best of these that is its *ergon*. He then identifies the *ergon* of a doctor to be health and the *ergon* of a sea captain to be safety;[24] yet he also identifies the *ergon* of the thinking part of the soul as 'truth', earlier glossed by him as 'thinking truly' (ἀληθεύειν).[25] Consequently, he understands the *ergon* of an X to be 'the best' that an X, *qua* X, is fit to achieve,

[22] Here it is also worth noting that new arguments for the authenticity of the *Protrepticus* fragments may be found in D. S. Hutchinson and M. R. Johnson, 'Authenticating Aristotle's *Protrepticus*', *Oxford Studies in Ancient Philosophy*, 29 (2005), 193–294.

[23] I rely on the text and translation of I. Düring (ed. and trans.), *Aristotle's Protrepticus: An Attempt at Reconstruction* (Göteborg, 1961), but with some alterations to the translation.

[24] Presumably, the many things that Aristotle thinks a doctor, for example, can achieve will be health but also healing, and all the various activities that form a part of healing (rubbing, purging, etc.).

[25] Since Aristotle first describes a case where something has only one capacity, the καί that links 'most exact truth' and 'thinking truly about what is' is epexegetic. This suggests that what is achieved is a certain true activity: thinking truly or judging truly. I take this interpretation to dovetail with the remarks we find in *NE* 6. 2, where we read that the *ergon* of the thinking parts of the soul is truth and that the virtues of these parts are what enable it to think most truly (μάλιστα ἀληθεύσει, 1039^{b}13). Though I cannot here argue for this view, I think that Aristotle does not conceive of truth, in its primary sense, as something that lies outside the activity of thinking (cf. *Metaph*. E 4, 1027^{b}25–7). For a different view see P. Crivelli, *Aristotle on Truth* (Cambridge, 2004), who maintains that true and false things (πράγματα) 'contribute to explaining what it is to be true or false for thoughts and sentences' (7). Crivelli does not discuss *Protr.* B 65 or *NE* 6. 2. For scholars who find Crivelli's claims about true and false πράγματα problematic see the reviews of *Aristotle*

whether it be beyond its activity (as in the case of a doctor or sea captain) or the activity itself (as in the case of the thinking part of the soul).

In the *Eudemian Ethics* Aristotle goes into more detail about what he takes an *ergon* to be. Nevertheless, the *Protrepticus* account already differs from that of Plato. The reason is as follows. When Plato in the *Republic* speaks of the *ergon* of X as what X can alone achieve or what it can achieve best (ἄριστα and κάλλιστα), the notion of 'best' is with respect to a comparison class of things that can achieve similar *erga*. But when Aristotle in the *Protrepticus* speaks of the *ergon* of X as what is 'best' (βέλτιστον), the notion of 'best' is with respect to a comparison class of things that X, *qua* X, can achieve. This thought is developed in the *Eudemian Ethics*.

5. Aristotle's understanding of an *ergon* in the *Eudemian Ethics*

Scholars generally agree that the *Eudemian Ethics* was written before the *Nicomachean Ethics* but after the *Protrepticus*.[26] In the *ergon* argument of the *Eudemian Ethics* we find what is probably the clearest case of Aristotle affirming that the *ergon* of an X is an activity in some cases and a product in others in accordance with the sort of thing the X is. The crucial passage runs:

It is clear that the *ergon* is better than the state or the disposition; but *ergon* is said in two ways [λέγεται διχῶς]. In some cases, there is an *ergon* beyond the employment:[27] for example, a house is the *ergon* of the housebuilding art and not the activity of housebuilding, and health is the *ergon* of the doctoring art and not the activity of healing or doctoring. In other cases, the employment is the *ergon*: for example, seeing is the *ergon* of vision, and

on Truth by M. Wheeler in *Journal of the History of Philosophy*, 44 (2006), 469–70, and by U. Coope in *Notre Dame Philosophical Reviews* (2005) ⟨http://ndpr.nd.edu/news/24902-aristotle-on-truth/⟩.

[26] Here I take it for granted that the *Eudemian Ethics* precedes the *Nicomachean Ethics*. However, if we assume the opposite, that will only strengthen my argument. This is because the distinction made in the *Eudemian Ethics* is also made in the *Protrepticus* (at B 65), which every scholar acknowledges to have been written before the *Nicomachean Ethics*. Thus, if we assume that the *Eudemian Ethics* is a later work of Aristotle, there will be evidence that Aristotle subscribes to the alternative concept of an *ergon* both before and after the *Nicomachean Ethics*.

[27] 'Employment' translates χρῆσις. The employment is of the power (vision, the doctoring art, the housebuilding art, etc.), and I do not think that the word need imply that there must be a user that is distinct from the power.

active understanding [of mathematical truth] is the *ergon* of mathematical knowledge. And so it follows that, when a thing's employment is its *ergon*, the employment is better than the state. (*EE* 2. 1, 1219ᵃ11–18)

This passage is rarely discussed. However, Reeve briefly gives what would presumably be a preferred interpretation for those who advocate the *ergon*-as-function reading of *NE* 1. 7. Reeve suggests that Aristotle is here noting that the term '*ergon*' is 'act/result ambiguous'.[28]

This seems to me highly doubtful. For if Aristotle were noting that '*ergon*' is act/result ambiguous, he could easily have done so by saying that there is one sense in which a house is the *ergon* of the housebuilding art and another sense in which housebuilding is. Yet he does not do this. Instead, when he mentions activities that are *erga*, he only mentions activities that do *not* issue in products: for example, seeing is the *ergon* of vision. And when he mentions products that are *erga*, he goes out of his way to say that the activities that issue in these products are *not erga*. He states: 'a house is the *ergon* of the housebuilding art and *not* the activity of housebuilding, and health is the *ergon* of the doctoring art and *not* the activity of healing or doctoring' (1219ᵃ14–16, emphasis added). Thus, Aristotle seems to be saying that when a thing's proper activity is for the sake of a product, the *ergon* of that thing is its product, *not* its proper activity.

Notice also how the argument begins: 'It is clear that the *ergon* is better than the state or disposition' (1219ᵃ11–13). It is only *after* making this claim that Aristotle draws the distinction between two types of *erga*: *erga* that are beyond activities and *erga* that are activities. With this distinction in hand, he concludes: 'So it follows that, when a thing's employment is its *ergon*, the employment is better than the state' (1219ᵃ17–18). Aristotle's reasoning proceeds like this. (1) The *ergon* is better than the state. (2) The *ergon* is an activity in some cases but a product in others. Therefore, (3) when the *ergon* is an activity, the activity is better than the state. The implication is that, when Aristotle made the claim about 'the *ergon*' at the beginning of the passage ('the *ergon* is better than the state', 1219ᵃ12), he intended it to cover both sorts of *erga*, and thus was taking '*ergon*' to signify a single concept.

[28] C. D. C. Reeve, *Practices of Reason: Aristotle's* Nicomachean Ethics (Oxford, 1992), 123. Cf. M. R. Johnson, *Aristotle on Teleology* (Oxford, 2005), 87–8: 'the function is in fact a product of action, like shoes, or the action itself, like shoemaking'.

Where is the unity to be found? Helpfully, Aristotle says precisely where. Just before the quoted passage, he makes this claim about everything with an *ergon*: 'the end of each [thing] is its *ergon*' (τέλος ἑκάστου τὸ ἔργον, *EE* 2. 1, 1219ᵃ8), explaining that 'the end is best, as being an end' (τὸ γὰρ τέλος ἄριστον ὡς τέλος, 1219ᵃ10). Then he indicates what he takes an 'end' to be:

τέλος τὸ βέλτιστον καὶ τὸ ἔσχατον, οὗ ἕνεκα τἆλλα πάντα. (1219ᵃ10–11)

The end is the best in the sense of the last [thing] for the sake of which everything else [is *or* is done].

It is this idea that unifies the two ways in which *ergon* 'is said' (1219ᵃ13). In the case of the housebuilding art, the 'last [thing] for the sake of which everything else [is done]' is a house (not housebuilding). However, in the case of the eye, Aristotle thinks, the 'last [thing] for the sake of which everything else [is]' is seeing—and this is the activity itself.

Now if Aristotle had distinguished two senses of the word '*ergon*' we would expect him to give two corresponding accounts of what an *ergon* is, but he does not do this. He gives only this *one* account, and on this account certain proper activities (e.g. housebuilding and shoemaking) are not *erga*. We should also note, though we will discuss this more in the next section, that when Aristotle identifies the *ergon* of each thing as its end (*EE* 2. 1, 1219ᵃ8), he understands 'end' in a certain way. The *ergon* of something is the end for the sake of which that sort of thing exists or 'has being'—*qua* the sort of thing that it is. Thus, the *ergon* of the housebuilding art will be a house because a house is the end for the sake of which the housebuilding art, *qua* housebuilding art, exists or has being.

Now if one desired more confirmation that we have detected the contours of the concept of an *ergon* in the *Eudemian Ethics*, one need only consider the passage that immediately follows the stretch of text we have so far considered. There Aristotle writes:

> Having made these distinctions, let us say that a thing and its virtue have the same *ergon*, though in different ways. For example, a shoe is the *ergon* of the shoemaking art and of the activity of shoemaking. So if there is some virtue that is the virtue of shoemaking and of a good shoemaker, its *ergon* is a good shoe [τὸ ἔργον ἐστὶ σπουδαῖον ὑπόδημα]. The same holds in other cases also. Now let us assume that the *ergon* of the soul is to accomplish living,[29] and that this is an employment and a waking state, since sleep is

---

[29] Since Aristotle identifies the *ergon* of the excellent soul as 'good life' or 'good

The Concept of Ergon

an idle and inactive state. So, as the *ergon* of the soul and of its virtue must be one and the same, the *ergon* of the virtue is good living [ἔργον ἂν εἴη τῆς ἀρετῆς ζωὴ σπουδαία]. (*EE* 2. 1, 1219ᵃ18–27)

Notice that Aristotle in this passage does not indicate which meaning of the word '*ergon*' he is using, and that is because (as I have argued) he has not distinguished different meanings of the word. He has instead indicated the different sorts of things that an *ergon* can be. Now notice how the passage is structured. Aristotle first articulates a principle (1219ᵃ19–20): the *ergon* of something and that of its virtue are the same (presumably in *genos*, cf. *NE* 1. 7, 1098ᵃ8), though different (presumably because one is achieved well, cf. *NE* 1. 7, 1098ᵃ12). He then clarifies the principle by applying it to the case of the shoemaking art: the *ergon* of the shoemaking art is a shoe, while the *ergon* of its virtue is a good shoe (1219ᵃ20–3). He says this holds for other cases (1219ᵃ23), and then immediately applies it in the case of the soul: the *ergon* of the soul is living, and the *ergon* of its virtue is good living (1219ᵃ23–7). The implication is that when Aristotle spoke of 'the *ergon*' at the beginning of the passage ('let us say that a thing and its virtue have the same *ergon* but in different ways', 1219ᵃ19–20), he was assuming that the *ergon* of an X was in some cases an activity (e.g. the soul's living) but in other cases a product (e.g. the shoemaker's shoe) in accordance with the sort of thing the X is.

Why have scholars thought that Aristotle is here distinguishing different meanings of the word '*ergon*'? According to some translations, Aristotle actually says that *ergon* 'has two meanings' or 'has two senses' (λέγεται διχῶς, *EE* 2. 1, 1219ᵃ13).³⁰ However, because Aristotle has no word for 'reference' as opposed to 'meaning' or

living' (ζωὴ σπουδαία), we would expect him to identify the *ergon* of the soul as 'life' or 'living'. It may then come as a surprise to read in different translations that the *ergon* of the soul is 'to make things live' (M. Woods (trans. and comm.), *Aristotle: Eudemian Ethics, Books I, II, and VIII*, 2nd edn. [*Eudemian Ethics*] (Oxford, 2005)), 'to cause life' (H. Rackham (trans.), *Aristotle:* The Athenian Constitution, The Eudemian Ethics, On Virtues and Vices [*Eudemian Ethics*] (Cambridge, Mass., 1996)), 'to produce living' (J. Solomon (trans.), *Eudemian Ethics*, in *The Complete Works of Aristotle*, ed. Barnes, ii. 1922–81), etc. The Greek is 'τὸ ζῆν ποιεῖν'. My solution is to understand 'ποιέω' in the way that we argued Plato uses it in *Republic* 1: the verb, while retaining the same meaning, can indicate a 'doing' or a 'making' as the case may be. Consequently, Aristotle at *EE* 2. 1, 1219ᵃ24, is not saying that the *ergon* of the soul is to make things live, but rather to 'achieve' or 'accomplish' living, which would be the same as 'living' or 'life'.

³⁰ The first translation is that of Rackham, *Eudemian Ethics*, and the second is

'sense', these translations are highly problematic. A much safer rendering of 'λέγεται διχῶς' is 'is said in two ways',[31] for the idea need only be 'there can be two different things going on when we say [some word]'. This allows for the possibility that Aristotle at *EE* 2. 1, 1219^{a}13–17, is not making a distinction between two possible meanings but two possible referents—for 'the *ergon* of an X' can refer to an activity *or* a product. As I have argued, the line of thought in the passage suggests that Aristotle at *EE* 2. 1, 1219^{a}13, is using 'λέγεται διχῶς' in this latter way; moreover, he seems to use the phrase in the same way just a few pages earlier, at *EE* 1. 7, 1217^{a}35, where he discusses the two ways in which *prakton* ('achievable in action') 'is said'. Once we appreciate this, I believe we remove the last impediment that one might reasonably have to thinking that Aristotle in *EE* 2. 1 supposes the *ergon* of an X to be an activity in some cases but a product in others, depending on what the *ergon* is.

Now that we have outlined Aristotle's account, we are in a position to see how it addresses the difficulty present in Plato's accounts. As we saw, Plato did not obviously have the resources to pick out a house as opposed to housebuilding as the *ergon* of the housebuilding art. This gap was due to Plato saying that the *ergon* of X was what X can achieve best, where the notion of 'best' is with respect to a comparison class of things that can achieve similar *erga* (*Rep.* 1, 353 A 1–8). This allowed it to be possible that a housebuilder achieved a house best but also achieved housebuilding best. Aristotle closes this gap by giving an account of what an *ergon* is that employs the notion of 'best' differently. He says that if a thing has an *ergon*, 'the *ergon* of each [thing] is its end' (*EE* 2. 1, 1219^{a}8), and he clarifies this by saying 'the end is the best in the sense of [being] the last [thing] for the sake of which everything else [is *or* is done]' (*EE* 2. 1, 1219^{a}10–11). Here the notion of 'best' is with respect to a comparison class of other things that an X, *qua* X, can achieve, and the way that one of these things is best is by being the last thing for the sake of which. This provides resources to pick out house as opposed to housebuilding as the *ergon* of the housebuilder because it

that of Solomon, *Eudemian Ethics* and of B. Inwood and R Woolf (trans.), *Aristotle: Eudemian Ethics* (Cambridge, 2013).

[31] This is more or less how the phrase is translated in Woods, *Eudemian Ethics*, A. Kenny (ed. and trans.), *Aristotle:* The Eudemian Ethics (Oxford, 2012), and P. L. P. Simpson (trans.), *The* Eudemian Ethics *of Aristotle, Translated with Explanatory Comments* (New Brunswick and London, 2013).

is a house (and not housebuilding) that is the last thing for the sake of which a housebuilder, *qua* housebuilder, has being. There are also features of the text that suggest Aristotle is directly responding to Plato's account. Just after articulating his own account, Aristotle clarifies it by giving the very examples from *Republic* 1 (346 D 1–8)—the examples of the housebuilding art and the doctoring art—that Plato's account could not obviously accommodate, and Aristotle pointedly remarks that the *ergon* of the housebuilding art is a house, 'not housebuilding' (*EE* 2. 1, 1219ᵃ15), and that the *ergon* of the doctoring art is health, 'not healing or doctoring' (*EE* 2. 1, 1219ᵃ15–16).[32]

6. Aristotle's understanding of an *ergon* in the *De caelo*

In the *Eudemian Ethics* Aristotle seems to affirm that the *ergon* of something is the end for the sake of which that sort of thing exists or has being. This account also seems to be implicit in a line from Aristotle's natural philosophy, *De caelo* 2. 3, 286ᵃ8–9: 'Everything that has an *ergon* exists [*or* has being] for the sake of its *ergon*' (ἕκαστόν ἐστιν, ὧν ἐστιν ἔργον, ἕνεκα τοῦ ἔργου). If we pair this with the following passage from the *Politics*: 'The housebuilders' art exists [*or* has being] for the sake of a house' (ἔστι τῆς οἰκίας χάριν ἡ τῶν οἰκοδόμων τέχνη, *Pol*. 7. 8, 1328ᵃ33),[33] we get the very claim we detected in *EE* 2. 1: the housebuilding art exists for the sake of a house, which is its *ergon*.[34]

There are also reasons even within the *De caelo* to think that Aristotle is there employing the concept of an *ergon* that we detected in

---

[32] Thus, Aristotle does not agree with Plato's account of what an *ergon* is—*pace*, for example, H. H. Joachim, *Aristotle: The* Nicomachean Ethics. *A Commentary*, ed. D. A. Reese (Oxford, 1951), 48.

[33] Here Aristotle uses 'χάριν' instead of 'οὗ ἕνεκα', but this is of little importance. The context of the passage makes it clear that he considers the two expressions to be equivalent (cf. *Pol*. 7. 8, 1328ᵃ29).

[34] Aquinas seems to arrive at an interpretation along these lines. This is despite the fact that the Latin translation he was using apparently rendered '*ergon*' in this passage as 'operatio', which Aquinas understands as 'proper activity'. Aquinas notes that the line (so understood) cannot be fully correct. He then inadvertently gets at (what I take to be) the actual meaning of the Greek by qualifying the claim that 'each thing is for the sake of its proper activity' by saying, 'or at least [for the sake of] what issues from that proper activity, in the case of those things in which there is some work [*opus*] beyond the activity, as is said in *Ethics* 1' (*In libros De caelo et mundo*, lb 2 lc 4 n. 5 Busa).

the *Eudemian Ethics*. Now it is uncontroversial that Aristotle sometimes identifies the *ergon* of an X as an activity. In fact, just after he articulates the principle mentioned above, he implicitly identifies the *ergon* of the heavenly bodies as a certain 'eternal motion' (κίνησιν ἀΐδιον, 2. 3, 286ª10).[35] But consider these remarks that come later in the *De caelo*, where Aristotle criticizes certain philosophers for holding to their view even when it conflicts with the revealed phenomena:

[Some philosophers speak] as if certain [principles] did not require to be judged by their results [ἀποβαινόντων], and most of all from the end. And the end of the productive expertise is the *ergon* [τέλος δὲ τῆς μὲν ποιητικῆς ἐπιστήμης τὸ ἔργον]. (3. 7, 306ª14–16)

Scholars naturally understand 'the *ergon*' here to refer to the product of the productive art since this is what 'results' (306ª15). (Stocks, for example, translates '*ergon*' in this passage as 'product' but in *De caelo* 2. 3 as 'function'.[36]) But notice that Aristotle identifies the *ergon* of the productive art as that art's *end*, and remember that he earlier identified the *ergon* of each thing as the end for the sake of which it exists (*De caelo* 2. 3, 286ª8–9). This gives us reason for taking seriously the possibility that Aristotle is using the same concept of an *ergon* in both the passage from 2. 3, where he implicitly identifies the *ergon* of the heavenly bodies as an eternal motion (286ª10), and in the passage from 3. 7, where he implies that the *ergon* of a productive art is its product (306ª16). Consequently, he seems to be assuming that the *ergon* of an X may be an activity in some cases but a product in others, in accordance with the sort of thing the X is.

I also think that we can detect the alternative concept of an *ergon* in the very argument of *De caelo* 2. 3. Aristotle's task in this chapter is to explain why there are different motions among the heavenly bodies, and he does so by employing the teleological principle 'each thing with an *ergon* exists for the sake of its *ergon*' (2. 3, 286ª8–9). He first shows that since the activity of what is divine is 'eternal life' (ζωὴ ἀΐδιος, 286ª9), the *ergon* of a divine (heavenly) body will be an eternal motion, which must be motion in a circle (286ª10–12). This

---

[35] It is perhaps worth noting that this eternal motion (κίνησις) is a very special kind of motion (if a motion at all) because there is no internal reason for it to stop—a feature that Aristotle elsewhere seems to think holds of all motions.

[36] J. L. Stocks (trans.), *On the Heavens*, in *The Complete Works of Aristotle*, ed. Barnes, i. 447–511.

is the motion of the outer sphere, which carries the fixed stars. He then articulates a long chain of conditions necessary for this eternal motion, culminating in the claim that there must be an eternal process of terrestrial generation (286^b1–2). In order that there should be this eternal process of generation, Aristotle thinks, there must be different, oblique motions in the heavens (286^b2–4). These other motions belong to the inner spheres that contain the planets. The upshot is this. Because his explanation for the oblique motions of the inner spheres is that they exist for the sake of eternal terrestrial generation, it looks as if the terrestrial generation will be the *ergon* of these motions. Consequently, it looks as if the *ergon* of the outer sphere is its proper activity (namely, the eternal circular motion), while the *ergon* of the inner sphere containing planets is something *beyond* its proper activity (namely, the eternal process of terrestrial generation).[37]

7. Remarks on the expressions 'end of something' and '*ergon* of something'

When Aristotle identifies 'the end' of the doctoring art as health (*NE* I. I, 1094^a8), he is thinking of a certain end, namely, the end that is 'the last thing for the sake of which' the doctoring art, *qua* doctoring art, exists or has being. When Aristotle identifies—in the *Eudemian Ethics* and elsewhere[38]—the *ergon* of an X as 'the end of an X', he has this sort of end in mind. To clarify further Aristotle's thought, we will consider three questions that one might have at this point.

First, while in the *Protrepticus* Aristotle identifies health as the *ergon* of the *doctor* (B 65), in the *Eudemian Ethics* he identifies it as

---

[37] Here the language of 'product' to describe the *ergon* beyond the proper activity of something may be misleading. For, of course, in the case I have just described the *ergon* beyond the proper activity is still an activity (the eternal process of terrestrial generation). The point, though, is just that the proper activity of the inner spheres is not the end, but rather something beyond it. The reason this process of generation can be an end (even though it is a process) is because it is eternal and so is in a way something complete (cf. *NE* 10. 4, 1174^a19–21).

[38] Besides the passages we have already discussed, consider: 'the *ergon* is the end' (*Metaph.* Θ 8, 1150^a21), 'that for the sake of which [a house exists] is [its] *ergon* . . .' (*Metaph.* B 2, 996^b7), and 'if each body had the ability to progress but not to perceive, it would perish and would not reach its end, which is the *ergon* of its nature' (*DA* 3. 12, 434^a32–$^b1$).

the *ergon* of the *doctoring art* (2. 1, 1219ᵃ15). Is there much at stake in this difference? I do not think so. Aristotle uses both locutions because when he speaks of the *ergon* of the doctor, he is thinking of the doctor *qua* doctor, and what holds of a doctor *qua* doctor holds of him in virtue of his doctoring art. Aristotle more or less articulates this point in *Physics* 2. 3:

> It is always necessary to investigate the most precise cause of each thing, just as in other cases: for example, a man builds a house because he is a housebuilder, and a housebuilder builds a house on the basis of the housebuilding art [κατὰ τὴν οἰκοδομικήν]. (195ᵇ21–4)

The housebuilding art is that in virtue of which a housebuilder builds a house. And so if we identify the *ergon* of the housebuilding art as a house, we have thereby also identified the *ergon* of the housebuilder, *qua* housebuilder. 'The *ergon* of the housebuilding art' is a more exact locution, and so is Aristotle's preferred expression. Yet because such exactness is not always needed, he also speaks of 'the *ergon* of the housebuilder'.

Second, because 'the *ergon* of each thing is its end' (*EE* 2. 1, 1219ᵃ8) and the human good is the end of all things achievable in action (cf. *NE* 1. 2, 1094ᵃ18–22), does it follow that the human good is somehow the *ergon* of every achievable thing, including every art (the doctoring art, the housebuilding art, etc.)? It does not. Something can have more than one end, and the end that is the *ergon* is not the same as the end that is the human good. As we have seen, Aristotle's examples from *EE* 2. 1 indicate that the *ergon* of something is the end for the sake of which that *kind* of thing exists. Thus, in the case of the end that is the *ergon*, Aristotle circumscribes the 'for the sake of' relation to the thing in question—*qua* that kind of thing. For example, though the bridle-making art exists for the sake of a bridle, and a bridle exists for the sake of the activity of horse riding, it does not follow that the *ergon* of a bridle-maker is the activity of horse riding. (Horse riding would be the *ergon* of the horse rider, who uses the bridle.) Rather, the 'last [thing] for the sake of which' the bridle-maker does what he does, *qua* bridle-maker, is a bridle (cf. *EE* 2. 1, 1219ᵇ4). Even if the human good is the end of the various arts because it is the end of all achievable things, it is only the end of the various arts *qua* things achievable in action.[39]

Third, what reason does Aristotle have for identifying the end

[39] To see this more clearly, it may be helpful to ask and answer a few ques-

of the housebuilding art as a house and *not* housebuilding? In several places Aristotle draws an important distinction between complete activities (e.g. seeing and living) and incomplete activities (e.g. housebuilding and shoemaking), and he claims that while the former are ends, the latter are not ends but 'belong to the class of means to ends'.[40] There are a variety of ways to mark this distinction, but here is one that is derived from *Metaphysics* Θ 6. If one says 'I am building a house', that implies that one has *not yet* built that house. But if one says 'I am living', that does not imply that one has *not yet* done anything. Incompleteness is built into the activity housebuilding, while it is not built into the activity of living. Consequently, while there is no internal reason why an activity of living should stop, there is an internal reason why an activity of housebuilding should stop, and this is the *end* it is aimed at—a house.[41] The fact that Aristotle gives principled reasons for marking a distinction between these different kinds of proper activities shows that he also has principled reasons for thinking that housebuilding cannot be the end for the sake of which the housebuilding art, *qua* housebuilding art, exists. This in turn gives him a reason for identifying the *ergon* of the housebuilding art as a house and not housebuilding. For when X's proper activity is incomplete, X's *ergon* will be something further, typically a product, and

---

tions. What is the end for the sake of which the housebuilding art, *qua thing achievable in action*, exists? The human good. And what is the end for the sake of which the doctoring art, *qua thing achievable in action*, exists? Also, the human good. But what is the end for the sake of which the housebuilding art, *qua housebuilding art*, exists? The *ergon* of the housebuilding art: a house. And what is the end for the sake of which the doctoring art, *qua doctoring art*, exists? The *ergon* of the doctoring art: health. The addition of such '*qua*'-locutions is helpful because, though Aristotle clearly subscribes to these distinctions, he is often content just to speak of 'the end of an X' and let the context do the work of directing the reader's attention to one or other of these two ends.

[40] τῶν περὶ τὸ τέλος (*Metaph.* Θ 6, 1048^{b}19). For discussions of this distinction see M. F. Burnyeat, '*Kinēsis* vs. *Energeia*: A Much-Read Passage in (but not of) Aristotle's *Metaphysics*', *Oxford Studies in Ancient Philosophy*, 34 (2008), 219–92; S. Makin (trans. and comm.), *Aristotle:* Metaphysics Book Θ (Oxford, 2006), 141–54; and J. Beere, *Doing and Being: An Interpretation of Aristotle's* Metaphysics Theta (Oxford, 2009), 221–30.

[41] This explains why, even though it makes sense to say that someone *was building* a house but did not *build* a house, it does not make sense to say that someone *was living* but did not *live*. Likewise, while it does make sense to say that someone was learning French, but did not learn French, it does not make sense to say that someone was seeing but did not see. Cf. G. E. M. Anscombe, *Intention* (Cambridge, Mass., 2000), § 23.

when X's proper activity is complete, X's *ergon* will be its proper activity.

8. Aristotle's understanding of an *ergon* in the *Nicomachean Ethics*

We have so far seen that both Plato in the *Republic* and Aristotle in the *Protrepticus*, *Eudemian Ethics*, and *De caelo* appear to think that the *ergon* of an X is not always an activity, but instead an activity in some cases but a product in others, in accordance with the sort of thing the X is. Consequently, if in the *ergon* argument of the *Nicomachean Ethics* Aristotle were to assume that the *ergon* of an X is always a proper activity, he would be breaking with a precedent and this would call for explanation. However, as we will now see, there are good reasons for thinking that Aristotle in the *Nicomachean Ethics* still subscribes to his earlier understanding of an *ergon*.

Before we focus on the *ergon* argument itself, we should note a few considerations which suggest that the alterative concept of an *ergon* is in use in the *Nicomachean Ethics*. First, whenever Aristotle in the *Nicomachean Ethics* clearly identifies the *ergon* of a productive art (the shoemaking art, the housebuilding art, etc.), he identifies it not as the art's proper activity (shoemaking, housebuilding, etc.), but as its product (a shoe, a house, etc.).[42] Second, in the *De caelo* (2. 3, 286ᵃ8–9, and 3. 7, 306ᵃ14–16), the *Eudemian Ethics* (2. 1, 1219ᵃ8), and elsewhere Aristotle maintained that the *ergon* of X was 'the end of an X', or more specifically, the end for the sake of which an X, *qua* X, has being. If Aristotle in the *Nicomachean Ethics* still subscribes to this account of what an *ergon* is (and I see no reason to think he does not), then *NE* 1. 1 gives us good reason to think that Aristotle

---

[42] One example comes from Aristotle's discussion of benefactors and beneficiaries. Having just claimed that benefactors love their beneficiaries even if those beneficiaries are of no use to them, Aristotle says: 'The same is true of artisans because each is fond of his own proper *ergon* [τὸ οἰκεῖον ἔργον] more than it would be fond of him if it acquired a soul [ὑπὸ τοῦ ἔργου ἐμψύχου γενομένου]. This is most of all true in the case of poets, for they are extremely fond of their own poems, loving them as if they were their own children' (*NE* 9. 7, 1167ᵇ33–1168ᵃ2; cf. 6. 1, 1120ᵇ13–14). This text forms part of a rich chapter, but we need only notice two things. First, Aristotle implies that the proper *ergon* of certain artisans is a product beyond their activity: in the case of the poet, his *ergon* is his poem. Second, the phrase 'τὸ οἰκεῖον ἔργον' ('the proper *ergon*') used in the first sentence regularly signifies the *ergon* proper to something's nature. Cf. *NE* 6 (=*EE* 5). 1, 1139ᵃ16–17: 'the virtue [of something] is relative to its proper *ergon* [τὸ οἰκεῖον ἔργον]'.

The Concept of Ergon   249

is employing the alternative concept of an *ergon*. For one thing, he clearly identifies the ends of certain arts as products: 'Since there are many actions, arts, and sciences, there turns out to be many ends: health is the end of the doctoring art, a boat of the boat-building art, victory of generalship, and wealth of household management' (1094^{a}6–9).[43] But Aristotle also, just before these lines, explicitly states that the end of an X is an activity in some cases but a product in others, depending on what X is. The distinction is given pride of place, occurring at the very beginning of the *Nicomachean Ethics*:

Every craft and every enquiry, and likewise every action and decision, are thought to aim at some good. And so the good has been aptly dubbed: that for which all things aim. Yet there seems to be a difference among ends: some are activities [ἐνέργειαι], and others are certain *erga* beyond the activities [τὰ δὲ παρ' αὐτὰς ἔργα τινά]. Where there are certain ends beyond the actions [τέλη τινὰ παρὰ τὰς πράξεις], the *erga* in these cases are by nature better than the activities [ἐν τούτοις βελτίω πέφυκε τῶν ἐνεργειῶν τὰ ἔργα]. (1. 1, 1094^{a}1–6)

In the first two sentences of this passage Aristotle identifies the good of something with the end of that thing. He then draws a distinction among ends, noting that some are activities, while some are certain *erga* beyond the activities. With this distinction drawn, he notes that, in those cases where the *erga* are beyond the activities, the *erga* are better than the activities.

Although nearly every translation renders '*erga*' at 1094^{a}5–6 as 'products' (or some equivalent), it is not obvious that the word means this here. Instead, I think Aristotle uses the phrase 'certain *erga* beyond the activities' (1094^{a}4–5) to *refer* to products. He does so by the addition of 'beyond the activities', which would be somewhat redundant if '*ergon*' meant 'product' and which possibly signals that there are other *erga* which are not beyond the activities (i.e. because they are the activities). Aristotle's use of the indefi-

---

[43] Because he identifies the end of an X with the good of an X, Aristotle also identifies the good of the doctoring art to be health, of the housebuilding art a house, and of generalship victory (*NE* 1. 7, 1097^{a}15–22). Since Aristotle also writes, 'Every good is the *ergon* of an art' (*NE* 7 (=*EE* 6). 11, 1152^{b}19), it is reasonable to assume that the *ergon* of an X may be an activity in some cases, but a product in others. Although this quotation occurs in an objection that is not written in Aristotle's own voice, when he responds to the objection (*NE* 7 (=*EE* 6). 12, 1153^{a}24–7) he seems to assume that this particular claim is true. (Though I think that Aristotle employs the same concept and account of an *ergon* in both the *Eudemian Ethics* and the *Nicomachean Ethics*, I do not make any crucial use of passages from the common books in my arguments. However, I make some use of such passages, as I do in this footnote.)

nite article *tina* ('certain' or 'some') also suggests this, and I think we should be discomfited by the fact that the word is often downplayed and sometimes left untranslated. Irwin, for example, drops the *tina*, translating the line: 'others are products apart from the activities' (1094^{a}4–5). A reason for this is not hard to find. If one translates '*erga*' as 'products', and yet also translates the *tina*, the line seems off: 'Yet there seems to be a difference among ends: some are activities, and others are certain products beyond the activities' (1094^{a}3–5). One naturally wonders: why just *certain* products? Why not *all* products? When there is a product beyond the activity, is it not always the end?

Of course, one might think that Aristotle is trying to allow for the possibility of by-products (like the scraps a shoemaker makes while producing a shoe). But several factors make this unlikely.[44] One might also think that *tina* does not have much content, so that it does not even warrant being translated. But this seems unlikely if for no other reason than because Aristotle explains how he understands 'παρ' αὐτὰς ἔργα τινά' ('certain *erga* beyond the activities', 1094^{a}4–5) by immediately glossing it as 'τέλη τινὰ παρὰ τὰς πράξεις' ('certain ends beyond the actions', 1094^{a}5). Because the phrase *telē tina* clearly means 'certain ends', it makes sense to take *erga tina* as 'certain *erga*'

Now if we suppose Aristotle to be using the alternative concept of an *ergon*, the *tina* makes good sense: since *erga* can designate activities or products, Aristotle uses the word *tina* to indicate only those 'certain' *erga* that are beyond activities, namely products.[45]

---

[44] First, it is not at all obvious that Aristotle would use the word '*ergon*' to refer to a by-product, and I know of no occasion on which he does so. Second, if this were Aristotle's reasoning, we would expect him to add a similar qualification to ἐνέργειαι ('activities') at 1094^{a}4, but he does not. The reason we should expect this is because Aristotle would similarly think that even when the end of a thing is an activity, there may still be other activities (besides the end) that the thing does, *qua* that sort of thing (like the stretching of a dancer before dancing, or the playing of scales by a musician). Third, as I note in the main text, Aristotle seems to explain what he means by 'παρ' αὐτὰς ἔργα τινά' ('certain *erga* beyond the activities', 1094^{a}4–5) by immediately glossing it as 'τέλη τινὰ παρὰ τὰς πράξεις' ('certain ends beyond the actions', 1094^{a}5). The τινά in the latter phrase is clearly supposed to signal that there are other ends that are not beyond the actions, but rather are the actions (as Aristotle has just explained, 1094^{a}3–5). If the two phrases are expressing the same basic idea (as they seem to), then the τινά in the former phrase would naturally signal that there are other *erga* that are not beyond the activities, but rather are the activities.

[45] Even though I take the phrase ἔργα τινά at 1094^{a}5 to refer to products, that is not a good reason to translate the phrase as 'products'. This is because ἔργα τινά does

The Concept of Ergon   251

Note that if '*erga*' here really does mean 'products' the last sentence is surprisingly wordy. Surely Aristotle would have only needed to say: 'products are by nature better than the activities that produce them'. Instead, he seems to convey by means of the phrase 'in these cases' (ἐν τούτοις) that there are *other* cases in which the *erga* are not better than the activities; again, this is because the *erga*, in those cases, *are* the activities. This is the only use of the word '*ergon*' before the *ergon* argument, and by using it here, he directs his reader to think of *erga* as ends (just as he does in the *Eudemian Ethics*), and to think of certain (τινά) of these *erga* as products, namely those that are 'beyond activities'.

But even apart from the remarks on translation that I have just made, these first lines of the *Nicomachean Ethics* (as rendered in almost any contemporary translation) give us reason to think that Aristotle in the *ergon* argument is not speaking of a function by means of the word '*ergon*'.[46] Consider Section A once again. After reminding us that people agree in calling the best good achievable in action eudaimonia, Aristotle says we still need clarity on what this best good is. He suggests that we will attain this if we grasp the *ergon* of a human, and he offers an explanation for this suggestion:

This is because just as in the case of a flautist, a sculptor, and every artisan, and generally, in the case of whatever has an *ergon* and an action, the good, that is,[47] the well [τὸ εὖ], seems to be [found] in its *ergon*, the same would seem to be true for a human, if he has an *ergon*. (*NE* 1. 7, 1097^{b}25–8)

Scholars of course assume that Aristotle is here claiming that for anything with an *ergon* and an action, 'the good, that is, the well' is found in that thing's proper activity. But there is a serious problem with this assumption. As we just noted, Aristotle offers the *ergon*

not mean 'products', and we should be trying to translate what these words mean and not what they refer to.

[46] That is, even if one thought that '*erga*' in the first lines of *NE* 1. 1 meant 'products', the principle expressed in these first lines gives us good reason to think it is the alternative concept (as found in *Republic* 1, *EE* 2. 1, etc.) that must be present in *NE* 1. 7.

[47] I take the καί in 'τἀγαθὸν εἶναι καὶ τὸ εὖ' epexegetically, and recommend that we translate it either as 'that is' or 'in the sense of'. This interpretation is commonly assumed by translators and commentators alike. Note that at the beginning of *NE* 1. 2 Aristotle designates a sense of 'the good' by using καί in just this way. He writes: 'If there is an end of things achievable in action that we desire on account of itself, and other things on account of this, and we do not choose all things for the sake of something else . . . clearly this would be the good, that is, the best [good] [τἀγαθὸν καὶ τὸ ἄριστον]' (1094^{a}18–22).

argument as an attempt to determine the best good achievable in action (1097ᵇ22; cf. 1. 2, 1094ᵃ18–22, and 1. 4, 1095ᵃ16–17). And so when Aristotle says that for anything with an *ergon* and an action 'the good, that is, the well' is found in its *ergon* (1097ᵇ27), he must be assuming there is not another *sort* of thing that such an agent can achieve that is better than the *ergon*. However, the first lines of the *Nicomachean Ethics* plainly state that when the end is beyond the activity, the *ergon* is by nature better than the activity. That is, in the case of things that yield products, the products are better *sorts* of things than the activities that produce them. Thus, the best *sort* of thing that a sculptor can achieve is not sculpting, but a sculpture. And so if Aristotle is going to locate 'the good, that is, the well' anywhere it will need to be in the best *sort* of thing that an X, *qua* X, can achieve. The thought of Section A, then, will need to be something like this: just as the best achievement of a sculptor is found in his *ergon* (his sculpture), and that of a flute-player in his *ergon* (his performance), so the best achievement of a human will be found in his *ergon*, if he has one. Consequently, Aristotle is assuming that while the *ergon* of a flautist is an activity (his performance), the *ergon* of a sculptor is not an activity but a product (his sculpture).

In case anyone might consider this an outlandish suggestion, I now note that the alternative concept of an *ergon* seems to be presupposed in both of the two ancient commentaries on the *Nicomachean Ethics* that discuss the *ergon* argument. One of these is the earliest extant commentary on the *Nicomachean Ethics* (in fact, the earliest extant commentary on any of Aristotle's writings), dating from the second century AD. The commentator, very probably Aspasius, writes the following while commenting on Section A:

> If, then, the *ergon* of the shoemaking art is a shoe [ὑπόδημα], and we are searching for what the end of a human is, we will have to grasp the *ergon* of a human, *qua* human.[48]

Later he identifies the human *ergon* as an activity, and in particular a rational activity (18. 1–2). Thus, Aspasius seems to think that the *ergon* of an X may be a product in some cases (e.g. the shoe of a shoemaker) but an activity in others (e.g. the rational activity of a human) in accordance with the sort of thing the X is. The anonymous author of the ancient Greek paraphrase of the *Nicomachean Ethics* thinks the same. Here is how he rewords Section A:

[48] Aspas. *In EN* 17. 22–4 Heylbut.

The Concept of Ergon

For just as the good of every artisan is found in his *ergon* [ἐν τῷ ἔργῳ αὐτοῦ], the good of a flute-player in his performance [ἐν τῷ αὐλεῖν], and the good of a sculptor in the sculpture [ἐν τῷ ἀγάλματι] (and this generally holds for every *ergon* and action), so the human good is in the human *ergon*, if there is some *ergon* of a human, in so far as he is a human.[49]

The idea seems to be that while the *ergon* of the flute-player is an activity (his performance, τὸ αὐλεῖν), the *ergon* of a sculptor is not an activity but a product (the sculpture, τὸ ἄγαλμα). And so both Aspasius and the paraphraser—the only extant ancient commentators on the *ergon* argument of the *Nicomachean Ethics*—assume that Aristotle there employs the alternative concept of an *ergon*.

My arguments have so far primarily focused on the concept of an *ergon* used in Section A, but I now note that whatever concept of an *ergon* is used in Section A must be used throughout the *ergon* argument. Section A makes a claim about *whatever* has an *ergon* and an action; and the whole point is that, while this claim clearly holds for every artisan (1097ᵇ26), it will also hold true for a human, if he has an *ergon*. When Aristotle goes on to identify the human *ergon* as 'activity on the basis of reason or not without reason' (1098ᵃ7–8), the concept must stay the same. If this is so, and if I am right about what an *ergon* is, then it is an error to suppose that '*ergon*' in *NE* 1. 7 means 'function' or 'proper activity'. The *ergon* argument is not a 'function' argument.[50]

9. The translation of '*ergon*'

How, then, should we translate '*ergon*'? Any translation must at least be capable of applying either to an activity or to a product that is-

---

[49] Heliod. *In EN* 13. 22–6 Heylbut.

[50] One might consider it a mark against my interpretation that Aristotle just seems to assume that the *ergon* of a human is an activity. For if Aristotle is employing the standard concept of an *ergon*, on which every *ergon* is an activity, such an assumption would of course make sense. But if Aristotle is employing the alternative concept of an *ergon*, should he not seriously entertain the possibility that the *ergon* of a human is a product? I do not think so. Aristotle is employing a concept that he shares with Plato, who also assumes that while the *ergon* of the housebuilder is a product (*Rep.* 1, 346 D 3–4), the *ergon* of a human is an activity (353 D 3–8), and so we need not think that Aristotle would always need to determine afresh whether the *ergon* of an X is an activity or a product. Also, as we will discuss, the key reason why Aristotle needs to be employing the alternative concept is because this is the only way that Section A can be relevant to determining the best achievement of a human, and such a reason does not require that Aristotle seriously entertain the possibility that the human *ergon* is a product.

sues from an activity. 'Proper activity' or 'characteristic activity' obviously cannot cover the latter case. If 'function' is capable of doing so, I believe that is only due to an etymological branch of the word that is in important respects unrelated to the branch according to which it means 'proper activity'. With regard to the latter ('proper activity') branch, Barney correctly employs the word when she writes: 'shoemaking is a function'.[51] One translation that has the right semantic range is 'work' or perhaps 'proper work'. The *Oxford English Dictionary* divides the meanings of 'work' into two: as a kind of doing (s.v. I. 1–8) or as something made (II. 9–21). We can speak of a 'work of art' (say, a statue) but also the 'proper work' of a dancer (dancing).[52] Consequently, if we wish to articulate the pre-theoretical concept of an '*ergon* of an X' that Plato and Aristotle seem to share, it may help to think of it as the 'work of an X'.[53]

10. Two difficulties for the assumption that NE 1. 7 employs the alternative concept of an *ergon*

I will now address two reasons why someone might doubt the interpretation of the *ergon* argument in the *Nicomachean Ethics* that I have been sketching.

First, if Aristotle is using the alternative concept of an *ergon*, then when he identifies the *ergon* of the kitharist as the performance on the kithara (1. 7, 1098^{a}8–12), he is doing so precisely because this is the end of the kitharist, *qua* kitharist. Aristotle must, then, think that the proper activity of the kitharist is a complete activity, issuing in no distinct product. Difficulty arises, though, when we observe certain passages in which Aristotle appears to assume that the proper activity of every art (*technē*) is an incomplete activity, is-

[51] Barney, 'Human Function', 303.
[52] This is no accident since English 'work' and Greek '*ergon*' are cognate. See e.g. *OED*, s.v. *work*, n.
[53] '*Ergon*' is rendered as 'work' in both *NE* 1. 1 and *NE* 1. 7 in two recent translations: R. C. Bartlett and S. D. Collins (trans.), *Aristotle: Nicomachean Ethics, Translated, with an Interpretive Essay, Notes, and Glossary* (Chicago, 2011), and J. Sachs (trans.), *Aristotle: Nicomachean Ethics, Translated with Glossary and Introductory Essay* (Newburyport, 2002). However, both translations render 'τὸ εὖ' at *NE* 1. 7, 1097^{b}27, in a way that implies that the *ergon* in question is a proper activity. As for translations in French, *ouvrage* and *œuvre* are perhaps the best options, while in German probably *Werk* and *Leistung*, and in Italian *opera* and *operazione* (and to a lesser extent *lavoro*).

The Concept of Ergon

suing in a distinct product. Notably, in *NE* 6 (=*EE* 5). 4 (cf. *NE* 2. 4) he says that producing (*poiēsis*) and action (*praxis*) are different (1140ª2), and he seems to be assuming that action (*praxis*) is a kind of complete activity and producing (*poiēsis*) a kind of incomplete activity.[54] Art (*technē*), he further asserts, is a state of true reason concerned with producing (1140ª20–1), not action. Thus, he appears to assume that the proper activity of every art is an incomplete activity.[55] Given that the skill of the kitharist seems to be a relatively straightforward counter-example to this claim, there seem to be three interpretative options. First, it did not occur to Aristotle that someone might consider the skill of the kitharist (or the flute-player, etc.) to be a counter-example. Second, Aristotle thinks that the activity of the kitharist is an incomplete activity, issuing in a distinct product. Or third, Aristotle in *NE* 6. 4 is employing the term 'art' ('*technē*') in a restricted sense such that the skill of the kitharist is not an art but an expertise concerned with action.

I will argue in favour of the third option. Against the first we should note that Plato in *Republic* 10 distinguishes between a 'using [χρησομένην] art' (601 D 1) such as the art of flute-playing, and a 'producing [ποιήσουσαν] art' (601 D 2) such as the art of flute-making. Thus, there is reason to think that Aristotle is aware that someone might think that the activity of a kitharist is not an instance of production and so not an incomplete activity. Against the second option, consider this passage from *Magna Moralia* 1. 34:

When it comes to things produced and things acted, the power of producing and the power of acting are not the same. On the one hand, the expertises of producing have some other end beyond the producing [τῶν μὲν γὰρ ποιητικῶν ἐστί τι παρὰ τὴν ποίησιν ἄλλο τέλος]; for instance, beyond housebuilding, since that is the expertise of producing a house, there is a house as its end beyond the producing, and the same goes for carpentry and the other expertises of producing; but in the expertises of acting there is no other end beyond the acting [ἐπὶ δὲ τῶν πρακτικῶν οὐκ ἔστιν ἄλλο οὐθὲν τέλος παρ' αὐτὴν τὴν πρᾶξιν]; for instance, beyond the performance of the kitharist [κιθαρίζειν] there is no other end, but this is the end, the activity and the action. Practical wisdom, then, concerns action and things acted,

---

[54] Aristotle here relies on his lost 'popular discussions' (1140ª3), and so we cannot be sure of his reasoning.
[55] Because I have made use of the *Eudemian Ethics* and the *Nicomachean Ethics* in my overall argument, *NE* 6 (=*EE* 5). 4 is relevant to the discussion no matter which work I maintain is its proper home.

but art [τέχνη] concerns production and things produced . . . (1197ª5–10; cf. 2. 12, 1211ᵇ25–32)

Here Aristotle (or some Aristotelian)[56] clearly asserts that while there is an end beyond housebuilding, there is not an end beyond the performance of the kitharist.[57] And so there is reason to think that, according to Aristotle, the performance of the kitharist is not an incomplete activity and so not an instance of production. (Moreover, if the author of the *Magna Moralia* thinks that the *ergon* of an X is the end of an X, *qua* X, then he would naturally employ the alterative concept of an *ergon*.) In support of the third option, we should note that the author of the *Magna Moralia* passage uses the word 'art' in a restricted sense such that the skill of the kitharist is not an art but an expertise concerned with action. This is clear because the author states both that the activity of the kitharist is not an instance of production but an instance of action, and that 'art' is concerned with production and not action. Thus, it seems not unlikely that Aristotle is using the word 'art' in a similarly restricted sense in *NE* 6. 4.[58]

Second, Aristotle makes the claim of Section A about anything with 'ἔργον τι καὶ πρᾶξις' (1097ᵇ26), which one could understand either as 'an *ergon* and an action' or 'an *ergon*, that is, an action'. Several scholars assume the latter reading, which implies that Aris-

---

[56] For a defence of the Aristotelian provenance of the *Magna Moralia* see J. M. Cooper, 'The *Magna Moralia* and Aristotle's Moral Philosophy', in J. M. Cooper, *Reason and Emotion* (Princeton, 1999), 195–211.

[57] The Stoics also acknowledged that there are some arts (e.g. the arts of dancing and acting) for which the proper activity is the end (cf. Cic. *Fin.* 3. 24). See G. Striker, 'Antipater, or the Art of Living', in M. Schofield and G. Striker (eds.), *The Norms of Nature: Studies in Hellenistic Ethics* (Cambridge, 2007), 185–204.

[58] I believe what I have said above is enough to give us reason to think that in *NE* 1. 7 Aristotle supposes the kitharist, *qua* kitharist, to have no further end beyond his proper activity. Nevertheless, in *NE* 1. 7 Aristotle appears to consider the skill of the flute-player to be an art (τέχνη, 1097ᵇ25–7). How do we reconcile this with *NE* 6. 4? I think we must suppose that, while in *NE* 6. 4 Aristotle uses the word 'art' in the restricted sense whereby only productive expertises count as arts, in *NE* 1. 7 he uses 'art' in a broader sense whereby non-productive practical expertises can count as arts. Independent confirmation that in *NE* 1. 7 Aristotle uses the word in this broader way comes from combining two observations. First, the restricted sense of 'art' corresponds to a restricted sense of 'action' (πρᾶξις) on which an incomplete activity such as housebuilding is not an action but a producing (ποίησις). Second, *NE* 1. 7 implies that a sculptor, and indeed every artisan, has an action (1097ᵇ25–7). Consequently, since Aristotle uses 'action' in *NE* 1. 7 not in the restricted but in the broad sense, he would naturally use 'art' in the broad sense as well.

The Concept of Ergon 257

totle assumes that the *ergon* of something is always an activity.[59] Both readings of the phrase are grammatically possible. However, there are reasons to question the latter reading,[60] and if one accepts my arguments about what an *ergon* is, one should go for the former reading instead. If after adopting the former reading one should then wonder why Aristotle speaks here (and at 1097^{b}29) of 'action', I suggest the following explanation.[61] Aristotle makes it very clear that he is looking for the best thing *achievable by humans in action* (πρακτὸν ἀνθρώπῳ), where 'action' seems to be an activity that partakes of reason to some extent. And so it is likely that Aristotle makes the claim of Section A only about those things that can achieve things in action—that is, only about those things that have both an *ergon* and an action (1097^{b}26), where 'action' is not just a thing's proper activity but the sort of proper activity that partakes of reason. The principle of Section A, then, is probably not here applied to just anything with an *ergon*, including artefacts.[62]

---

[59] For example, M. Nussbaum, 'Aristotle on Human Nature and the Foundations of Ethics', in J. E. J. Altham and R. Harrison (eds.), *World, Mind and Ethics: Essays on the Ethical Philosophy of Bernard Williams* (Cambridge, 1995), 86–131 at 112, translates ἔργον τι καὶ πρᾶξις (1097^{b}26) as 'function or activity', and writes: 'What would naturally be meant by the 'function or activity' of a certain sort of craftsman would be that craftsman's characteristic activity *qua* that sort of craftsman—the activity or activities in virtue of which he is, and is counted as, a craftsman of that sort.'

[60] For example, if we take καί epexegetically at *NE* 1. 7, 1097^{b}26 and 1097^{b}29, it looks as if the phrases should be understood as 'including extensions for an *ergon*. The first (ἔργον τι καὶ πρᾶξις rendered as 'an *ergon*', i.e. an action') will have it that every *ergon* is an action, while the second (ἔργα τινὰ καὶ πράξεις rendered as 'certain *erga*, i.e. actions') will have it that only certain *erga* are actions (the implication being that some *erga* are not actions). Moreover, neither Aspasius nor the ancient paraphraser takes καί at 1097^{b}26 this way.

[61] Besides the explanation that I offer in the main text, note that καί may be quasi-epexegetic, such that the phrase should be understood as 'including action'. (The same explanation could hold for 'καὶ πράξεις' at 1097^{b}29.) The rationale for this would be that Aristotle wants to make it clear that an *ergon* can be an action, and he might think such clarification helpful because he earlier (at *NE* 1. 1, 1094^{a}5) used the word '*erga*' to refer to products.

[62] *Pace* e.g. Lawrence, 'Fallacious?', 206: 'the principle [in Section A] is being generalized over all functional items, including artifacts'. I do not mean to deny that Aristotle sometimes uses the word 'πρᾶξις' to mean something like 'proper activity', but I do not think he does so in *NE* 1. 7. Instead, I think that the use in *NE* 1. 7 is more like the one we find at *NE* 6 (=*EE* 5). 2, 1139^{a}19–20: 'it is clear that wild animals [θηρία] have perception but no share in action [πράξεως]'.

11. Towards an 'achievement' interpretation of the *ergon* argument at *NE* 1. 7

Any interpretation of the *ergon* argument largely turns on how one interprets its first section—what I have been calling 'Section A':

SECTION A

This is because just as for a flautist, a sculptor, and every artisan, and generally, for whatever has an *ergon* and an action, the good, that is, the well [τὸ εὖ], seems to be [found] in its *ergon*, the same would seem to be so for a human, if he has an *ergon*. (*NE* 1. 7, 1097ᵇ25–8)

Though I cannot here fully justify my doing so, I take the claim of Section A to be this:

CLAIM OF SECTION A

For anything with an *ergon* and an action, the good in the sense of the excellent achievement (τἀγαθὸν καὶ τὸ εὖ) is found in its *ergon*.

Like many others, I take *to eu* of an X to be the *ergon* of an X achieved well (cf. *NE* 1. 7, 1098ᵃ12; 2. 6, 1106ᵇ12). But, of course, unlike many others, I do not think an *ergon* is always an activity. Consequently, I think that the alternative concept of an *ergon* should lead us to understand *to eu* as meaning something like 'the excellent accomplishment' or 'the excellent achievement', where this can be either an excellent activity or an excellent product.[63] I also think that the excellent achievement is found *in* the *ergon* in the way that a species is found *in* a genus (cf. *Phys.* 6. 3, 210ᵃ18).[64] And so one could also understand the claim of Section A to be:

---

[63] I am here offering an alternative to the common way of interpreting 'τὸ εὖ' as 'the doing well'. My interpretation lines up nicely with the way Aristotle uses 'τὸ εὖ' and 'τὸ εὖ ἔχον ἔργον' in *NE* 2. 6, 1106ᵇ8–14, a passage that recalls the *ergon* argument of *NE* 1. 7 by developing the connection between virtue and 'the excellent *ergon*' that was first introduced there.

[64] This interpretation of 'is in' falls between the two interpretations currently available in the secondary literature. Some scholars think that when Aristotle says the well 'is in' the *ergon*, he means that the well 'consists in' or 'is' the *ergon* (cf. R. Kraut, *Aristotle on the Human Good* (Princeton, 1989), 312). Others think that he means that the well 'depends on' the human *ergon* (cf. Irwin, *Ethics*, 183). Though I cannot argue for this here, I take the latter claim to be too weak to allow Aristotle to arrive at his definition, and I take the former claim to be one that Aristotle considers false.

The Concept of Ergon 259

for anything that has an *ergon* and an action, the good in the sense of the excellent achievement is its *ergon* achieved well. Section A, then, locates the right class or genus within which to find the human good, that is, the best thing achievable by a human. Aristotle reasons that just as a sculptor's excellent achievement will be in his *ergon* (which is a sculpture, *not* sculpting), so will his best achievement. And just as a human's excellent achievement will be in his *ergon* (which is activity of the part of the soul having reason), so will his best achievement—that is, the human good.

This puts us in a position to reconstruct the *ergon* argument in such a way that it is both valid and plausible. Below I list the premisses and conclusions of the *ergon* argument roughly in the order in which they are found or implicitly found in the text, omitting some subarguments (the arguments that a human has an *ergon*, and the argument that the human *ergon* is an activity of the rational part of the soul) as well as some clarifications (e.g. Aristotle's explication of 'rational part of the soul'). After each premiss I indicate in parentheses the sections of the text to which the premiss corresponds.[65]

(P1) The human good is the best achievement of a human (1097^b22–3; cf. *NE* I. 1–2).

(P2) The best achievement of a human is the excellent achievement of a human with any better-making features that there may be. [assumption]

(C1) The human good is the excellent achievement of a human with any better-making features that there may be. [from (P1) and (P2)]

(P3) For anything that has an *ergon* and an action, the excellent achievement of that thing is its *ergon* excellently achieved (1097^b25–8 [=CLAIM OF SECTION A]).

(P4) A human being has an *ergon* and an action. [From subargument in 1097^b28–33]

(C2) Therefore, the excellent achievement of a human being is the human *ergon* excellently achieved. [from (P3) and (P4)]

(P5) The *ergon* of a human being is activity of the part of the hu-

---

[65] As I understand it, Aristotle does not explicitly state (P2) because he takes it (and thus the conclusion (C 1)) to be obvious. He does not state (P7) because he has articulated his understanding of what it is to be 'end-like' (τέλειον) earlier in *NE* I. 7, at 1097^a15–$^b6$. He does not state (P8) for similar reasons, though he does partially articulate the premiss just after the conclusion of the argument at 1098^a18–20.

man soul having reason (1098ᵃ7–8). [From subargument in 1097ᵇ33–1098ᵃ4]

(C3) Therefore, the excellent achievement of a human being is activity of the part of the soul having reason, achieved excellently. [from (C2) and (P5)]

(P6) For an *ergon* to be achieved excellently is for it to be achieved on the basis of virtue/excellence (1098ᵃ15; cf. 1098ᵃ8–11).

(C4) Therefore, the excellent achievement of a human being is activity on the basis of the virtue of the part of the human soul having reason (1098ᵃ16–17). [from (C3) and (P6)]

(P7) Activity on the basis of the virtue of the part of the human soul having reason is better if it is achieved on the basis of the best and most end-like virtue, if there are more virtues than one (cf. 1097ᵃ28–30).

(P8) Activity on the basis of virtue of the part of the human soul having reason is better if it occurs in an end-like [i.e. complete] life (1098ᵃ18–20; cf. 1097ᵃ28–30).

(C5) Therefore, 'the human good turns out to be activity of the [rational part of the human] soul on the basis of virtue, and if there are more virtues than one, on the basis of the best and most end-like virtue, and moreover in an end-like [i.e. complete] life' (1098ᵃ16–18). [from (C1), (C4), (P7), (P8)]

Several features of my reconstruction distinguish it from all others currently on offer.[66] I take two of these features to be of central importance, but here I will discuss just one of them:[67] on my recon-

---

[66] Perhaps surprisingly, there are relatively few explicit reconstructions of the *ergon* argument: P. Glassen, 'A Fallacy in Aristotle's Argument about the Good' ['Fallacy'], *Philosophical Quarterly*, 7 (1957), 319–22 at 320; D. S. Hutchinson, *The Virtues of Aristotle* (London and New York, 1986), 55; A. Gomez-Lobo, 'The Ergon Inference', *Phronesis*, 34 (1989), 170–84 at 182; D. Achtenberg, 'The Role of the *Ergon* Argument in Aristotle's *Nicomachean Ethics*', in J. P. Anton and A. Preus (eds.), *Essays in Ancient Greek Philosophy IV* (Albany, NY, 1991), 59–72 at 62–3; M. Pakaluk, *Aristotle's* Nicomachean Ethics*: An Introduction* (Cambridge, 2005), 80; C. Natali, '*Posterior Analytics* and the Definition of Happiness in *NE* I', *Phronesis*, 55 (2010), 304–24 at 317; and P. Gottlieb, *The Virtue of Aristotle's Ethics* (Cambridge, 2009), 66–7.

[67] The other feature of central importance is that on my reconstruction Aristotle distinguishes the excellent achievement of a human from the best achievement. The excellent achievement of a human is 'activity of the soul on the basis of virtue', and when Aristotle adds the two criteria 'if there are more virtues than one, on the basis of the best and most end-like virtue' and 'in an end-like [i.e. complete] life' he is listing further requirements that something must meet if it is to be the best achievement

The Concept of Ergon   261

struction, the key explanatory middle term of the argument is 'the best achievement of a human'.[68]

Recall that before the *ergon* argument Aristotle makes it abundantly clear that for something to be the human good is for it to be the best thing *achievable* by humans in action (cf. 1. 2, 1094ª18–22; 1. 4, 1095ª16–17). Aristotle characterizes the nature of the human good in no other way than this.[69] Consequently, because the conclusion of the *ergon* argument is a definition of the human good, the key explanatory middle term of the argument ought to be 'the best achievement of a human'. However, no current interpretation supposes this to be the middle term. The reason, I believe, is as follows. Since scholars have assumed that Aristotle's concept of an *ergon* is the concept of a proper activity, they have been unable to interpret Section A in such a way that it is relevant to determining the best achievement of a human. They have heard Aristotle as saying that for a sculptor, flautist, and every artisan, 'the good, that is, the well' is found in their respective *proper activities*. Because the best achievement of a sculptor is clearly not found in his activity of

---

of a human, which is the human good (and not merely the excellent achievement). Current reconstructions suppose that the proper conclusion of the argument is 'activity of the soul on the basis of virtue' (what I take to be the excellent achievement of a human) and that the two criteria are merely optional elucidations of that conclusion. See the reconstructions listed in the previous footnote as well as the influential (though brief) statement of this 'implicit criteria view' by J. Ackrill, 'Aristotle on Eudaimonia', in A. Rorty (ed.), *Essays on Aristotle's Ethics* (Berkeley, 1980), 15–34 at 27. Although I do not agree with the implicit criteria view, my interpretation of Section A can be made compatible with it so long as one identifies the best accomplishment of a human with the excellent accomplishment of a human.

[68] What is an 'explanatory middle term'? In an Aristotelian syllogism there are three terms, and the middle term is the one that drops out in the conclusion. Consider: 'Shelters for belongings are roofed. Barns are shelters for belongings. Therefore, barns are roofed' (see J. Barnes (trans. and comm.), *Aristotle: Posterior Analytics* (Oxford, 1993), 231). The middle term is 'shelters for belongings'. Here the middle term is also explanatory because it is in virtue of being a 'shelter for belongings' that a barn is roofed. Above I speak of the *key* explanatory middle term, and that is because, even though there are several middle terms in the argument, 'the best achievement of a human' (as used in the argument from (P1) and (P2) to (C 1)) is the one that provides the direct link to 'the human good'.

[69] Indeed, even though Aristotle says 'eudaimonia most of all seems to be this sort of thing [i.e. the best and most end-like good]' (*NE* 1. 7, 1097ª34), he never says that for something to be the human good is for it to be eudaimonia. Though I cannot argue for this here, I think there is good reason to believe that the human good and eudaimonia are not coextensive. For example, God is the primary instance of eudaimonia but does not possess the human good since this is the best thing achievable *by humans* in action.

sculpting but in his sculpture (or sculptures), scholars have had to come up with a different key middle term for the *ergon* argument. They have proposed 'the virtue of a human',[70] 'the flourishing of a human',[71] 'the successful functioning of a human',[72] etc. Barney, for example, supposes both that the human good is the flourishing of a human, and that the claim of Section A is: for anything with an *ergon* and an action, the flourishing of that thing is its *ergon* accomplished well.[73] Barney's interpretation might initially seem attractive. However, when we bear in mind that, according to Aristotle, for something to be the human good is for it to be the best good *achievable* by humans in action, we see that Barney's proposal (as well as any other that does not employ the alternative concept of an *ergon*) is unacceptable. When Aristotle arrives at his definition of the human good, he must do so not because this is the flourishing of a human or because this is the successful functioning of a human, but rather because this is the best achievement of a human.

To appreciate this point, consider the following requirement for any (charitable) interpretation of the *ergon* argument: it must ensure that if the human good is an activity, it is a complete activity. This is because an incomplete activity is essentially for the sake of something else, and the human good, in virtue of being the human good, is an end that is not such as to be chosen for the sake of something else. Thus, because the *ergon* argument is offered as the explanation for why the human good is defined as it is, the argument should ensure that if the human good is an activity, it is a complete activity. However, only my interpretation of the argument does this. I think that Aristotle employs the alternative concept of an *ergon* (on which, if the *ergon* is an activity, it must be a complete activity), and that he supposes that for any X with an *ergon* and an action, the best achievement of an X is a certain excellent version of its *ergon*. Contrast this with, for example, Barney's interpretation. She thinks that Aristotle employs the standard concept of an *ergon* and

---

[70] Cf. Glassen, 'Fallacy'. Glassen has in mind human virtue when he speaks of the 'goodness of a human'.   [71] Cf. Barney, 'Human Function'.

[72] Cf. Lawrence, 'Fallacious?'. Lawrence also sometimes speaks of 'the success of a human' but assumes that this is equivalent to the 'functioning successfully of a human'.

[73] Barney, 'Human Function', 311, gives this interpretation of Section A: 'If an *x qua x* has as its function to ϕ, then the good *of* an *x qua x*—its flourishing as an *x*—consists in ϕ-ing well.' She assumes that the good of a human, *qua* human, is 'the human good'.

that he supposes that for any X with an *ergon* and an action, the flourishing of an X is its functioning well. Thus it could turn out that the flourishing of an X is an incomplete activity: for example, the flourishing of a sculptor is sculpting well. Though the 'flourishing of a human' turns out to be a complete activity, that is just a coincidence. On Barney's interpretation, nothing about Aristotle's reasoning requires it to be a complete activity. Consequently, I contend that we need to assume that Aristotle is employing the alternative concept of an *ergon* if he is to be plausibly interpreted as giving the right *sort* of explanation for defining the human good as he does.

Why is grasping the correct explanation so important? Aristotle quite generally maintains that one understands (*epistasthai*) *that* something is the case only when one grasps the explanation for *why* it is the case.[74] He would, then, appear to maintain that one understands his definition of the human good (*NE* 1. 7, 1098^{a}16–18) only when one grasps the explanation for why the human good is defined as it is. I have argued that we can grasp this explanation—that is, the *ergon* argument—only if we suppose Aristotle to be employing the alternative concept of an *ergon*.

12. Conclusion

In this paper I have attempted to clear the way for a new interpretation of Aristotle's famous *ergon* argument in *NE* 1. 7. In doing so I have argued for several theses: (1) the *ergon* of an X is an activity in some cases but a product in others, in accordance with the sort of thing the X is; (2) Plato and Aristotle share this basic concept of an *ergon*, but differ in their accounts of what an *ergon* is; (3) Aristotle's account of an *ergon* is 'the end for the sake of which an X, qua X, exists'; and (4) the alternative concept of an *ergon* allows the

---

[74] See *Post. An.* 1. 2, 71^{b}30–1 (cf. *Metaph. A* 1, 981^{a}30–^{b}10, and *Phys.* 1. 1, 184^{a}10–16). In *NE* 6. 3 Aristotle says that one can have ἐπιστήμη ('expert knowledge' or 'understanding'), strictly speaking, only about things that do not admit of change—that is, only in theoretical matters. However, in the same passage he implicitly acknowledges that there are states that resemble knowledge in the strict sense (*NE* 6. 3, 1139^{b}18–19), and he applies the word ἐπιστήμη both to practical and to productive expertises at various places in the *Nicomachean Ethics* (e.g. 1. 2, 1094^{b}2–7; 7. 3, 1147^{b}13–17) and in the *Metaphysics* (e.g. *A* 1, 981^{b}8–9; *E* 2, 1026^{b}4–5). Thus, it is defensible to suppose that, according to Aristotle, one can have understanding (or something like understanding) of ethical truths and that such understanding would require grasping the explanation for why that truth held.

key explanatory middle term of the argument to be what it in fact ought to be, 'the best achievement of a human'. A full explication and evaluation of this 'achievement' reading still await us, but I believe I have here given reasons to take the reading seriously.

Centre Léon Robin

BIBLIOGRAPHY

Achtenberg, D., 'The Role of the *Ergon* Argument in Aristotle's *Nicomachean Ethics*', in J. P. Anton and A. Preus (eds.), *Essays in Ancient Greek Philosophy IV* (Albany, NY, 1991), 59–72.

Ackrill, J., 'Aristotle on Eudaimonia', in A. Rorty (ed.), *Essays on Aristotle's Ethics* (Berkeley, 1980), 15–34.

Allen, R. E. (trans.), *Plato:* The Republic (New Haven and London, 2008).

Annas, J., *An Introduction to Plato's* Republic (Oxford, 1981).

Anscombe, G. E. M., *Intention* (Cambridge, Mass., 2000).

Barnes, J. (trans. and comm.), *Aristotle:* Posterior Analytics (Oxford, 1993).

Barnes, J. (ed.), *The Complete Works of Aristotle* (Princeton, 1995).

Barney, R., 'Aristotle's Argument for a Human Function' ['Human Function'], *Oxford Studies in Ancient Philosophy*, 34 (2008), 293–322.

Barney, R., 'Socrates' Refutation of Thrasymachus', in G. Santas (ed.), *The Blackwell Guide to Plato's* Republic (Oxford, 2006), 44–62.

Bartlett, R. C., and Collins, S. D. (trans.), *Aristotle:* Nicomachean Ethics, *Translated, with an Interpretive Essay, Notes, and Glossary* (Chicago, 2011).

Beere, J., *Doing and Being: An Interpretation of Aristotle's* Metaphysics Theta (Oxford, 2009).

Bloom, A. (trans.), *The* Republic *of Plato*, 2nd edn. (New York, 1991).

Bodéüs, R. (trans.), *Aristote: l'Éthique à Nicomaque* (Paris, 2004).

Broadie, S. (comm.), and Rowe, C. (trans.), *Aristotle:* Nicomachean Ethics [*Ethics*] (Oxford, 2002).

Burnyeat, M. F., '*Kinēsis* vs. *Energeia*: A Much-Read Passage in (but not of) Aristotle's *Metaphysics*', *Oxford Studies in Ancient Philosophy*, 34 (2008), 219–92.

Coope, U., review of Crivelli, *Aristotle on Truth*, in *Notre Dame Philosophical Reviews* (2005) ⟨http://ndpr.nd.edu/news/24902-aristotle-on-truth/⟩.

Cooper, J. M., *Reason and Human Good in Aristotle* [*Human Good*] (Indianapolis and Cambridge, 1986).

Cooper, J. M., 'The *Magna Moralia* and Aristotle's Moral Philosophy', in J. M. Cooper, *Reason and Emotion* (Princeton, 1999), 195–211.
Cooper, J. M., with Hutchinson, D. H. (ed.), *Plato: Complete Works* (Indianapolis and Cambridge, 1997).
Crisp, R. (ed. and trans.), *Aristotle:* Nicomachean Ethics (Cambridge, 2000).
Crivelli, P., *Aristotle on Truth* (Cambridge, 2004).
Destrée, P., 'Comment démontrer le propre de l'homme? Pour une lecture "dialectique" de *EN* I, 6', in G. R. Dherbey and G. Aubry (eds.), *L'Excellence de la vie* (Paris, 2002), 39–61.
Düring, I. (ed. and trans.), *Aristotle's* Protrepticus*: An Attempt at Reconstruction* (Göteborg, 1961).
Gigon, O. (trans.), *Aristoteles: Die Nikomachische Ethik* (Düsseldorf and Zurich, 2001).
Glassen, P., 'A Fallacy in Aristotle's Argument about the Good' ['Fallacy'], *Philosophical Quarterly*, 7 (1957), 319–22.
Gomez-Lobo, A., 'The Ergon Inference', *Phronesis*, 34 (1989), 170–84.
Gottlieb, P., *The Virtue of Aristotle's Ethics* (Cambridge, 2009).
Grube, G. M. A. (trans.), *Republic*, rev. C. D. C. Reeve, in *Plato: Complete Works*, ed. Cooper, 971–1223.
Hutchinson, D. S., *The Virtues of Aristotle* (London and New York, 1986).
Hutchinson, D. S., and Johnson, M. R., 'Authenticating Aristotle's Protrepticus', *Oxford Studies in Ancient Philosophy*, 29 (2005), 193–294.
Inwood, B., and Woolf, R. (trans.), *Aristotle*: Eudemian Ethics (Cambridge, 2013).
Irwin, T. H. (trans.), *Aristotle:* Nicomachean Ethics*, Translated with Introduction, Notes and Glossary* [*Ethics*], 2nd edn. (Indianapolis and Cambridge, 1999).
Irwin, T. H., *Plato's Ethics* (Oxford, 1995).
Joachim, H. H., *Aristotle: The* Nicomachean Ethics. *A Commentary*, ed. D. A. Reese (Oxford, 1951).
Johnson, M. R., *Aristotle on Teleology* (Oxford, 2005).
Kenny, A. (ed. and trans.), *Aristotle:* The Eudemian Ethics (Oxford, 2012).
Korsgaard, C., 'Aristotle on Function and Virtue' ['Function and Virtue'], *History of Philosophy Quarterly*, 3 (1986), 259–79.
Kraut, R., *Aristotle on the Human Good* (Princeton, 1989).
Lawrence, G., 'Is Aristotle's Function Argument Fallacious?' ['Fallacious?'], *Philosophical Inquiry*, 31 (2009), 191–224.
Lee, H. D. P. (trans.), *Plato:* Republic (New York, 2007).
Lindsay, A. D. (trans.), *Plato:* The Republic (New York, 1976).
Makin, S. (trans. and comm.), *Aristotle:* Metaphysics Book Θ (Oxford, 2006).

Natali, C., '*Posterior Analytics* and the Definition of Happiness in *NE* I', *Phronesis*, 55 (2010), 304–24.
Nussbaum, M., 'Aristotle on Human Nature and the Foundations of Ethics', in J. E. J. Altham and R. Harrison (eds.), *World, Mind and Ethics: Essays on the Ethical Philosophy of Bernard Williams* (Cambridge, 1995), 86–131.
Pakaluk, M., *Aristotle's* Nicomachean Ethics*: An Introduction* (Cambridge, 2005).
Rackham, H. (trans.), *Aristotle:* Nicomachean Ethics (Cambridge, Mass., 1934).
Rackham, H. (trans.), *Aristotle:* The Athenian Constitution, The Eudemian Ethics, On Virtues and Vices [*Eudemian Ethics*] (Cambridge, Mass., 1996).
Reeve, C. D. C., *Action, Contemplation, and Happiness: An Essay on Aristotle* (Cambridge, Mass., 2012).
Reeve, C. D. C. (trans.), *Plato:* Republic [*Republic*] (Indianapolis and Cambridge, 2004).
Reeve, C. D. C., *Practices of Reason: Aristotle's* Nicomachean Ethics (Oxford, 1992).
Ross, W. D. (trans.), *Nicomachean Ethics*, rev. J. O. Urmson, in *The Complete Works of Aristotle*, ed. Barnes, ii. 1729–1867.
Sachs, J. (trans.), *Aristotle:* Nicomachean Ethics*, Translated with Glossary and Introductory Essay* (Newburyport, 2002).
Shorey, P. (trans.), *Plato:* Republic*, Books I–V* (Cambridge, Mass., 1937).
Simpson, P. L. P. (trans.), *The* Eudemian Ethics *of Aristotle Translated with Explanatory Comments* (New Brunswick and London, 2013).
Slings, S. R. (ed.), *Platonis Rempublicam recognovit brevique adnotatione critica instruxit* (Oxford, 2003).
Solomon, J. (trans.), *Eudemian Ethics*, in *The Complete Works of Aristotle*, ed. Barnes, ii. 1922–81.
Stocks, J. L. (trans.), *On the Heavens*, in *The Complete Works of Aristotle*, ed. Barnes, i. 447–511.
Striker, G., 'Antipater, or the Art of Living', in M. Schofield and G. Striker (eds.), *The Norms of Nature: Studies in Hellenistic Ethics* (Cambridge, 2007), 185–204.
Vlastos, G., 'Justice and Happiness in the *Republic*', in G. Vlastos, *Platonic Studies* (Princeton, 1973), 111–39.
Waterfield, R. (trans.), *Plato:* Republic (Oxford, 1993).
Wheeler, M., review of Crivelli, *Aristotle on Truth*, in *Journal of the History of Philosophy*, 44 (2006), 469–70.
Woods, M. (trans. and comm.), *Aristotle:* Eudemian Ethics*, Books I, II, and VIII*, 2nd edn. [*Eudemian Ethics*] (Oxford, 2005).

ARISTOTLE ON ESSENCE AND HABITAT

JESSICA GELBER

1. Introduction

ARISTOTLE was aware that organisms have parts and organs that are well suited to exercising their distinctive vital capacities, such as their capacities for locomotion, reproduction, self-maintenance, and perception. The presence of those well-suited parts and organs is, Aristotle thinks, no accident. These parts are present for the sake of those vital activities and functions they are used to perform:

Since every instrument is for the sake of something, and each of the parts of the body is for the sake of something, and what they are for the sake of is a certain action, it is apparent that the entire body too has been constituted for the sake of a certain complete action. For sawing is not for the sake of the saw but the saw for sawing; for sawing is a certain use. So the body too is in a way for the sake of the soul, and the parts are for the sake of the functions in relation to which each of them has naturally developed. (*PA* 1. 5, 645^{b}14–20, trans. Lennox)

Aristotle was also aware that organisms have, by and large, parts and organs that are well suited to life in a certain kind of habitat.[1] (By 'habitat' I mean an ecological environment characterized both

© Jessica Gelber 2015

I am grateful to the organizers and participants of the 36th Annual Workshop in Ancient Philosophy, particularly my commentator, Eve Rabinoff, as well as to Anna Marmodoro and members of her seminar in Oxford, for their extremely helpful suggestions for improvement. I also benefited greatly from discussions with Michael Caie, Kim Frost, Devin Henry, Joe Karbowski, Sean Kelsey, Jim Lennox, Hille Paakkunainen, Kara Richardson, and Joel Yurdin. Brad Inwood also deserves many thanks for his editorial assistance and advice. I would especially like to express my gratitude to Kathleen C. Cook.

[1] I am oversimplifying matters here in speaking as though an organism has only a single habitat, since Aristotle distinguishes several respects in which something might be, for example, a water-, marsh-, or land-dweller. As Aristotle discusses in *HA* 7 (8). 2, an animal might be a water-dweller with respect to feeding, but a land-dweller with respect to cooling, for instance. This becomes relevant for Aristotle when he is discussing (e.g. in *PA* 4. 13) kinds that 'tend to both sides'—ones that have one habitat for certain vital activities and a different habitat for others. My

by abiotic features such as moisture, light, and temperature, and by biotic ones, such as the availability of certain kinds of plants and animals as food or shelter, or the presence of predators or rivals.) His biological works contain numerous references to the co-ordination between the parts or organs that a kind of organism uses to exercise its vital capacities, and the conditions in the habitat in which it does so. For instance, he notes that the hard lining of the camel's mouth allows it to consume the type of vegetation—viz. thorny cactus plants—that grow in the deserts where the camel lives (*PA* 3. 14, 674^{a}22–^{b}5), that the flat beak of certain marsh birds is useful for digging up roots in the mud (*PA* 4. 12, 693^{a}11 ff.), and that birds that live near water can swim more easily because of the webbing between their toes (*PA* 4. 12, 694^{b}6 ff.). Reflection on these facts quite naturally leads us to ask what accounts for the fit between these organisms and their habitats. I will call such a question a 'question of fit'. But Aristotle, despite his awareness of those same facts, never asks any such question.[2]

discussion of habitat is consistent with this complication, and so for the most part I will overlook it. (For discussions of these kinds, which are sometimes called (perhaps misleadingly) 'dualizers', see D. M. Balme, 'Aristotle's Use of Division and Differentiae', in A. Gotthelf and J. G. Lennox (eds.), *Philosophical Issues in Aristotle's Biology* [*Issues*] (Cambridge, 1987), 69–89; A. Gotthelf, 'First Principles in Aristotle's *Parts of Animals*' ['First Principles'], in Gotthelf and Lennox (eds.), *Issues*, 167–98, repr. in A. Gotthelf, *Teleology, First Principles, and Scientific Method in Aristotle's Biology* [*Teleology*] (Oxford, 2012), 153–85; J. G. Lennox, 'Divide and Explain: The *Posterior Analytics* in Practice', in Gotthelf and Lennox (eds.), *Issues*, 90–119, repr. in J. G. Lennox, *Aristotle's Philosophy of Biology: Studies in the Origins of Life Science* [*Biology*] (Cambridge, 2001), 7–38; J. G. Lennox, '*Bios* and Explanatory Unity in Aristotle's Biology' ['*Bios*'], in D. Charles (ed.), *Definition in Greek Philosophy* (Oxford, 2010), 329–55; J. G. Lennox, 'Βίος, Πρᾶξις, and the Unity of Life' ['Πρᾶξις'], in S. Föllinger (ed.), *Was ist 'Leben'? Aristoteles' Anschauungen zur Entstehung und Funktionsweise von Leben. Akten der Tagung vom 23.–26. August 2006 in Bamberg* (Stuttgart, 2010), 239–59.)

[2] Asking what accounts for the fit between organisms and their habitats is not the same as asking why organisms are found in habitats to which they are well suited. Questions of fit are questions of the form 'Why are fish so well suited to life in water?', rather than 'Why are fish found in water?'. Call questions of this latter sort 'distribution questions'. One way to see that these questions are distinct is by noting that one could answer all of the questions of fit and yet still not have an answer to distribution questions: we could understand why there is a fit between fish and water, but still wonder why it is that fish are actually living in water, rather than eking out their existence in some less than ideal circumstances. I suspect that the tendency to conflate these two questions is in part explained by the fact that we usually answer both questions by appeals to an organism's evolutionary history. Although Aristotle does not ask either of these sorts of question, my focus here is only on why he does not raise questions of fit.

It is unlikely that Aristotle thinks this 'fit' (as I am calling it) between organisms and their habitats is merely a lucky coincidence. In *Physics* 2. 8 he rejects the idea that regularly occurring, beneficial arrangements of parts within the body—such as our teeth being arranged suitably for biting and grinding food—could be merely due to chance. So, it is natural to expect that Aristotle would consider the beneficial co-ordination between organisms and their habitats to be equally non-accidental. The co-ordination between the parts of the body is not sufficient to explain the survival and flourishing of a kind; if the kind does not have a co-operative habitat, having teeth that are suitable for biting and grinding, for example, would be of little use.

Darwinians and Creationists have ready explanations. The former can tell an evolutionary story about how organisms evolved to be the way they are; the latter can appeal to an Intelligent Designer's grand plans for producing such a good fit. On the assumption that Aristotle is neither a Darwinian nor a Creationist, however, these answers are not available to him.

In what follows I will first consider two possible strategies for reconstructing Aristotle's answer to questions of fit. The first is going to appeal to a global or cosmic version of natural teleology. The second will give the conditions in various habitats an efficient-causal role in shaping the character of the organisms living in them. Neither of these approaches, as I will argue, provides an attractive answer.

What I will propose instead is a way of understanding Aristotle's views about the essences of living substances, i.e. the 'what-it-is-to-be' for living creatures, that explains why he would not ask any questions of fit. In short, my proposal will be that habitat is partially constitutive of the vital capacities that comprise a kind's essence. Consequently, whereas *we* might think that questions of fit are urgent, for Aristotle those questions would not arise. For, just as asking why swimming takes place in water evinces some confusion about what swimming is, Aristotle would think that asking a question of fit betrays a misunderstanding about what the objects of natural science are. Swimming is a kind of movement that takes place—essentially—in water. So, too, all of an organism's psychic capacities are ones that take place—essentially—in certain types of environment. The various activities that comprise the life of a kind of organism cannot even be specified without referring to the habitats in which those activities are performed. The way of thinking about the essences of living kinds that I will attribute to Aristotle yields a richer and more nuanced view about natural substances than the abstract and programmatic discussions in the *Physics* suggest.[3]

2. Global teleology

One approach to answering questions of fit is to read Aristotle as endorsing a 'cosmic' or 'global' version of natural teleology in the way advocated by David Sedley.[4] On Sedley's view, the beneficial coordination between organisms and their habitats is to be explained teleologically. The conditions that make life possible—especially human life—are such as they are for the sake of doing just that:

> Clearly the world as a whole is structured in many ways that are regularly beneficial to life, including the availability of natural resources, and the eternally recurrent intertransformation of the four simple bodies that underlies the weather cycle, this latter dependent in turn on the daily and annual cycles of the sun. If Aristotle conceded that these advantageous cosmic structures require no teleological explanation, he would be playing into the hands of his opponents by implying that advantageous structures in individual organisms might equally well be understood as nonpurposive.[5]

Although Sedley's interpretation is subtler and more complicated than I can do justice to here,[6] I take the crux of it to be the following. In Sedley's view, Aristotle holds that goal directedness in

[3] It will simply be false, *pace* S. Waterlow, to say that Aristotle thinks the conditions in a certain habitat merely 'provide the stage' (S. Waterlow, *Nature, Change, and Agency in Aristotle's* Physics [*Nature*] (Oxford, 1982), 38) or 'arena' (ibid. 33) in which an individual substance's activities are carried out, or that Aristotle does not consider positive descriptions of those conditions important to understanding the natures of living organisms (ibid. 33).

[4] See D. Sedley, 'Is Aristotle's Teleology Anthropocentric?' ['Anthropocentric'], *Phronesis*, 36 (1991), 179–96; '*Metaphysics* Λ', in D. Charles and M. Frede (eds.), *Aristotle's* Metaphysics Λ: *Proceedings of the Fourteenth Symposium Aristotelicum* (Oxford, 2000), 327–50; *Creationism and its Critics in Antiquity* [*Creationism*] (Berkeley, 2007); and 'Teleology, Aristotelian and Platonic', in J. G. Lennox and R. Bolton (eds.), *Being, Nature, and Life in Aristotle: Essays in Honor of Allan Gotthelf* (Cambridge, 2010), 5–29.

[5] Sedley, *Creationism*, 196.

[6] I am glossing over, in particular, the anthropocentric aspect of Sedley's interpretation: 'Nature is anthropocentric to the extent that man is the ultimate *beneficiary*, while god remains the ultimate object of aspiration, that which all lesser beings strive to imitate' (Sedley, 'Anthropocentric', 180). On Sedley's interpretation, all natural

nature extends beyond the development and characteristic behaviours of individual substances and to the cosmos considered as a whole. Not only the reproduction and maintenance of individual living beings, but also the motions of celestial bodies, the cycles of elemental transformation, and sublunary weather patterns are goal-directed processes.

The shared goal of all these natural phenomena, furthermore, is the emulation of the Unmoved Mover's perfect activity, which each thing does in its own way. A living organism emulates divine actuality by reproducing another like itself.[7] The elements do this by continual, cyclical transformation into each other.[8]

It is important to note that on Sedley's interpretation, moreover, it is not merely the shared striving to emulate god's perfect actuality that ensures and so explains that good order will obtain among all the parts of the cosmos.[9] After all, the fact that the Unmoved Mover serves as the 'metaphysical magnet'[10] drawing all things towards it is surely compatible with a lack of co-ordination. In order for that shared goal to be providing a genuine explanation, there needs to be some connection between the single, common aim and the co-ordination and fit between natural entities. Without such a connection, there is nothing that guarantees that order will emerge. Sedley forges a link, on Aristotle's behalf, between each natural entity's aim to emulate god's perfect actuality and their mutual co-ordination (including organisms' fit with their habitats) by positing a 'cosmic

phenomena ultimately aim to emulate god's perfection, but natural phenomena are for the sake of humans—the highest species—in the sense that they benefit humans. (For the distinction between *aim* and *beneficiary* see *DA* 2. 4, 415^{a}23–^{b}7, 415^{b}15–21; *Phys.* 2. 2, 194^{a}33–6; *Metaph.* Λ 7, 1072^{b}1–4.)

[7] Cf. *GA* 2. 1, 731^{b}31–732^{a}1; *DA* 2. 4, 415^{a}25 ff.
[8] *GC* 2. 10, 337^{a}1 ff.; *Meteor.* 1. 9, 346^{b}35 ff.
[9] The idea that a shared aim gives rise to co-ordination is expressed by I. Bodnár, who writes that 'Aristotle submits that there is a joint-arrangement, that every single entity is jointly arranged in relation to all the others and that this joint-arrangement arises due to the fact that each of these entities is related to the single entity at the pinnacle of this arrangement' (I. Bodnár, 'Teleology across Natures' ['Teleology'], *Rhizai*, 2 (2005), 9–29 at 22). Similarly, M. Leunissen claims that in Aristotle's view, the 'goodness, order, and joint arrangement of the cosmos as a whole *emerge* from the goal-directed actions of the individual parts of the cosmos towards the same end, the Unmoved Mover' (M. Leunissen, *Explanation and Teleology in Aristotle's Science of Nature* [*Explanation*] (Cambridge, 2010), 47).
[10] This phrase is borrowed from C. Kahn, 'The Place of the Prime Mover in Aristotle's Teleology', in A. Gotthelf (ed.), *Aristotle on Nature and Living Things* [*Nature*] (Pittsburgh, 1985), 183–205 at 184.

nature', over and above the individual natures. On Sedley's interpretation, every part of the cosmos strives to emulate god's perfect activity. This striving by any given part of nature, however, does not take place in a vacuum, but within a larger system. The larger system of which each is a part constrains or determines what the best possible emulation of god's perfect activity consists in, just as an organism's entire body constrains what optimal functioning of any particular part of it will involve. So, for instance, the lung is an organ for cooling. But how that cooling function is best carried out is in large part dependent upon what the other body parts are like. Optimal cooling is not necessarily the highest degree of cooling; what is optimal depends on factors such as the degree of heat in an organism's heart. So too, what the best possible emulation of god's perfection can be for any part of nature is determined by its place in the universe as a whole.

Sedley's proposal, then, is that the whole universe is analogous to an individual organism. Like an individual organism, the universe has a nature, over and above the individual natures. And this 'cosmic nature' co-ordinates its parts such that each part is able to emulate god's perfect activity in the best possible way:

> Just as the nature of an animal can be invoked to explain why it has the parts that it does, including some that are at the service of others, so too the nature of the world, including the sublunary realm's complex goal-directed structure with man at its apex, can be invoked to explain why it contains the species, weather-systems, and other amenities that it does.[11]

What this interpretation makes room for is an explanation of the co-ordination between organisms and their habitats. Given that each part of nature is striving to imitate god's perfection, and that what such imitating involves depends on its place in the cosmos, it will turn out that the co-ordination between organisms and their habitats is simply a permanent feature of the well-ordered world, just

---

[11] Sedley, *Creationism*, 203. Sedley's evidence for his interpretation is primarily the analogy drawn in *Metaph*. Λ 10, 1075^{a}11–25, between the universe and armies (and households), where the 'joint-arrangement' of the components appears to be explained by their being 'jointly arranged in relation to one thing'. Although Aristotle does not say as much explicitly, we can imagine that the soldiers in an army are arranged in relation to each other—there is beneficial co-ordination among their actions—in virtue of their sharing the same goal, perhaps obeying the orders of the general. For discussions of Sedley's treatment of this passage see Bodnár, 'Teleology', 17–21, and R. Wardy, 'Aristotelian Rainfall or the Lore of Averages' ['Rainfall'], *Phronesis*, 38 (1993), 18–30 at 23–6.

as the 'teleological functioning of the parts of the body constitutes a permanent symbiotic interrelation'.[12]

An interpretation of Aristotle's teleology such as Sedley's may provide an answer, for Aristotle, to questions of fit. But there are reasons to wonder whether this is really Aristotle's view. There is, as Sedley's critics have pointed out, at least a *prima facie* tension between the idea that there is a cosmic nature, analogous to the natures of individual living beings, and Aristotle's metaphysics of substance.[13] Aristotle says in the *Physics* that only substances have natures (192^b32–3). So, if the cosmos is to have a nature, it must be a substance, which seems to imply that the inhabitants of the cosmos are parts of that substance. But Aristotle also appears to think that parts of substances are not substances, or at least are only substances in potential (*Metaph. Z* 16, 1040^b5 ff.). If so, this threatens the status of living things—given that they are parts of the cosmos—as paradigmatic substances (cf. *Metaph. Z* 7, 1032^a19; *Z* 8, 1034^a4; *H* 3, 1043^b21–3).

Sedley's interpretation has also been criticized for its rejection of what has been called Aristotle's 'teleological axiom' that 'nature does what is best among the possibilities for *the animal's own being*'.[14] Aristotle's reference to the final cause in *Physics* 2. 7, 198^b8–9, as being what is 'better thus, not simply, but in relation to the being of each thing', is taken by many scholars as explicitly restricting the scope of goal-directed natural processes to those that benefit the same natural entity as that which undergoes the process.[15] Although there are ways of reading Aristotle's claim in *Physics* 2. 7 that are amenable to Sedley's view,[16] Aristotle's practices in his biological works—where there are very few passages that do not clearly con-

---

[12] Sedley, 'Anthropocentric', 187.

[13] See Wardy, 'Rainfall', and Bodnár, 'Teleology', for objections to the existence of a cosmic nature in Aristotle's ontology.

[14] J. G. Lennox, *Aristotle: On the Parts of Animals I–IV. Translated with an Introduction and Commentary* [*Parts*] (Oxford, 2001), 341.

[15] See L. Judson, 'Aristotelian Teleology' ['Aristotelian'], *Oxford Studies in Ancient Philosophy*, 29 (2005), 341–66 at 359–62, and Lennox, *Parts*, 341. D. M. Balme claims that Aristotle's statement in *Physics* 2. 7 'cannot be reconciled' with global teleology (*Aristotle: De partibus animalium I and De generatione animalium I* (*with Passages from II. 1–3*). *Translated with Notes, with a Report on Recent Work and an Additional Bibliography* [*De partibus*] (Oxford, 1992), 96). Aristotle makes similar remarks at *IA* 2, 704^b15–17, and *GA* 5. 8, 788^b20–5.

[16] Sedley suggests that the contrast intended between better 'simply' and better 'in relation to each being' is that between being better relative to some being or other and being better 'absolutely', and takes Aristotle to be denying Plato's view in the

form to that 'axiom'—is thought to tell against such an alternative reading.[17]

I will add to the list of worries the fact that Aristotle does not seem to offer any argument for the existence of a cosmic nature. As I understand it, Aristotle's argument for positing goal-directed natures that co-ordinate the parts of individual organisms relies heavily on observations of the regularity with which these beneficial structures are produced.[18] In an eternal, ungenerated universe there is no analogous reproductive regularity to be observed. Consequently, the same kind of argument as he gives for goal-directed individual natures cannot be applied in the case of a cosmic nature. It might be Aristotle's view that the whole universe has a nature like the natures of individual organisms, and that this cosmic nature is responsible for the beneficial distribution of organisms in suitable habitats. If that is his view, however, it is one for which he does not appear to give an argument. And this is surprising, given that he clearly sees the need to argue against those who deny that there are individual, goal-directed natures.

These criticisms of Sedley's interpretation are not decisive. However, in the light of the fact that his interpretation requires quite

Timaeus that features of the world can be intrinsically good, and 'not because they do anyone any good' ('Anthropocentric', 190).

[17] As M. Leunissen interprets Aristotle, this teleological axiom applies only to cases of what she calls 'primary teleology', but not to what she calls 'secondary teleology'. On her interpretation, cases of secondary teleology are cases of 'any agent—internal or external—making use of things available by nature for its own good, such as living beings using each other as food' (*Explanation*, 25). This distinction might provide a way to read various comments (such as that at *PA* 4. 13, 696^{b}24 ff., where Aristotle claims that the placement of the dolphin's mouth is for the sake of preserving other animals) in a way that does not conflict with the teleological axiom, since one can maintain that these are cases of secondary teleology, and the axiom applies only to primary teleology. Unfortunately, however, I do not think appealing to secondary teleology will provide a satisfying answer to questions of fit. For the answer would be that the habitat is for the sake of the kind—though only in the secondary way—in that 'the formal nature of one natural being appropriates the potentials available in another natural being in order to use it for its own benefit' (ibid. 48). That is, the sense in which the habitat is for the sake of the organisms is that the habitat gets used by or is useful for organisms. However, since questions of fit are questions about *why* a habitat is useful for an organism, such an answer would seem merely to restate the *explanandum*.

[18] For a discussion of the relevance of regular reproduction from seed in Aristotle's argument for natural teleology see A. Code, 'The Priority of Final Causes over Efficient Causes in Aristotle's *PA*', in W. Kullmann and S. Föllinger (eds.), *Aristotelische Biologie: Intentionen, Methoden, Ergebnisse* [*Biologie*] (Stuttgart, 1997), 127–43.

controversial assumptions, a proposal for how Aristotle would answer questions of fit that presupposes it is not appealing.[19]

3. Adaptation

Sometimes Aristotle speaks about an organism's habitat in a way that strongly suggests a causal and explanatory account running from facts about a habitat to facts about an organism's parts and features. In *PA* 4. 12, for instance, he says that 'Some birds are long-legged. The cause [*aition*] of this is their marsh-dweller way of life' ($694^{b}12$). Comments such as this indicate that Aristotle thinks there is a causal account proceeding from facts about the habitat to facts about the body parts and features of the living organisms in it.

As is well known, Aristotle thinks there are four ways of being a cause, so there is a question about which he means to be referring to here. If one were tempted to read this as signalling an efficient-causal account, as opposed to a formal- or final-causal one,[20] further support might be garnered from the fact that there are other passages in which an efficient-causal role is given to environmental conditions such as climate. For example, *GA* 5. 3 contains a description of the way variations in hair thickness result from differences in the temperature and humidity of a given region. The reason organisms have hair at all is protection, but how thick or thin, straight or curly the hair is depends on factors such as the amount of heat and fluidity present while it is forming. So, for example, Scythians and Thracians have straight hair, in part because the surrounding air is moist, whereas those who live in hot and dry regions such as Ethiopia have curly hair ($782^{b}33$–$783^{a}1$). And in *GA* 4. 2 facts about climate and a region's water are said to play a role in determining the sex of an embryo ($767^{a}28$–35). In addition, Mariska Leunissen has recently argued that Aristotle holds a version of what she calls 'environmental determinism' about the development of character.[21] Leunissen argues that in Aristotle's view, an organism's *ethos* or natural character—its being timid, mild, courageous, gentle, intelli-

---

[19] The interpretation that I will be arguing for is, in fact, compatible with Sedley's, but it does not require it.

[20] I will argue that this should be read as a teleological explanation.

[21] M. Leunissen, 'Aristotle on Natural Character and its Implications for Moral Development' ['Character'], *Journal of the History of Philosophy*, 50 (2012), 507–30 at 509.

gent, or stupid—is causally determined by 'external environmental factors'.[22]

So, in certain cases, Aristotle may hold that an organism's features are efficient-causal effects of conditions in its environment. Those cases, however, are importantly different from the ones I am concerned with here. In each of those examples just mentioned, there is a material-efficient causal account that goes from environmental factors, by way of the organism's elemental composition or bodily 'blend' (*krasis*), to some characteristic or feature. Here the environment is thought to influence the outcome via its causal influence on the quality of the material constitution of an organism. Questions of fit, however, are about the co-ordination between habitat and the parts that are suited to performing their functions in those habitats, and it is doubtful that a similar efficient-causal account can be given for those.

There are at least three reasons for this doubt. First, Aristotle gives no indication that he thinks that a causal story going from the effects of climate on the organism's bodily blend to the organism's part or feature could be told about the long legs of the marsh-dweller bird. It is equally unclear that he thinks that this could be the case for the flat beaks of the swamp-dweller, vegetarian birds (*PA* 4. 12, 693^{a}11 ff.) and the webbed feet of the aquatic birds (*PA* 4. 12, 694^{b}6 ff.), or the hard roof of the mouth and multiple stomachs of the thorny-food-eating[23] camel (*PA* 3. 14, 674^{a}22–^{b}5). Unlike, for example, hair thickness, there is no attempt on Aristotle's part to explain how temperature and humidity give rise to variations in the shapes and structures of these sorts of parts or organs. At least in the case of hair thickness, Aristotle appeals to rates of evaporation and amounts and qualities of moisture being evaporated. Second, even if there were some way to tell such a story, it would need to include the environment's efficient-casual effect on the organisms' activities and functions. For Aristotle thinks that the character of the function that a part is used to perform is explanatorily prior to

---

[22] Leunissen argues that an organism's natural character depends on its elemental 'blend', which blend is in turn 'changeable by efficient-causal changes due to aging and disease, diet, and external environmental factors' ('Character', 509). Leunissen cites *Pol.* 7. 7, 1327^{b}18–38, as evidence that Aristotle thinks the natural character traits of an individual human 'depend on the climate where it lives' (ibid.).

[23] See Lennox, '*Bios*', 338–9 n. 14, for a discussion of the tight connection between the 'material constitution of the food source' and an organism's habitat. I am accepting Lennox's suggestion that references to nourishment be read as emphasizing the habitat rather than the food.

the character of the part. Third, this would not explain why an organism's parts and activities should turn out to be suitable in those conditions. That is, the fact that some part of an animal is a result of certain efficient-causal influences in no way guarantees that the part will be beneficial to the animal in the conditions that exert this causal influence.

Is there some other way—that is, other than environmental influence on the bodily blend—in which organisms' features can be considered as effects of the conditions in their environments? Some scholars claim that the sorts of examples just cited are instances of adaptation by an organism to its environment.[24] If we take 'adapt' simply to mean 'change in response to the environment', it seems reasonable that Aristotle would think there are plenty of ways that an organism can do this. There are, for instance, extended discussions of the ways different kinds of organisms respond to seasonal changes by hibernating (*HA* 7 (8). 14–17) and migrating (*HA* 7 (8). 12–13).

There is, however, a limit to the kinds of change an individual organism's nature could undergo in response to its environment. And changes to an organism's body parts that are needed to perform certain functions seem to lie well beyond that point. The problem with this idea is not merely the fact that it seems implausible to think that an organism could grow longer legs in response to finding itself in a marsh in the way it might go into hiding in response to a drop in temperature, or that a bird could develop webbing between its toes in response to living in water, just as it might fly to warmer regions when winter arrives.[25] The problem with this as an interpretation of Aristotle is that changes such as those in the size, shape, or position

[24] Judson, 'Aristotelian', 355 n. 46; Lennox, *Parts*, 331; Leunissen, *Explanation*, 42.

[25] Lamarck, after all, thought this was the case: 'We find in the same way that the bird of the water-side which does not like swimming and yet is in need of going to the water's edge to secure its prey, is continually liable to sink in the mud. Now this bird tries to act in such a way that its body should not be immersed in the liquid, and hence makes its best efforts to stretch and lengthen its legs . . . The bird which is drawn to the water by its need of finding there the prey on which it lives, separates the digits of its feet in trying to strike the water and move about on the surface. The skin which unites these digits at their base acquires the habit of being stretched by these continually repeated separations of the digits; thus in the course of time there are formed large webs which unite the digits of ducks, geese, etc., as we actually find them. In the same way efforts to swim, that is to push against the water so as to move about in it, have stretched the membranes between the digits of frogs, sea-tortoises, the otter, beaver, etc.' (J. B. Lamarck, *Zoological Philosophy: An Exposition with*

of body parts would require changes in the functions and activities those parts are needed to perform: the functions and activities have, in Aristotle's view, causal and explanatory priority over the parts. And, I submit, an organism cannot modify its essential vital activities within a single lifespan.[26]

The idea that there can be adaptations of essential activities would be reasonable, perhaps, given the assumption that species evolve over time. If species evolve—if some species go out of existence and new species come to be—there is nothing obviously incoherent about there being modifications to essential activities and functions. Yet although there may be nothing in Aristotle's theory that is inconsistent with evolution, there is no evidence that Aristotle does think species evolve. The consensus view, on the contrary, is that Aristotle believes in the permanence and fixity of the species—that the world has always contained the kinds of organisms it does—and that this would be the most reasonable position to take, given the lack of palaeontological evidence in his day.[27] In order to accept that Aristotle's answer to questions of fit is that 'the kind adapted to its environment', we must then be willing to endorse the view that, according to Aristotle, species evolve. However, since the latter view is unattractive, so consequently is the former.

4. Habitat and essence

So far, I have considered two possible, though problematic, answers to questions of fit. The first answer requires the assumption that Aristotle's ontology includes an overall, cosmic nature. The second answer is hard to square with Aristotle's belief that functions are prior to parts, as well as his views about the fixity of kinds.

regard to the Natural History of Animals, translated, with an introduction by Hugh Elliot (London, 1914), 119).

[26] This does not mean that an organism will not behave differently in different circumstances. However, not all differences in behaviour are manifestations of differences in vital capacities. I discuss this further below, in sect. 6.

[27] See e.g. J. Cooper, 'Aristotle on Natural Teleology', in M. Nussbaum and M. Schofield (eds.), *Language and Logos: Studies in Ancient Greek Philosophy Presented to G. E. L. Owen* (Cambridge, 1982), 197–222 at 202 ff.; J. G. Lennox, 'Kinds, Forms of Kinds, and the More and the Less in Aristotle's Biology', in Gotthelf and Lennox (eds.), *Issues*, 339–59 at 359, repr. in Lennox, *Biology*, 160–81 at 178; Balme, *De partibus*, 97–8.

Here I want to consider a different, more promising strategy, one that shows why questions of fit are, in effect, the wrong sort of questions to expect Aristotle to be asking, given his conception of living substances. This strategy, in short, is to reconceive of the relation between habitats and organisms. In my view, Aristotle considers habitat to be partially constitutive of the capacities that comprise a kind's essence, and not merely an external or enabling condition under which an organism can exercise its essential capacities. An attractive feature of this interpretation is that it explains why Aristotle would not raise any questions of fit: there is no need to ask why an animal is well suited to the habitat in which it lives if its habitat is already included in what it is to be an animal of that kind.

The idea that habitat is part of an organism's essence, and that habitat accordingly plays an explanatory role in scientific investigations about the kind, is not original with me. Long ago, for example, Allan Gotthelf noted that the elephant's being a marsh-dweller is one of the 'multiple essential features' that Aristotle appeals to in his complicated explanation of the elephant's distinctive trunk.[28] And in recent papers Jim Lennox has pointed out that a kind's 'way of life' or *bios*—of which habitat is one important aspect—'is occasionally identified as a fundamental feature of its *being*; and particular *divisions* of ways of life as general differentiae are likewise aspects of the essence of *forms* of those kinds'.[29]

As both Gotthelf and Lennox have pointed out, *History of Animals* and *Parts of Animals* contain frequent references to the environment in which an organism performs various activities, such as feeding or cooling, in a way that strongly suggests that performing those activities in that habitat is, in Aristotle's view, simply part of the kind's nature. On the basis of such references, it would appear that Aristotle thinks that it is part of the being or essence of the kind to perform those activities in certain habitats. And if this is, in fact, how Aristotle is thinking about living substances and their habitats, it is no surprise that he never explicitly raises any questions of fit, questions which seemed so pressing to later biologists and philosophers such as Darwin.

---

[28] A. Gotthelf, 'The Elephant's Nose: Further Reflections on the Axiomatic Structure of Biological Explanation in Aristotle' ['Elephant'], in Kullmann and Föllinger (eds.), *Biologie*, 85–96 at 91, repr. in A. Gotthelf, *Teleology, First Principles, and Scientific Method in Aristotle's Biology* (Oxford, 2012), 186–96 at 192.

[29] Lennox, '*Bios*', 348, and '$Πρᾶξις$', 252.

The general idea that a kind's essence will include its habitat is appealing, but the plausibility of this interpretation of Aristotle depends on how it is developed in detail. One would hope that this general idea could be made precise in a way consistent with Aristotle's other views. In particular, since Aristotle appears to identify an organism's essence with its soul (DA 2. 4, 415^{b}8–15)—its capacities for engaging in vital activities—we need an account of how habitat is related to those capacities comprising soul.

Gotthelf, unfortunately, does not address how the multiple essential features appealed to in explanations are related to one another. His focus is on examining the structure of those explanations, with a view to showing that they do have, at least implicitly, the sort of structure described in the *Posterior Analytics*. In particular, Gotthelf is interested in presenting evidence that Aristotle's biological writings consider certain features that are appealed to in various explanations to be essential features that would be part of a kind's definition.[30] Such features are what Gotthelf refers to as the 'givens', features of a kind that explain the presence or character of its other features but that are not 'explained anywhere else in *PA*, and for each of which there is good theoretical or intuitive reason to think that Aristotle considered them explanatorily basic and thus essential to the subject kind'.[31] Gotthelf claims that being a marsh animal is among those unexplained explainers of the elephant's trunk,[32] but does not say how that fact about the elephant is related to its other essential features.[33] As Gotthelf's concern in

[30] In Gotthelf's view, in fact, Aristotle in his biology considers many more features than psychic functions to be part of the being or essence of a kind. Gotthelf thinks that in addition to 'standard soul-functions', Aristotle includes in the οὐσία certain body parts, 'dimensional' features such as, perhaps, size and shape of certain limbs, and 'the blend of material elements that constitutes the animal' (A. Gotthelf, 'Notes towards a Study of Substance and Essence in Aristotle's *Parts of Animals* ii–iv' ['Notes'], in Gotthelf (ed.), *Nature*, 27–54 at 48, repr. in Gotthelf, *Teleology*, 217–40 at 238). This, as Gotthelf says, puts pressure on 'strongly functionalist interpretations of Aristotelian form' ('Notes', 53–4 n. 22 = *Teleology*, 233 n. 27).

[31] Gotthelf, 'Elephant', 86 (= *Teleology*, 188). Gotthelf is at times more circumspect about whether references to a kind's οὐσία are to be taken as references to its essence or τὸ τί ἦν εἶναι (see e.g. 'Notes', 51 n. 5 and 52 n. 11 = *Teleology*, 219–20 n. 4 and 223 n. 12.)   [32] 'Elephant', 87 (= *Teleology*, 188).

[33] Elsewhere Gotthelf entertains the idea that where an organism eats is not a 'given' but rather is explained by the kind of food it must eat ('First Principles', 192–3 = *Teleology*, 179). Although eating a sort of food might be a 'given', Aristotle also appears to hold that organisms' food must have 'an elemental blend like their own' (ibid. 193 = *Teleology*, 179). This suggests to Gotthelf that 'the blend of material *elements* makes it causally necessary that an animal feed in a certain place' ('Notes',

these papers is not to say *how* but rather only *that* such features are essential, the idea is not developed in sufficient detail for our purposes. Lennox's recent work on *bios*, on the other hand, which can be seen as one way to develop the general idea that essence includes habitat, does say more about the relationship between a kind's habitat and its psychic activities. On Lennox's interpretation, *bios* is the 'single essential feature of organisms . . . that accounts for the *integration* of the many physical and functional differences that make different kinds of animals what they are'.[34] Lennox argues that *bios*, though not mentioned in works such as the *Physics* or in the methodological discussions in Aristotle's biological treatises, is given a prominent role in both *History of Animals* and *Parts of Animals*. In the former it is one of the four main differentiae around which the data Aristotle presents there are organized. And in *Parts of Animals* it plays an ineliminable role in explaining why different animals' parts vary in particular ways. Strictly speaking, the character of the body parts is teleologically explained by the functions they are used to perform, but on Lennox's interpretation a kind's *bios* determines what its vital functions have to be like. That latter role, according to Lennox, is crucial to Aristotle's scientific study of animal parts because Aristotle is acutely aware that explanations of individual parts by reference to individual functions are not sufficient to explain the survival and flourishing of an organism. For the functions too must be co-ordinated or integrated so that they all work together.[35] By appealing to *bios* Aristotle can explain 'why a particular kind of animal has just the set of functions it has'[36] and so can account for the unity of an animal's many activities and functions: Aristotle conceives of a kind's functions and activities as unified and co-ordinated by its *bios*. Habitat, on this view, is related to a kind's essential functions

53 n. 20=*Teleology*, 231 n. 24). 'Watery' animals, for instance, must feed in water. However, the elemental constitution of a given region is not necessarily the same as a habitat. The fact that something must eat 'watery' food does not entail that it live in a marsh as opposed to, for example, a lake or seashore. For this reason, I do not take the passages cited by Gotthelf (*HA* 589^{a}5–8; *Resp.* 14; *PA* 669^{a}9–11; and *GC* 335^{a}10) to be clear evidence that a kind's elemental blend explains its having a certain habitat.

[34] '*Bios*', 333.
[35] See e.g. Lennox, '*Bios*', 350–1, and '$Πρᾶξις$', 254: 'The way of life of an animal demands a coordination of the many "structure/function complexes" that make up the animal. Without that coordination . . . you do not have an organism, i.e. a living unity.'   [36] Lennox, '*Bios*', 333, and '$Πρᾶξις$', 239.

by being an aspect of a whole *bios* that determines what the kind's essential functions have to be like.

Lennox is certainly right to stress the importance, for Aristotle and the modern biologist alike, of accounting not only for the morphological fit of parts to functions but also for the fit between functions. Moreover, scattered remarks that Aristotle makes suggest that he takes himself to be addressing how the parts are co-ordinated with one another, and not merely how the parts are suited for particular functions. There are, however, two reasons that might make one hesitate to accept Lennox's interpretation.

First, it is not clear how this talk of 'integrating' and 'co-ordinating' is supposed to be made precise, or what it means for activities to be unified 'due to' the *bios*. Lennox's language ('accounts for', 'explains', 'enforces coordination', 'demands') suggests a causal relation, and in particular the sort of causal and explanatory relation that soul bears to an animal's characteristic behaviours and the functions of its parts. Lennox is clear, however, that he does not think that a kind's *bios* is equivalent to its soul or essence. And he is clear that he does not think that a kind's essential activities are 'due to' the *bios* in the sense that they are for the sake of the *bios*. But since it is neither a formal- nor a final-causal relation, nor presumably an efficient- or material-causal relation, it is not clear how this co-ordinating or integrating role is meant to correspond, if at all, to the quadruple causal framework discussed in the *Physics*. The nature of the causal and explanatory role that *bios* plays is, then, somewhat elusive.

Second, as Lennox also notes, there are reasons to wonder how such a complex way of life, with all its many aspects, can be a unitary feature. This is problematic since, according to Lennox, Aristotle's motivation for introducing such a feature as *bios* was to provide unity to the whole host of functions and activities that comprise a living being's soul or essence. But in order to do this unifying work, the *bios* must somehow form a unity itself. Given that a kind's *bios* involves so many different things, it appears that we have just pushed the question back to one about the 'unity of the diverse features of the animal's way of life'.[37]

These obstacles to accepting Lennox's interpretation, though not trivial, are not insurmountable. My interests are more narrowly delimited here, however, and so I would like instead to explore an-

---

[37] Lennox, '*Πρᾶξις*', 259.

other option for construing the relationship between habitat and essential psychic activities that could be compatible with, though it does not require, the stronger view advocated by Lennox.

An alternative way to pursue the same general strategy—i.e. the strategy that builds habitat into the essence by assigning it a role in determining what a kind's essential functions and activities must be like—would be to fill in the details as follows. Since a kind's essence is identified with soul, which is a set of capacities for engaging in vital activities, we can think about essences in terms of sets of capacities. Capacities, moreover, can be considered at varying levels of generality. For instance, pastry chefs and barbecue masters both have the general capacity to cook food. However, they each have that capacity in different, more specific ways. One has the pastry-chef cooking capacity, the other has the barbecue-master cooking capacity. What determines the precise character of their respective capacities are factors such as where and on what ingredients the capacities are exercised. That is, their capacities are different in virtue of differences in the medium in which their capacities are exercised (oven vs. grill) and differences in the objects upon which they are exercised (flour, butter, sugar vs. meat). Similarly, birds share a general capacity to walk. However, walking in a marsh and walking on rocky cliffs are very different activities. The specific form of walking exhibited by the crane, for example, will differ from that of a falcon in virtue of particular features of the habitat—the marsh—in which the crane's walking occurs.[38]

Habitat, according to this proposal, gets into the essence by serving as a determinant of the precise way in which organisms have their vital capacities.[39] Marsh-dweller birds, for instance, are

[38] Just to be clear, the genus–species relationship that obtains between the general capacity to walk and the species of walking exhibited by the marsh-dweller is not to be construed as one that treats 'marsh-dweller' as a *differentia* of the general capacity. Not every genus–species relationship is one for which there is an independent, extra feature that gets added to the genus to yield a new species. A bird is a specific way of being an animal, but a bird is not animal+some *differentia*; a bird is a determinate way of being an animal. Just so, being a marsh-dweller bird is not being a bird+some *differentia*; being a marsh-dweller is a determinate way of being a bird. For a helpful discussion of this contrast between different kinds of genus–species relationships see A. Ford, 'Action and Generality', in A. Ford, J. Hornsby, and F. Stoutland (eds.), *Essays on Anscombe's* Intention (Cambridge, Mass., 2011), 76–104 at 82–90. In Ford's terminology, I take the specific capacities to stand in 'categorial' genus–species relationships to the general ones.

[39] An organism's natural habitat cannot, of course, be the only thing serving to determine how the organism has its capacities. There are likely to be several

not just birds with certain capacities that happen to be exercised best in marshes. Marsh-dweller birds are birds that have those capacities in the marsh-dweller way. That is, 'the marsh-dweller way' is a specification of the way the organism has its vital capacities.

According to this understanding of the relation between essential capacities and habitat, it is natural to read Aristotle's references to organisms' habitats as references to the specific or determinate way they have their vital capacities, such as locomotion. For instance, 'marsh-dweller way of life' is, on my proposal, a reference to the way the bird has its essential vital capacities—in the marsh-dweller way. Consequently, when Aristotle claims that being a marsh-dweller is the cause of some birds having long legs (at *PA* 4. 12, 694^{b}12, cited above), he is giving a teleological explanation. It is not that the marsh-dweller birds have long legs for the sake of being in marshes. Rather, they have long legs for the sake of exercising their distinctive capacities, such as their capacity to walk in a certain way. And that Aristotle takes himself to be giving a teleological explanation in this passage is evinced by his commenting in the very next sentence that 'nature makes the instruments to fit the function, not the function to fit the instruments' (694^{b}13–14). It is for the sake of walking in a certain way—the way a marsh-dweller bird must walk—that those birds have long legs.

5. 'External' conditions and capacities

In case one is sceptical about including spatially external elements in the essence of a living being, Aristotle's account of perception provides a useful model.[40] Aristotle thinks that perceptual organs, such as eyes, are defined by the perceptual capacities they are for. And perceptual capacities are essentially defined by reference to their proper external objects. To understand what an eye is, you must know what sight is. To know what sight is, you must know that it is *of colour*. Similarly, hearing is of sounds, and taste of flavours (*DA* 2. 6, 418^{a}11–13). Not only is this an example of Aris-

---

determinants. Otherwise, all organisms in a certain habitat would have their essential capacities in the same way, which they do not.

[40] I owe thanks to Eve Rabinoff for suggesting perception as a model for the way that something 'external' gets to be 'internal'.

totle building something spatially external into the specification of a capacity, but his account of perceptual capacities also exemplifies how something external can determine the precise character of a capacity. For the nature of a perceptual capacity's proper object determines what that capacity has to be like, though not by being an efficient cause (as external objects are efficient causes of perceptual episodes). Rather, given that the objects are a certain way, something can be a perceiver only if it has organs with powers that stand in the right relation to the character of those objects. A sighted eye, for instance, has the power or capacity to see, and this power it has, Aristotle says, is a certain ratio.[41] This is because colour, the *per se* object of vision, is a certain ratio of light to dark. This explains why plants do not perceive: they do not have a mean (*mesotēs*)—the proper ratio—and so cannot be receptive of the form of a sensible object (e.g. the form of a colour, which is a certain ratio) without the matter. So there is a quite clear sense in which the capacity to see is what it is in virtue of its objects being what they are.[42]

Aristotle's account of perception, then, shows us how the *object* of a capacity determines what the capacity is like. In addition, it exemplifies how the *context* in which a capacity is exercised does so as well. For there is a further feature of Aristotle's account of perception that is relevant to this discussion, namely, the medium in which perceptual capacities are exercised. Vision, hearing, and smell are, essentially, capacities for doing certain things or being affected in certain ways under certain conditions, e.g. in a transparent medium. And the ways that organisms have their perceptual capacities will be different in different media. For example, some animals smell in water and some smell in air. Both water-dwellers and land-dwellers have the same capacity to smell, Aristotle says, but they smell in different media and so have it in different ways.[43] One does so by breathing, which is analogous to opening one's eyelids, and the other perceives smell in the watery medium directly. The medium is not merely the 'enabling' condition for the exercise of an organism's perceptual capacities: the character of the medium affects

---

[41] *DA* 2. 11, 424ᵃ4–6: 'perception is like a certain ratio [μεσότητα] between opposites among the perceptibles. And on account of this it discerns the perceptibles. For the mean [μέσον] is able to discern [κριτικόν].' See also *DA* 2. 12, 424ᵃ28 ff.

[42] Thanks to Joel Yurdin for helpful discussions about this.

[43] See *De sensu* 5, 444ᵇ20–8. Since both kinds of organisms perceive odours—the *per se* objects of smell—they both have this perceptive power, 'but perhaps not in the same way' (ἀλλ' οὐ τὸν αὐτὸν ἴσως τρόπον).

the nature of the capacity. Analogously, on my account, habitats are not merely external or enabling conditions under which organisms exercise vital capacities: the character of the habitat is built into the specification of the particular way the kind has its vital capacities.[44]

6. Natural changes

The way that Aristotle's account of perception builds spatially external features into the specification of the capacities is helpful, I have suggested, in showing the plausibility of the interpretation I am offering. As is the case with perception, specifying what any other vital capacity is must include spatially external factors, such as habitat. As I will now discuss, the analogy with perception is also helpful in shedding important light on certain philosophical and methodological assumptions in Aristotle's scientific practices.

It follows from the way I have been suggesting that Aristotle conceives of the relationship between an organism's habitat and its essence that the nature of a living organism, and the changes that are due to that nature, cannot be understood in abstraction from the context in which it essentially belongs. Just as one can make sense of the changes and activities that constitute the life of an organism only when understood in the context of an entire life cycle, and not when viewed at a single moment in time, those changes and activities will make sense only when considered in the light of the conditions that are essentially implicated in them. Living substances are what they are partially in virtue of the spatially external factors that living substances have the capacities *on which* to act and *by which* to be affected. Consequently, in so far as natural science aims to understand those changes and activities that constitute the lives of

---

[44] This is not the place to embark on a full discussion of Aristotle's comments in *Metaphysics* Θ 5, but scholars have taken him to be asserting there something like the view that enabling conditions are not external to but definitive of the capacity they enable. It is identified as the 'more interesting reading' of two ways of understanding 1047^{b}35–1048^{a}2, discussed by S. Makin, *Aristotle:* Metaphysics *Book Theta* (Oxford, 2006), 103 ff. Similarly, J. Moline states that Aristotle 'conceives of the force of a true capacity claim as being narrowly circumscribed by the circumstances under which the capacity in question is in fact manifested. He thinks of what some would call "external interferences" not as limitations upon the exercise of a capacity which one possesses in any case; rather he conceives of them as circumscribing and defining more narrowly the capacity itself, as refuting inexact conceptions of the capacity in question' (J. Moline, 'Provided Nothing External Interferes', *Mind*, 84 (1975), 244–54 at 249). See also T. Johansen, *The Powers of Aristotle's Soul* (Oxford, 2012), 75–8.

living organisms, it is the business of a natural scientist to study living organisms in their natural habitats.

The requirement that living organisms be studied in their natural habitats has far-reaching implications for our assessment of Aristotle's practices in his natural science. It has been alleged to be a weakness of Aristotle's natural science that it does not consider the changes an organism might undergo when removed from its habitat—including changes in its behaviour—to be ones that exhibit its nature or essence. Solely what an organism does in its natural setting is thought to manifest its essence. His view has been contrasted unfavourably with our current belief that an organism's changes in all types of circumstances, not merely its usual or typical ones, are 'equally natural to it'.[45] Waterlow has criticized Aristotle's exclusive focus on what an organism does in its natural habitat as follows:

What more understandable for a virtual pioneer in natural philosophy than to assume that the natures of things can be read off from such changes alone, and to consign all other reactions to the category of the 'incidental', as reflecting nothing intrinsic in the objects that suffer them, but only the tendency of an interfering force? . . . But a notion with plausible illustrations is not necessarily a coherent concept capable of actual instantiation, and we may well doubt the sense, as well as the scientific usefulness, of a view which obliges us to identify the changes natural to a given object with a mere *sub-class* of those occurring in it through perfectly natural causes.[46]

As Waterlow sees it, Aristotle's failure to consider the changes that take place in non-typical circumstances as natural is an unfortunate consequence of his metaphysical views about natural substances. Natural substances differ from artefacts in that they have natures—'inner principles of change and rest'—and so can be the sources of their own changes. This implies that although external factors might play a role in determining whether or not some change occurs in an organism, they have no part to play in shaping the character of the change, according to Waterlow. This leads Aristotle to ignore the influence that non-typical conditions exert on an organism's changes, Waterlow claims, since those conditions would have no bearing on the kinds of changes of which an organism's nature can be the source. If he were to allow external conditions to shape or determine organisms' natural changes, according to Wa-

[45] Waterlow, *Nature*, 35. [46] Waterlow, *Nature*, 30.

terlow's diagnosis, it would threaten their status as causally autonomous substances with internal principles of change:

> If the nature of a natural substance is exhibited in the changes whose character it autonomously determines, then in these changes the only role left to the external conditions is that of permitting the change or not hindering it. It follows that if the conditions do hinder it, the resulting situation, whether it is a new change or quiescent state, does not exhibit the substantial nature.[47]

And this conclusion—that changes in different conditions do not exhibit a kind's nature—is a mistake, according to Waterlow.[48] For, as she points out, surely the changes an organism undergoes in all sorts of circumstances are equally changes that are natural for it.

I agree that Aristotle thinks the changes an organism undergoes outside of its natural habitat do not exhibit its essential nature. But I disagree about the relationship natural habitat stands in to essence, and so disagree that this is a mistake for Aristotle. I think that Aristotle is viewing habitats as partially constitutive of essential capacities, rather than merely the background conditions that might permit or hinder their exercise. Accordingly, since it is part of the essence of a kind to dwell in certain habitats, the idea that its changes in alternative circumstances do not exhibit its nature is not a naïve mistake, but rather a substantive thesis.

If I am correct, Aristotle has every reason to think that what organisms do in their habitats constitutes changes that reveal their essences, and what they do in other situations does not. Attending once again to the parallels with perception helps us to see why this is so. For an organism's capacities are related to its natural habitat in the way that a sighted eye's power to see is related to the transparent medium in which it exercises that power. The changes that an eye undergoes in the absence of a transparent medium are, surely, changes that are possible for it. However, not every change that it is possible for something to undergo is one for which it has an essential capacity, and only those changes which are the exercises of essential capacities can reveal its essence.[49] Given that Aristotle thinks vision

---

[47] Waterlow, *Nature*, 29.

[48] Waterlow, *Nature*, 34: 'But it is surely a crude mistake to think that an object's unitary nature is manifested only in behaviour of a *single* observable pattern.'

[49] This line of thought is in the spirit of suggestions made by A. D. P. Mourelatos, 'Aristotelian Powers and Modern Empiricism', *Ratio*, 9 (1967), 97–104, about Aristotle's conception of capacities that are constitutive of a φύσις.

essentially takes place in a transparent medium, a sighted eye in the dark is not performing its essential function. Since an eye in the dark is not doing what it is of the essence of an eye to do, whatever it does is not revealing anything about its essential nature or function. And it is the eye's essential nature or function that Aristotle, in trying to understand the natural world, is concerned to understand.

Similarly, an organism outside of its natural habitat will undergo various changes and may very well survive, but it is not living the life distinctive of its kind. Those things that it can do in alternative habitats are not, for Aristotle, capacities constitutive of its essential nature, any more than what an eye can do in the dark is among the eye's essential capacities. An eye in the dark is not exercising some other capacity that it has; it is trying, and failing, to exercise its perceptual capacity. So too, a fish flopping on the shore is not exercising some other locomotive capacity; it is trying, and failing, to exercise its capacity to swim.

Just to be clear, knowing what an eye does in the dark can be useful in an investigation of eyes, of course. And it is certainly the case that Aristotle thinks that what we observe organisms doing outside of their habitats is relevant to scientific enquiry. For instance, the fact that fish choke out of water (as Aristotle reports) is useful in a scientific investigation into their distinctive way of cooling themselves (with water, through gills). This bit of data is, in fact, employed by Aristotle to refute the view that fish respire by drawing air from the surrounding water (*Resp.* 3, 471^{b}12 ff.). Although it is relevant for a natural scientist to know that a fish chokes out of water, a fish has no essential capacity to do this. Choking out of water does not reveal the fish's essence or exhibit its nature.

Thinking that how a creature behaves in other habitats does not reveal its essence is a mistake only if one thinks of habitats as simply background conditions that permit or hinder a kind's essence to be realized. If instead, as I have argued, it can be essential to natural substances that they perform their vital activities in certain habitats, trying to learn about the nature of those organisms by seeing what they do outside of their habitats would be like trying to learn about an eye in pitch darkness.

Thus Aristotle's refusal to consider what organisms do in nonnatural settings as changes that reveal their essences, if the proposal argued for here is correct, is justified. A human living outside of a *polis* is either 'worse or greater than human' (*Pol.* 1. 2, 1253^{a}2–4), and it is a human life that Aristotle cares about understanding. A flourishing human life, Aristotle thinks, essentially involves living in a certain sort of habitat. The same goes for other living beings.

7. Conclusion

I began by observing that Aristotle is aware of the advantageous fits between organisms and their natural habitats. It would be surprising if he thought this to be coincidental, given how vehemently he insists that beneficial arrangements of parts within organisms cannot be merely lucky coincidences. And it would not only be surprising: it runs counter to the way Aristotle talks about beneficial correlations between organisms and where they dwell. For instance, he says that 'residents by seas and rivers and lakes include all the web-footed; for nature itself seeks what is suitable' (*HA* 8 (9). 12, 615^{a}24–6).

This comment indicates that for Aristotle it is 'nature itself' that ensures the fit between web-footed creatures and living near water. But this is ambiguous. It is possible to read this as claiming that, as a view such as Sedley's would have it, a global nature is responsible for the fit. And it is also possible to read this as claiming that the individual natures of the sea, river, and lake residents are responsible, perhaps because they can respond to their environments by forming webbed feet. But neither of these readings is attractive. As I argued, in order to make an appeal to global teleology provide a satisfying answer, the view that there is a cosmic nature must be attributed to Aristotle, which is controversial. And an attempt at an answer running from environmental factors to the organisms' parts can be successful only if the environment can cause changes to the essential functions those parts are needed to perform. Yet that requires some notion of adaptation over time, which appears to conflict with Aristotle's view that kinds are fixed and eternal.

What I proposed instead is that Aristotle considers a kind's natural habitat to be built into the character of its essential capacities. As I read that remark in *History of Animals*, he is claiming that the natures of those sea-, river-, and lake-dwellers are responsible for their useful webbed feet, just in the way that the natures of humans are responsible for humans having the arrangement of teeth that we do. So, I think we should not hear comments about the habitat in which an organism lives as references merely to the 'arena' in which an animal exercises its capacities, but rather as elliptical references to those vital capacities that are constitutive of their being the kinds of organisms that they are.

If we take on board this suggestion about how to conceive of an organism's habitat in relation to its vital capacities, the answer to questions of fit is obvious and trivial. For now the form of our question is not 'Why are birds that have these parts and natural capacities so well suited to living in marshes?', but rather 'Why are birds that have their natural capacities in the marsh-dweller way so well suited to living in marshes?'. And asking that latter sort of question is like asking why swimmers are so well suited to moving in water, or why it is colour that vision perceives. As questions about how the parts of a swimmer's body fit together, or about the structure of the eye, these are perfectly fine questions, and ones for which Aristotle has answers. But if these are questions about the fit between a certain sort of movement (swimming) and where it is exercised, or about why perception is of perceptibles, I think we would not ask them. So, if I am right that Aristotle thinks an organism's habitat is built into its essence, this is exactly how he would hear questions of fit, and thus it is unsurprising that he never raises them.[50] For those are questions that Aristotle would have considered absurd, just as he thought it absurd to ask 'why the curable, when moved and changed *qua* curable, progresses towards health and not towards whiteness' or 'why fire is carried upwards and earth downwards' (*De caelo* 4. 3, 310^b16 ff.).

University of Pittsburgh

BIBLIOGRAPHY

Balme, D. M., *Aristotle:* De partibus animalium *I and* De generatione animalium *I (with Passages from II. 1–3). Translated with Notes, with a Report on Recent Work and an Additional Bibliography* [*De partibus*] (Oxford, 1992).

[50] I. Bodnár makes a similar suggestion about why we do not find Aristotle trying to explain interspecies teleological relationships in his biological works. Bodnár claims that the description of the ways of life and characteristic activities of biological organisms 'will also set out those elements of their habitat which contribute to the well-being of these animals. Accordingly, the description of biological natures already contains the way the animal, in a teleological manner, meshes in with its environment' (Bodnár, 'Teleology', 27).

Balme, D. M., 'Aristotle's Use of Division and Differentiae', in Gotthelf and Lennox (eds.), *Issues*, 69–89.

Bodnár, I., 'Teleology across Natures' ['Teleology'], *Rhizai*, 2 (2005), 9–29.

Code, A., 'The Priority of Final Causes over Efficient Causes in Aristotle's *PA*', in Kullmann and Föllinger (eds.), *Biologie*, 127–43.

Cooper, J., 'Aristotle on Natural Teleology', in M. Nussbaum and M. Schofield (eds.), *Language and Logos: Studies in Ancient Greek Philosophy Presented to G. E. L. Owen* (Cambridge, 1982), 197–222.

Ford, A., 'Action and Generality', in A. Ford, J. Hornsby, and F. Stoutland (eds.), *Essays on Anscombe's Intention* (Cambridge, Mass., 2011), 76–104.

Gotthelf, A. (ed.), *Aristotle on Nature and Living Things* [*Nature*] (Pittsburgh, 1985).

Gotthelf, A., 'First Principles in Aristotle's *Parts of Animals*' ['First Principles'], in Gotthelf and Lennox (eds.), *Issues*, 167–98; repr. in Gotthelf, *Teleology*, 153–85.

Gotthelf, A., 'Notes towards a Study of Substance and Essence in Aristotle's *Parts of Animals* ii–iv' ['Notes'], in Gotthelf (ed.), *Nature*, 27–54; repr. in Gotthelf, *Teleology*, 217–40.

Gotthelf, A., *Teleology, First Principles, and Scientific Method in Aristotle's Biology* [*Teleology*] (Oxford, 2012).

Gotthelf, A., 'The Elephant's Nose: Further Reflections on the Axiomatic Structure of Biological Explanation in Aristotle' ['Elephant'], in Kullmann and Föllinger (eds.), *Biologie*, 85–96; repr. in Gotthelf, *Teleology*, 186–96.

Gotthelf, A., and Lennox, J. G. (eds.), *Philosophical Issues in Aristotle's Biology* [*Issues*] (Cambridge, 1987).

Johansen, T., *The Powers of Aristotle's Soul* (Oxford, 2012).

Judson, L., 'Aristotelian Teleology' ['Aristotelian'], *Oxford Studies in Ancient Philosophy*, 29 (2005), 341–66.

Kahn, C., 'The Place of the Prime Mover in Aristotle's Teleology', in Gotthelf (ed.), *Nature*, 183–205.

Kullmann, W., and Föllinger, S. (eds.), *Aristotelische Biologie: Intentionen, Methoden, Ergebnisse* [*Biologie*] (Stuttgart, 1997).

Lamarck, J. B., *Zoological Philosophy: An Exposition with regard to the Natural History of Animals*, translated, with an introduction by Hugh Elliot (London, 1914).

Lennox, J. G., *Aristotle: On the Parts of Animals I–IV. Translated with an Introduction and Commentary* [*Parts*] (Oxford, 2001).

Lennox, J. G., *Aristotle's Philosophy of Biology: Studies in the Origins of Life Science* [*Biology*] (Cambridge, 2001).

Lennox, J. G., 'Bios and Explanatory Unity in Aristotle's Biology' ['Bios'], in D. Charles (ed.), *Definition in Greek Philosophy* (Oxford, 2010), 329–55.

Lennox, J. G., 'Βίος, Πρᾶξις, and the Unity of Life' ['Πρᾶξις'], in S. Föllinger (ed.), *Was ist 'Leben'? Aristoteles' Anschauungen zur Entstehung und Funktionsweise von Leben. Akten der Tagung vom 23.–26. August 2006 in Bamberg* (Stuttgart, 2010), 239–59.

Lennox, J. G., 'Divide and Explain: The *Posterior Analytics* in Practice', in Gotthelf and Lennox (eds.), *Issues*, 90–119; repr. in Lennox, *Biology*, 7–38.

Lennox, J. G., 'Kinds, Forms of Kinds, and the More and the Less in Aristotle's Biology', in Gotthelf and Lennox (eds.), *Issues*, 339–59; repr. in Lennox, *Biology*, 160–81.

Leunissen, M., 'Aristotle on Natural Character and its Implications for Moral Development' ['Character'], *Journal of the History of Philosophy*, 50 (2012), 507–30.

Leunissen, M., *Explanation and Teleology in Aristotle's Science of Nature* [*Explanation*] (Cambridge, 2010).

Makin, S., *Aristotle: Metaphysics Book Theta* (Oxford, 2006).

Moline, J., 'Provided Nothing External Interferes', *Mind*, 84 (1975), 244–54.

Mourelatos, A. D. P., 'Aristotelian Powers and Modern Empiricism', *Ratio*, 9 (1967), 97–104.

Sedley, D., *Creationism and its Critics in Antiquity* [*Creationism*] (Berkeley, 2007).

Sedley, D., 'Is Aristotle's Teleology Anthropocentric?' ['Anthropocentric'], *Phronesis*, 36 (1991), 179–96.

Sedley, D., '*Metaphysics Λ*', in D. Charles and M. Frede (eds.), *Aristotle's Metaphysics Λ: Proceedings of the Fourteenth Symposium Aristotelicum* (Oxford, 2000), 327–50.

Sedley, D., 'Teleology, Aristotelian and Platonic', in J. G. Lennox and R. Bolton (eds.), *Being, Nature, and Life in Aristotle: Essays in Honor of Allan Gotthelf* (Cambridge, 2010), 5–29.

Wardy, R., 'Aristotelian Rainfall or the Lore of Averages' ['Rainfall'], *Phronesis*, 38 (1993), 18–30.

Waterlow, S., *Nature, Change, and Agency in Aristotle's Physics* [*Nature*] (Oxford, 1982).

INDEX LOCORUM

Alexander of Aphrodisias
[*In Aristotelis Metaphysica commentaria*], ed. Hayduck
456. 31: 168 n. 3
457. 3–8: 208–9 n. 116
457. 20–1: 168 n. 3
457. 22: 168 n. 3
457. 25–6: 168 n. 3
457. 27: 168 n. 3
457. 33–6: 177 n. 41
457. 36–458. 1: 169 n. 10, 173 n. 29
457. 38–9: 168 n. 3
458. 4–5: 168 n. 3
458. 8–9: 168 n. 7
458. 10–15: 174 n. 32
458. 18–19: 213–14 n. 130
598. 1–4: 178 n. 42
598. 4–6: 178 n. 44
598. 4: 178 n. 44
598. 5–6: 178 n. 44
600. 39: 186 n. 68, 186 n. 69

Andocides
1. 14: 172 n. 23

Antiphanes, ed. Koch
fr. 56. 1: 172 n. 24

Aquinas
In duodecim libros Metaphysicorum Aristotelis expositio, ed. Cathala–Spiazzi
1223: 173 n. 27, 173 n. 29
1230–40: 191 n. 82
1241: 211 n. 125
1243: 213 n. 129
In libros De caelo et mundo, ed. Busa
lb 2 lc 4 n. 5: 243 n. 34
Sententia libri Ethicorum, ed. Busa
1. 10 n. 2: 230 n. 11

Aristophanes
Frogs
1052: 173 n. 28

Aristophon, ed. Koch
fr. 9. 4: 172 n. 24

Aristotle
Categories
1^a20–$^b6$: 209 n. 118
1^b25–7: 211
1^b25: 211
2^a7–10: 177 n. 41
4^a23–8: 170–1 n. 16
4^a23–6: 169 n. 11
4^a26–8: 170 n. 12
4^a36–$^b2$: 170–1 n. 16
4^b8–10: 169 n. 11
6^a35: 49
6^a36–$^b10$: 49 n. 34
6^b15–18: 50 n. 35, 51
6^b28–7^b14: 46
6^b28–35: 49 n. 34, 55 n. 44
6^b34: 50 n. 36, 50–1 n. 37
7^a15–17: 49 n. 34
7^a31–$^b9$: 48, 53 n. 41
7^b15 ff.: 49 n. 34
11^a20–33: 52–3 n. 40, 55 n. 44
12^b6–15: 193 n. 89, 200–1 n. 104
14^a27: 190
14^b13–22: 204 n. 108
14^b14–22: 169 n. 11
14^b24: 180 n. 56, 190 n. 77
15^a11: 180 n. 56
16^a6–8: 193 n. 89
19^a33: 193 n. 89
De anima
407^a6–10: 169 n. 9
408^a6: 180 n. 56
408^a9: 180 n. 56
415^a23–$^b7$: 270–1 n. 6
415^a25 ff.: 271 n. 7
415^b8–15: 280
415^b15–21: 270–1 n. 6
418^a11–16: 170 n. 12
418^a11–13: 284
424^a4–6: 285 n. 41
424^a28 ff.: 285 n. 41
427^b11–14: 170 n. 12
427^b20–1: 170 n. 12

427^b24–6: 171 n. 17
428^a1–4: 170 n. 12
428^a3–5: 170 n. 12
428^a3–4: 170 n. 12
428^a11: 170 n. 12
428^a12: 170 n. 12
428^a16–19: 170 n. 12
428^a16–18: 170 n. 12
428^b2–9: 170 n. 12
428^b10–17: 170 n. 12
428^b18–30: 170 n. 12
430^a26–$^b6$: 169 n. 9
430^a26–8: 176
430^a27–8: 211 n. 125
430^b26–31: 175
430^b29–30: 170 n. 12
431^a15–16: 210 n. 122
432^a11–12: 211 n. 125
434^a32–$^b1$: 245 n. 38
De caelo
280^b25–281^a1: 189
280^b31–2: 189
281^a3: 189
286^a8–9: 243, 244, 248
286^a9: 244
286^a10–12: 244
286^a10: 244
286^b1–2: 245
286^b2–4: 245
306^a14–16: 244, 248
306^a15: 244
306^a16: 244
310^b16 ff.: 291
De generatione animalium
731^b31–732^a1: 271 n. 7
767^a28–35: 275
779^a3: 216 n. 137
782^b33–783^a1: 275
788^b20–5: 273 n. 15
De generatione et corruptione
319^b8–14: 214 n. 133
335^a10: 280–1 n. 33
337^a1 ff.: 271 n. 8
338^a17–338^b1: 117
338^a18: 117
De incessu animalium
704^b15–17: 273 n. 15
De insomniis
458^b10–13: 170 n. 15
De interpretatione
16^a9–18: 169 n. 11, 170 n. 14, 171 n. 19, 177 n. 41, 210 n. 124
16^a19–20: 170 n. 14

16^b6–8: 170 n. 14
16^b33–17^a4: 170 n. 14
17^a1–5: 169 n. 11
17^a8–12: 170 n. 14
17^a8–9: 170–1 n. 16
17^a11–12: 170 n. 13
17^a38–$^b23$: 207 n. 111
17^a38–$^b1$: 192 n. 86, 194
18^a13–17: 217 n. 139
19^a7–22: 169 n. 10
19^a33: 169 n. 11
20^b13–26: 217 n. 139
23^a27–39: 170–1 n. 16
23^a27–30: 170 n. 13
23^a38: 170 n. 12
24^b1–7: 170–1 n. 16
24^b1–2: 171 n. 20
De partibus animalium
644^a27–8: 192 n. 86
645^b14–20: 267
669^a9–11: 280–1 n. 33
674^a22–$^b5$: 268, 276
693^a11 ff.: 268, 276
694^b6 ff.: 268, 276
694^b12: 275, 284
694^b13–14: 284
696^b24 ff.: 274 n. 17
De respiratione
471^b12 ff.: 289
14: 280–1 n. 33
De sensu
442^b8–10: 170 n. 12
444^b20–8: 285 n. 43
Eudemian Ethics
1217^a35: 242
1217^b25–1218^a1: 210 n. 123
1219^a8: 240, 242, 246, 248
1219^a10–11: 240, 242
1219^a10: 240
1219^a11–18: 238–9
1219^a11–13: 239
1219^a12: 239
1219^a13–17: 242
1219^a13: 240, 241, 242
1219^a14–21: 230
1219^a14–16: 239
1219^a15–16: 243
1219^a15: 243, 246
1219^a17–18: 239
1219^a18–27: 240–1
1219^a19–20: 241
1219^a20–3: 241
1219^a23–7: 241

Index Locorum

1219^{a}23: 241
1219^{a}24: 240–1 n. 29
1219^{b}4: 246
1226^{a}1–4: 170 n. 12
1226^{a}31: 216 n. 136
Historia animalium
589^{a}5–8: 280–1 n. 33
615^{a}24–6: 290
Magna Moralia
1187^{a}21: 216 n. 136
1197^{a}5–10: 255–6
1211^{b}25–32: 256
Metaphysics
981^{a}30–^{b}10: 263 n. 74
981^{b}8–9: 263 n. 74
981^{b}10–13: 27
996^{b}7: 245 n. 38
999^{b}33–1000^{a}1: 192 n. 86
1010^{b}2–3: 170 n. 12
1010^{b}14–26: 170 n. 12
1012^{a}2–5: 177 n. 40, 216
1015^{a}14: 180 n. 56
1015^{b}12: 180 n. 56
1017^{a}7–^{b}9: 167–8 n. 2
1017^{a}31–5: 200–1 n. 104, 219 n. 142
1017^{a}31–2: 171 n. 21, 219 n. 142
1018^{a}1–4: 192 n. 86
1021^{a}25–6: 179 n. 51
1023^{a}8–11: 216 n. 136
1023^{a}11–13: 209 n. 118
1023^{b}29–32: 192 n. 86
1024^{b}6–8: 182
1024^{b}17–21: 189, 196
1024^{b}17–18: 192–3 n. 87
1024^{b}18–19: 198, 200
1024^{b}18: 208 n. 114
1024^{b}19–20: 200–1 n. 104
1024^{b}19: 208 n. 114
1024^{b}20: 192–3 n. 87
1024^{b}21: 197 n. 93, 198, 198–9 n. 98
1024^{b}24–5: 196
1024^{b}25: 197 n. 93
1025^{b}3–4: 167
1026^{a}33–^{b}2: 167
1026^{a}37: 168 n. 6
1026^{b}4–5: 263 n. 74
1026^{b}13–14: 214
1026^{b}21: 214 n. 131
1027^{b}17–1028^{a}4: 168–9
1027^{b}18–19: 201, 207, 208–9 n. 116, 209
1027^{b}18: 208–9 n. 116
1027^{b}19–26: 168 n. 4
1027^{b}19–23: 208
1027^{b}19–20: 209
1027^{b}19: 208 n. 114
1027^{b}20–3: 208
1027^{b}20: 208–9 n. 116, 209
1027^{b}21–2: 208 n. 113, 208–9 n. 116
1027^{b}21: 178 n. 49, 208 n. 113, 208 n. 114, 208–9 n. 116
1027^{b}22–3: 209 n. 117
1027^{b}22: 208–9 n. 116
1027^{b}23: 212
1027^{b}24–5: 217
1027^{b}25–9: 174 n. 32
1027^{b}25–7: 170, 183, 209, 237–8 n. 25
1027^{b}25: 209
1027^{b}26–7: 210
1027^{b}27–8: 174, 175, 177, 177 n. 41
1027^{b}27: 192 n. 85, 210
1027^{b}28–9: 179, 181, 218
1027^{b}28: 177
1027^{b}29–1028^{a}4: 210
1027^{b}29–33: 169 n. 10
1027^{b}29–31: 210
1027^{b}29–30: 176 n. 38, 214
1027^{b}29: 173, 174
1027^{b}31–3: 176 n. 38, 210, 211
1027^{b}31: 173, 174, 179, 198–9 n. 98, 210, 211
1027^{b}34–1028^{a}1: 214, 214–15 n. 134, 218
1028^{a}1–2: 213
1028^{a}2: 213, 214–15 n. 134
1028^{a}4–6: 168 n. 8
1028^{a}10–14: 167–8 n. 2
1028^{a}10–11: 168 n. 8
1030^{b}11–12: 182 n. 61
1032^{a}12–13: 182 n. 61
1032^{a}19: 273
1034^{a}4: 273
1038^{b}11–12: 192 n. 86
1038^{b}16: 192 n. 86
1040^{b}5 ff.: 273
1040^{b}25–6: 192 n. 86
1041^{a}17–18: 202 n. 106
1041^{a}22: 202 n. 106
1042^{b}26–7: 198 n. 96
1043^{b}21–3: 273
1045^{b}32–4: 167–8 n. 2
1045^{b}36: 180 n. 56
1047^{b}35–1048^{a}2: 286 n. 44
1048^{b}19: 247 n. 40
1049^{a}29–30: 214 n. 133
1050^{b}8–34: 179 n. 51

1051^a34–$^b9$: 178–9
1051^a34–$^b3$: 204
1051^a34–$^b2$: 167–8 n. 2, 182, 187, 191
1051^a34: 178 n. 42, 181
1051^a35–$^b1$: 179 n. 51
1051^a35: 179 n. 51, 182
1051^b1–3: 183, 194
1051^b1–2: 179
1051^b1: 179 n. 51, 181
1051^b2–3: 185, 200, 208 n. 115
1051^b3–5: 195, 204
1051^b3–4: 195
1051^b4–5: 195, 196
1051^b5: 178 n. 49, 185 n. 65
1051^b6–9: 204
1051^b6: 204
1051^b9–17: 185, 199 n. 100, 204
1051^b9–11: 185
1051^b9: 185 n. 65
1051^b10: 185 n. 65
1051^b11–13: 185, 208 n. 115
1051^b11–12: 184
1051^b12–13: 185
1051^b13–17: 185
1051^b13–14: 169 n. 11, 170 n. 12
1051^b17–1052^a4: 175
1051^b17–22: 185, 192
1051^b18–21: 200–1 n. 104
1051^b19–20: 185, 194, 200–1 n. 104, 208 n. 115
1051^b19: 184
1051^b20–1: 185, 192, 200–1 n. 104
1051^b20: 192
1051^b21–2: 185
1051^b22–1052^a4: 186
1051^b22–3: 186
1051^b32: 177 n. 41
1051^b33–5: 185, 186, 208 n. 115
1051^b33–4: 184
1051^b35: 198–9 n. 98
1052^b19: 180 n. 56
1053^b5: 180 n. 56
1065^a21–4: 215
1065^a22: 216 n. 136
1065^a23: 198–9 n. 98
1069^b26–8: 167–8 n. 2
1072^b1–4: 270–1 n. 6
1075^a5–10: 176 n. 38
1075^a11–25: 272 n. 11
1089^a26–8: 167–8 n. 2
1089^b23–4: 214 n. 133
1150^a21: 245 n. 38

Meteorologica
338^b24: 216 n. 137
338^b25: 216 n. 137
339^a5: 216 n. 137
339^a21: 216 n. 137
343^b1: 116
343^b18–19: 116
346^b35 ff.: 271 n. 8

Nicomachean Ethics
1039^b13: 237–8 n. 25
1094^a1–6: 249
1094^a3–5: 250, 250 n. 44
1094^a4–5: 249, 250, 250 n. 44
1094^a4: 250 n. 44
1094^a5–6: 249
1094^a5: 230, 250, 250 n. 44, 250–1 n. 45, 257 n. 61
1094^a6–9: 249
1094^a8: 245
1094^a18–22: 246, 251 n. 47, 252, 261
1094^a18–20: 228
1094^a22: 228
1094^b2–7: 263 n. 74
1095^a16–17: 252, 261
1095^a17–22: 228
1096^a25–34: 210 n. 123
1097^a15–$^b6$: 259 n. 65
1097^a15–22: 249 n. 43
1097^a28–30: 260
1097^a34: 261 n. 69
1097^b22–4: 228
1097^b22–3: 259
1097^b22: 252
1097^b25–8: 228, 251, 259
1097^b25–7: 256 n. 58
1097^b25: 228
1097^b26: 216 n. 136, 230, 253, 256, 257, 257 n. 59, 257 n. 60
1097^b27: 230, 252, 254 n. 53
1097^b28–33: 229–30 n. 10, 259
1097^b29: 257, 257 n. 60, 257 n. 61
1097^b33–1098^a4: 260
1098^a7–8: 230, 253, 260
1098^a8–12: 254
1098^a8–11: 260
1098^a8: 241
1098^a11–12: 230
1098^a12: 229, 241, 258
1098^a15: 260
1098^a16–18: 227, 260, 263
1098^a16–17: 260
1098^a18–20: 259 n. 65, 260
1106^b8–14: 258 n. 63

Index Locorum

1106ᵇ10: 230
1106ᵇ12: 258
1111ᵇ31–4: 170 n. 12
1111ᵇ33–4: 210 n. 122
1120ᵇ13–14: 248 n. 42
1124ᵇ6: 170 n. 12
1133ᵃ7–10: 230
1139ᵃ16–17: 248
1139ᵃ19–20: 257 n. 62
1139ᵇ15–18: 170 n. 12, 170–1 n. 16, 171 n. 20
1140ᵃ2: 255
1140ᵃ3: 255 n. 54
1140ᵃ20–1: 255
1142ᵇ11: 170 n. 12
1142ᵇ12–15: 170 n. 15
1147ᵇ13–17: 263 n. 74
1151ᵇ3–4: 170 n. 12
1152ᵇ19: 249 n. 43
1153ᵃ24–7: 249 n. 43
1167ᵇ33–1168ᵃ2: 248 n. 42
1174ᵃ19–21: 245 n. 37
Physics
184ᵃ10–16: 263 n. 74
190ᵃ31–ᵇ3: 118 n. 22
190ᵃ33: 118 n. 22
190ᵇ3: 118 n. 22
192ᵇ32–3: 273
194ᵃ33–6: 270–1 n. 6
195ᵃ33–ᵇ6: 53 n. 41
195ᵇ21–4: 246
198ᵇ8–9: 273
208ᵃ14–16: 193–4 n. 90
210ᵃ18: 258
210ᵃ20–1: 209 n. 118
210ᵃ21–3: 216 n. 136
Politics
1253ᵃ2–4: 289
1328ᵃ29: 243 n. 33
1328ᵃ33: 243
Posterior Analytics
71ᵃ23–4: 192 n. 86
71ᵇ21–2: 109
71ᵇ30–1: 263 n. 74
73ᵃ28–9: 142 n. 61
88ᵇ32–89ᵃ4: 170 n. 12
90ᵇ33–4: 217 n. 139
100ᵇ5–9: 170 n. 12
123ᵃ15–19: 170 n. 12
Prior Analytics
24ᵃ10–11: 161
24ᵃ11–15: 161
24ᵃ11: 142
24ᵃ14–15: 142
24ᵃ16–17: 161, 217 n. 139
24ᵃ28–9: 217 n. 139
24ᵃ30: 161
24ᵇ20: 113
24ᵇ22–6: 110, 113
24ᵇ22–3: 162
24ᵇ22: 114
24ᵇ23–4: 138 n. 53
24ᵇ24–6: 126, 146
24ᵇ24: 114
24ᵇ28–30: 131, 141, 142 n. 61, 207 n. 111
24ᵇ29: 137 n. 52
24ᵇ30: 139
25ᵃ4–5: 182 n. 61
25ᵃ7: 133 n. 44
25ᵃ11: 133 n. 44
25ᵃ15: 133 n. 44
25ᵃ16: 133 n. 44
25ᵃ18: 133 n. 44
25ᵃ19: 133 n. 44
25ᵇ37–40: 119, 130
25ᵇ39–40: 136
25ᵇ40–26ᵃ2: 119, 130, 139
25ᵇ40: 136
26ᵃ2: 120, 133 n. 44
26ᵃ13: 118 n. 21
26ᵃ23–6: 148
26ᵃ23–5: 119, 130
26ᵃ24: 136
26ᵃ25–7: 119, 130
26ᵃ27: 136
26ᵃ39–40: 130 n. 35
26ᵇ18: 118
26ᵇ24: 130 n. 35
26ᵇ26: 118
26ᵇ27: 130 n. 35
26ᵇ28–30: 148
26ᵇ29: 118 n. 21
26ᵇ30: 128, 158
27ᵃ5–9: 120
27ᵃ8–9: 126
27ᵃ9–18: 126
27ᵃ12–13: 120
27ᵃ15–16: 155
27ᵃ16: 118, 148
27ᵃ17: 127, 149
27ᵃ23: 118
27ᵃ36: 120
28ᵃ1: 118
28ᵃ4: 118 n. 21, 129
28ᵃ22: 120

300   Index Locorum

28^a26–8: 111
28^a36: 118
28^b30: 118
29^a11: 118
29^a23–6: 147
29^b6–8: 158
29^b36–30^a3: 122
29^b36–7: 121
30^a3–5: 122
30^a6–14: 122
30^a15–23: 136, 154–5
30^a17–23: 121
30^a17–20: 122
30^a21–3: 122, 137
30^a21: 137
30^a22: 137, 137 n. 52, 138, 139, 144, 155
30^a29–30: 182 n. 61
30^a37–$^b1$: 150
30^a40–$^b1$: 123
30^a40: 150
30^b1–2: 121, 123, 125
30^b11–13: 152
30^b13: 150
31^a30: 150
31^a37: 150
31^b17: 150
31^b20: 150
31^b28–9: 182 n. 61
32^a29–$^b1$: 156 n. 69
32^b38–33^a1: 121
32^b39: 123
32^b40–33^a1: 123
33^a1–5: 121
33^a1: 123
33^a3–5: 123
33^a17–20: 147 n. 63
33^a21–7: 156
33^a23–5: 121
33^a23: 124
33^a24–5: 124
33^a25–7: 121
33^a27–34: 147 n. 63, 156
33^a27: 124, 125
33^b25–9: 127–8 n. 33
33^b25–8: 124
33^b28–9: 147 n. 63
33^b33–40: 124
33^b33–6: 121, 124, 151, 154
33^b34–5: 1551
33^b34: 150, 151
33^b36–40: 121
33^b36: 124

34^a1–5: 128
34^b19–35^a2: 127–8 n. 33
34^b25–6: 127–8 n. 33
35^a1–2: 127–8 n. 33
35^a30–5: 121, 124
35^a35–6: 124, 125
35^b23–6: 121, 159
35^b25: 124
35^b38: 147 n. 63
36^a1: 129
36^a2–7: 121, 124
36^a6–7: 124
36^a17–25: 121
36^a17–21: 125
36^a39–$^b2$: 121, 125
40^b30–1: 217 n. 139
43^a25–32: 192 n. 86

Protrepticus
B 65: 237, 237–8 n. 25, 245

Sophistici elenchi
165^a6–8: 193 n. 89
169^a7–8: 217 n. 139
169^a10–11: 217 n. 139
169^a14: 217 n. 139
175^a8–9: 193 n. 89
177^a31–2: 193 n. 89
178^a25–7: 193 n. 89
178^b24–9: 169 n. 11, 170 n. 12
178^b37–9: 192 n. 86
179^a8–10: 192 n. 86
181^b23–4: 217 n. 139

Topics
103^a9–10: 193 n. 89
107^a3–12: 210 n. 123
111^a14–20: 170 n. 12
141^b19–22: 231

Asclepius
In Aristotelis Metaphysicorum libros I–VI commentaria, ed. Hayduck
373. 32: 168 n. 3
374. 7–8: 176–7 n. 39
374. 18–21: 213–14 n. 130

Aspasius
In Ethica Nicomachea commentaria, ed. Heylbut
17. 22–4: 252 n. 48
18. 1–2: 252

Cicero
De finibus
3. 24: 256 n. 57

Index Locorum

Demosthenes
8. 45: 172 n. 24

Euclid
Elements
1, def. 15: 15
1, def. 16: 15
1, prop. 1: 14
1, prop. 2: 14
1, prop. 3: 14
1, prop. 4: 14
1, prop. 5: 14
1, prop. 7: 14
1, prop. 8: 14
1, prop. 9: 14
1, prop. 10: 14
1, prop. 11: 14
1, prop. 13: 14
1, prop. 15: 14
1, prop. 16: 14
1, prop. 26: 14
1, prop. 29: 14
1, prop. 34: 14

Euripides
Electra
346: 173 n. 28

Heliodorus
In Ethica Nicomachea paraphrasis, ed. Helbut
13. 22–6: 253 n. 49

Herodotus
1. 95. 1: 173 n. 28
1. 116. 5: 173 n. 28
5. 50. 2: 171 n. 22
5. 106. 4: 171 n. 22
7. 209. 1: 171 n. 22
9. 11. 3: 171 n. 22

Isaeus
10. 17: 172 n. 24

Isocrates
Antidosis
201. 4: 7

Plato
Charmides
167 E 1–2: 49 n. 34, 50
168 B–C: 50–1 n. 37
168 B 2–3: 49 n. 34
168 B 5–D 1: 46
168 B 5–8: 49 n. 34
168 C 1–3: 46
168 C 4–5: 49 n. 34
168 C 9–10: 49 n. 34
168 D 1–3: 46
168 D 6–E 1: 46
Cratylus
385 B 10: 171 n. 22
428 D 5–6: 171 n. 22
Crito
43 C 4: 172 n. 23
47 B 12: 172 n. 23
Euthydemus
284 A 5–8: 171 n. 22
284 C 2–6: 171 n. 22
286 A 2–3: 171 n. 22
Euthyphro
7 C 6: 172 n. 23
Gorgias
468 B 1–E 5: 40 n. 8
Meno
70 A 1–71 A 7: 9
71 B 3–4: 9, 17
72 C 6–D 1: 9
72 C 7–8: 9
77 B 6–78 B 2: 40 n. 8
80 D 5–E 5: 10
82 D 8–E 2: 10
82 E 2–83 E 10: 10
84 A 1–2: 10
84 D 3–85 B 7: 10
84 E 4–85 B 2: 10–11
84 E 4–85 A 1: 13
85 C 9–D 1: 12
85 C 10–11: 16
85 E 1–3: 18
88 B 4: 9 n. 16
88 C 2: 9 n. 16
98 A 3–8: 7–8
98 A 3–6: 1
Parmenides
133 C 8: 48 n. 31
134 A 3–B 1: 49 n. 34, 50 n. 36
134 A 9: 50–1 n. 37
138 B 5–6: 117
138 D 5: 117
139 D 1–E 3: 117
139 E 7–149 A 6: 116–17
139 E 7: 116
139 E 9–140 A 1: 117
140 C 6–7: 117
140 D 3: 117

302 Index Locorum

161 E 5–162 A 1: 171 n. 22
Phaedo
65 C 10: 172 n. 23
68 D 10: 172 n. 23
Phaedrus
262 B 2–3: 171 n. 22
Protagoras
328 A 7–C 2: 100
354 C 4: 40 n. 8
358 B 6–D 4: 40 n. 8
358 C 6–E 2: 40 n. 8
Republic
346 D 1–8: 236, 243
346 D 1–6: 233–4
346 D 3–4: 253 n. 50
346 D 5: 235
352 D 9–E 3: 235
352 E 3–4: 232, 233 n. 18, 236
352 E 3: 235
352 E 4: 232 n. 16, 235
353 A 1–8: 242
353 A 9–11: 233 n. 18
353 A 9: 232, 232 n. 15
353 A 10–11: 233, 234 n. 19, 235, 236
353 A 10: 235
353 A 11: 232 n. 16, 235
353 C 6–7: 234 n. 19
353 D 3–8: 253 n. 50
353 D 3–7: 234 n. 19
389 C 4–5: 171 n. 22
413 A 7–8: 171 n. 22
421 D 9–E 5: 234 n. 19
421 D 12: 234 n. 19
435 C 5: 37 n. 1
435 E 1: 37 n. 1
436 B 9–439 C 9: 37 ff.
436 B 9–C 2: 39, 50
437 B 1–4: 50
437 B 1–C 9: 39
437 C 1–2: 48
437 C 3: 48
437 C 7–9: 50
437 D–E: 43 n. 19
437 D 1–E 6: 39
437 D 7–E 6: 51 n. 38
437 E 7–438 A 5: 39, 41
438 A 7–D 9: 37
438 A 7–B 2: 39, 46, 49, 51
438 A 7: 50
438 A 8–B 2: 50
438 B 4–D 9: 49
438 C: 52 n. 39
438 C 6–D 8: 52

438 C 6–9: 50 n. 36
438 C 7–8: 52 n. 39
438 C 7: 52 n. 39
438 D 7: 50
438 E 5: 48, 50 n. 36
439 A 1–7: 53, 55–6
439 A 1–2: 50, 55 n. 45
439 A 4–B 1: 41 n. 11
439 B 3–C 8: 54
439 B 3–6: 39
439 B 8–C 1: 54
439 C 3–5: 39
439 C 6–8: 39
439 E 1: 37 n. 1
441 C 6: 37 n. 1
442 B 10: 37 n. 1
442 C–D: 41
442 C 4: 37 n. 1
443 D 3: 37 n. 1
505 D–506 A: 41
511 D 6–8: 20 n. 29
571 C–572 B: 41
580 D–581 A: 41
597 A 1–7: 234 n. 19
601 D 1–E 2: 234, 255
601 D 2: 255
602 D 6–E 2: 234 n. 19
603 A 9–B 3: 234 n. 19
Sophist
237 B 7–E 7: 201
240 D 9–241 A 2: 201
240 D 9–10: 171 n. 22
255 C–D: 48 n. 31
Symposium
199 C 4–5: 49
199 D 1–5: 47
199 D 4: 47
199 D 7: 48
199 E 3–4: 47
200 A 5: 49 n. 34, 50
Theaetetus
151 E 8–152 C 6: 62
152 C 8–D 2: 94
152 D 2–E 1: 68 n. 12, 92–3
152 D 2: 93
153 D 8–154 A 4: 75 n. 29
153 E 4–154 A 4: 68 n. 12
156 C 7–157 A 4: 76 n. 31
156 C 7–E 7: 75 n. 29
156 D 2–157 C 1: 68 n. 12
157 A 7–C 1: 93 n. 64
158 B 2–E 5: 72
158 E 6: 69 n. 17

Index Locorum

159 B 2–E 5: 72, 74 n. 26, 75 n. 29
159 C 4–D 6: 76 n. 31
160 B 3: 93
160 B 5–D 3: 68 n. 12
160 B 5–C 2: 93
160 B 8–C 2: 88 n. 53
160 C 7–D 3: 76 n. 31
160 C 7: 69 n. 17
161 D 2–162 A 3: 64, 102
161 D 2: 69 n. 17
162 A 4–C 2: 66 n. 8
162 C 8–D 1: 73 n. 25
165 E 1–4: 100 n. 76
166 A–168 C: 97
166 A 7–B 2: 65
166 C–167 D: 66
166 C 2–9: 65
166 C 2–7: 68 n. 12
166 D 1–167 D 2: 79–80
166 D 1–7: 65
166 D 7–E 4: 73
166 E 2–167 A 8: 64
166 E 2–4: 73 n. 25
166 E 4–167 A 6: 88 n. 53
167 A 7–8: 171 n. 22
167 C 4–7: 64
167 C 4–5: 73 n. 25
167 D 2–3: 84 n. 46
167 D 5–168 C 2: 65
168 C 2–169 A 1: 66 n. 8
170 A 6–171 D 7: 66 n. 7
170 D 4–E 6: 73
170 D 5–6: 69 n. 17
170 E 4–5: 69 n. 17
170 E 9: 69 n. 17
171 A 6–9: 64
171 A 9: 171 n. 22
171 C 5–7: 69 n. 17
171 E 1–3: 73 n. 25
172 A 1–C 1: 64
172 A 1–B 6: 83 n. 44
172 C–177 C: 97
172 E 2–173 B 2: 97
177 C 6–D 7: 83 n. 44
177 C 7–8: 73 n. 25
178 A 5–179 B 5: 82 n. 41
188 D 3–4: 171 n. 22
188 D 8–10: 171 n. 22
189 A 10–B 6: 171 n. 22
199 B 8–9: 171 n. 22
201 D 2–3: 50 n. 36
204 E 11: 48 n. 31

Scholia in Aristotelem, ed. Brandis
739^{a}21–2: 169 n. 10

Sextus Empiricus
Adversus mathematicos
8. 310: 118–19 n. 23

Sophocles
Electra
584: 173 n. 28

Thucydides
1. 142. 6–7: 6 n. 11
2. 87. 4: 6 n. 11
7. 21. 3. 1–22. 1. 1: 6

Xenophon
Oeconomicus
19. 17: 172 n. 24

Notes for Contributors to Oxford Studies in Ancient Philosophy

1. Articles should be submitted with double line-spacing throughout. At the stage of initial (but not final) submission footnotes may be given in small type at the foot of the page. Page dimensions should be A4 or standard American quarto (8½× 11″), and ample margins (minimum 1¼″ or 32 mm) should be left.

2. Submissions should be made as a file in PDF format attached to an e-mail sent to the Editor. Authors are asked to supply an accurate word-count (*a*) for the main text, and (*b*) for the notes. The e-mail which serves as a covering letter should come from the address to be used for correspondence on the submission. A postal address should also be provided. If necessary, arrangements for alternative means of submission may be made with the Editor. Authors should note that the version first submitted will be the one adjudicated; unsolicited revised versions cannot be accepted during the adjudication process.

The remaining instructions apply to the final version sent for publication, and need not be rigidly adhered to in a first submission.

3. In the finalized version, the text should be double-spaced and in the same typesize throughout, **including displayed quotations and notes**. Notes should be numbered consecutively, and may be supplied as either footnotes or endnotes. Any acknowledgements should be placed in an unnumbered first note. Wherever possible, references to primary sources should be built into the text.

4. **Use of Greek and Latin.** Relatively familiar Greek terms such as *psychē* and *polis* (but not whole phrases and sentences) may be used in transliteration. Wherever possible, Greek and Latin should not be used in the main text of an article in ways which would impede comprehension by those without knowledge of the languages; for example, where appropriate, the original texts should be accompanied by a translation. This constraint does not apply to footnotes. Greek must be supplied in an accurate form, with all diacritics in place. A note of the system employed for achieving Greek (e.g. GreekKeys, Linguist's Software) should be supplied to facilitate file conversion.

5. For citations of Greek and Latin authors, house style should be followed. This can be checked in any recent issue of *OSAP* with the help of the Index Locorum. The most exact reference possible should normally be employed, especially if a text is quoted or discussed in detail: for example, line references for Plato (not just Stephanus page and letter) and Aristotle (not just Bekker page and column).

6. In references to books, the first time the book is referred to give the initial(s) and surname of the author (first names are not usually required), and the place and date of publication; where you are abbreviating the

title in subsequent citations, give the abbreviation in square brackets, thus:

> T. Brickhouse and N. Smith, *Socrates on Trial* [*Trial*] (Princeton, 1981), 91–4.

Give the volume-number and date of periodicals, and include the full page-extent of articles (including chapters of books):

> D. W. Graham, 'Symmetry in the Empedoclean Cycle' ['Symmetry'], *Classical Quarterly*, NS 38 (1988), 297–312 at 301–4.
>
> G. Vlastos, 'A Metaphysical Paradox' ['Metaphysical'], in G. Vlastos, *Platonic Studies*, 2nd edn. (Princeton, 1981), 43–57 at 52.

Where the same book or article is referred to on subsequent occasions, usually the most convenient style will be an abbreviated reference:

> Brickhouse and Smith, *Trial*, 28–9.

Do *not* use the author-and-date style of reference:

> Brickhouse and Smith 1981: 28–9.

7. Authors are asked to supply *in addition*, at the end of the article, a full list of the bibliographical entries cited, alphabetically ordered by (first) author's surname. Except that the author's surname should come first, these entries should be identical in form to the first occurrence of each in the article, including where appropriate the indication of abbreviated title:

> Graham, D. W., 'Symmetry in the Empedoclean Cycle' ['Symmetry'], *Classical Quarterly*, NS 38 (1988), 297–312.

8. If there are any unusual conventions contributors are encouraged to include a covering note for the copy-editor and/or printer. Please say whether you are using single and double quotation marks for different purposes (otherwise the Press will employ its standard single quotation marks throughout, using double only for quotations within quotations).

9. Authors should send a copy of the final version of their paper in electronic form by attachment to an e-mail. The final version should be in a standard word-processing format, accompanied by a note of the word-processing program used and of the system (**not just the font**) used for producing Greek characters (see point 4 above). This file must be accompanied by a second file, a copy in PDF format of the submitted word-processor file; the PDF file must correspond **exactly** to the word-processor file. If necessary, arrangements for alternative means of submission may be made with the Editor. With final submission authors should also send, in a separate file, a brief abstract and a list of approximately ten keywords.